Feminist Philosophy of Religion

'*Feminist Philosophy of Religion* is a crucial addition to this important field of study. Anderson and Clack have succeeded in demonstrating not only the inherent vibrancy of feminist philosophy of religion, but also its potential for transforming mainstream philosophy of religion.'
Nancy Tuana, Professor of Philosophy, Penn State University, and co-editor of *Hypatia: A Journal of Feminist Philosophy*

Feminist philosophy of religion has developed in recent years because of the identification and exposure of explicit sexism in much of the traditional philosophical thinking about religion. The struggle with a discipline shaped almost exclusively by men has led feminist philosophers to redress the problematic biases of gender, race, class and sexual orientation of the traditional subject.

   Feminist Philosophy of Religion: Critical Readings brings together new and key writings on the core topics and approaches to this growing field. Each essay exhibits a distinctive theorectical approach and the readings appropriate insights from the fields of literature, theology, philosophy, gender and cultural studies. Beginning with a general introduction, Part One of the Reader explores important approaches to the feminist philosophy of religion, including psychoanalytic, poststructuralist, postmetaphysical and epistemological frameworks. In Part Two the authors survey significant topics including questions of divinity, embodiment, autonomy and spirituality, and religious practice. Supported by explanatory prefaces and an extensive thematic bibliography, *Feminist Philosophy of Religion: Critical Readings* is an important resource for this new area of study.

   Essays by: Pamela Sue Anderson, Ellen T. Armour, Tina Beattie, Beverley Clack, Vrinda Dalmiya, Dorota Filipczak, Nancy Frankenberry, Harriet A. Harris, Amy Hollywood, Grace M. Jantzen, Alison Jasper, Fionola Meredith, Kathleen O'Grady, Melissa Raphael, Janet Martin Soskice, Heather Walton.

Pamela Sue Anderson is Fellow in Philosophy, Regent's Park College, Oxford University. She is author of *A Feminist Philosophy of Religion: The Rationality and Myths of Religious Belief* (1998). **Beverley Clack** is Senior Lecturer in Religious Studies and Philosophy, Oxford Brookes University. She is author of *Sex and Death* (2002).

Feminist Philosophy of Religion

Critical Readings

Edited by

Pamela Sue Anderson and
Beverley Clack

Routledge
Taylor & Francis Group

LONDON AND NEW YORK

First published 2004
by Routledge
2 Park Square, Milton Park, Abingdon, Oxon, OX14 4RN

Simultaneously published in the USA and Canada
by Routledge
711 Third Ave, New York NY 10017

Routledge is an imprint of the Taylor & Francis Group

Transferred to Digital Printing 2006

Typeset in Perpetua and Bell Gothic by
Wearset Ltd, Boldon, Tyne and Wear

British Library Cataloguing in Publication Data
A catalogue record for this book is available from the British Library

Library of Congress Cataloging in Publication Data
A catalog record for this book has been requested

ISBN 0-415-25749-2 (hbk)
ISBN 0-415-25750-6 (pbk)

Contents

Contributors

Pamela Sue Anderson is Fellow in Philosophy, Regent's Park College, University of Oxford. Her publications include *Ricoeur and Kant: Philosophy of the Will* (1993) and *A Feminist Philosophy of Religion: The Rationality and Myths of Religious Belief* (1998).

Ellen T. Armour is Associate Professor and Chair of Religious Studies at Rhodes College, Memphis, Tennessee. Her publications include *Deconstruction, Feminist Theology and the Problem of Difference: Subverting the Race/Gender Divide* (1999). She is currently co-editing a volume on Judith Butler.

Tina Beattie is a lecturer in Christian Studies at the University of Surrey Roehampton. Her latest book is *God's Mother, Eve's Advocate: A Marian Narrative of Women's Salvation* (2002).

Beverley Clack is Senior Lecturer in Religious Studies and Philosophy at Oxford Brookes University. Her publications include *Sex and Death* (2002), *Misogyny in the Western Philosophical Tradition* (1999) and *The Philosophy of Religion*, co-authored with Brian R. Clack (1998).

Vrinda Dalmiya is Associate Professor of Philosophy at the University of Hawaii. She has published articles on ethics and feminist epistemology. Her research seeks to develop an epistemology based on care in dialogue with both analytic and feminist theory.

Dorota Filipczak is a lecturer in English Literature and Culture at the University of Lódz in Poland. Her publications include *The Valley of the Shadow of Death: Biblical Intertext in Malcolm Lowry's Fiction* (1999).

Nancy Frankenberry is the John Phillips Professor of Religion at Dartmouth College, Hanover, New Hampshire. She is the author of *Religion and Radical Empiricism* (1987), co-editor of *Language, Truth and Religious Belief* (1999) and editor of *Radical Interpretation in Religion* (2002).

Harriet A. Harris is Chaplain of Wadham College, Oxford, and Honorary University Fellow of the University of Exeter. She is author of many articles in the philosophy of religion and philosophical theology. Her books include *Fundamentalism and Evangelicals* (1998).

Amy Hollywood is Professor of Theology and the History of Christianity, University of Chicago. She is the author of *The Soul as Virgin Wife: Mechthild of Magdeburg, Marguerite Porete, and Meister Eckhart* (1995) and *Sensible Ecstasy: Mysticism, Sexual Difference, and the Demands of History* (2001).

Grace M. Jantzen is Research Professor of Religion, Culture and Gender at the University of Manchester. Her publications include *Becoming Divine: Towards a Feminist Philosophy of Religion* (1998), *Power and Gender in Christian Mysticism* (1995), and her current project is *Death and the Displacement of Beauty*.

Alison Jasper is Lecturer in Religious Studies at the University of Stirling. Her publications include *The Shining Garment of the Text: Gendered Readings in the Prologue of John* (1998). Her current research is in the areas of feminist theology and the teaching of religious studies.

Fionola Meredith holds a Ph.D. in Scholastic Philosophy from Queen's University Belfast, where she teaches feminist theory. She works for Women into Politics, an organisation promoting the greater inclusion of women in public life in Northern Ireland, and is a columnist in the political journal, *Fortnight*.

Kathleen O'Grady is Research Associate at the Simone de Beauvoir Institute, Concordia University, Montreal, and Director of Communications for the Canadian Women's Health Network. She is co-editor of *French Feminists on Religion: A Reader* (2002) and *Religion in French Feminist Thought* (2003).

Melissa Raphael is Principal Lecturer in Theology and Religious Studies at the University of Gloucestershire. Her publications include *Theology and Embodiment: The Post-Patriarchal Reconstruction of Female Sacrality* (1996) and *The Female Face of God in Auschwitz: A Jewish Feminist Theology of the Holocaust* (2003).

Janet Martin Soskice is the University Reader in Philosophical Theology at Cambridge University. Recent articles include 'Blood and Defilement: Reflections on Jesus and the Symbolics of Sex' in Kendall and Davis's *The Convergence of Theology*, and 'Trinity and Feminism' in *The Cambridge Companion to Feminist Theology* (2002).

Heather Walton is Lecturer in the School of Divinity at Glasgow University. She co-edits the journal *Theology and Sexuality*, and her publications include *Women Writing the Divine: Literature, Theology and Feminism* (forthcoming, 2004).

Acknowledgements

The editors would like to thank the following: Janet Martin Soskice for permission to reprint 'Love and Attention', which was originally published in Michael McGhee (ed.) *Philosophy, Religion and the Spiritual Life*, Cambridge: Cambridge University Press, 1992, pp.59–72; Indiana University Press for permission to reproduce Vrinda Dalmiya, 'Loving Paradoxes: A Feminist Reclamation of the Goddess Kali', which was originally published in *Hypatia*, 15: 1 (Winter 2000): 125–150; Princeton University Press for permission to reproduce Nancy Frankenberry, 'Philosophy of Religion in Different Voices', which was originally published in Janet A. Kourany (ed.) *Philosophy in a Feminist Voice: Critiques and Reconstructions*, 1998, pp.173–192; Cambridge University Press for permission to reproduce Grace M. Jantzen, 'What's the Difference? Knowledge and Gender in (Post)Modern Philosophy of Religion', which was originally published in *Religious Studies*, 32: 4 (1996): 431–484; Sheffield Academic Press for permission to reproduce 'Struggling for Truth', *Feminist Theology*, 28 (September 2001): 40–56. An earlier version of Kathleen O'Grady's essay appeared as 'The Pun or the Eucharist? Eco and Kristeva on the Consummate Model for the Metaphoric Process', *Literature and Theology: An International Journal of Theory, Criticism and Culture* (Oxford University Press), 11: 1 (March 1997): 93–115.

We would also like to take this opportunity to thank Helen Reynolds for her help in preparing this manuscript, and Paul Hunt and Robert Lindsey for their support and encouragement.

General introduction

My images are about struggling out of containment, reaching out and opening up as opposed to masking or veiling.

Judy Chicago[1]

IN CERTAIN FIELDS OF STUDY, feminism is thought to be a thing of the past: discrimination against women is no longer a live issue. However, as we look back over the past five years or so since the publication of the first two monographs on feminist philosophy of religion,[2] it is undeniable that feminism is not finished: indeed, it has barely begun in this context. The field continues to exclude women in thought and practice. In fact, the problem with defining the subject itself – i.e. philosophy of religion – is indicative of this situation. It is virtually impossible to give a definition without reinforcing, one way or another, the devaluation of terms associated with the female. One method (logical proofs or other rational demonstrations) and one model (traditional theism), excluding any association with the body, are assumed by the Anglo-American tradition of philosophy of religion. If we present a new definition of the field, we are told, 'Well, that is not really philosophy of religion – but go ahead if you want to'; if we give a definition compatible with the lively debates in contemporary philosophy of religion concerning God's existence, his attributes and the justification of theistic beliefs, then we find ourselves unable to relate much, if anything, that we think about love and truth, or reason and emotion, to these traditional debates. So it might seem easier to say, 'Well, this is really feminist theology – or thealogy', thereby feeling comfortable and content in a totally separate field from those who are real *philosophers* of religion. We strongly resist all of these alternatives. Thus we insist upon asserting that this is a book on feminist *philosophy of religion* edited, and contributed to, by women who are *feminists*.

In writing feminist *philosophy*, we each have a self-conscious approach or method for doing philosophy of religion; as *feminists*, we each seek to write from a concrete context, to communicate, connect and collaborate with each other. We seek a transformation of the field by *the inclusion of* women and marginalized others, of those things associated with the female,[3] of methods thought to be impossible for women,[4] and of material content which has been left out of debate or reflection, as a source of anxiety.[5]

For example, we no longer feel happy with objectivity that is male-neutral.[6] The search for truth must include an awareness of our subjectivity and the limits of our ability to be objective. So, we are reconfiguring central concepts and core concerns, including reason, emotion, desire, mortality, natality, autonomy, heteronomy, singularity and multiplicity.

One way to realize how far we are from achieving feminist goals is to imagine the majority of philosophy chairs, professors, and authors of philosophy of religion textbooks, monographs or essays in anthologies on philosophy of religion being women. In practice, we see the reverse is true: men constitute by far and away the majority of past and present philosophers of religion. Women simply lack the social and material markers which would give them any epistemic authority in the field. It is not unusual for a woman attending a philosophy of religion conference to be mistaken for the woman in charge of the bookstalls. We still find new books coming out on or about philosophy of religion in which there are no female contributors,[7] no mention of feminism,[8] no discussion of emotion, sexual or romantic love, care or justice, beauty or birth. Presumably the response to pointing out such omissions would be 'What do such topics have to do with religion?'

Yet who defines *religion*? Who identifies what necessarily binds us together? Who precisely serves as an authority on how philosophical method should be applied to religion? Who knows the truth? Who is wise? Who is a trustworthy witness? Who matters to us? Who is divine? And how do we stand in relation to the infinite conceived as both immanent and transcendent? To what do we aspire? For whom do we yearn? Which practices, or rituals, form us? And to what end? Which practices develop our most binding relationships? Even our definitions become part of our critical self-reflection. We grapple concretely and critically with 'religion', 'philosophy' and even our definitions of 'feminist'. A common characteristic of our self-definition as feminist philosophers of religion, then, is that we grapple with such fundamental questions.

These are feminist questions; and they are also questions about philosophy, and of its relevance for religion. The questions addressed in this book include these and many more: what makes our voices different? What's the difference when, with an awareness of our gender(ing), we ask 'whose knowledge'? What about our desires and longings? Why have our emotions and feelings been excluded from debates in philosophy of religion? Why don't Anglo-American philosophers of religion listen to French philosophers? Or German? What about Indian practices and rituals? How might these shape our spiritual practices, and who we are? Sexual difference is something which has been repressed and/or excluded: but what about race? Ethnicity? Why are philosophers of religion white, male, mainly Protestant – virtually always Christian – Western and largely Anglo-American? In fact, once we start asking questions of difference, we must also acknowledge our own exclusion of race, of Eastern Europe, of the Orient, and so on.

It is characteristic of each contributor to this anthology that she seeks to be self-reflective, self-critical and self-conscious about her thinking and acting, but also about her philosophical method and approach to the concepts of religion(s) and the concerns of those marginalized or forgotten. So retrieval goes along with recon-figuration; difference along with uniqueness or singularity; discord along with concord; discontinuity along with continuity; uncertainty often more than certainty – which is how it should be as long as we seek to be creative and transformative in our feminist approaches to philosophy of religion.

We chose not to give up either the 'feminist' in our title or the 'philosophy of religion'. It may well be that feminist theology has been more open to feminist philosophy of religion – but this book is not for theologians alone. It is for philosophers of every persuasion and for every theorist who wants to think critically, imaginatively, attentively and reflexively about religious rituals and beliefs about the body, the divine, the material world, spirituality, temporality, love and truth. Essentially philosophy of religion done by feminists and for women and men, has as its focus that which makes up our fundamental nature and our relationships to what we find undeniable: that we are born, we love, suffer loss, long for love which endures, and we die. Ultimately, we feminist philosophers of religion all struggle – struggle with the truth, struggle with ourselves, with love, divine and human. Our struggling is at the heart of our listening and of our grappling with that which is difficult, with our past and what we have been taught. We grapple for a future which is beautiful, just, good and true to all of us. Our vision is real – there is no illusion; we do not expect that beauty, justice, goodness and truth will be easy to achieve; in fact, our goal is not achievable, but without it we would not be able to hope that knowing the difference is possible, and hence, a liveable ideal for moving towards what could be.

This book is the result of collaboration over a number of years during which we, the editors, have suffered our own losses, have loved and enjoyed, thought and rethought about birth, death, life and divine love. We have found support and energy from each other, but also from each of the contributors who joined and stayed with our collaborative thinking as feminist philosophers of religion. Judy Chicago's *The Dinner Party*, which provides the cover illustration for this collection, is thus an apt image of what feminist philosophy of religion involves. Just as Chicago's work considers feminist history as a meeting of women in the convivial setting of a dinner party, where agreements and disagreements, life and love, are discussed over food and wine, so we see feminist philosophy of religion as a collabo-rative exercise where we share and challenge each other about what it means to be female, practitioners of philosophy, and part of this world, here and now. We hope that this volume will enable the reader to join us in this discussion.

Notes

1   Judy Chicago, cited in 'The Dinner Party to Receive Permanent Home: Brooklyn Museum of Art – Brooklyn NY April 23, 2002', at http://www.judychicago.com/index.html (accessed on 23 October 2002).
2   P.S. Anderson, *A Feminist Philosophy of Religion: The Rationality and Myths of Religious Belief,*

Oxford: Blackwell, 1998; and G. Jantzen, *Becoming Divine: Towards a Feminist Philosophy of Religion*, Manchester: Manchester University Press, 1998.

3   See Genevieve Lloyd, *The Man of Reason: 'Male' and 'Female' in Western Philosophy*, 2nd edn, London: Routledge, 1993, for examples of the way in which Western philosophizing has associated femaleness with emotion and the body, thus excluding women from engagement with the 'male' categories of reason and the mind.

4   See, for example, excerpts from Kant and Schopenhauer which suggest that a woman *qua* woman cannot be a philosopher, in B. Clack (ed.) *Misogyny in the Western Philosophical Tradition*, Basingstoke: Macmillan, 1999.

5   So, abjection, defilement, slime: fearful things, yet things which are of deep concern for men and women.

6   Anderson, *A Feminist Philosophy of Religion*, p. 13.

7   In his 'comprehensive' and 'authoritative' overview of the field at the beginning of the twenty-first century, Brian Davies includes 65 essays, each is put under an appropriate topic, including seven topics which cover the standard issues of traditional theism, and there is no female contributor on her own; the only woman listed, Eleanor Stumpf, has written an article with her male collaborator, Norman Kretzman; see B. Davies, *Philosophy of Religion: A Guide and Anthology*, Oxford: Oxford University Press, 2000. We must admit that Charles Taliaferro and Paul J. Griffiths have published another anthology, presenting a new range of essays and topics by both men and women, including theist, atheist and (a few) feminist essays; see C. Taliaferro and P.J. Griffiths (eds) *Philosophy of Religion: An Anthology*, Oxford: Blackwell, 2003. And yet, unlike this present collection of essays, all of their edited essays have been previously published in the mid- to late twentieth-century, so generally their collection still does not reflect the major changes in contemporary philosophical or feminist scholarship.

8   See A.C. Thiselton, *A Concise Encyclopedia of the Philosophy of Religion*, Oxford: Oneworld, 2002, where few women are referenced with no mention of feminism or, indeed, of any feminist philosophers of religion.

PART ONE

Approaches to feminist philosophy of religion

Chapter 1

FEMINIST APPROACHES

Nancy Frankenberry

PHILOSOPHY OF RELIGION IN DIFFERENT VOICES

■ From **PHILOSOPHY OF RELIGION IN DIFFERENT VOICES**, in Janet A. Kourany (ed.) *Philosophy in a Feminist Voice: Critiques and Reconstructions*, 1998, pp. 173–192.

Nancy Frankenberry offers two historically different points of view on philosophy of religion, documenting the earliest elements for a feminist philosophy of religion. First of all, this chapter contains material reprinted from Frankenberry's reflections upon the situation in 1994 when women in theology were strongly motivated spiritually and practically to make certain feminist inroads into philosophical debates about religion and sexism. At the time, the patriarchal force in the field of philosophy of religion was formidable enough to marginalize these feminist debates; not only was the practice of philosophy of religion shaped largely by white, male European Protestant analytical philosophers, but the virtually exclusive focus of their practice was the justification of belief in the patriarchal God of traditional Christian theism. Frankenberry responded to this situation with both a critique of the masculinist conception of God and a partial reconstruction of the field, which drew upon the emerging voices of women differing according to class, race, religion, ethnicity and sexual orientation. Second, the chapter includes Frankenberry's significant Addendum, written especially for this book, on the changing situation at the beginning of the twenty-first century (pp. 20–24). Again, Frankenberry attempts a partial reconstruction of the exemplary writings of women, which have emerged in the field: aiming, now, to move women's voices to the centre of philosophical debates. As these voices are being heard evermore clearly, women philosophers have begun to shape distinctive feminist approaches to contemporary philosophy of religion.

History shows that the moral degradation of woman is due more to theological superstitions than to all other influences together.

Elizabeth Cady Stanton[1]

God alone can save us, keep us safe. The feeling or experience of a positive, objective, glorious existence, the feeling of subjectivity, is essential for us. Just like a God who helps us and leads us in the path of becoming, who keeps track of our limits and infinite possibilities – as women – who inspires our projects.

Luce Irigaray[2]

RANGING FROM THE SCALDING critique of Stanton to the reconstructive reflections of Irigaray, feminist philosophy of religion has been marked by a complex set of relations to the subject matter of religion, as well as to the discipline of philosophy. For those who find that the backlash against feminism and the revival of the religious right threaten to contribute as much to 'women's degradation' as old 'theological superstitions' do, Stanton's reasoning is still persuasive: the Word of God is the word of man, used to keep women in subjection and to hinder their emancipation. For others, who tend to identify with communities of faith and resistance, gynocentric efforts to create a possible space for the divine hold considerable appeal. Whether offering critique or reconstruction, women are (re)writing philosophy of religion today according to a variety of strategies whose overall rationale was articulated more than a hundred years ago by Anna Julia Cooper, an African-American feminist who appealed to the creation of a wholeness of vision:

It is not the intelligent woman vs. the ignorant woman, nor the white woman vs. the black, the brown, and the red – it is not even the cause of woman vs. man. Nay, it is woman's strongest vindication for speaking that *the world needs to hear her voice*. It would be subversive of every human interest that the cry of one half of the human family be stifled. Woman . . . daring to think and move and speak, – to undertake to help shape, mold and direct the thought of her age, is merely completing the circle of the world's vision.[3]

My purpose in this essay is to consider the ways in which philosophy of religion is currently being written in different voices and to offer a critique of the dominant direction of the discipline. By critique I mean the practice, as described by Jeffner Allen and Iris Marion Young, of showing the limits of a mode of thinking by forging an awareness of alternative, more liberating, ideas, symbols, and discourses.[4] Although I will suggest ways in which gender as an analytic category and gender studies as a body of knowledge cannot only challenge but also enrich and inform the methodological and substantive assumptions of philosophers of religion, I do not mean to suggest that gender hierarchy comprises a simple or exclusive category of analysis.[5] Given the interflowing streams of class, race, ethnicity, age, sexual orientation, and nationality that shape the complex modalities of social experience, it is unlikely that any one factor could ever suffice as a single or unitary focal point. And of course women cannot be presumed to speak in a single voice or to share a uniform 'experience.' Nevertheless, gender constitutes perhaps the most fundamental factor creating human difference, and it remains among the most ignored philosophically.

In the history of the philosophy of religion, gender bias has long operated to shape the ways in which the traditional problems and orientations of the field have been constructed. Like the cultural phenomenon of religion itself, philosophy of religion not only originated in a male tradition of production and transmission, with a history of excluding and devaluing women, but it has also been defined by many concepts and symbols marked as 'masculine,' which stand in oppositional relation to those marked as 'feminine.' Unlike the cultural phenomenon of religion, however, which is embedded in multiple cultural contexts, philosophy of religion has been largely Eurocentric and Anglo-American in its orientation. In addition to gender bias, its ethnocentrism constitutes the second major weakness of the field. For a long time, philosophy of religion has been written from a standpoint not unlike that of the Reverend Thwackum, the character in Henry Fielding's novel *Tom Jones*, who announced: 'When I say religion, I mean the Christian religion, and when I say the Christian religion, I mean the Protestant religion, and when I say the Protestant religion, I mean the Church of England!' If not always the Church of England, it is for the most part Protestant Christianity that has been conflated with 'religion' in the modern period of philosophy of religion. Most philosophers when they consider the field no doubt think of the standard topics and problems treated in the more familiar anthologies and textbooks: arguments for and against the existence of God; the nature and attributes of deity; the validity of religious knowledge claims; the question of theodicy; the justifiability of religious belief and language; the hope of immortality; the relation of faith and reason; evaluation of the nature of religious or mystical experiences, and so forth. Called upon to teach a course in philosophy of religion, many philosophers are likely to turn to the classic texts in the field, updated by contemporary readings, most of which conform in one way or another to Parson Thwackum's definition.

Undaunted by two such severe deficiencies – gender bias and ethnocentrism – the dominant Anglo-American analytic school of philosophy of religion has proved surprisingly healthy. Whereas at the midpoint of the twentieth century philosophy of religion was virtually defined by the assumptions and methods of logical positivism and empiricism, in the last few decades new and technically rigorous contributions by religiously committed philosophers have enlivened old theistic arguments. After long decades of dormancy when logical positivism seemed to yield only negative conclusions in the philosophy of religion, a resurgence of interest in traditional theism is occurring in mainstream philosophy of religion.[6] Thanks to the work of a variety of analytic philosophers, we now know, for example, that modal logic can be used to formulate a more perspicacious version of the ontological argument, that Bayesian models of probability can breathe new life into inductive justifications of religious belief, that rational choice theory can propel Pascal's wager once again to center stage, and that language-game analysis can offer a prima facie justification of religious language. Such developments, imported from other areas of philosophy, have prompted Richard Gale to suggest that 'philosophy of religion is to the core areas of philosophy – logic, scientific methodology, the philosophy of language, metaphysics, and epistemology – as Israel is to the Pentagon. The former are a proving ground for the weapons forged in the latter.'[7] Far from the days of wondering what Athens has to do with Jerusalem, philosophy and religion now appear to have entered a period of détente as comrades-in-arms. None of the new and sophisticated military hardware, however, engages the questions posed by feminist inquiry or aims at disarmament of the sexist elements of the traditional theistic model. Instead, in the work of philosophers such as Richard Swinburne, Alvin Plantinga, William Alston, and D.Z.

Phillips, philosophy of religion has been deployed in defense of the cogency of a standard form of Western monotheism, in the service of a conception of 'God' that is patriarchal, and in the vested interests of staunchly traditional forms of Christianity.[8]

Philosophy of religion [. . .] needs to shed both its gender bias and its ethnocentrism if it is to open out in new directions adequate to the twenty-first century. Not only is much of its content sexist and patriarchal, but its understanding of religion is parochially defined and monoculturally impaired. By contrast, the constructive contours of several new research programs that I will trace in this chapter offer an exciting potential for reshaping the field.

The problem of God and the critique of philosophy of religion

With its very subject matter – religion – so notoriously riddled with misogyny and androcentrism, the philosophy of religion can hardly ignore questions of gender ideology. Indeed, gender bias in religion has not been accidental or superficial. Elizabeth Johnson likens it to a buried continent whose subaqueous pull shapes all the visible landmass; androcentric bias has massively distorted every aspect of the terrain and rendered invisible, inconsequential, or nonexistent the experience and significance of half the human race.[9] Of all the manifold forms sexism takes, none has been more pernicious than the religious and theological restrictions on women's lives. For philosophers studying the intellectual effects and belief systems of religions, the opportunity to critique and correct sexist and patriarchal constructions in this field is as ample as it is urgent, given the ubiquitous presence of gender ideology in all known religions. Not one of the religions of the world has been totally affirming of women's personhood. Every one of them conforms to Heidi Hartmann's definition of patriarchy as 'relations between men, which have a material base, and which, though hierarchical, establish or create interdependence and solidarity among men that enable them to dominate women.'[10] All sacred literatures of the world display an unvarying ambivalence on the subject of women. For every text that places well-domesticated womanhood on a religious pedestal, another one announces that, if uncontrolled, women are the root of all evil. Religion thus comprises a primary space in which and by means of which gender hierarchy is culturally articulated, reinforced, and consolidated in institutionalized form. Religion is hardly the only such space, of course, but it appears to have been a particularly persistent and recurrent way of undergirding and sanctifying gender hierarchy in the West.

Not only does gender bias saturate the subject matter of philosophy of religion but it also permeates its practice, in ways that range from the sublime to the recidivist. On the recidivist side, a series of familiar lapses appears: the dearth of female authors in the leading journals or standard textbooks; the almost complete absence of attention to feminist philosophy on the part of mainstream authors, male and female; the exclusively male-authored and monochromatic complexion of the standard anthologies of readings and editorial boards. Even the use of inclusive language has been remarkably slow in finding its way into the scholarly publications and conceptual patterns of the field.[11] It is not unusual to find authors who discuss concepts of justice and fairness at length, using throughout the male pronoun. The 'simple matter of pronouns,' as Elizabeth Kamarck Minnich has remarked, 'contains the whole of our problem, and there is no shortcut to fixing it. Every time we stumble over a pronoun, we stumble over the root problem that entangles the dominant tradition in its own old errors.'[12] The dominant tradition, however, has barely begun to register the seriousness of the feminist criticism of patriarchal religious language.

This lapse is most apparent at the sublime end of the scale, where discussion of the problem of God, a topic that has been standard fare for all schools of philosophy of religion, epitomizes the pervasive gender bias infecting the field. Long a linchpin holding up other structures of patriarchal rule, the concept of a male God has been judged by every major feminist thinker, including Mary Daly, Rosemary Radford Ruether, Naomi Goldenberg, Judith Plaskow, Julia Kristeva, and Luce Irigaray, to be both humanly oppressive and, on the part of believers, religiously idolatrous. Why should a single set of male metaphors be absolutized as though supremely fitting about the subject? Contrary to the literary gesture of writers hoping to avoid sexist language with ritual disclaimers, it has not been persuasive simply to declare that the concept of God transcends gender and, therefore, 'he' is not literally male, and then to presume that all can go on as before. The problem remains that once the masculine has been raised to the universal human, beyond gender, the feminine alone must bear the burden of sexual difference.

Despite the de-anthropomorphizing efforts of many generations of theologians and philosophers, the sign God remains stubbornly gendered male in Western thought. Philosophers of religion have sometimes marked a distinction between the crudely anthropomorphic language of myth and popular piety, on the one hand, and the loftily conceptual and gender-neutral language of philosophy, on the other hand, while failing to account for the fact that the *Vorstellung*, or image, of a male personage is firmly inscribed in every major philosophical *Begriff*, or concept, of deity in the West, and the referent in the long history of philosophical arguments both for and against the existence of God is for the most part subliminally envisioned as male. Whether taken as real or unreal, inferred validly or invalidly, experienced directly or projected illusorily, the divine identity in classical theism has been unmistakably male. More problematically, the supreme, ruling, judging, as well as loving, male God envisioned as a single, absolute subject and named Father has been conceived as standing in a relation of hierarchical domination to the world. In ways both implicit and explicit, this has tended in turn to justify various social and political structures of patriarchy that exalt solitary human patriarchs at the head of pyramids of power. Drawn almost exclusively from the world of ruling-class men, traditional theistic concepts and images have functioned effectively to legitimate social and intellectual structures that grant a theomorphic character to men who rule but that relegate women, children, and other men to marginalized and subordinated areas. The discursive practices that construct the divine as male have been so intimately connected to the production of ideologies which devalue all that is not male that they have formed a constitutive element in the oppression of women and other "Others." Mary Daly pronounces the perfect apothegm on this form of sexism when she writes, 'If God is male, then the male is God.'[13]

At the same time, the problem of gender bias is more subtle than the dominance of male signifiers for deity alone indicates. It encompasses other topics and gender-inflected categories of traditional philosophy of religion, as well as the basic conceptual tools assumed in this field. Like a prism that refracts all the surrounding light, the gendering of God has skewed the way in which other problems in philosophy of religion have traditionally been constructed. The problem of *religious language*, for example, is frequently cast in terms of the meaning and use of metaphors and models, and questions of reference and truth. But the metaphors and models employed by mainstream philosophers of religion often trade uncritically on intrinsically hierarchical patterns of relations. Metaphors such as Father, King, Lord, Bridegroom, Husband, and God-He go unmarked. Let an occasional female model or metaphor intrude into this homosocial circle and it will immediately be remarked upon, usually producing nervous laughter in the classroom. In considerations of the so-called *divine attributes*, none receives more discussion in the literature than that of 'omnipotence,' by which some version of 'perfect power' is meant. In the eleventh century, Peter Damian could quote approvingly the biblical passage "O Lord, King Omnipotent, all things are placed in your power, and there is no one who is able to resist your will' as he argued that divine omnipotence is even able to 'restore a virgin to purity after her fall.'[14] In twentieth-century studies, 'perfect power' has not improved any.[15] On standard definitions of the concept of omnipotence, ranging from 'unilateral power to effect any conceivable state of affairs' to more moderate 'self-limiting power,' the kind of power in question is in principle one of domination, or power-over, and has been persistently associated with the characteristics of ideal masculinity. Like the two favorite heroes of modern philosophy, the Cartesian cognitive subject and the Kantian autonomous will, an omnipotent deity reflects the mirror image of idealized masculinist qualities. At the same time, philosophical arguments on behalf of the concept of divine aseity or self-sufficiency reinforce the disparagement of reciprocal power relations that is characteristic of patriarchy in its social and intellectual expressions. Among contemporary schools, only process philosophers of religion have explicitly argued against the attribute of omnipotence on the grounds that it is conceptually incoherent, scientifically superfluous, and morally offensive in its association of the divine with Male Controlling Power.[16]

In a related way, the topic of *theodicy* has also been deeply shaped by male-defined constructions of power and interest. The very form of the question, How can an all-powerful deity permit evil? implies a meaning of 'all-powerful' that is embedded in a discourse of domination. Also exemplary are the types of evil overlooked in the many hypotheticals, counterexamples, and possible worlds that are generated in discussions of theodicy by male philosophers. Misogyny and rape rarely make the list of evils. The whole drift of theodicy as an intellectual exercise points back to the question of God, and rarely to the world of cruelty and suffering.[17]

Philosophical debates on the topic of *immortality*, it could be argued, have also been deeply shaped by androcentric interests – centering on self-perpetuation and individual, rather than collective, survival. Charlotte Perkins Gilman, rightfully regarded as a foremother in feminist philosophy of religion, located the gender difference in *His Religion and Hers* (1923) this way: 'To the death-based religion, the main question is, "What is going to happen to me, after I am dead?" – a posthumous egoism. To the birth-based religion, the main question is, "What is to be done for the child who is born?" – an immediate altruism.'[18] Forgiving Gilman for the simplicity of her anthropology, we see her point. In philosophically emphasizing the absolute transcendence of God over the world, the dominating and all-encompassing nature of the divine power, and the splendid self-sufficiency and independence of the divine will, classical philosophical theism produced a perfect reflection of patriarchal consciousness in which it is

possible today to see only 'man.' Religiously, as well, classical theism's entire repertoire of beliefs concerning God, creation, redemption, and future hope have been
interwoven with characteristics that are oppressive to half of the human race.

A still deeper critique involves the differentiation of embedded levels of bias and
androcentrism in the crucial assumptions, methods, and norms of traditional philosophy of religion. Rooted in an ancient dualistic worldview whose philosophical inadequacy has been harder to detect, until recently, than its social and legalistic inequities,
Western religious categories have been inextricably bound up with 'a certain metaphysical exigency,' as Derrida calls it. The metaphysical worldview that once supported the
sacred canopy may have lost all cogency for the modern mind, along with the arguments of medieval Scholastics that sailors cannot kiss their wives good-bye on Sundays,
or hangmen go to heaven, but the dualisms associated with that worldview have continued to haunt the philosophical imagination, betraying an androcentric bias. Beginning with Greek philosophy's equation of the male principle with mind and reason and
act, the female principle was left with only a contrasting identification in terms of
matter, body and passion and potency. The subsequent history of Western philosophy,
despite major conceptual shifts, displayed a characteristic logic and form. Taking the
form of hierarchical opposition, the logic of binary structuring mutually opposed such
elements as mind and body, reason and passion, object and subject, transcendental and
empirical. As argued by any number of feminist philosophers, these hierarchical oppositions are typically gender-coded. Body, matter, emotions, instincts, and subjectivity
are coded as feminine, while mind, reason, science, and objectivity are coded as masculine.[19] Western monotheism has constructed the meaning of 'God' in relation to
'world' around these binary oppositions of mind/body, reason/passion, male/female.
In this way, not only religion in the West but also traditional philosophy of religion
remain complicitous with the very system of gender constructs and symbolic structures
that underlie women's oppression.[20] In the binary opposition between 'God' and
'world,' 'God' occupies the privileged space and acts as the central principle, the One
who confers identity to creatures to whom 'He' stands in hierarchical relation. Oppositional pairing of God/world has served in turn to organize others, such as heaven and
earth, sacred and profane. The widespread dichotomy of sacred/profane, employed by
many authors, thus comes already encoded with the hierarchical oppositions of
male/female and masculine/feminine onto which it is mapped, along with the structurally related pairs, white/black and heterosexual/homosexual.[21] The first term in
each pair is sacralized, while the second is rendered profane.

Along with the broad dissemination of the foregoing critique has come an increasing awareness that the relation between symbolic structures, on the one hand, and
gender constructions, on the other, cannot be specified in terms of a single explanatory
model. The power of symbolic orders to invoke and reinscribe implicit gender understandings works in varied and complex ways, as shown in recent studies. Emphasizing
the polysemic and multivalent quality of religious symbols, Caroline Bynum's work, for
example, stresses the ability of a symbol to hold different meanings for different
people. Never a simple matter of sheer reflection of the social order, the relation
between society and symbol, or between psyche and symbol, is open-ended. Relations
of reversal or inversion of actual social structures may also obtain, making it risky for
the interpreter to posit a single unidirectional cause-and-effect relation between symbol
and social setting. As Bynum points out, meaning is not so much imparted as it is

appropriated 'in a dialectical process whereby it becomes subjective reality for the one who uses the symbol,' allowing for the possibility that 'those with different gender experiences will appropriate symbols in different ways.'[22] An important implication of this is that no necessary correlation can be assumed between goddess-worshipping cultures and actual egalitarian social structures in the lives of females and males of that culture. Similarly, the male Father God may open up a range of different interpretative possibilities for both women and men. In culturally specific and historically unstable ways, religious symbols, even of the male Father God, have been useful in resisting and subverting the social order, not only in reflecting or reinforcing it. In light of these considerations, it is risky to generalize across cultures, religious traditions, or historical periods with respect to the different ways in which males and females appropriate or construct religious symbolism. More detailed historical and philosophical analyses are needed of the relations between symbolic structure and gender constructions.[23]

Although mainstream philosophers have so far failed to take explicit account of the gendered dynamics of religious thought, for over two decades a variety of other scholars, including biblical exegetes, theologians, ethicists, and feminist philosophers of religion, have produced an extraordinary explosion of research resulting in feminist theologies, critical hermeneutics of suspicion, and woman-affirming writings on spirituality. In these, 'the problem of God' reappears as a crucial site of reconstruction to which I selectively attend in the next section.

Reconstructing the meaning of the divine

The medieval theologian Hildegard of Bingen, struggling to capture her vision of the Spirit of God, wrote with a cascade of vivid images, a mélange of metaphors. As rendered by Elizabeth Johnson in the following passage, Hildegard's vision encompasses many of the themes that appear in the writing of twentieth-century feminist writers. The divine spirit, according to Hildegard, is the very life of the life of all creatures; the way in which everything is penetrated with connectedness and relatedness; a burning fire who sparks, ignites, inflames, kindles hearts; a guide in the fog; a balm for wounds; a shining serenity; an overflowing fountain that spreads to all sides. 'She is life, movement, color, radiance, restorative stillness in the din. Her power makes all withered sticks and souls green again with the juice of life. She purifies, absolves, strengthens, heals, gathers the perplexed, seeks the lost. She pours the juice of contrition into hardened hearts. She plays music in the soul, being herself the melody of praise and joy. She awakens mighty hope, blowing everywhere the winds of renewal in creation.'[24] This, for Hildegard in the eleventh century, is the mystery of the God in whom humans live and move and have our being.

Eight centuries later, Paula Gunn Allen has written in similarly provocative language of the spirit that is pervasive of her Languna Pueblo/Sioux peoples: 'There is a spirit that pervades everything, that is capable of powerful song and radiant movement, and that moves in and out of the mind. The colors of this spirit are multitudinous, a glowing, pulsing rainbow. Old Spider Woman is one name for this quintessential spirit, and Serpent Woman is another . . . and what they together have made is called Creation, Earth, creatures, plants and light.'[25]

In Ntozake Shange's well-known play, a tall black woman rises from despair and cries out, 'i found god in myself and i loved her, i loved her fiercely.'[26] Alice Walker, in a frequently citied passage in *The Color Purple*, voices a similar note as Shug recounts to Celie the epiphany that came over her when she learned to get the old white man off her eyeball:

> It? I ast.
> Yeah, It. God ain't a he or a she, but a It.
> But what do it look like? I ast.
> Don't look like nothing, she say. It ain't a picture show. It ain't something you can look at apart from anything else, including yourself. I believe God is every-thing, say Shug. Everything that is or ever will be. And when you can feel that, and be happy to feel that, you've found It.[27]

In recent theological constructions, Rosemary Ruether has worked with the unpronounceable written symbol 'God/ess,' used to connote the 'encompassing matrix of our being' that transcends patriarchal limitations and signals redemptive experience for women as well as for men. Modeling God for a nuclear age, Sallie McFague has experimented with metaphors of God as Mother, Lover, and Friend of the world which is conceived of as God's own body. Correlating the Tillichean notion of the power of being with the empowerment women know in freeing themselves from patriarchy, the early Mary Daly posited God as 'Verb,' a dynamic becoming process that energizes all things. Using process philosophy's categories, Marjorie Suchocki has given new resonance to the meaning of Whitehead's metaphors of God as 'the lure for feeling' whose 'power of persuasion' aims to effect justice and peace. Blurring the lines between psychological, somatic, and religious experiences, Luce Irigaray projects a concept of 'the feminine divine' grounded in the morphology of women's bodies in all their multiplicity and fluidity.[28] Significantly in all the cases cited here, contemporary women's articulation of a relation between God and the world depicts the divine as continuous with the world rather than as radically transcendent ontologically or meta-physically. Divine transcendence is seen to consist in total immanence. But images and metaphors are not philosophical concepts, and the reference range of 'the divine' as it appears in these and other feminist writings is not always clear. While theologians are frequently satisfied to work imaginatively with symbols, images, and metaphors, without regard to the question *what* the symbols are symbolic *of*, philosophers of reli-gion normally seek more precision and conceptual clarification.

On the difficult question of the meaning and reference of God-talk, two contemporary schools of philosophy of religion offer potentially promising reconstruc-tive and revisionist avenues. Both the tradition that employs the classical ontology of being, extending from Thomas Aquinas to Paul Tillich and the early Mary Daly, and the tradition that employs an ontology of becoming, extending from Alfred North White-head to Charles Hartshorne, John Cobb Jr., Marjorie Suchocki, and Catherine Keller, afford systematic conceptual schemes for explicating the metaphors that appear in various contemporary writings concerning 'the sacred' and any of its variants, such as 'the divine,' 'spirit,' 'God,' 'transcendence,' or 'higher power.' Both traditions can be modified, moreover, according to qualifications I will suggest, and thereby seen to con-verge in a single conceptual model, rendered as 'creativity' in Whitehead's system and as being *(esse)* in Aquinas's.

The school of thought known as process philosophy has been re-writing philosophy of religion in a radically different voice for several decades, providing the basis for a revisionist theism that is better termed 'panentheism,' or all-in-god. Preeminently among those who have labored in this cenury to construct a coherent philosophy of God that is also consistent with scientific cosmology and evolutionary theory, process philosophers of religion have produced, in addition, a model relatively free of sexism and androcentrism. The underlying values of the process worldview are organic, relational, dynamic, and embodied. Whitehead's 1929 elaboration of the idea that 'it is as true to say that God creates the World as that the World creates God'[29] anticipated the themes of interrelatedness and mutual conditioning that feminist philosophy has developed in multiple ways in recent decades.[30]

In the process paradigm everything comes into being by grasping or 'prehending' antecedently actualized things to integrate them into a new actualized thing, its own self. Supplanting substance philosophy's idea that it takes an agent to act, process philosophy proposes a model whereby agents are the results of acts and subjects are constituted out of relations. Quantum units of becoming achieve momentary unity out of a given multiplicity in a never-ending rhythm of creative process whereby 'the many become one and are increased by one.'[31] Creativity within each occasion is spontaneous, the mark of actuality, and free, within the limits determined by its antecedent causes. Creativity unifies every many and is creative of a new unifying perspective that then becomes one among the many. In a process ontology, creativity is ultimate reality not in the sense of something more ultimate behind, above, or beyond reality but in the sense of something ultimately descriptive of all reality, or of what the biologist Charles Birch and the theologian John B. Cobb Jr. call 'the Life Process.'[32] As a category, creativity is the 'ultimate of ultimates' in Whitehead's words, but as such it is only an abstraction, the formal character of any actual occasion. Creativity as concrete, however, signifies the dynamism that is the very actuality of things, their act of being there at all. Everything exists in virtue of creativity, but creativity is not any *thing*.

The proposal to view the divine as equivalent to creativity marks a crucial departure from Whitehead's own notion of God as an actual entity in the process of becoming, but it acquires support from its correlation with the tradition that employs the language of being, rather than becoming, to explicate the meaning of the divine. In its classical medieval synthesis in Aquinas, this tradition conceptualizes the divine as *esse ipsum* and holds that in God essence and existence are one; that is, God's very nature is *esse*, to be. Everything that exists does so through participation in divine being, or being itself. Although for Aquinas and classical thinkers, being was thought to be already concretized in a single source that was supremely actual, precisely this assumption undergoes modification in the shift from a substance metaphysics to one in which processive-relational categories are taken as ultimate. Desubstantialized and freed from static fixity in neo-Scholastic metaphysics, being signifies the source and power of all that exists. Dynamized and pluralized according to the process paradigm, being does not repose in an originary source antecedent to every event; rather, it constitutes the very act of be-ing, of liv-ing, of exist-ing in the present moment as a new one emergent from an antecedent many. As such, being or creativity is inherently relational and processive. It is immanent within each momentary event as its spontaneous power; and it is also transcendent to that event of becoming in the sense that it is never exhausted by the forms in which it is found but is always potentially a 'more' that is 'not yet' actualized. As long as being, like creativity, is not construed as something a being *has* but rather as what it means *to be* at all, the identification of God with being in the West can be understood to point to sheer livingness or that which energizes all things to exist. Although no-thing particular in its own right, being is the very actuality of things, their act of being there at all. Being-itself is therefore not construed as a particular being, thus ruling out pictorial theism's anthropomorphisms; it is not the sum of beings, thus ruling out pictorial theism's anthropomorphisms; it is not the sum of beings, thus ruling out a simple aggregration; it is not a property of things nor an accidental quality, not a substance, and not a class of things.

Articulating this tradition in light of recent feminist writings about God, Elizabeth Johnson explicates the concept of *esse* to signify 'pure aliveness in relation, the unoriginate welling up of fullness of life in which the whole universe participates.'[33] Like the theologian–philosopher of religion Paul Tillich, Johnson understands the symbol God to refer to the creative ground of all that is and the re-creative ground of the energy to resist nonbeing toward the good that may yet be, the future promised but unknown. For Johnson the religious 'naming toward God' as 'Holy Mystery' is not an utterly agnostic gesture but analogical in that the dynamic and immanental idea of God is the idea of that which energizes all things. The concept of God as *esse* within this ontological framework refers to the sheer actuality of things, an act common to all things. Dynamic and living, being is yet elusive. Signifying the moment-to-moment reality in virtue of which everything exists, the philosophical concepts of creativity (as explicated by Whitehead) and of *esse* (as explicated dynamically) are useful for interpreting what philosophy of religion in a new and different voice could mean by 'divine reality,' 'holy mystery,' 'empowering spirit,' and a variety of other metaphors and symbols.

By providing a unifying concept that articulates a common feature of various experiences of the presence and absence of empowerment, reconstruction of the concept of God along the lines adumbrated here can illuminate and give coherence to the varieties of women's and men's experiences at three levels: the personal and interpersonal; social systems and institutional structures; and the all-encompassing natural world. Any person, for example, who survives horrible crime, assault, war, or famine, and who wants to praise the power or powers that permit her being in the face of nonbeing, experiences the meaning of creativity, of being, even if she can no longer give credence to the faith of the fathers. Anyone who experiences life's fresh starts of vitality and freedom, of courage renewed, or of love restored in unlikely circumstances, encounters the mystery of the divine. All those women and men who in their sheer grit to keep on keeping on find the strength to march, organize, protest, sue, walk out, tear down, make peace, or rebuild, are animated by the spirit. And anyone who has ever felt awe before the power of ocean and sky, the majesty of mountain, the peace of prairie, or the wildness of any part of nature's terrible beauty, has been stirred by the same living God.[34]

While revisionist and depatriarchalized philosophies of God will clearly continue to engage some philosophers of religion, others are willing to see even that topic cease to hold center stage in future philosophies of religion. As new waves of historicism and antiessentialism begin to register among a new generation of postanalytic philosophers of religion, dissatisfaction is developing with the way in which the traditional table of contents has been constructed. Michael McGhee, for example, criticizes the tendency of philosophers silently to assimilate questions about religion to questions about 'belief in the existence of God.' Complaining of the slippery slope whereby philosophers slide from 'religion' to religious 'belief' and from that to 'belief in God,' McGhee laments the way that 'philosophical reflection about religion is transformed without a pause into reflection on the existence of God, and questions about the rationality of belief, the validity of the proofs, and the coherence of the divine attributes cannot be far behind.' The established methodology that causes this slide may be historically understandable in terms of the influence of natural theology on philosophy of religion, but the real issue, McGhee notes, 'is whether such preoccupations should remain central to the philosophy of religion, and, if not, what should replace them.'[35] Strong examples of alternative preoccupations from recent work are considered in the next sections.

Engendering new philosophies of religion

Two major thematic concerns serve to distinguish the new generation of texts from mainstream analytic philosophy of religion. First, the body, a recurrent theme in a variety of recent interdisciplinary studies, figures as the material or symbolic basis for much new writing, in contrast to the fiction of disembodied subjectivity that marks most mainstream epistemology.[36] Second, analysis of the complex relations between power and knowledge recurs in the new philosophies of religion, in contrast to the dominant paradigm's failure to take seriously enough the social processes that construct subjectivity, the discursive practices that construct the discipline of philosophy itself, and the relations of power that inform both.

Reinclusion of the embodied character of subjectivity produces, for example, such subtle and provocative investigations as Paula Cooey's *Religious Imagination and the Body*. Giving the body a major epistemological role as medium, Cooey explores its ambiguous double role as site and as sign, and demonstrates how wide a range of new inquiries can be opened up for philosophy of religion by this focus. Among the new questions that emerge from the conjuction of the body, sexuality, and religious experience are those that Cooey formulates for further study; they are worth quoting at length to highlight the difference between a religious epistemology oriented to embodied subjectivity and mainstream ones in which such questions never get posed in connection with the topic of mystical or religious experience:

> What role does eroticism play in mystical experience? Given contemporary claims that sexual exploration liberates and empowers, are there material and historical relations between mystical self-transcendence and disciplined transgression of sexual taboos, and, if so, what are they? What kinds of meaning and value do such experiences produce? How does acknowledging the involvement of sexuality in mystical experiences, whether sexuality is suppressed or exercised, materially affect the central symbols or concepts themselves? Does acknowledging the involvement of the body in mystical experiences tell us anything new about the role of central symbols as place-setters, or the prescription of limits on language itself? Given that transgression may include violence perpetrated by a self upon the self or others, how does disciplined transgression of sexual taboos (for example, sadomasochistic practices) relate to other contexts of violence (for example, torture, war, domestic violence, and rape)? Does the occurrence of

sexual transgression in the context of a religious symbol system substantively differ from any other context? What does it mean that believers attribute wrath, carnage, sexual transgression, erotic behavior, and sexual acts to their deities? Does the absence of such attributions simply mask and deny the reality of the violence of human existence?[37]

In another kind of body-based study, Howard Eilberg-Schwartz's provocative work *God's Phallus and Other Problems for Men and Monotheism* is indicative of a new alliance of philosophy of religion with gender studies and social theory, rather than with natural theology and speculative metaphysics.[38] Dozens of feminist studies over the past twenty-five years have explored the way in which male deities authorize male domination in the social order. Written mostly by women, these studies typically have attended to the way in which a male divinity undermines female experience by both legitimating male authority and deifying masculinity. Left unconsidered until very recently has been the question whether a male divinity generates certain dilemmas and tensions for the conception of masculinity, rendering its meaning unstable. Overturning the conventional assumption that Jewish monotheism centered on an invisible, disembodied deity, Eilberg-Schwartz shows through careful analysis of numerous myths that ancient Israel did image God in human form, while at the same time veiling the divine phallus.

Two consequences in particular arise for masculinity in a religious system that imagines a male deity with a phallus. First, the dilemma of homoerotic desire is posed when men worship a male God in a culture based on heterosexual complementarity. Although the expression of divine-human intimacy is couched in the language of male-female complementarity, it is males, not females, who enter in to the convenantal marriage with the deity. Collectively, Israelite men were constituted discursively as 'she' and were said to be 'whoring' when they strayed from monotheism (monogamy) into idolatry (adultery). Suppression of the homoerotic impulse in the divine-human relationship, however, could take several forms: hiding and veiling the body of God through prohibitions against depicting God; feminizing Israelite males so that they could assume the role of God's wife; and exaggerating the way in which women are 'other' so as to minimize the ways in which men are made into others of God.

The solution of imagining Israel as a metaphoric woman, in an exclusive relation to the divine maleness, may have solved the first dilemma of homoerotic desire only by generating another. The second major dilemma for masculinity is posed by being made in the image of a sexless Father God in a culture defined by patrilineal descent. The sexlessness of a Creator Father God sets up major tensions for men who must procreate. In contrast to the Christian religion, whose different logic of a God fathering a Son could render a human father irrelevant, Hebrew logic placed great importance on the human father, generating tension around a Father God who was thought to be sexless and therefore without a son. When the dilemma of homoerotic desire is again posed for Christian men in relation to a male Christ's body, it, too, is avoided by speaking collectively of the Christian community as a woman.

Just as feminist theorists have yet to explore fully the question of how a male God is problematic for men's conceptions of self, feminist critique has left unthought the difference between God as male and God as Father, according to Eilberg-Schwartz. Strict focus on the ways in which a masculine image of God undermines female experience tends 'to conflate human and divine masculinities into one undifferentiated symbol.'[39] Differentiating between images of male deities and images of father deities, Eilberg-Schwartz contends that the maleness of God may have different implications than the fatherliness of God. Fatherly images of God can and should be used, he argues, 'but only if equally powerful female images are also celebrated.' Repudiating the incorporeal, distant God that helped to generate the hierarchical associations of masculinity and femininity, he favors an image of 'a tender loving Father who faces and embraces the child,' in the apparent expectation that a loving and embodied God may support a different kind of masculinity, one more capable of intimacy and tenderness.[40]

An indication of another new direction available to philosophers of religion appears in the growing influence of poststructuralist criticism, which accords great significance to the webbed relations of language, experience, power, and discourse. The links frequently assumed among these terms, however, leave a lot of open, untheorized space. Mary McClintock Fulkerson brilliantly exposes and attempts to fill these gaps in *Changing the Subject*, a study of women's discourses, feminist theology, and the import of the poststructuralist revolution. One of the most powerful insights of the post-structuralist discourse analysis that Fulkerson deploys is its challenge to three inadequate notions of language, gender, and power: (1) the idea that linguistic signs re-present the thing; (2) the Cartesian assumption of the subjective consciousness as the origin of meaning; and (3) the understanding of power only in terms of external, unidirectional, and negative oppression. Poststructuralist method also critiques the related liberal logic of inclusion that appeals to 'women's experience' as though it is an unproblematic or uncoded content of some kind. All such strategies and methods, Fulkerson shows, fail to recognize and account for the multiplicity of differences among myriad subject positions. In contrast to the liberal humanist goal of accommodating as many 'different voices' as possible, discourse analysis seeks a more radical reading of the ways 'voice' itself is produced and knowledge is power. In order to flesh out the multiple orderings that create differences in women's positions, a major epistemic shift is needed, one that has already been more fully accomplished by theologians and literary critics than by philosophers of religion. According to Fulkerson, taking into account the inextricable and multiplicative character of the link between knowledge and the social relations out of which knowledge emerges changes the question, as well as the subject. The question is not, for example, whether a given religious belief system is oppressive or liberating to women. Such generic and wholesale frames need to be replaced by more complex appreciation of the construction of multiple identities according to different locations in the social formation of patriarchal capitalism.

Calling explicit attention to the priority of interpretive interest on the part of scholars, Fulkerson examines the way that social relations and politcal elements in the form of postindustrial capitalism and modern disciplinary technologies are implicated in the construction of both readers and texts. In this account, signifying processes constitute the very objects that philosophers of religion consider and often reify as natural. At the same time, philosophers of religion occupy social positions of power, which further construct their own complex identities, discourses, and desires. Therefore, philosophies that regard language or ideas as straightforward reflections of, or homologous with, the social relations of their proponents turn out to be quite inadequate. Equally, the pretense to be interest-free belies the situated, interested nature of all knowing and disguises the way the philosopher of religion's own theoretical discourse is impacted by power.

Fleshing out the multiple orderings that create differences in women's positions should result in a clarification of what is at stake in appeals to 'women's experience,' often taken as a 'source' and/or 'norm' for feminist thought in an earlier generation of texts. Rather than as a 'content' that is representative of a natural realm of women's consciousness, religious or otherwise, 'women's experience' can be understood as constructed from 'converging discourses, their constitution by differential networks, and their production of certain pleasures and subjugations.'[41] There is, therefore, no essential woman, or inner consciousness, or natural body that transcends all particularities to which one can appeal in order to join women together in a shared dilemma/oppression and a shared vision of emancipation. Experience is not the origin of (feminist) philosophy of religion in the sense of offering evidence for its claims, but the very reality that needs to be explained. Similarly, in theorizing the link, for example, between the maleness of divine imagery and the legitimation of male dominance, what needs to be *explained* is how the maleness of divine imagery gets distributed and interrelated with material realities, and *how* the discourse itself carries out the oppression of women.

Once the false universal of 'women's experience' or 'human experience' is replaced with Fulkerson's 'analytic of women's discourses,' philosophers of religion can begin to consider the specific productions of positions for women, asking such questions as: What discourses construct the middle-class white churchwoman's positions? The poor Pentecostal woman preacher's? The liberal academic liberation feminist's? In extended accounts of Appalachian Pentecostal women preachers' discourse and of the discourse of Presbyterian women's groups, Fulkerson illuminates how these two very diverse women's subject positions have wrestled with a religious tradition in ways both liberating and constraining. By approaching the world of faith as a system of discourses, rather than as representational interpretations or cognitive belief claims, she displays how women's faith positions can be constitutive of their emancipatory practices. The call stories and worship performances of poor Pentecostal women ministers, accompanied by ecstatic and bodily displays of joy, produce particular forms of resistance to patriarchal constraints, just as the faith practices of middle-class Presbyterian housewives produce other possibilities for transgression, pleasure, and desire.

The merit of this methodological shift for philosophy of religion is a greatly enhanced display of the complexity of gender discourse, of the constraints and resistances found in faith practices, and of the social conditions of signification. Above all, poststructuralist criticism has the merit of fully displaying a feminist commitment to the situated character of knowledge. Unlike mainstream analytic philosophy, it creates space in which it is possible to ask what philosophy of religion has occluded from its angle of vision by virtue of the abstract and distanced discourse that characterizes it. The problem is not that philosophy of religion employs abstractions; all theoretical discourse must employ critical and abstract reasoning. The problem occurs when philosophy's abstractions are presented as disembodied and independent of the philosopher's social position, as though innocent of the philosopher's own complicity in the power/knowledge relation. Failing to pursue the implications of the central insight that discourse (including the very discourse of mainstream analytic philosophy of religion) produces meaning effects, philosophers of religion are unlikely to be able to problematize their own writing.

Even as she invokes a feminist theological principle that 'only that which supports the full humanity of women is revelatory,' Fulkerson points out that 'the standard for "full humanity" is precisely what we do not have or know.'[42] Her use of a poststruc-turalist account of discourse rules out the possibility of claims that can be validated outside of particular communities and their languages. Appealing to nonfoundational-ism, the position that eschews the search for justifying beliefs or experiences that can in turn support other beliefs derived from them, Fulkerson apparently does not find it necessary to offer reasoned arguments for the faith claims and theological commitments she both makes and invokes.[43] This aspect of the method of discourse analysis may be more or less disturbing to philosophers or religion insofar as they find the project of proving or defending the existence or non-existence of God to be an interesting one. Fulkerson clearly does not. The pertinent discursive practices she analyzes are those of resistance, survival, agape, and hope – practices, she freely admits, that *assume* the existence of God rather than problematize it.

How far discourse analysis such as Fulkerson's can go toward ever *subverting* the belief structures of Pentecostal women ministers or Presbyterian housewives remains an open question. Are certain structures of belief more emancipatory or enslaving than others? When the object of belief is assumed to be unreal, can the language of transcendence still be retained as poetic probes? Might women-centered beliefs and gynocentric practices deconstruct and show the partiality of masculinist models of deity? This constellation of questions is at the heart of another new direction available to philosophy of religion, appearing at the intersection of philosophy, psychoanalytic theory, and French feminist thought. An increasingly influential source for those who would fashion a more inclusive philosophy of religion is the work of Luce Irigaray, whose explicit insistence on the importance of the religious dimension to the creation of women's subjectivity and self-transcendence stands in some contrast to other analyses, such as Simone de Beauvoir's. Indeed, Irigaray goes so far as to claim: 'Divinity is what we need to become free, autonomous, sovereign. No human subjectivity, no human society has ever been estab-lished without the help of the divine. There comes a time for destruction. But, before destruction is possible, God or the gods must exist.'[44] The gynocentric models of 'God or the gods' that Irigaray favors go hand in hand with the project of a new ethics of sexual difference that would recognize the subjectivity of each sex instead of symbolically split-ting the maternal to the feminine and the spiritual to the masculine.

But how are Irigaray's recent calls for 'a feminine divine' to be understood? Although a number of critical analyses of Irigaray's texts and their implications for Anglo-American philosophy of religion are beginning to appear,[45] the work of Amy Hollywood is perhaps the most lucid and philosophically important of these. Holly-wood's analysis discloses that Irigaray's acceptance of a Feuerbachian projection theory of religion, in which God is the projection of human wishes, attributes, and desires, complicates her efforts to construct a new 'feminine divine.' 'What Irigaray appears to forget,' Hollywood notes, 'is Feuerbach's central claim (and the grounds for his hope that the hold of religion might be *broken*): for religious projection to function, its mechanism must be hidden so that its object might inspire belief.'[46] Irigaray recognizes that the 'exposure' of this mechanism has not destroyed religion for many, and hence asserts the importance of adequate projections. But how is such projection possible or meaningful for those, like Irigaray herself, who assume that the object of belief is unreal? If Irigaray maintains a Feuerbachian human referent for her own projection of religious discourse in terms of female representations of the divine, the feminine divine, too, would seem to facilitate its own destruction. What possibilities does this leave for female transcendence? Can belief be simultaneously posited *and* decon-structed? Can the strong female subjectivity created in and by a mystic such as Teresa of Avila become available to women *without* Teresa's acceptance of a transcendent Other who is the divine? Because transcendence for Irigaray is associated with the 'male' and a sacrificial economy, it is not clear how women are expected to claim the new subject-ivity that she thinks religion, reconstituted, can offer. According to Hollywood, 'Her ambivalence with regard to belief and transcendence leads her immediately to decon-struct the very deities she invokes.' For all of its intriguing promise, this gynocentric project in philosophy of religion creates distinctive tensions, leading Hollywood to inquire 'how far the immanent can be re-inscribed as the site of transcendence without returning to the logic of sacrifice and bodily suffering seemingly endemic to the incar-national theologies of Christianity.' There is also the related question of 'whether belief can be mimed without re-inscribing women into a logic of the same such as that which Irigaray sees underlying Christianity.[47]

Insofar as preoccupation with the very concept of belief itself stands at the center of much modern philosophy of religion, Irigaray's 1981 essay entitled 'Belief Itself' is of special interest.[48] In Amy Hollywood's reading of this allusive text, 'Irigaray argues that the constitution of the normative subject of religion and philosophy depends on the mastery and silencing of the mother('s) body, and hence the denial of real differences between the sexes and between subjects.[49] Irigaray's argument is not only the familiar feminist one that the *object* of belief is male-defined but also the more radical claim that the *structure* and discourse of belief itself are masculinist and in need of deconstruction. Irigaray's development of this argument relies upon critical appropriations of psycho-analysis and Derridean reading practices to show how the related issues of embodiment and presence and absence are implicated in the formation of the subject, belief, and sexual difference. The constitution of normative (Western, bourgeois) subjectivity depends on the association of the body with the mother and femininity and an always incomplete and ambivalent mastering, concealment, or denial of the mother's body. Freud's own account of the *fort-da* game ('gone'-'there') played by his grandson, Ernst, exposes the relationship between belief and the little boy's mastery of the mother's presence and absence, concealedness and unconcealedness. Despite her apparent absence, she is there, the boy comes to believe, and in so believing he experiences his own power. For Irigaray, God, as the Father and the source of meaning, is the object of a belief first articulated in the (male child's) attempt to master the mother's absence; according to Hollywood's gloss, the dismantling of the subject as master, then, implies a concomitant deconstruction of the object of belief.

In the final analysis, it may be that Irigaray refuses simply to reduce the divine to Feuerbachian new 'ego ideals' projected for women, for on her own terms this could only mean a reversion to the logic of the same and negation of the possibility of radical alterity. Not wanting to negate the divine entirely, as she also wants to hold out the hope to women of transcendence, Irigaray can be interpreted as reinscribing a religious language that leads neither to theism nor to atheism but, rather, to a dialectic of immanence and transcendence that is strongly reminiscent of certain medieval Christian mystics. The medieval mystics Mechthild, Hadewijch, and Marguerite Porete are important as well to Amy Hollywood because, among other things, they afford philo-sophy or religion new ways of talking about the divine or the sacred that do not in any way assume an 'object of belief' along hierarchical lines of verticality.[50]

As is evident from even this limited discussion, the effort of engendering philosophy of religion anew in the different voices noted here raises new questions, identifies alternative kinds of issues as relevant, and focuses attention on the value judgments, the political effects, and the power dimensions of philosophical work in this field. One important way in which women, in conjunction with other elided groups and perspectives, hope to change the contours and texture of mainstream philosophy of religion consists in making epistemological questions an explicit point of focus. What has the status of knowledge? What gets valorized as worth knowing? What are the criteria evoked? Who has the authority to establish meaning? Who is the presumed subject of belief? How does the social position of the subject affect the content of religious belief? What is the impact upon religious life of the subject's sexed body? What do we learn by examining the relations between power, on the one hand, and what counts as evidence, foundations, modes of discourse, and forms of apprehension and transmission, on the other hand? In view of the intimate connection of power/knowledge, how do we handle the inevitable occlusion that attends all knowledge production? What particular processes constitute the normative cultural subject as masculine in its philosophical and religious dimensions? Questions such as these have not previously been asked in philosophy of religion; their answers will depend upon the intellectual capaciousness and undisciplined, because interdisciplinary, freedom of a new generation of philosophers.

Addendum 2002

Since the time the above was first written in 1994, and published in 1998, much has changed. I cannot encompass in this brief space all the intervening literature, but I hope to highlight several landmarks and emerging themes, and then to raise some very broad questions that seem to me more urgent today than eight years ago.

Happily, we can point to vital signs that feminist philosophy of religion is maturing as a distinct field. The first indication of this is the appearance of two book-length studies: Pamela Sue Anderson's (1998) *A Feminist Philosophy of Religion: The Rationality and Myths of Religious Belief* and Grace M. Jantzen's (1999) *Becoming Divine: Towards a Feminist Philosophy of Religion*.[51] Another measure of the increasing vitality of feminist philosophy of religion is the publication of such collections as *Feminist Interpretations of Mary Daly*, devoted to an overdue assessment of one of the most original authors in the field, and *Feminist Interpretations of Soren Kierkegaard*, containing critical analyses by different feminists of the 'father of religious existentialism.'[52] Unlikely even ten years ago, the first volume of a major reference work covering 1900–2000, the *Handbook of Contemporary Philosophy of Religion*, published by Kluwer, concludes with a chapter on feminist philosophy of religion as represented by Mary Daly, Sally McFague, Luce Irigaray, Julia Kristeva, Pamela Sue Anderson, and Grace Jantzen.[53] Finally, volumes like the present one, conceived and edited by Pamela Sue Anderson and Beverley Clack, are stimulating new thinking on a variety of topics at the intersections of feminism, philosophy, and religion as these are being reconfigured in the twenty-first century.

Of course, some things have not changed. Analytic philosophy of religion to a man continues to ignore the questions and alternatives proposed by feminist philosophers of religion; and feminists in other areas of philosophy for the most part continue to neglect the subject of religion, arguably the most multiply intersecting variable in the construction of gender, sexuality, and subjectivity. The rise of religious fundamentalisms in all religions throughout the world has made an understanding of religion politically urgent and ethically important for feminist theory in general, not only because this has been accompanied by the promotion and enforcement of traditional gender roles, the explicit intent of which has entailed the subordination of women, but also because women of all classes and in all corners of the world are active and pious participants within religious traditions, not simply passive victims. Likewise, feminist scholars interested in postcolonial studies have addressed race, gender, and sexuality in the context of colonialism, but until recently, ignored the critical importance of religion to these dimensions. The wide-ranging studies in the 2002 collection, *Postcolonialism, Feminism, and Religious Discourse*, begin to redress this omission, encompassing contributions from feminist scholars who are Native American (Cherokee), Chinese, Botswanan, Turkish, Jewish, African-American, and Euro-American.[54] More such multicultural and multireligious anthologies are needed.

If Anderson's *A Feminist Philosophy of Religion* and Jantzen's *Becoming Divine* are any indication, several generalizations about the current state of feminist philosophy of religion can be risked. First, the standard division between Anglo-American philosophy and Continental philosophy, still apparent in mainstream philosophy, is evaporating in feminist philosophy of religion. Both Anderson and Jantzen engage a wide variety of texts and problems typically identified with both styles of philosophy. Second, the influence of French feminisms on the work of Anglo-American feminist philosophers of religion is strong and likely to remain unabated for some time.[55] In particular, Irigaray's work inspires by far the most commentarial, critical, or constructive attention. Third, in 2002 it is evident that the 'feminism' in feminist philosophy of religion is still largely 'white feminism.' Race constitutes an unthematized ground of what Ellen Armour has called 'whitefeminism's white solipsism.'[56]

Fourth, a thoroughgoing critique of epistemology-centered philosophy is at work in contemporary feminist philosophy of religion, strikingly similar to that found in classical American pragmatism. Both Anderson and Jantzen replace the disembodied subject or mind or consciousness posited by traditional philosophy ('rationalism') with an understanding of subjectivity or consciousness as a historical artifact rather than an absent cause. In common with a host of other feminist philosophers, they insist that the condition of reason or truth or knowledge is not abstraction from particular, historically determinate circumstances, that is, from the locations and effects of desire, but rather immersion in them. In doing so, each makes explicit the central theme of feminism that men no longer monopolize the resources of rationality, that the self-mastering 'man of reason' is no longer the only subject who speaks. On questions of the justifiability of religious belief – previously centerstage in philosophy of religion – Anderson and Jantzen, as well as other feminists, are divided. Jantzen argues that the category of belief and questions about the justification of religious belief can be dismissed as comprising nothing but part of the masculine symbolic. Anderson, although her intention is *not* to *justify* theistic beliefs, does not so swiftly dismiss such questions; her analysis of issues related to reason, objectivity, and desire recognizes that the gendered – often sexist and racist – nature of our social and physical locations supports the need for better, or less distorted, philosophical reflection. Reconfiguring religious belief as shaped by a cognitive sensibility of 'yearning,' she illustrates this by way of the myths of

Mirabai, the legendary Hindu poetess–saint, and Antigone, the mythical figure of Greek tragedy.

A fifth theme in contemporary feminist philosophy of religion focuses on the body and serves to join feminist philosophy of religion to the work of other feminists who have been trying to rethink the materiality of the body and to show that, as Judith Butler says, bodies matter. Nuanced studies of the linkages between bodies, discourse, and power in religious contexts are still in short supply in the literature of philosophy of religion, although important investigations are being produced by feminist theorists in related disciplines, as Saba Mahmood's work shows.[57]

Building on the theme of corporeal subjectivity, a sixth theme in the literature interrogates possibilities for human transcendence, whether of the body whose pain and pleasure has been disastrously associated in the past with the feminine, or of the body politic in its present local, nation–state, or international political constrictions. How far can we get beyond where we are now? What can humans hope for? In most feminist philosophy of religion, 'transcendence' is conceptualized in temporal, this-worldly terms, along horizontal, rather than vertical, lines of movement. As the future transcends the past, possibility transcends actuality. 'Becoming divine' as a possibility not-yet-actualized hints at a feminist future in the absence of an antecedently-given actual divinity. Many feminists trace the fundamental philosophical problem of the Western ontotheological tradition to a fatal category mistake – it confused ideals with agents and possibilities with actualities. Detailing the problematics of monotheism, Laurel Schneider suggests in *Re-Imagining the Divine* that the construction of a monistic polytheism better suits the sensibilities of religious feminism.[58]

A great deal of what we have learned in the last 20 years about embodiment, sexuality, subjectivity, and the imaginary is either derived from or associated with psychoanalytic discourses. This context gives rise to a cluster of substantive questions around which lively debate swirls in 2002. Here I will mention only three of the most pressing questions, to which I can offer only tentative suggestions: (1) the primacy of sexual difference; (2) the project of projecting a 'feminine divine'; and (3) the precise relation of psychoanalytic concepts to philosophical analysis in feminist philosophy of religion.

On the first question, Irigaray and her sympathetic readers have maintained that sexual difference is the salient question of our time.[59] But does this assumption unduly homogenize the spectrum of possibilities at just the time when new genealogies of bodies and identities are being invoked by various queer theorists, poststructuralist feminists, and historicists who are calling into question the primacy of sexual difference? In that case, the dyads male–female and their mapping to masculine–feminine are constitutive exclusions that feminist philosophy of religion can no longer presume now that new questions about the reality of human sexual dimorphism pose a challenge to the continued use of the sex–gender distinction once so useful to feminist thought itself.[60]

Related to this are questions about the point of and the prospects for articulating a 'female divine.' Those who doubt the desirability of such a projection prefer to see feminist philosophy of religion restrict itself to 'critique' and leave 'reconstruction' to the theologians. This is a fine line to walk. On the understanding of the 'female divine' as a de-transcendentalized horizon of human possibilities inclusive of the hope of women's full emancipatory transformation, its very utopian quality raises further questions about the relation between symbolic orders and real conditions of life. Even if a fully imagined 'female divine' appears, why should anything at all follow from this for the cultural, economic, or political status of actual women? Current feminist ways of thematizing a relation between sexual difference and divine alterity are most often lyrical, leaving open or undecidable the important philosophical question, What is the ontological status of the object of belief, especially when that object is deliberately constructed?[61] It seems that no one has yet developed a systematic position on this question that is at once philosophical and feminist and applicable to an understanding of religion as something other than 'ideology.'

A third set of questions arises out of the prominence of psychoanalytic concepts in feminist thought in general and in feminist philosophy of religion in particular. Even acknowledging the plentiful feminist interventions already made in post-Freudian and post-Lacanian psychoanalytic theory, the philosophical examination of psychological phenomena is unfinished feminist business. It is, after all, the psychoanalytic perspective that has presented sexual difference as a natural and irreducible difference, and it is psychoanalytic discourses that have replaced or reinterpreted standard religious language in the West for much of the last century. In what ways are its main categories – the unconscious, transference, repression, sublimation, condensation – explanatory? What, for that matter, is the status of hermeneutical 'interpretation' in contrast to 'explanation' in terms of causes? And what are the culturally and historically contingent limitations of the French poststructuralist psychoanalytic theories whose current deployment in feminist philosophy of religion has been conspicuous? Can feminist philosophies of religion afford to leave unexamined its own sweeping appeal to such concepts as a masculinist imaginary and a feminist symbolic?

Speaking for myself, and from a North Atlantic location, I look to an emerging convergence of feminist and pragmatist agendas. Indebted to the pioneering work of Charlene Haddock Seigfried in *Pragmatism and Feminism: Reweaving the Social Fabric*, pragmatist–feminist philosophy of religion is a relatively new development.[62] On its philosophical side, both pragmatist philosophy and feminism share such important features as: a strong critique of scientistic positivism; resistance to fact–value dichotomies; reclamation of the experiential and epistemic import of aesthetics; analyses of dominant discourses in light of forms of social domination; linkage of theory and practice; interest in the theoretical primacy of concrete experience; repudiation of the spectator stance of philosophical indifference; and an interrogation of the social–political effects of the social sciences. On its religious side, the pragmatist tradition offers untapped resources for feminist reconstruction, ranging from the explicit philosophies of religion in the classical writings of Peirce, James, Dewey, Santayana, and Mead, to the implicit ones in the current revival of pragmatism on both sides of the Atlantic. Summing up the religious import of American pragmatism in its first millennium, John Stuhr sees that pragmatism has constituted 'a forced relocation, a long march, of traditional notions of transcendence and spirituality,' rather than, as its critics charge, an abdication of any hopes of transcendence at all. Pragmatism, according to Stuhr, 'has relocated transcendence *within* immanence, relocated spirit *within* nature, relocated absolutes *within* inquiry, relocated affirmation *within* negation, relocated salvation *within* community.' Just as succinctly, Stuhr lists the chief products of pragmatism's naturalization processes:

> truth without the problems of certainty; justification without the problems of foundations; nature and access to it without the problems of supernaturalism or

solipsism; values without the problems of absolutism or arbitrariness; and distinctively religious or spiritual experience without idealism, dualism, or institutional religion.[63]

It seems to me that this compendium comprises an agenda ripe for philosophical unpacking and feminist elaboration. Forced relocation – under naturalistic and feminist auspices – ought to be the name of the game from now on.

Notes

1 Elizabeth Cady Stanton, 'Has Christianity Benefitted Women?' *North American Review* 140 (1885): 389–90.

2 Luce Irigaray, 'Divine Women,' in *Sexes and Genealogies*. Trans. Gillian C. Gill (New York: Columbia University Press, 1993), p. 67. I am indebted to Amy Hollywood for calling this quotation to my attention.

3 Anna Julia Cooper, 'A Voice From the South,' in *Schomburg Library of Nineteenth-Century Black Women Writers* (New York: Oxford University Press, 1988 [1892]), pp. 121–23.

4 Jeffner Allen and Iris Marion Young, eds, *The Thinking Muse: Feminism and Modern French Philosophy* (Bloomington: Indiana University Press, 1989).

5 Neither do I intend to invoke a distinction between gender and sex that allows naturalized assumptions about the sexed body to go unquestioned.

6 Indicative of this resurgence is the volume *Contemporary Perspectives on Religious Epistemology*, edited by R. Douglas Geivett and Brendan Sweetman (New York: Oxford University Press, 1992). Significantly, this volume consists entirely of contributions from twenty-four male authors and includes not a single female author. The epistemological perspectives represented in this volume are uniformly concerned with traditional modes of Christian belief. For an argument that Anglo-American philosophers are now addressing an expanded range of topics, see Eleonore Stump's claim that new work in philosophy of religion is currently characterized, first, by 'a broad extension of subjects seen as appropriate for philosophical scrutiny' and, second, by 'a willingness to bridge boundaries with related disciplines.' But what Stump means by 'new work' is that 'philosophers have gotten up their courage and ventured into such areas as providence, creation, conservation, and God's responsibility for sin,' and by 'related disciplines' she refers only to theology and biblical studies. Cf. Eleonore Stump, ed., *Reasoned Faith: Essays in Philosophical Theology in Honor of Norman Kretzmann* (Ithaca, N.Y.: Cornell University Press, 1993), p. 1.

7 Richard Gale, *On the Nature and Existence of God* (Cambridge: Cambridge University Press, 1991), p. 2.

8 See, for example, Richard Swinburne, *The Coherence of Theism* (Oxford: Clarendon, 1977); Swinburne, *The Existence of God* (Oxford: Clarendon Press, 1979); Swinburne, *Faith and Reason* (Oxford: Clarendon Press, 1981); Alvin Plantinga, 'Is Belief in God Properly Basic?' *Nous* 15, no. 1 (1981); 41–52; Plantinga, 'Reason and Belief in God,' in Alvin Plantinga and Nicholas Wolterstorff, eds, *Faith and Rationality* (Notre Dame: University of Notre Dame Press, 1983); Plantinga, *Warrant: The Current Debate* (New York: Oxford University Press, 1993); Plantinga, *Warrant and Proper Function* (New York: Oxford University Press, 1993); William P. Alston, *Perceiving God: The Epistemology of Religious Experience* (Ithaca, N.Y.: Cornell University Press, 1991); and D.Z. Phillips, *Faith after Foundationalism* (London: Routledge, 1988). See also Phillips's uncritical assumption that the Christian God exhibits the three characteristics of 'independence of the way things go, unchangeability, and immunity from defeat,' in 'Faith, Skepticism, and Religious Understanding,' in Ann Loades and Loyal D. Rue, eds, *Contemporary Classics in Philosophy of Religion*. (La Salle, Ill.: Open Court, 1991), pp. 123–38.

9 See Elizabeth A. Johnson, *She Who Is: The Mystery of God in Feminist Theological Discourse* (New York: Crossroad, 1993).

10 Heidi Hartmann, 'The Unhappy Marriage of Marxism and Feminism: Toward a More Progressive Union,' in Lydia Sargent, ed., *Women and Revolution: The Unhappy Marriage of Marxism and Feminism* (Boston: South End Press, 1981), p. 14.

11 For example, John Hick's widely used text, *Philosophy of Religion* (Englewood Cliffs, N.J.: Prentice-

Hall, 1989), now in its fourth edition, went through three editions before the author amended it with more inclusive language. Despite Hick's explanation in the 1983 preface that he has 'desexized' (sic) his language, it is apparent that conceptually his notion of God is still what Lacan calls the 'good old God,' the Father, the omnipotent One of classical theism.

12   Elizabeth Kamarck Minnich, *Transforming Knowledge* (Philadelphia: Temple University Press, 1990), p. 175.

13   Mary Daly, 'Feminist Post-Christian Introduction,' in her *The Church and the Second Sex*, 2d ed. (New York: Harper and Row, 1975), p. 38.

14.   Peter Damian, 'On Divine Omnipotence,' in John F. Wippel and Allan B. Wolter, eds, *Medieval Philosophy* (New York: Free Press, 1969), pp. 143–45.

15.   John Mackie's definition may stand as representative: 'We might suggest that "God is omnipotent" means that God can do anything that is logically possible. . . . So omnipotence includes the power to make X to be only where there is no contradiction either in X itself or in making X to be. . . . if God is omnipotent every coherently describable activity or production is within his power.' See his 'Omnipotence' in Linwood Urban and Douglas N. Walton, eds, *The Power of God: Readings on Omnipotence and Evil* (New York: Oxford University Press, 1978), pp. 76, 77.

16   See in particular John B. Cobb Jr. and David R. Griffin, *Process Theology: An Introductory Exposition* (Philadelphia: Westminster Press, 1976); Charles Hartshorne, *Omnipotence and Other Theological Mistakes* (Albany: State University of New York Press, 1984); and Marjorie Suchocki, *The End of Evil: Process Eschatology in Historical Context* (Albany: State University of New York Press, 1988).

17   This is the point of Marilyn Thie's critique in 'Epilogue: Prologomenon to Future Feminist* Philosophies of Religions,' in *Hypatia: A Journal of Feminist Philosophy* 9, no. 4 (Special Issue on Philosophy of Religion, edited by Nancy Frankenberry and Marilyn Thie; Fall 1994): 234. For two important exceptions, see Wendy Farley, *Tragic Vision and Divine Compassion: A Contemporary Theodicy* (Louisville, Ky.: Westminster/John Knox Press, 1990), and Kathleen M. Sands, *Escape from Paradise: Evil and Tragedy in Feminist Theology* (Minneapolis, Minn.: Fortress Press, 1994).

18   Charlotte Perkins Gilman, *His Religion and Hers* (New York: Century, 1923), p. 46.

19   See Susan Bordo, *The Flight to Objectivity: Essays on Cartesianism and Culture* (Albany: State University of New York Press, 1987); Sandra Harding and M. B. Hintikka, eds, *Discovering Reality: Feminist Perspectives on Epistemology, Metaphysics, Methodology, and Philosophy of Science* (Dordrecht: Reidel, 1983); Luce Irigaray, *This Sex Which Is Not One* (Ithaca, N.Y.: Cornell University Press, 1985); and Genevieve Lloyd, *The Man of Reason* (London: Methuen, 1985).

20   Inevitably, I am conflating my critique of mainstream philosophy of religion with a critique of its subject matter, Western monotheistic religious beliefs. When religion is construed this narrowly, philosophy of religion acquires an impaired view of what is appropriate for its philosophical scrutiny.

21   For a development of this theme in connection with the work of Durkheim and Weber, see Victoria Lee Erickson, *Where Silence Speaks: Feminism, Social Theory, and Religion* (Minneapolis, Minn.: Fortress Press, 1993).

22   Caroline Walker Bynum, Stevan Harrell, and Paula Richman, *Gender and Religion: On the Complexity of Symbols* (Boston: Beacon Press, 1986), p. 9.

23   For a preliminary analysis in connection with three models of divinity, see Nancy Frankenberry, 'Classical Theism, Panentheism, and Pantheism: The Relation between God Construction and Gender Construction,' *Zygon Journal of Science and Religion* 28, no. 1 (March 1993): 29–46. For a brief discussion of why such analysis is not more common in philosophy of religion, see my 'Introduction: Prolegomenon to Future Philosophies of Religion,' *Hypatia: A Journal of Feminist Philosophy* 9, no. 4 (Special Issue on Philosophy of Religion, edited by Nancy Frankenberry and Marilyn Thie; Fall 1994): 1–14.

24   Johnson, *She Who Is*, pp. 127–28. Cf. Hildegard of Bingen, *Scivias*, trans. Mother Colubia Hart and Jane Bishop (New York: Paulist Press, 1990).

25   Paula Gunn Allen, *The Sacred Hoop: Recovering the Feminine in American Indian Traditions* (Boston: Beacon Press, 1986), p. 22.

26   Ntozake Shange, *for colored girls who have considered suicide/when the rainbow is enuf* (New York: Macmillan, 1976), p. 63.

27   Alice Walker, *The Color Purple* (New York: Harcourt Brace Jovanovich, 1982), pp. 177–78.

28   See Rosemary Radford Ruether, *Sexism and God-Talk* (Boston: Beacon Press, 1983); Sallie McFague, *Models of God: Theology for an Ecological, Nuclear Age* (Philadelphia: Fortress Press, 1987); Mary Daly, *Beyond God the Father* (Boston: Beacon Press, 1973); Marjorie Suchocki, *The End of Evil: Process Eschatology in Historical Concept* (Albany: State University of New York Press, 1988); and Irigaray, *Sexes and Genealogies*.

29   Alfred North Whitehead, *Process and Reality*, corrected edition, eds, David R. Griffin and Donald Sherburne (New York: Free Press, 1978), p. 348.

30   An excellent account of these themes in process philosophy from a feminist perspective is found in Catherine Keller, *From a Broken Web: Separation, Sexism, and Self* (Boston: Beacon Press, 1986). See also Nancy Howell, 'The Promise of a Process Feminist Theory of Relations,' *Process Studies* 17 (Summer 1988): 78–87.

31   Whitehead, *Process and Reality*, pp. 31–34, 342–51.

32   Charles Birch and John B. Cobb Jr., *The Liberation of Life: From the Cell to the Community* (Cambridge: Cambridge University Press, 1981).

33   Johnson, *She Who Is*, p. 240. Given other aspects of Johnson's ontology, however, it is unlikely that she would favor the radically pluralized and temporalized interpretation of creativity/*esse* that I recommend here.

34   A more developed treatment of the concept of the divine as creativity would consider the ways in which divine power is not always and everywhere 'good' in any unambiguous sense. While the power of being may always be good, what is is not always good. While creativity is an ontological good, it may also turn out to be a practical or social evil in context.

35   Michael McGhee, 'Introduction,' in Michael McGhee, ed., *Philosophy, Religion and the Spiritual Life* (Cambridge: Cambridge University Press, 1992), p. 1.

36   For important critiques of the dominant tradition's neglect of what constitutes a real, socially located epistemic subject, see Lorraine Code, *What Can She Know? Feminist Theory and the Construction of Knowledge* (Ithaca, N.Y.: Cornell University Press, 1991); Jane Duran, *Toward a Feminist Epistemology* (Savage, Md.: Rowman and Littlefield, 1991); and Terence W. Tilley, *The Wisdom of Religious Commitment* (Washington, D.C.: Georgetown University Press, 1995).

37   Paula M. Cooey, *Religious Imagination and the Body: A Feminist Analysis* (New York: Oxford University Press, 1994), p. 127.

38   It is also indicative of the fact that the 'different voice' in which philosophy of religion is being written is not limited to the female register.

39   Howard Eilberg-Schwartz, *God's Phallus and Other Problems for Men and Monotheism* (Boston: Beacon Press, 1994), pp. 5–6.

40   Ibid., pp. 239, 240.

41   Mary McClintock Fulkerson, *Changing the Subject: Women's Discourses and Feminist Theology* (Minneapolis, Minn.: Fortress Press, 1994), p. 115.

42   Ibid., p. 103.

43   See, for example, ibid., pp. ix, 7, 24 n. 10, 29, 372–77. This assimilation of 'theology' to 'testimony' is mistaken, in my judgment; the crisis of legitimation of theology's cognitive claims cannot be so easily circumvented.

44   Irigaray, *Sexes and Genealogies*, p. 62.

45   In particular, see C. W. Maggie Kim, Susan M. St. Ville, and Susan M. Simonaitis, *Transfigurations: Theology and the French Feminists* (Minneapolis, Minn.: Fortress Press, 1993); Philippa Berry and Andrew Werncik, eds, *Shadow of Spirit: Postmodernism and Religion* (New York: Routledge, 1992); and Elizabeth Grosz, *Sexual Subversions: Three French Feminists* (Sydney: Allen and Unwin, 1989).

46   Amy M. Hollywood, 'Beauvoir, Irigaray, and the Mystical,' *Hypatia: A Journal of Feminist Philosophy* 9, no. 4 (Special Issue on Philosophy of Religion, edited by Nancy Frankenberry and Marilyn Thie; Fall 1994): 175. Cf. Ludwig Feuerbach, *The Essence of Christianity*, trans. George Eliot. (New York: Harper Torchbooks, 1957).

47   Hollywood, 'Beauvoir, Irigaray, and the Mystical,' pp. 176–77.

48   Luce Irigaray, 'Belief Itself,' in *Sexes and Genealogies*, pp. 25–53.

49   Amy M. Hollywood, 'Deconstructing Belief: Irigaray and the Philosophy of Religion' (paper presented at the annual meeting of the American Academy of Religion, Chicago, November 1994).

50   For an extended analysis, see Amy M. Hollywood, *Soul as Virgin Wife: Mechthild of Magdeburg, Marguerite Porete, and Meister Eckhart* (South Bend, Ind.: Notre Dame University Press, 1995).

51   P.S. Anderson, *A Feminist Philosophy of Religion: The Rationality and Myths of Religious Belief* (Oxford: Blackwell, 1998); G. Jantzen, *Becoming Divine: Towards a Feminist Philosophy of Religion* (Bloomington: Indiana University Press, 1999). A third book-length study that appeared in this same period is D. Hampson, *After Christianity* (Valley Forge, Pa.: Trinity Press International, 1997), a work I would locate within feminist theology (or a/theology) rather than within feminist philosophy of religion. Written from a non-religious and anti-theological point of view, the main burden of Hampson's

argument, delivered with considerable brio, historical sweep, and philosophical reflection, is that Christianity is 'untrue' and 'immoral.'

52 *Feminist Interpretations of Mary Daly*, S. Hoagland and M. Frye, eds. (University Park: Pennsylvania State University Press, 2000); *Feminist Interpretations of Soren Kierkegaard*, C. Leon and S. Walsh, eds. (University Park: Pennsylvania State University Press, 1997). Both volumes appear in a remarkable series, *Re-Reading the Canon,* under the general editorship of N. Tuana. In addition to Daly and Kierkegaard, feminist re-interpretations of the Western canon are now available on Plato, Arendt, Beauvoir, Wollstonecraft, Foucault, Hegel, Derrida, Kant, Aristotle, Descartes, Hume, Nietzsche, Wittgenstein, Dewey, Gadamer, Levinas, Ayn Rand, Heidegger, Sartre, and – of particular interest to philosophers of religion – St. Augustine.

53 See E.T. Long, *Twentieth-Century Western Philosophy of Religion 1900–2000* (Dordrecht/Boston/London: Kluwer Academic Publishers, 2000).

54 *Postcolonialism, Feminism, and Religious Discourse*, L. Donaldson and Kwok Pui-lan, eds. (New York/London: Routledge, 2002). See also *The Postcolonial Bible*, R.S. Sugirtharajah, ed. (Sheffield: Sheffield Academic Press, 1998).

55 For but one recent example, see *French Feminists on Religion*, M. Joy, K. O'Grady, J. Poxon, eds. (New York: Routledge, 2001).

56 E. Armour, *Deconstruction, Feminist Theology, and the Problem of Difference: Subverting the Race/Gender Divide* (Chicago: The University of Chicago Press, 1999), 5. In light of feminist discourse's rupture between race and gender, it remains imperative that feminist philosophies of religion amount to more than a white-privileged women's version of a formerly white-privileged men's philosophical project.

57 For an exemplary study from a feminist anthropologist of religion, see Saba Mahmood, 'Feminist Theory, Embodiment, and the Docile Agent: Some Reflections on the Egyptian Islamic Revival,' *Cultural Anthropology* 16 (2000): 202–36.

58 See L.C. Schneider, *Re-Imagining the Divine: Confronting the Backlash against Feminist Theology* (Cleveland, Ohio: The Pilgrim Press, 1998), ch. 7.

59 See, for example, L. Irigaray, *An Ethics of Sexual Difference*. Trans. C. Burke and G.C. Gill (Ithaca: Cornell University Press, 1993), and Irigaray, *I Love to You*. Trans. Alison Martin (New York: Routledge, 1996).

60 See C.E. Gurdorf, 'The Erosion of Sexual Dimorphism: Challenges to Religion and Religious Ethics,' *Journal of the American Academy of Religion*, 69, 4 (December 2001), 863–91.

61 Writing some time ago on the parallels between theological construction of God-concepts and the social construction of gendered subjectivity, I suggested that both constructions happen to converge on the interrogation of the extent to which something that is socially and historically constructed, and known to be so, can also be personally appropriated and lived out with a measure of authenticity (see reference in note 23 above). I still think that formulation makes sense, but I would clarify further the several distinct senses in which, as William James put it, 'that which is real in its effects must be accounted real.'

62 See C.H. Seigfried, *Pragmatism and Feminism: Reweaving the Social Fabric* (Chicago: University of Chicago Press, 1996); C.H. Seigfried, ed., *Feminist Interpretations of John Dewey* (University Park: Pennsylvania State University Press, 2001); Erin McKenna, *The Task of Utopia: A Pragmatist and Feminist Perspective* (Rowman & Littlefield Publishers, 2001); S. Sullivan, *Living Across and Through Skins: Transactional Bodies, Pragmatism, and Feminism* (Bloomington: Indiana University Press, 2001); M. Lock and P.A. Kaufert, eds, *Pragmatic Women and Body Politics* (Cambridge: Cambridge University Press, 1998). For the use of a pragmatist–feminist perspective in theological studies, see S.G. Davaney, *Pragmatic Historicism: A Theology for the Twenty-First Century* (Albany: State University of New York Press, 2000); and Rebecca S. Chopp, *The Power to Speak: Feminism, Language, God* (Crossroad/Herder & Herder, 1989).

63 John J. Stuhr, 'Life Without Spirituality, Philosophy Without Transcendence,' *The Hedgehog Review* 3/3 (Fall 2001), 66–67.

Chapter 2

A PSYCHOANALYTIC APPROACH

Grace M. Jantzen

WHAT'S THE DIFFERENCE? KNOWLEDGE AND
GENDER IN (POST)MODERN PHILOSOPHY OF
RELIGION

■ From **WHAT'S THE DIFFERENCE? KNOWLEDGE AND GENDER IN (POST)MODERN PHILOSOPHY OF RELIGION**, *Religious Studies*, 32: 4 (1996): 431–48.

Grace Jantzen adopts a psychoanalytic approach to philosophy of religion by locating the difference gender makes in the unconscious. Jantzen insists that the distinctiveness of contemporary Continental philosophy rests in knowing how to access this gendered difference, which has been ignored at the peril of Anglo-American philosophers of religion. Her contention is that, in resisting this approach on 'the Continent' (which for her is essentially France), analytic philosophers of religion continue to repress crucial content – content that will make all the difference to the shape of a feminist philosophy of religion. Jantzen's argument is unequivocal: we can and must undo this repression with greater self-awareness. In her words, 'it is necessary to be in touch with emotion, bodiliness and sexuality, in short with that which psychoanalytic theory has labeled the feminine . . . it is necessary also to become aware of the manifestations of both repression and vulnerability in social and global contexts and the ways in which difference is implicated with power: such issues as emerge in awareness of gender, race and colonialism' (p. 34).

DONNA HARAWAY, IN HER 'Manifesto for Cyborgs', issues a warning that in the post-modern world where grand narratives increasingly fail and subjects are seen to be irremediably fragmented, 'we risk lapsing into boundless difference and giving up on the confusing task of making a partial, real connection. Some differences are playful; some are poles of world historical systems of domination. Epistemology is about knowing the difference.'[1] Such an account of epistemology, which sees its central task to be a knowledge of the significance of difference and a capacity to discern between innocent and oppressive forms of difference, is perhaps not one that would most readily occur to British philosophers of religion. It is, however, an account which has resonances both with many contemporary Continental thinkers and with feminist epistemologists. Notwithstanding the many areas of divergence between and among these groups, on two points at least they converge: that the recognition and discernment of difference has become inescapable for epistemology; and that of the differences which must be dealt with, gender difference has a paradigmatic status.

Contemporary Continental thought, particularly that deriving from France, is often referred to by the terms 'postmodern' or 'poststructural' and their variants, in a doubtful if convenient derivation from Lyotard's account of *The Postmodern Condition*.[2] Yet as soon as one begins to read the thinkers lumped together under these labels, the vast differences among them become apparent. Indeed, many of the thinkers unhappily joined together under the term 'postmodern' explicitly reject the label. It is therefore important to ask, as Judith Butler does,

> Is there, after all, something called postmodernism? Is it an historical characterization, a certain kind of theoretical position, and what does it mean for a term that has described a certain aesthetic practice now to apply to social theory . . . ? Who are these postmodernists? Is this a name that one takes on for oneself, or is it more often a name that one is called . . . ?[3]

Butler suggests, I believe correctly, that the term is far too frequently used as a refusal to take the writers in question seriously, whether as an excuse to jump on some sort of 'postmodern bandwagon' or, more often, as a technique of dismissal, as when Ernest Gellner says that postmodernists and feminists, between them, have manufactured a 'pseudo-crisis' of reason which actually amounts to nothing more than 'sturm und drang und tenure.'[4] Such blanketing techniques, used by either side, labelling each other as trendy and reactionary respectively, are not going to be very helpful: in any case, there are plenty of them already, without my adding to them. What is needed is a much more piecemeal approach, looking carefully at particular aspects of Continental thought on difference and gender and the ways in which they challenge British philosophy of religion. In one paper, I can do no more than make a very modest start in this task; but I hope that it will be of interest in itself, and also serve as an invitation to further reading and critical study of the richly varied primary texts. This is all the more important because whereas Continental thought is being taken up by British thinkers in linguistics and cultural studies and in its implications for Biblical studies and hermeneutics, few philosophers of religion have so far taken it seriously. One reason for this is the deep channel that separates England from France when it comes to conceptualizing what religion is, and therefore what constitutes philosophy of religion and how it should be conducted. In this paper I would like to sketch something of that divide, in order that we may approach contemporary Continental thought, particularly its emphasis on difference and gender, with fewer misconceptions and greater chance of appreciation and understanding.

In the following sketch, I shall use 'British' as shorthand for the Anglo-American analytic tradition in philosophy of religion with its heavy investment in the philosophical theology of Christianity, and 'French' as shorthand for the strands of thought associated with structuralism and its aftermath, and recognize in advance that I am lumping together, under each label, thinkers who are in fact quite disparate and who in important ways disagree with one another. Also, of course, there are a few British philosophers of religion who have been deeply influenced by contemporary Continental thinking (Don Cupitt comes to mind) and a few Continental thinkers, such as Vincent Brümmer, whose methodology is not differentiable from what I am labelling 'British'. I am using 'British' and 'French' as shorthand for divergent methodologies, rather than as adjectives describing where people live, though there is considerable correspondence between the two.

1 Constructing the discipline of philosophy of religion

A central preoccupation of many British philosophers of religion, as well as of American strands such as those influenced by Alvin Plantinga, is with the nature and existence of God, where 'God' is understood along the lines of traditional Christian doctrine: a being other than the world or anything in it who is its creator, omnipotent, omniscient, and benevolent. In what has become known as the 'realist'–'antirealist' debate, the contested question is whether belief in God signifies belief that such a transcendent being objectively exists, or whether expression of belief in God is something more like a subject's positioning of herself over against whatever might happen, whether or not there is a transcendent referent for the term 'God'. The latter position is, as we shall see, rather closer to Continental thought forms than the former.

Among those who take the realist position, the question of the existence of this God, then, is seen as a question of objective fact. Though the existence of such a being might be the most important of all facts, and indeed their cause, in terms of its status *as* a fact it is not different from other facts. If it is true, it is one more fact within the world of facts; if it is false, the rest of the world of facts stays just the same, since it is after all *from* that world of facts that the evidential debate is conducted. The difference between a theist and an atheist, on this account, is that the theist accepts as a fact one item which the atheist denies, namely the existence of God. Hence one can pass from atheism to theism or vice versa by the addition or subtraction of one fact, while the rest of the facts remain untouched. This is of course *not* to say that the addition or subtraction of that fact is without profound implication for how the individual's life is conducted, and in that sense has a bearing on other facts. But believers and atheists can share in scientific theories, laboratory experiments, economic strategies, and social policies: their disagreement regarding God's existence is an additional fact, external to the class of facts about the world, and best left to the private realm of religion. This is true even in the moral realm: for example, in *Responsibility and Atonement* Richard Swinburne separates his inquiry into two parts: first the development of a moral theory which rests largely on critical intuition and is not specifically Christian, and second, an analysis of what follows if we add to this the premises of traditional Christian doctrine.[5] Although he holds that such addition does make a moral difference especially in such things as making worship a duty, the moral theory developed in the first part of the book functions in what Philip Quinn has described as an 'Archimedean fixed point',[6] a basis for theological evaluation precisely *because* it holds for theists and nontheists alike.

One of the tasks of philosophy of religion, then, is to consider whether it is rational to believe in God. This task can be approached in various ways: with Richard Swinburne in a quasi-calculation of the probabilities of the existence of God, for example, or, quite differently, with the idea that the existence of God is a properly basic belief, as Alvin Plantinga holds, perhaps grounded, as William Alston argues, in mystical perception, a concept modelled on the sensory perception of empirical objects. Although I do not want to minimize the differences between these philosophers, I suppose that from a Continental perspective they all look very much alike, in their preoccupation with a putative transcendent being and how belief in such a being could be justified.

Moreover, they all proceed, not only as though the central question of philosophical theism is the question of whether or not God exists (as an objective fact), but also as though the philosopher who weighs the evidence or perhaps ponders basicality or mystical perception is, unproblematically, a rational subject. This subject has experiences, whether sensory or mystical, and is capable of weighing up those experiences (perhaps with a little help from philosophical experts) and deciding on the basis of them whether or not it is rational to believe that God exists. Exactly the same assumption of the rationality of the subject obtains, moreover in relation to what some philosophers of religion consider to be the logically prior issue of the coherence of theism, the conceptual investigation of the simultaneous attribution of the traditional predicates of the divine. Such issues as the embodiedness and cultural embeddedness of the knowing subject, differences between subjects whether in terms of power, gender, or social status, or the effects of the unconscious or of ideology on claims to knowledge are not taken as central to the debate.

All of this presupposes, moreover, that it is possible to speak of these subjects of rationality and their experiences, and indeed of God, in ordinary human language. Granted, the question of how finite human language can refer to the infinite is a question which many British philosophers of religion grapple with, recognizing that an appeal to analogy or metaphor at least requires explication. It is no accident, either, that those English-speaking philosophers of religion like D. Z. Phillips, who take seriously Wittgenstein's remarks on language games which have close affinities to Continental semiotics, are seen to destabilize a good deal of traditional philosophy of religion. With the exception of such Wittgensteinians, however, and in spite of some recognition of the problem of reference, a great deal of contemporary philosophy of religion proceeds as though the difficulties in speaking of or referring to God can be overcome, and that, at least at a rough and ready level, we can adequately understand what is meant by such putative divine attributes as omnipotence, omniscience and goodness.

In much Continental thought, each of these terms – God/religion, the subject, and language – are held self-evidently to be vastly more problematic and complicated than they are taken to be in British philosophy of religion. Contemporary Continental thinkers such as Derrida, Irigaray and Kristeva, for all their differences, take as inescapable the conceptual terrain mapped out by the 'masters of suspicion' Nietzsche, Marx and Freud, and the complications of this terrain by Saussure, Lacan and Althusser – to let these names stand for many. This is not to say that they suppose that the positions adopted by these thinkers are beyond dispute, but rather that they cannot be ignored. To ignore is to be ignorant. The importance of the unconscious, and therefore of longing, projection and repression in any significant human relation and therefore certainly in religion; the inescapability of ideology and social construction and therefore the dynamics of power and dominance in religion; the continuous play of signifiers in an ever-shifting constellation of meaning, and therefore the problem of reference or relation to the signified; the interweaving of violence and the sacred and the all-pervasiveness of sexual dynamics of masculinity and femininity; the inescapable responsibility of intellectuals for the ethical and political uses that will be made of our words and our silences: all these themes are in their view fundamental for any non-naive philosophy of religion. Moreover, all of these are, in their view, always already implicated in anything that could *count* as 'empirical evidence' or as 'logical coherence' – and implicated even more obviously in who gets to do the counting.

Such assumptions are quite literally foreign to many British philosophers of religion, and I do not wish to suggest that they are beyond challenge. Indeed, the French thinkers I have mentioned are themselves often sharply critical of the 'masters of suspicion' and their followers. The differences in what is at stake in their critiques and how they are pursued, however, are revealing. In British writing, what often happens is that specific arguments about religion in Freud or Marx or Nietzsche are challenged by a combination of appeal to empirical evidence and logic. Thus, for example, John Hick in his book *An Interpretation of Religion*, devotes a few pages to criticisms of some particular arguments about the nature of religion offered by Durkheim and Freud. Having dispensed with these arguments to his satisfaction, Hick then proceeds to an account of religion which treats human subjectivity, experience and language relatively unproblematically.[7] From the perspective of current French philosophers, who are also, like Hick, deeply concerned about the nature of religion, such an approach would appear simplistic. This is not to say that they would defend Freud or Marx or Durkheim at the points where Hick attacks them: as already said, they also develop searching critiques of these thinkers.[8] But in French thinking, the force of the 'masters of suspicion' is not so much in their detailed arguments, which may often fall into mistakes, but rather in the ways in which they show Enlightenment assumptions about the rational subject, language and religion to be radically destabilized by the combined factors of the unconscious and socially constructed ideology. Unless we recognize the extent to which assumptions of such destabilization forms the background to the philosophy of religion of Kristeva (or Irigaray, or Derrida, or Foucault, for all their differences), that philosophy will remain as incomprehensible to us as British realism and empiricism seem astonishing to them. In the interests of promoting understanding, I shall make some highly schematic remarks about the ways in which this destabilization is related to issues of difference and of gender, and is seen to affect the three areas highlighted in my comments about British philosophy of religion: the subject, language and God/religion.

2 Decentring the subject

The work of Freud and Lacan has shown that subtending the 'rational' and 'autonomous' ego beloved of Kant and his followers is the unconscious, built out of the repression of unacceptable desires from early childhood onwards, and always returning to reveal itself in jokes, slips of the tongue, and above all dreams. The desires of the unconscious are desires of and for the body, focused initially on the body of the mother, and subsequently on all the others who stand in for the (m)other. But since the conscious, rational ego was built upon the repression and mastery of those desires, that mastery will extend to all those who stand for the mother, all the (m)others who at an unconscious level suggest to the subject the desires that have been repressed. In Lacanian psychoanalytic theory, moreover, the subject *qua* subject is always masculine, since it is individualized out of its primordial unity with the mother by means of identification with the Law of the Father in the Oedipal phase of childhood development. In so far as women become subjects – which is only imperfectly and against the grain – it is by becoming masculinized, speaking men's language, playing male roles by male rules, or by accepting female roles of motherhood and service designed for them by males.

Hence, the subject's efforts at mastery are directed toward the feminine, all that is identified with the (m)other: actual women, otherness in race or sexuality, and, dramatically, 'Mother Nature' whose domination is taken up as a sacred task. The mastery of all these is a necessary corollary to the repression of the desire for the mother by which the subject constitutes itself as a separate and rational ego. Furthermore, in this effort toward mastery the ego will bond with and project itself into any structures of kinship or institutions of society which will facilitate such repression: thus are the structures of civilization built up. Difference, of which gender difference is the paradigm, is perceived as a challenge to mastery. Hence the Continental view is that any understanding of religion and the concept of God must take seriously the extent to which conceptualizations of the divine are male projections serving the interests of repression of desires and the mastery of (m)others.

Although any specific allegation of projection, notoriously those found in Freud's *Totem and Taboo*,[9] can be usefully explored and perhaps challenged, Continental thinkers take it for granted that once we have admitted the existence of the unconscious, as we must, then we can no longer philosophize as though we are uncomplicated rational subjects. Our very existence is built upon difference, as we define our conscious selves over against others. Nor can we suppose that God is an uncomplicated divine subject, our mirror image writ large. The idea that we can tabulate characteristics of human personhood, and then ask to what extent such characteristics might apply to God and how they would have to be modified in the divine case, even granted a quite complicated doctrine of analogy, would seem to French thinkers quite impossible. All the same, to say that the concept of God of western Christianity carries huge loads of projection is not necessarily to say that it is false: Irigaray, for instance, urges that women should engage in conscious and deliberate projection of a female divine as an antidote to a relentlessly male deity, and in an effort to reach toward the horizon of our gendered becoming.[10] It is, however, to say that any account of God must be treated with a hermeneutic of suspicion both in terms of its provenance and in terms of the strategic purposes it serves. They would perhaps not be surprised at reading, as I did in the *Church Times* a year or two ago, a bishop explaining that 'in the Christian tradition God is a relatively genderless male deity'.

The insistent question for Continental thinkers, then, is how at a conscious level to relate to the unconscious. It is possible to repress it, to deny its importance for the philosophy of religion. But a basic theme of psychoanalysis is the 'return of the repressed', the intrusion of that which was meant to be silenced into speech and behaviour. One of the techniques of Continental writers like Derrida and Irigaray is to demonstrate what *really* was on an author's mind, at an unconscious level, as that is revealed in the metaphors, turns of phrase, or lacunae in the text. This 'reading the margins' can be infuriating to British philosophers of religion, since it is not engaging with the argument of the text but rather ferreting out the desires of the subtext, engaging, therefore, at a level of unacknowledged and perhaps unacknowledgeable motivation rather than at a level of acknowledged argument.

On the other hand, the relation to the unconscious need not be one of repression or denial. It can instead be openness and vulnerability to difference, so that the conscious and the unconscious can be integrated. In this way that which erupts from unconscious depths is a creative wellspring rather than a threatening volcano, and desire and rationality can be strongly connected rather than struggling against each other. But for this to be the case, it is necessary to be in touch with emotion, bodiliness, and sexuality, in short with that which psychoanalytic theory has labelled the feminine. Moreover, for this to have integrity, it is necessary also to become aware of the manifestations of both repression and vulnerability in social and global contexts and the ways in which difference is implicated with power: such issues as emerge in awareness of gender, race and colonialism. The effort toward integration has led to some highly creative work in the philosophy of religion, which connects it to issues of ethics and politics: some examples are Irigaray's 'Divine Women',[11] and Kristeva's development of 'herethics' in 'Stabat Mater'.[12] It can, however, have bizarre results as well. So, for example, we find Derrida in *Spurs* trying to 'write like a woman'[13] – a gesture simultaneously radical and hugely problematic. (What is a man doing trying to write like a woman while women themselves – Irigaray, Kristeva, Cixous – are still being silenced, even in his own work? Why doesn't he rather try to write like a man – not a universal sexless subject but an embodied male human being in a specific, not universal, context, who takes actual women and their work seriously?)

One of the points of contention around the theme of the decentring of the subject is the status of the self in relation to agency and moral responsibility. The phrase 'the death of the subject' is sometimes bandied about as though any recognition of the discursively constructed nature of the subject carries with it the loss of possibility of agency or accountability, since there is no pre-given 'I' who acts and who can be held accountable for my action. This, however, is to misunderstand what is going on. The point of rejecting a pre-given 'I', a self which is not constructed in the matrix of power constituted by discourse of gender, race, class and sexuality within a particular historical context, is not to say that there are no 'subjects' and certainly not to deny them agency and accountability. It is, rather, negatively, to ask what purposes of power are being served by insisting on a pre-given self rather than to have one's eyes opened to the extent to which our privileged subjecthood may be bought at the expense of the abjection of others; and positively, it is to say that subjects, *complete with* agency and accountability, are constituted within and by a context, a context which importantly involves exclusion, since one constitutes oneself by distinguishing oneself from the other – initially from the mother. Selfhood is premised on difference, and cannot occur in a vacuum. The important question, then, is how that difference will be construed: will it be in terms of mastery or respect, belittling or celebration?

3 'Structured like a language'

The Continental emphasis on the unconscious is coupled with an emphasis on historical and social locatedness which shapes and frames the subject. This emphasis is heavily indebted to linguistic theory, especially the structuralist semiotics of Saussure[14] and Jakobson,[15] as well as to theories of ideology derived from Marx via Althusser and others. Very broadly speaking, the difference from British philosophy of religion in this respect is the recognition that all experience, indeed all conceptualization and speech, is always already constructed with the concrete cultural and material frame. There can be no such thing as neat experience, uncontaminated by perspective and assumption, whether that is sensory experience or religious experience. Just as the words I use must be selected from the vocabulary of the language in which I speak for them to count as words at all rather than unintelligible babble, so also any experience I claim as evidence for a belief can only be identified as such within a cultural repertoire, and is, along with the beliefs themselves, in large measure socially constructed.

The words 'structure' and 'construction' keep appearing; and indicate the great debt that current Continental thought owes to structuralism, an approach especially associated with Saussure and Lévi-Strauss.[16] Structuralism can be summarized as the theory that every social practice is structured like a language. What this means is that social practices are not spontaneous eruptions out of nowhere: they are determined by rules of procedure – what we might call the 'grammar' of the practice. It means also that the practice signifies something of importance within the culture, and that the particular rules of the practice stand in arbitrary relation to that which is signified.

Thus for example the practice of religious sacrifice serves in many societies both as a method of bonding among those who participate in the ritual and perhaps eat the food of the sacrificial victim, and as a way of excluding others by not permitting them to partake. There are very precise rules about what must and must not be done, and by whom, in sacrifices ranging from animal slaughter in primitive religions to the Catholic mass. Yet these rules are arbitrary in relation to the symbolic function they serve: in one society only the most revered men are permitted to eat the brains of the victim and the liver is given to those of low esteem, while in another society exactly the reverse occurs, yet with the same social meaning. Similarly, the sounds of one language differ from those of another and are arbitrary in their designation. This arbitrariness, however, does not mean that in any given language one can use sounds to mean whatever one likes and expect to be understood; just as the social rules and practices of a society, though arbitrary in the sense that they could be different in some other society, are not open to individualistic reinterpretation. One cannot just decide to feed the consecrated host to one's dog in a Catholic mass and expect observers to take that action as having no particular meaning.

The assumption of structuralist linguistics is coupled with broad acceptance of Lacanian psychoanalytic theory which, as sketched above, accepts that the Symbolic, including language, civilization, religion, at least in their western manifestations, are identified with the masculine. The example of sacrifice graphically illustrates this: in a vast range of societies sacrifice can only be performed by a man, and if women can partake at all, they can do so only in conditions strictly controlled by men. Thus one of the social functions of sacrifice is to bond the men of power together and to exclude or control slaves, foreigners, and women, whose blood is often seen as a pollutant. So prevalent is this structure across divergent cultures that Nancy Jay has described sacrifice as a 'remedy for having been born of a woman'.[17] Sacrifice is thus taken as an extreme example of the masculinist construction of the Symbolic in which difference, paradigmatically gender difference, is crucial.

But if this were all that could be said, then there would be no way of breaking out of it. A structuralist account of language (where language stands for the Symbolic in general) is profoundly conservative, seeing language as homogeneous and therefore paralysed when it comes to any confrontation with the other. The only thing the ego can do is attempt mastery. Contemporary Continental thinkers are deeply concerned with the ways in which the dominant groups, whether political, ecclesiastical, intellectual, or racial have sought to master the various 'others', often with great brutality, to their own impoverishment, and the ways in which religion has been part of those structures of domination. Yet such attitudes of oppression enacted by the mastering ego are indicative of a failure to encounter and be enriched by the alterities within ourselves: we remain 'strangers to ourselves', as Kristeva entitles one of her recent books,[18] and rather than celebrating the elements of difference and foreignness, we are threatened by them, seek to repress and master them, and hence to repress anyone – the other race, sex, sexuality – that serves to remind us of our own alterities.

The poststructuralist move is to recognize that social practices, including language, though structured according to rules which imply attitudes of mastery, nevertheless also carry within themselves the resources necessary to transgress the boundaries of the dominating establishment and to begin to develop alternative ways of thinking and being.[19] I see this as the shorthand way of distinguishing contemporary poststructuralism from the structuralist thought preceding and to a large extent shaping it: poststructuralists seek ways, from *within* the structures of the Symbolic, to disrupt or transgress those structures, thus destabilizing them in the interests of justice: a brilliant and outrageous example is Derrida's *Dissemination*, where he disrupts Lacanian gender structures and their compulsory heterosexuality by showing what happens when the autonomy of the male self is taken literally.[20] This interest in destabilizing from within is why poststructuralists are so interested in excess, transgression, free play, even madness. They draw upon Surrealists, the *avant garde*, the Marquis de Sade. They look at prisons and at mental hospitals; they explore bodiliness and sexuality in many forms, not just as an aspect of their 'private lives' but as part of their philosophical enterprise of seeking ways to destabilize the dominant ego and its structural manifestations, and thus make room for the celebration of alterities. This can and sometimes does tip over into nihilism, as in Baudrillard,[21] or into an amoral and relativistic free-play, as in Mark Taylor's (mis)appropriation of Derrida for a 'transgressive' philosophy of religion which is so busy smashing icons that it has not one word to say about issues of injustice. But in the work of many poststructuralist writers the exploration of the excessive or transgressive serves a very serious moral purpose indeed. I am personally particularly interested in the (different) ways in which Irigaray and Kristeva explore women's mystical experience as excessive, disruptive of the stable and oppressive structures of religious language, doctrine and practice, and thereby opening new horizons of the imminent divine that will be able to celebrate rather than repress alterities of sex, race and sexuality.[23]

The effort toward ways of dealing with oppressive structures is also one of the reasons why French thinkers adopt writing styles which we in Britain may well find opaque and exasperating. Rather than writing in straightforward prose, developing arguments with clearly defined premises and conclusions, French writers tend to use allusive, often poetic style, sometimes allowing themselves to free-associate on a theme to see what comes up, almost as one would in a therapy session where one was allowing the unconscious to emerge. Since British philosophers are for the most part given to a philosophical methodology whereby arguments are presented, attacked, defended, and counterattacked, clarity and precision of presentation is of great importance.

French thinkers, however, see this as already buying into the structuring of rationality which they are seeking to destabilize by their insistence on the unconscious and the structures of ideology. At best, as in Irigaray's *Speculum* or Kristeva's *Powers of Horror*, the allusive method is wonderfully illuminating of possibilities, though it must be granted that at the hands of less competent or less morally committed writers the line between brilliance and self-indulgence is easily crossed.[24] Even at its best, however, British philosophers can find this writing extremely heavy going, partly because of the difference of style of argument, and partly also because the multiple allusions tend to assume a thorough knowledge of French literature and philosophy of the past five hundred years (and sometimes, also that of Russia, Italy and former Eastern Bloc countries): it is like trying to read Milton without benefit of the Bible or Shakespeare. Partly, this just means that one has to do a great deal of very pleasant homework reading history and novels and poetry (and looking at paintings and sculpture) in order to understand what they are getting at. The difficulty I have with it is that it sometimes seems to be addressed only to those who have the leisure and educational privilege to engage in such cultural pursuits, and in this sense can be elitist – though as compared with the use of Bayes's theorem to assess the probability of the existence of God, I should think it is accessible to far more people.

Coupled with the issues raised by structuralism, Continental thinkers are acutely aware that the framing of experience, and therefore the development of any discipline or body of knowledge, is intertwined with issues of power and authority. On what grounds are people considered to be experts in any field? The straightforward answer is that people are experts if they know a great deal about it. But as soon as it is recognized that the 'experts' are also the ones who develop, define and police the field, the connection between knowledge and power which Foucault so tellingly explored becomes obvious.[25] At this point there is also a connection back to the unconscious, since the exercise of authority will reflect the desires, quite probably repressed and unacknowledged, of those in power. If those desires include a strong need to deny the relevance of the body, to repress sexuality and the (m)other, in short to refuse differences, then the structures of civilization as they are defended and upheld by those in authority are bound to be bad news for women, blacks, and gays, and poor people of all countries.

Broadly speaking, and with many variations, French thinkers have taken it as given that this applies to the history of Christendom, not only in ecclesiastical structures but also in theology and philosophy of religion. Where British thinkers prefer to deal in terms of developing and defending arguments for or against specific religious beliefs, French thinkers are acutely conscious of the ideology and social construction of those beliefs, and insist on asking who benefits and who loses out, not only from the beliefs themselves, but even from conducting the conversation in this way. Many British thinkers are worried about the relativist consequences of French procedure, and what may be perceived as continual side-stepping of the substantive issues of theology and the philosophy of religion. French thinkers ask how it comes about that these particular issues are the ones that are construed as 'substantive' issues in the first place, while others such as those having to do with gender and other forms of difference are marginalized. Such questioning disrupts the whole idea of a quest for religious (or any other) realities by means of the employment of Enlightenment rationality, with its unproblematic and implicitly masculine subject and the philosophical methods it employs. Both method and goal French thinkers would see as prime examples of socially constructed projection of repressed masculinist desires. Given such utterly different starting points between British and French thinkers, it is hardly surprising that without very great good will and considerable effort, everyone winds up with a headache.

Although a complete discussion of the question of relativism would take me far beyond the bounds of this paper, it is important to note that in this regard French thinkers have not always been well served by their Anglo-American admirers: Richard Rorty, for example, and Mark Taylor espouse a relativism which they consider derivative from Derrida, but which is arguably very far from Derrida's own thought.[26] Derrida's emphasis on deconstruction, in fact, is one which British philosophers of religion might find congenial. In his 'Force of Law: the "Mystical Foundation of Authority"'[27] Derrida shows how it is necessary to investigate the ways in which justice has been construed in different historical contexts, and in particular how what has counted as 'justice' has all too often served the interests of those who were doing the counting. But such a deconstruction of justice is necessary precisely in the *name* of justice and for its sake: and this is so even though we can be quite clear that we are never going to arrive at a neutral or uncontextual transcendent account of justice. Whatever account of justice we propose will itself always need deconstruction, and so on, *ad infinitum*; but although we can never say that we have arrived, or are already perfect, this is not the same as to say that any account we develop is unusable, let alone that one account of justice is as good as another. Though Derrida does not make the comparison, this is not far from Eckhart's comment, 'For God's sake, rid me of God,' at least if that is interpreted to mean that whatever concepts of God we may develop, we must always also recognize that they are provisional and partial and if viewed as final they become idolatry: in the name of God it is necessary to deconstruct God.

4 God and religion

But if the subject of religious belief is destabilized by the unconscious, and the language of religion is socially and ideologically framed, what about God? What, according to Continental thinkers, is religion itself? Again, there are many variations, but some common themes emerge. First, it is taken as obvious that 'good old God', as Lacan calls him, is a masculinist projection subtending the phallocentric structures of civilization; there are arguments about detail here, but the central point is hardly disputed among current French thinkers.[28] But that is by no means to dismiss the divine, or religion. On the contrary, thinkers like Irigaray and Kristeva and (I think) Derrida would see the 'British style' belief in God and discussions about that God's existence and nature not just as simplistic but as profoundly irreligious. This is not merely because British philosophers of religion do not engage with the psychoanalytic and political issues already raised, which Continental thinkers consider essential to any intellectually responsible stance. It is also because they would hold that to think of the existence of God as a fact among other facts, even if the most important one, is to trivialize it right out of religious significance. Continental thought would thus see British philosophy of religion as largely secular and empiricist in its treatment of the question of God's existence as one more fact about a world which is otherwise the same for theists and atheists.

Their approach, instead, is to shift the understanding of religion to the idea that the basic values, myths and rituals of any civilization are in fact its religion. Religion in some form, thus, is a necessary basis for any civilization. In some ways we can see religion and the unconscious as parallel in their thought: we could say that in their view as the unconscious subtends the rational subject, so religion subtends civilization. The question, therefore, is not *whether* we as a society will be religious, but *how*, just as the question is not whether we as individuals have an unconscious, but how we relate to it. This accounts for a comment such as the following by Irigaray:

> It seems we are unable to eliminate or suppress the phenomenon of religion. It reemerges in many forms, some of them perverse: sectarianism, theoretical or political dogmatism, religiosity. . . . Therefore, it is crucial that we rethink religion, and especially religious structures, categories, rules, and utopias, all of which have been masculine for centuries. Keeping in mind that today these religious structures often appear under the name of science and technology.[29]

Such an attitude explains the prominence of religious themes in Continental thought, even among thinkers who would look with suspicion on the very idea of a 'specialty' in philosophy of religion. The writings of Lacan are peppered with Biblical quotations and religious allusions, not often commented upon by his English expositors who, while discussing his psychoanalytic and philosophical ideas, seem largely to have assumed the Anglo-American secularist stance which I think French writers hold to be impossible. From a certain perspective, also, Derrida's work can arguably be seen as an exercise in apophatic theology. Some British and American feminist writers are alive to the importance of religion for Irigaray and Kristeva.[30] With these exceptions, however, the religious ideas of Continental thinkers are largely unexplored or marginalized by English-speaking writers who discuss their ideas, probably because many of the English writers who do engage with French thought are sociologists or linguists, and are not particularly interested in religion, while philosophers of religion have for their part left them severely alone. Thus what may be one of the most creative aspects of their work is ignored.

One of the reasons for this may be that British philosophers of religion do not see why that which subtends civilization should necessarily be called religious: why should we not rather reserve the term for that which has to do with God and God's relations to the world? In part this is a question of stipulation, though once again it is obvious that stipulation carries a great weight of power and ideology: think for instance of the way Smart or Hick speaks of 'major world religions' – meaning primarily Christianity, Islam, Judaism, Buddhism and Hinduism – and thereby marginalize tribal and aboriginal religions, though historically and perhaps even now these would have more adherents than those systems which are labelled 'major'. One does not have to be unduly cynical to suppose that the history of this country as a 'Christian' colonial power has something to do with how easily we find these stipulations 'normal'.

Be that as it may, Continental thinkers might point out that, whatever name is given to it, the ultimate values and myths that subtend a civilization are of enormous significance, and that if societies or subgroups within them are worshipping money or science or football, then it is far more intellectually responsible for thinkers to notice and interpret this than to shrug it off as not really about religion and therefore not our specialist concern. Whether one thinks that such things as ongoing sexism and racism, the wars in Bosnia and Chechnya or the tenuous peace in Northern Ireland, are manifestations of genuine religion or an aberration of it, even on a most generous reading, Christendom has lent itself to incalculable injustice over the centuries. Is it not urgent that an account of the nature of religion take this on board? Once again, British philosophers are likely to see Continental thinkers as lacking in rigour and discipline, and lapsing into sociology and politics, while French thinkers might see British philosophers of religion as much too narrow in approach, refusing to engage with the real religious issues of our time while frittering away energy discussing things that don't have much bearing on people's lives, and thereby in effect supporting the status quo. It should not be forgotten that most of the French thinkers I have mentioned inherited the ideals, though not the precise content, of the political commitment of Jean-Paul Sartre and Simone de Beauvoir. Many of them were on the barricades in 1968, and have worked hard for political and social projects such as the welfare of Algerian immigrants, the lifting of the USSR's heavy hand in Poland and Czechoslovakia, the right of French women to contraception and abortion, and the humanizing of conditions in mental hospitals and prisons. This political engagement, and the ways in which the institutions of church and university enabled them or failed them in their efforts, informs all their thinking; indeed, they would consider it part of an intellectual's duty to be engaged at a practical, not only at a theoretical level.

I am aware of how sketchy is this summary of some of the differences of approach of British and French thinkers on the themes of the subject, language, and God/religion. Everything I have said requires deepening; and for almost every generalization about both British and French philosophers, exceptions could easily be found. Furthermore, even to give such a sketch, with rather simplistic pigeon holes, already places me very firmly on English-speaking terrain: I cannot imagine any French thinker making such a survey or even having much sympathy with it. They would surely want to know what desires and whose interests are being served by an attempt to button down, however provisionally, the shifting signifiers in the way that I have done.

My excuse is that I believe that we (i.e. English-speaking philosophers of religion) have a great deal to learn from them, but that differences of style and basic assumptions and starting positions often make their work inaccessible to us. Unless we recognize and allow for some of these differences, we won't begin to see what they are on about. And whether in the end we agree or disagree, I believe that we are greatly impoverished if we refuse to engage at all. Epistemology, especially in the philosophy of religion, is inescapably about 'knowing the difference'.

Notes

1   Donna Haraway, 'A Manifesto for Cyborgs: Science, Technology and Socialist Feminism in the 1980s', in Linda J. Nicholson (ed.), *Feminism/Postmodernism* (London and New York: Routledge, 1990), pp. 202–3 (first published in 1985 in *Socialist Review*, no. 8).

2   Jean François Lyotard, *The Postmodern Condition: a Report on Knowledge*, trans. G. Bennington and Brian Maaumi (Minneapolis: University of Minnesota Press, 1984).

3   Judith Butler, 'Contingent Foundations: Feminism and the Question of "Postmodernism"', in *Feminist Contentions*, ed. Seyla Benhabib, Judith Butler, Drucilla Cornéll and Nancy Fraser (London and New York: Routledge, 1995).

4   Ernest Gellner, *Postmodernism, Reason and Religion* (London and New York: Routledge, 1992).

5   Richard Swinburne, *Responsibility and Atonement* (Oxford: Clarendon Press, 1989).

6   Philip L. Quinn, 'Swinburne on Guilt, Atonement, and Christian Redemption', in Alan G. Padgett

(ed.), *Reason and the Christian Religion: Essays in Honour of Richard Swinburne* (Oxford: Clarendon Press, 1994).

7   John Hick, *An Interpretation of Religion: Human Responses to the Transcendent* (London: Macmillan, 1989), ch. 7.

8   See, for example, Luce Irigaray, *Speculum of the Other Woman* (Ithaca, N.Y., and London: Cornell University Press, 1985) for a sustained critique of Freud; and Jacques Derrida, *Spectres of Marx: The State of the Debt, the Work of Mourning, and the New International*, tr. Peggy Kamuf (London: Routledge, 1994) for reflections on Marxist thought in the aftermath of the Soviet Union and the Eastern Bloc.

9   Sigmund Freud, *Totem and Taboo*, in his *The Origins of Religion*, tr. James Strachey (Penguin Freud Library, vol. 13; Harmondsworth: Penguin, 1985).

10   Luce Irigaray, 'Divine Woman', in *Sexes and Genealogies*, tr. Gillian C. Gill (New York: Columbia University Press, 1993).

11   Luce Irigaray, 'Divine Women', in her *Sexes and Genealogies*.

12   Julia Kristeva, 'Stabat Mater', in her *Tales of Love*, tr. Leon S. Roudiez (New York: Columbia University Press, 1987); reprinted in Toril Moi (ed.), *The Kristeva Reader* (Oxford: Blackwell, 1986).

13   Jacques Derrida, *Spurs: Nietzsche's Styles*, tr. Barbara Harlow (Chicago: Chicago University Press, 1978).

14   Ferdinand de Saussure, *General Course in Linguistics*, tr. Roy Harris (London: Duckworth, 1983).

15   Roman Jakobson, *Fundamentals of Language* (The Hague: Mouton, 1956).

16   The primary texts here are Ferdinand de Saussure, *General Course in Linguistics*, and Claude Lévi-Strauss, *The Savage Mind* (English tr.; London: Weidenfeld and Nicolson, 1966). For useful secondary literature see Jonathan Culler, *Saussure* (London: Collins, Fontana Modern Masters, 1976); John Sturrock, *Structuralism*, 2nd edn (London: Fontana, HarperCollins, 1993); Eve Tavor Bannet, *Structuralism and the Logic of Dissent: Barthes, Derrida, Foucault, Lacan* (London: Macmillan, 1989).

17   Nancy Jay, *Throughout Your Generations Forever: Sacrifice, Religion, and Paternity* (Chicago: University of Chicago Press, 1991), p. xxiii.

18   Julia Kristeva, *Strangers to Ourselves*, tr. Leon S. Roudiez (New York: Columbia University Press, 1993).

19   See, for example, Julia Kristeva, *Revolution in Poetic Language*, tr. Leon S. Roudiez (New York: Columbia University Press, 1993).

20   Jacques Derrida, *Dissemination*, tr. Barbara Johnson (Chicago: University of Chicago Press, 1981).

21   See among others, Jean Baudrillard, *Fatal Strategies*, tr. Philip Beitchman and W.G.J. Niesluchowski (London: Pluto, 1990); *The Transparency of Evil: Essays on Extreme Phenomena*, tr. James Benedict (London: Verso, 1993).

22   Mark Taylor, *Erring: A Postmodern A/theology* (Chicago: University of Chicago Press, 1984).

23   Luce Irigaray, *Speculum of the Other Woman*, tr. Gillian C. Gill (Ithaca, N.Y.: Cornell University Press, 1985), pp. 191–240; and Julia Kristeva, *Tales of Love*.

24   As I think it does, for example, in Mark Taylor, *Erring*.

25   As for example in his essays in Michel Foucault, *Power/Knowledge: Selected Interviews and Other Writings 1972–1977*, ed. Colin Gordon (New York: Harvester Wheatsheaf, 1980).

26   Richard Rorty, *Contingency, Irony and Solidarity* (Cambridge: Cambridge University Press, 1989); and Mark Taylor, *Erring*. For a discussion of Rorty, see Richard J. Bernstein, 'Rorty's Liberal Utopia' in his *The New Constellation: The Ethical-Political Horizons of Modernity/Postmodernity* (Cambridge: Polity Press, 1991).

27   Jacques Derrida, 'Force of Law: the "Mystical Foundation of Authority"', in Drucilla Cornell *et al.* (eds), *Deconstruction and the Possibility of Justice* (New York: Routledge, 1992).

28   For Lacan's view, see his 'God and the *Jouissance* of The Woman', in Juliet Mitchell and Jacqueline Rose (eds), *Feminine Sexuality: Jacques Lacan and the École Freudienne* (Basingstoke: Macmillan, 1982). The idea derives broadly from Freud, of course, especially his *The Future of an Illusion*.

29   Luce Irigaray, 'Women, the Sacred, Money', in her *Sexes and Genealogies*, p. 75.

30   See for example David Crownfield (ed.), *Body? Text in Julia Kristeva: Religion, Women, and Psychoanalysis* (Albany: State University of New York Press, 1993); Kathryn Bond Stockton, *God Between Their Lips: Desire Between Women in Irigaray, Bronte, and Eliot* (Stanford, Cal.: Stanford University Press, 1994); C.W. Maggie Kim *et al.* (eds), *Transfigurations: Theology and the French Feminists* (Minneapolis: Augsburg Fortress, 1993).

Chapter 3

A POST-STRUCTURALIST APPROACH

Ellen T. Armour

A DECONSTRUCTIVE APPROACH TO FEMINIST PHILOSOPHY OF RELIGION: RACE, SEX, AND POST(?)MODERNITY

Like Jantzen, Ellen Armour turns to the Continent, and French philosophers in particular, for her post-structuralist approach to feminist philosophy of religion. But Armour focuses specifically on the race/gender divide. She is unsatisfied with the 'whitefeminism' which has been unable to recognize its own racial coloring. She offers an innovative account employing Derrida against himself and against all those white females who need to recognize the racial biases which continue to exclude non-whites from the discipline. Crucially, she appropriates Derrida's claim that 'there is nothing outside the text' for a critical unraveling of 'the text' which is Western metaphysics. Armour not only makes a highly significant social statement about the racism inherent in the earliest forms of feminist theology, but her creative use of deconstruction gives the philosophically minded a challenge. She carves out anti-racist tools for feminists from the unlikely sources of Derrida and Irigaray.

IN THIS CHAPTER, I UNDERTAKE to illustrate the benefits of one approach (my own) to feminist philosophy of religion through what is variously described as post-structuralist or deconstructive philosophy. Traditionally, philosophy of religion has drawn on analytic philosophy as its primary resource and concerned itself with shoring up religion by submitting faith claims to rational scrutiny. Those beliefs were deemed sound for which arguments could be mounted that met the rigorous standards of philosophical logic. A number of feminists trained in analytic philosophy of religion have offered astute criticisms of traditional philosophy of religion (Grace Jantzen, Pamela Sue Anderson, Morny Joy, to name a few) and have turned to Continental philosophy to address those weaknesses. They see in Continental philosophy (and psychoanalysis, a cognate field) a route that offers access to resources that can address the lacunae they find in traditional philosophy of religion. Attending to the question of sexual difference reveals traditional philosophy of religion in a new light. It raises questions about the philosophical imaginary (Jantzen) and puts questions about the view from nowhere (Anderson) in a new context, for example.

To the concern with sexual difference I add an explicit focus on racial differences, as well. My interest in race and feminism was sparked by my own experience of an institutional failure to give race the attention it needed. I was at Vanderbilt during the late 1980s, a particularly difficult period in the divinity school's history. The institution had played a significant role in the civil rights struggle in the 1960s and early 1970s. In the spring of 1960, there was a showdown between the Board of Trust and the divinity school faculty over expelling James Lawson, an African-American divinity student and civil rights activist. (Lawson had brought unwelcome attention to the university through his leadership and defense of sit-ins at Nashville businesses.) The dispute was eventually resolved in Lawson's favor, but at a particularly dark point in the negotiations, many of the divinity school faculty proffered their resignations. In the 1970s, the divinity school faculty led a protest of the university's decision to host the Davis Cup tennis tournament, which included a team from South Africa (still under apartheid at the time). However, in the late 1980s, this same institution was forced to confront its failure to sustain the legacy of the past by critiques raised of then-current practices by then-current students of color. I participated in several cross-racial coalitions to help the school address its problems. In the process, I found out that, feminism's claims notwithstanding, cross-racial coalition work was at least as difficult for women as for men. It seemed to me that the dynamics that frustrated our attempts to work across racial lines called into question certain claims made by feminist theologians, in particular. Many of these theologians (Rosemary Ruether, for example) came to feminism through the civil rights movement. They described feminist theology as distinct from other forms of liberation theology in that it sides with 'the oppressed of the oppressed; namely, women of the oppressed.'[1] Their work suggested that a common desire for liberation and a common understanding of the source of oppression unproblematically bound women together across color lines. However, my experience suggested that race lines fractured rather than bound women together – even women of good intention and similar political sensibility. It seemed to me that we were caught in patterns not of our own making that probably ran deep in the fabric of our cultural context and history. Trying to account for that difficulty and to overcome it was a direct impetus behind my book, *Deconstruction, Feminist Theology, and the Problem of Difference: Subverting the Race/Gender Divide.*[2] I turn to deconstruction as a resource for addressing these problems.

A book by a white feminist on the subject of race in 1999 may seem untimely.[3] After all, feminist theology and theory had been contending with criticisms of our inability to consistently incorporate race and other differences into our work in our discipline for several years. In fact, these criticisms had prompted many of the most significant debates within feminist thought in the 1980s and 1990s. However, my analysis of the outcome of these debates suggested that little progress had been made. Indeed, the very strategies designed by white feminists to overcome our blindness went astray – as a matter of course. The debates over the so-called 'problem of essentialism' provided a particularly telling example. The problem of essentialism arose, in part, out of a response to criticisms from women of color. These scholars argued that white feminists assumed that, at bottom, what it meant to be a woman was essentially the same for all women. Racial differences added an extra dimension, but they did not alter the fundamental experience of being a woman. White feminists acknowledged the critique as justified. We identified the assumption that all women are the same with what came to be known as biological essentialism; that is, assuming that femininity was grounded ultimately in women's bodily nature. Locating women's identity in culture (i.e. gender) rather than nature (i.e. sex), we assumed, made room for differences of all sorts to matter, whether explicitly addressed or not. Essentialism was the problem, not race.

In practice, simply avoiding making claims about women's nature produced disappointing results. Rather than actually dealing with differences between women, white feminists policed each other's texts in search of symptoms of the disease of biological essentialism. This focus perpetuated a myopic tendency to think of difference in the abstract, not as a feature of the concrete historical realities of women's lives and the practices that sustain them. White feminist thought continued to suffer from a double erasure of race; white feminists were unable to sustain attention to African-American feminists' insights and remained blind to whiteness as a racial mark that shaped their own work. It was as though race and gender constituted two sides of a chasm whose bridge kept disappearing into a fog. What goes under the name of feminism, I argued, is more aptly named 'whitefeminism.'

It seemed to me that the forces at work exceeded and even ran counter to the intentions of whitefeminists. My investigation raised questions about the relationship between authors and texts, and texts and contexts that, I argued, needed to be addressed. We assume that authors are the masters of their texts, deciding what goes in and what stays out, what receives attention and what does not. Yet, it seemed to me that whitefeminists were decidedly unable to master not just the topic of race, but its very dynamics. It seemed as though something were conspiring to keep race and gender on opposite sides of a divide. How might one gain some purchase on that 'something' in order to expose and disrupt it?

For answers to these questions, I turned to deconstruction as practiced by Jacques Derrida and Luce Irigaray. Given their reputation in the academic circles of feminism and religion, they probably seem like unlikely aids to my project. Theologians and philosophers of religion associated deconstruction with nihilism. The initial volume of essays on deconstruction and theology asserted that deconstruction was, 'in the final analysis *the death of God put into writing*.'[4] Feminists gave a wary nod to deconstruction as a critical practice that exposed texts' hidden interests, but feared that it undercut any grounds for normative claims that are essential to feminist practice. Irigaray's work had come to the attention of Anglophone feminists at the height of debates over essentialism, and that timing definitively shaped reception of her work. Irigaray's many references to the multiple sites of pleasure on the female body caused a number of Anglophone feminists to charge her with biological essentialism. Others, however, saw in her invocation of multiplicity (note the title of her second book, *This Sex Which Is Not One*[5]) important potential for thinking women's diversity.

My own approach to their work was hardly uncritical. Neither of these thinkers had overcome the race/gender divide in their own work. Derrida takes on both race and gender, but in separate (though often parallel) places. Irigaray's evocations of diversity remained mostly abstract. When concretized (as in the Italian feminist movement), they did not cross racial lines. However, I saw in both thinkers' work taken together important strategies for addressing the problems in whitefeminism. These strategies involve what Derrida calls double reading and writing. Double reading sifts through the Western philosophical tradition and its contexts in search of assertions of mastery *and* signs of resistance to that mastery. Insofar as double reading uncovers what is already occurring, it reveals a double writing at work in this tradition and its contexts. Applying these strategies to these thinkers' own work uncovered insights and resources for moving beyond the race/gender divide. Double reading and writing also describe the approach I took toward reading Derrida and Irigaray. I read their work both for their own submission to mastery and resistances to it; for signs of their work's inscription by the divide between race and gender, and resistance to it.

'Nothing outside the text?'

I began with the (in)famous mantra associated with Derrida's work, 'there is nothing outside the text.' Derrida's insight could not be reduced to its nihilistic stereotype — that there is nothing outside of language. Rather, as deployed by Derrida, this phrase spoke to a way of understanding the relationship between text and author, text and context that provided a theoretical framework for understanding whitefeminism's predicament. The 'text' outside of which there is 'nothing' is not a literal text, but rather a context that shapes our knowing and our doing. That context is constituted by certain hierarchical dualisms (spirit/matter, ideal/real, presence/absence, intelligible/sensible, reason/emotion). The first item in each pair is valued above the second item. These dualisms come together to constitute dominant strands in the fabric of Western thought. All our thinking, writing, and doing occurs in a context shaped by these dualisms, including our thinking about gender and race. Masculine/feminine and white/black also constitute hierarchical dualisms that align with these other dualisms in destructive ways. Together, these dualisms that govern our concepts of race and gender constitute an economy of sameness that is ontotheological and phallogocentric. At the heart of this economy lie two figures, man and God, who mirror each other. Man is the master of language, able to mean what he says and to say what he means. His ability to do so rests upon the assumed existence of a God whose Word *is* Being. It is no coincidence that the *theos* that founds *ontos* (whose *logos* is *ontos*) is male. As ground of being, this god founds the (less secure) link between being and language that constitutes man's subjectivity. Man further secures his subjectivity by establishing boundaries between himself and his 'others.' Not coincidentally, those others turn out to be marked as different through sex or race.

Because this text is the very context in which we are embedded, Derrida's work suggests that it writes us at least as much as we write it. I argue that whitefeminism is itself a mirror image of these same dynamics. Like man, the woman who lies at the heart of whitefeminist concerns is defined in terms of her sexed and raced others. For all of feminism's insistence on providing a platform from which (all) women can contest the multiple oppressions that constrain them, whitefeminism's woman seems clearly to be the product of a very specific time and place. The figure of woman that dominates whitefeminists' texts is the descendant of the woman idealized by the nineteenth-century 'cult of true womanhood.' Pretty, pious, and pure, the pedestal from which she guarded home and hearth was also a prison locking her away from involvement with the masculine public sphere. Although arguably the two waves of the feminist movement have liberated many women from this role (whitefeminists themselves exemplify that) in our daily lives, she remains our model of oppression. Although long ago recognized by feminists as man's 'other,' this woman's own racial 'other' has remained largely invisible to whitefeminists. Using the work of African-American feminist theorists, historians, and literary scholars such as bell hooks, Hazel Carby, and Hortense Spillers (among others), I argue that whitefeminism's woman and that of African-American womanhood were defined in opposition to one another. Deemed, by definition, ugly rather than pretty, promiscuous rather than pure, black women were exploited rather than protected. In the words of Hortense Spillers, they are 'twin actants on a common psychic landscape.'[6] Whitefeminism's blindness to race is a consequence of the subject position we have inherited from the racist and sexist context that produced these two concepts of women. We fail to recognize whiteness as a racial mark and pass over black women in our political and theoretical work, in part, because our very subject position depends upon it. We require the mirror of black femaleness to establish our identity, a 'fact' that must be both continually reasserted (but under cover) in order to function.

Subverting the race/gender divide

Deconstruction is not just a diagnostic tool, but also a curative tonic. In addition to what seemed to me an accurate diagnosis of whitefeminism's affliction, I found in deconstruction strategies for overcoming race's double erasure. Both Derrida and Irigaray claim that occupying the underside of the economy of sameness accords the context's 'others' some subversive potential. They exploit that potential – although to limited liberative effect – in the figures of the text's sexed or raced 'others.' Whitefeminism's other, it seemed to me, held within her similar subversive potential. Indeed, the ground cleared by my reading of Derrida and Irigaray made possible readings of African-American feminists' work that could register within a whitefeminist context as subverting the race/gender divide. Their work not only contests African-American womanhood, but white womanhood, as well. In doing so, they carry feminism toward its 'end' in two senses. First, they both expose and subvert the division between white and black womanhood. Harriet Jacobs' slave narrative is a case in point. The heroine bespeaks a desire for sexual purity, an attribute associated with white women by the cult of true womanhood. Such work loosens the wedge that separates these notions of womanhood thereby furthering the (im)possible promise of feminism to provide a platform from which women can resist the variety of oppressions they face.

Playing on Derrida's use of the double meaning of *pharmakon* ('remedy' and 'poison'), the cure I offer is hardly comforting or conclusive.[7] This deconstructive approach does not produce, at long last, the inclusive vision of the unity of women that feminism desires. Rather than paving over the fissures out of which the race/gender divide emerges, this approach deepens them, in a sense. That is, it attempts to keep 'woman' open as a site where differences can come to the fore and be contested. Such an aim offers no guarantees; in fact, even as it arises out of feminism's own founding aim (resisting the varieties of oppression that women face), it asserts the inescapability of the risks of that very project. The platform called for by such a project is constituted not by a seamless ground of sameness, but by fissures and ruptures through which differences emerge that require negotiation. Deconstruction, then, is not a practice in which one engages merely to clear ground for difference; rather, one continues to engage it as a strategy of vigilance on behalf of sexual and racial differences over and against an economy of sameness that would contain or erase them.

The future of deconstruction, feminism, and religion

Deconstructive feminist theology and/or philosophy of religion should now be concerned with promoting racial/sexual differences. That task requires first a reimmersion in the crucible of modernity that produced whitefeminism in the first place, but in order to break out of it.

I have become increasingly convinced that developing economies that can sustain attention to sexual and racial differences will require finding genuinely postmodern ways of thinking about and dealing with religion. Let me say what I mean and then describe what's led me to this conviction. Modernity posed significant challenges to religious authority on many fronts, not the least of which was the challenge posed by modern science to the claim that God was the ground of all that is. In the face of this challenge, religion relocated its claims in the God/man relationship.

Consider this very rough account of the conception of man's relationship to God which was produced by modern philosophers. The presence of the thought of infinity in the cogito establishes God's existence, according to Descartes. Inaccessible to speculative knowledge, according to Kant, God is relocated to the realm of practical reason. To continue to be moral in the face of an unjust world, human beings must posit a god who ensures that good triumphs in the end. Schleiermacher asserts that the truth of religion lies in religious experience, which is, at its heart, the feeling of absolute dependence. It is but a short distance from relocating the truth of religion in the religious subject to Feuerbach, Freud, and Nietzsche: that is, to the notion that the idea of a supreme being fulfills some psychological need for the human being. Hence, the question of the relationship between faith and reason – an issue as old in philosophy of religion as Christian apologetics, at least – is brought to something of an impasse. Whether God really exists or is simply a human projection ultimately can't be decided on rational grounds (though either position can be justified on rational grounds). At best, *pace* William James, one can conclude that it makes as much sense as not to live one's life as if God were real or, *pace* Soren Kierkegaard, faith exceeds reason. In either case, faith is placed beyond the reach of reason and becomes a matter (as it has, in the modern West) of personal belief and private practice.

Certain hallmarks, then, came to characterize the modern concept of religion – the god/man duo sustained by the mechanism of projection, the opposition between faith and reason, theism and atheism – to which modern theology and philosophy of religion respond.[8] Though I cannot make the arguments in full here, I would argue that these hallmarks are implicated in the economies of racial and sexual indifference that also came to characterize modernity.[9] Insofar as these economies are imbricated in the modern view of religion (and vice versa), I would argue that the (im)possible possibility of religion on the other side of ontotheology rises or falls with the (im)possible possibility of enabling sexual and racial differences to flourish. Recall that at the heart of the economy of sameness that produces and sustains economies of racial and sexual indifference resides that hallmark of religious reflection, the god/man duo. Or, restated in Derridean language, metaphysical humanism and ontotheology are two sides of the same coin. Indeed, I would argue that the (im)possible possibility of religion on the other side of ontotheology rises or falls with the (im)possible possibility of enabling sexual and racial differences to flourish.

In *Becoming Divine*, Jantzen exposes traditional philosophy of religion's dependence upon the god/man duo and links it directly to this discipline's inability to open itself toward sexual differences.[10] I would argue that, although it takes different forms, her critique could be extended to much of what goes under the name of Continental philosophy of religion. In recent years, philosophers like John Caputo, Richard Kearney, Jean-Luc Marion, Gianni Vattimo and Merold Westphal have found in the Continental tradition a rich resource for religious reflection.[11] These scholars attempt to take seriously the critiques of religion that emerge from this tradition while also drawing on what they see as resources for furthering religious reflection. Of particular pertinence to their work are the attention given to religion by Martin Heidegger and certain of his successors (Derrida and Emmanual Levinas, in particular). They find that these thinkers offer a fresh perspective on religion that seems particularly appropriate for our era. However, Caputo *et al.* are engaged in work that seems to share the broad aims of traditional philosophy of religion. Though they draw on Continental rather than analytic philosophy, they, too, subject to philosophical scrutiny the specific contents of religious faith in order to justify, purify, and strengthen it.[12] To their credit, these philosophers seek to shore up a Christianity characterized by resistance to fundamentalisms of various kinds as well as a positive concern for social justice. However, that commitment is articulated in largely abstract terms (philosophically as a concern for 'the other,' religiously as a concern for 'the widow and the orphan').[13] Sexual and racial differences – when they are thematized explicitly at all – figure most often as an automatic outgrowth of unmooring religion from its traditional sources of security.[14]

Most of these scholars think Christian religious reflection suffers from an ancient disease born of its early contact with the corrupting influence of Greek philosophy. Importing Plato and Aristotle sent Christianity astray. It came to rely overmuch on (Greek) reason and lost touch with its (Jewish) roots in faith. According to this account of Christianity's history, the tradition winds up (ironically, I would argue, given the modern alignment of religion as reason's opposite) beholden to modernism with its confidence in self-mastery and metanarratives. Deconstruction tempers Christianity's modernist hubris by exposing the limits of reason, of metanarratives, of plenitude and presence and (re)creates space for faith's re-emergence. The faith that re-emerges centers around belief in and fidelity to a transcendent Father God who, while he grounds the world by giving himself to it as its creator, redeemer, and sustainer, is never fully available to human grasp – a fact that religious folk tend to forget, these scholars argue. Deconstruction, then, clears away yet another idolatry – ironically, by using philosophy against itself.

Insofar as their work exposes the limits and failures of modernism, these philosophers position themselves legitimately as postmodern. Nevertheless, it seems to me that their work remains beholden to the legacy of modernism. At the limits of reason appears faith, its binary opposite. The God who lies beyond knowing remains the Father God of the god/man duo. He may give of himself in an inexhaustible stream, according to Jean-Luc Marion (to take one example), but his gift grounds ever more securely the line of fathers and sons that constitute traditional religious authority.[15]

Feminist religious reflection is not immune from a related criticism. That the god/man duo is implicated in sexual indifference is hardly a new insight to feminist theologians and philosophers of religion. Mary Daly said it early and well: 'If God is male, then the male is god.'[16] That this insight is a commonplace, however, also sounds a cautionary note. Challenging masculine imagery for God and the masculine constructions of the human being who relates to this god – both central aspects of whitefeminist religious reflection – has done little if anything to ensure attention to differences between women. This suggests that simply contesting the content of images of God and constructions of human being isn't enough to disrupt the economy of sameness that they sustain. Substituting feminine images for masculine images (God the mother for God the father, for example) and broadening the palette of what counts as human to include sexual difference may only replace one standard of sameness with another leaving, as Irigaray warns, the system of phallogocentrism in place.

Beyond projection

Generally these contemporary proposals for new approaches to philosophy of religion through Continental philosophy leave projection untouched as the mechanism that sustains the divine/human relationship, an approach that, by its very nature, sustains sameness rather than difference. However, I have become increasingly convinced that this way of construing the relationship of the divine and human not only closes off sexual and racial difference, but is inadequate to lived religious experience. Central to this shift in my thinking has been my experience working with the Project on Lived Theology.[17] This project connects academics with activists on the basis of common interests. The group of which I was a part focused on cross-racial coalition work (though issues of sexual differences also came up frequently). Meeting and talking with male and female activists of various ethnic backgrounds whose religious convictions motivated and sustained their work for justice across racial lines confirmed for me the inadequacy of the theory of projection for understanding the way human beings relate to the divine. Commitment to a very traditional Father God impelled and sustained commitments to working with and on behalf of folk defined as racial 'others.' This was true even for minority women (who hardly saw themselves in this traditional god). This is not to suggest that masculine concepts and images of God are benign after all; allegiance to this God did appear to have predictable negative effects on activists' dealing with sexual differences (women's issues and homophobia). It does suggest, however, that feminist philosophy of religion and theology need a more nuanced approach to God-talk than the one-size-fits-all Feuerbachian projection model.[18]

Having rejected certain approaches, then, to deconstructive feminist philosophy of religion, what would I propose instead? Derrida describes deconstruction as 'an incision . . . [that] can be made only according to lines of force and forces of rupture that are localizable in the discourse to be deconstructed.'[19] When approached from a concern for sexual and racial differences, certain ruptures in the modernist paradigm of religion – often sexually and racially marked – appear in the work of Irigaray, Derrida, Heidegger, and even certain Continental philosophers of religion. That religion and sexual difference coincide in Irigaray's work is not particularly surprising. That such intersections appear in the work of philosophers for whom sexual and racial differences are hardly primary concerns is perhaps more surprising. Much of my recent work has focused on reading these interventions together in order to begin to sketch the possibilities of a common future for religion beyond ontotheology and sexual and racial difference. In the closing pages of this chapter, I will describe in brief compass what this work has yielded.

In *Belief Itself*, Irigaray argues that belief (which she defines as holding something to be true despite prima facie evidence to the contrary) plays a critical role in sustaining the economy of sexual indifference.[20] Two scenes prove symptomatic of belief's function; one obviously religious (the Eucharist), one ostensibly non-religious (Freud's account of the fort/da game). Her analysis suggests that belief functions in both contexts as the linchpin in a phallogocentric economy funded by an economy of sacrifice centered around unacknowledged mourning for the maternal body.

Irigaray's analysis of belief identifies a rupture within the modernist paradigm of religion. First, the narrative of modernity as confining religion to a separate and discreet sphere is called into question. Belief appears in a context that claimed to have resolutely separated itself from religion. Irigaray's analysis also belies the claim that belief per se lies beyond ontotheology. In both scenes, belief turns out to be the mechanism that secures the link between man and truth on which both scenes depend. At the same time, it affirms (though with a twist) the insight of much Continental philosophy of religion that belief points the way toward moving beyond ontotheology. Uncovering the resources that sustain ontotheology in the first place makes it possible to mine them for moving religion beyond ontotheology.

When considered in light of Irigaray's work on belief, Derrida's quasi-autobiographical text, 'Circumfession' (his contribution to a joint venture with Geoffrey Bennington entitled *Jacques Derrida*), can be productively read as pointing the way beyond ontotheology.[21] In *Jacques Derrida*, Bennington (a translator, interpreter, and personal friend of Derrida) undertakes to introduce the uninitiated to Derrida's thought via excurses on specific themes and topics. As counterpoint to what he describes repeatedly as Bennington's very ontotheological project, Derrida offers 'a supposedly idiomatic, unbroachable, unreadable, uncircumcised piece of writing, held not to the assistance of his father, as Socrates would say, but to my assistance at the death of a mother' ('Circumfession,' 194). Derrida's decision to center this text around the loss of his mother reads as more than fortuitous. The maternal body offers an escape from ontotheology because of its hidden role in sustaining it. Derrida's work with this body is intriguing, as well, when read against this background. Rather than a loss obscured and (supposedly) mastered, 'Circumfession' lays bare a loss acknowledged and unmasterable; one that opens onto a series of further wounds – past and anticipated – including Derrida's own death-to-come.

Another aspect of Irigaray's work also opens up important avenues for feminist philosophy of religion. In *An Ethics of Sexual Difference*, Irigaray invokes religion as an important element in an economy of difference rather than sameness. She describes us as waiting for a new god, whose coming will inaugurate

> another epoch in history.... This creation would be our opportunity ... by means of the opening of a *sensible transcendental* that ad-vents through us, of which *we would be* the mediators and bridges. Not only in mourning for the dead God of

Nietzsche, not waiting passively for the god to come, but by conjuring it up among and across us, within and between us, as resurrection or transfiguration of blood, of flesh, through a language and an ethics that is ours.[22]

The very notion of a sensible transcendental turns on its head conventional associations of divinity with transcendence *of* materiality; in its place, Irigaray evokes a divine transcendence *in* materiality. Similarly, conjuring a god between us turns on its head projecting a god in front of us.

In other texts, Irigaray reads the philosophical tradition for evidence of sensible transcendentals in the form of the fundamental elements of pre-Socratic philosophy hidden beneath the surface (water in Nietzsche's case, air in Heidegger's, for example). They are transcendent in that they constitute the milieu essential to the philosopher's fundamental insights or principles, yet their function as essential ground goes unremarked in the philosopher's own work. As transcendents that appear through the cracks of our cultural imaginary, they offer potential for grounding economies of difference rather than sameness. Unlike the phallus, the current standard of value in our economy, sensible transcendentals are not, properly speaking, one thing or many things. Thus, they thematize a between – a not-so-solid ground upon which or in the midst of which relationships between differends can potentially establish themselves and flourish. The fact that the sensible transcendentals are also linked to religious imagery (air with breath, fire with spirit, in Christianity) also gives them capacity to be used as resources for alternative construals of divinity, both in concept and in practice.[23]

I have also explored the potential of sensible transcendentals (specifically in Heidegger's work) for the dual project of moving religion beyond ontotheology and enabling sustained attention to sexual and racial differences. Taking a cue from Derrida's analysis of the roles played by *Geist* (spirit) and *Geschlecht* (a multivalent term that covers various genres of human organization, including but not limited to race and gender) in Heidegger's work, I turned to one of his later essays on the poet Georg Trakl to investigate the interplay of religious motifs, sexual, and racial difference within Heidegger's attempts to escape ontotheology and metaphysical humanism.[24] While I conclude that Heidegger ultimately forecloses on the most radical possibilities opened up by his work, I find it significant that, like Derrida in 'Circumfession,' Heidegger turns to figures of racial and sexual difference to escape metaphysics and ontotheology.

Conclusion

What, then, do these ruminations suggest about the potential in post-structuralism for feminist philosophy of religion concerned with promoting sexual and racial differences? What will philosophy of religion – or religion itself, for that matter – look like on the other side of ontotheology and metaphysical humanism? First, the approach I have articulated here affirms that feminist philosophy of religion will need to court rather than ignore the social, historical, embodied context in which religion takes place. It will need to pay attention to lived religious experience – especially in contexts where religion funds sustained attention to sexual and racial differences (whether these be previous incarnations of religion or current ones). To fully mine these sites for the resources they offer, feminist philosophy of religion will need to expand its list of conversation partners. While philosophy will continue to be a vital one, the tools of historical investigation, cultural theory, and theories of religion are equally critical for inquiring into the work religion does and can do in the future. The work outlined in this chapter invites attention to religion as a cultural force and a communal practice, a matter not just of doctrine but of ritual. The approach I have outlined above also invites philosophy of religion to follow religion down a potentially transformative path beyond its modern preoccupations and conceptual structures. Following religion toward the future opened up by sexual and racial differences holds out the promise of transforming not only our relationships to ourselves and one another, but potentially the role religion plays in postmodernity.

Notes

1   R. Ruether, *Sexism and God-Talk: Toward a Feminist Theology*, Boston, MA: Beacon Press, 1983, p. 13.

2   E. Armour, *Deconstruction, Feminist Theology and the Problem of Difference: Subverting the Race/Gender Divide*, Religion and Postmodernism Series, edited by Mark C. Taylor, Chicago, IL: University of Chicago Press, 1999.

3   The summary of my book that appears here is a slightly revised version of one that appeared in 'Interpreting Practices, Sustaining Differences: Deconstruction as Hermeneutical Praxis,' in A. Wiercinski (ed.) *Beyond the Human and the Divine: Philosophical and Theological Hermeneutics*, Toronto: The Hermeneutic Press, Elan and Son, 2002, pp. 573–580.

4   C. Raschke, 'The Deconstruction of God,' in T.J.J. Altizer, M.A. Myers, C.A. Raschke, R.P. Scharlemann, M.C. Taylor, and C.E. Winquist (eds) *Deconstruction and Theology*, New York, NY: Crossroads, 1982, p. 3 (author's emphasis).

5   L. Irigaray, *This Sex Which is Not One*, trans. C. Porter and C. Burke, Ithaca, NY: Cornell University Press, 1985.

6   H. Spillers, 'Mama's Baby, Papa's Maybe: An American Grammar Book,' *Diacritics*, 1987 (17, no. 2); reprinted in A. Mitchell (ed.) *Within the Circle: An Anthology of African American Literary Criticism from the Harlem Renaissance to the Present*, Durham, NC: Duke University Press, 1994, pp. 454–481; see p. 474.

7   See 'Plato's Pharmacy,' in Derrida, *Dissemination*, trans. B. Johnson, Chicago, IL: University of Chicago Press, 1981.

8   Of course, the character and trajectory of those responses vary considerably. On the one hand, one thinks of post-Kantian Protestant liberalism (from Ritschl, for example, through Tillich) and the Barthian reaction to that tradition, but one also thinks of feminist theology (as noted above and the secular or death-of-god theology movements.

9   For more on the relationship between the God/man duo and sexual and racial indifference, see Armour, *Deconstruction, Feminist Theology and the Problem of Difference*, Chapters 2, 4, and 5. For more on the relationship between sexual indifference (including a footnote on racial indifference!) and the opposition between faith and reason, see my 'Beyond Belief? Sexual Difference and Religion After Ontotheology,' in J. Caputo (ed.) *The Religious*, Blackwell Readings in Continental Philosophy series, edited by S. Critchley, New York, NY: Blackwell Press, 2002, pp. 212–226. A brief summary of this essay appears below, pp. 49–51.

10 G. Jantzen, *Becoming Divine: Towards a Feminist Philosophy of Religion*, Bloomington, IN: Indiana University Press, 1999, pp. 27–32.

11 These are, of course, not the only philosophers and theorists of religion to draw on the Continental tradition. Charles Winquist, Edith Wyschogrod, and Mark Taylor also do so – with very different aims and very different results. Rather than shoring up a particular religious tradition, their work centers around exploring religious dimensions of culture (and cultural dimensions of religion). So, for example, Taylor's work examines issues connected to religion (transcendence, negation, etc.) but manifested in cultural phenomena as diverse as the Las Vegas hotel scene and computer technology. Wyschogrod also engages religious questions (for example, the embodiment of moral action, the meaning of death), but as embedded in rather than separate from culture. Her *Saints and*

Postmodernism: Revisioning Moral Philosophy, Religion and Postmodernism Series, Chicago, IL: University of Chicago Press, 1990, for example, looks into genres of religious writing related to the lives of the saints alongside texts from the modern and postmodern literary canon as she considers how morality comes to be. As this chapter develops, it will become clear that my work has more in common with theirs than with Caputo, *et al.*

12   I am necessarily painting with a broad brush, in what follows, which obscures some very real differences among these thinkers. For example, Richard Kearney finds both Caputo's and Marion's god too abstract and too distant to sustain religious faith; hence his proposal of 'the God who may be' as an alternative. The starting point for these scholars differs as well. Only Westphal explicitly names his starting point as a concern for the ongoing life of faith (see *Overcoming Onto-theology: Toward a Postmodern Christian Faith*, New York, NY: Fordham University Press, 2001). Both Caputo and Marion would claim to be philosophers first and religionists second. However, Marion's claim to be engaged purely in phenomenology for its own sake has been greeted with considerable skepticism by other philosophers in the field. See D. Janicaud, J.-F. Courtine, J.-L. Chrétien, M. Henry, J.-L. Marion, and P. Ricoeur, *Phenomenology and the 'Theological Turn': The French Debate*, New York, NY: Fordham University Press, 2000.

13   See, for example, J. Caputo, *The Prayers and Tears of Jacques Derrida: Religion Without Religion*, Philosophy of Religion Series, edited by M. Westphal, Bloomington, IN: Indiana University Press, 1997. pp. 337–339; R. Kearney, 'Introduction,' *The God Who May Be: A Hermeneutics of Religion*, Bloomington, IN: Indiana University Press, 2001, pp. 1–8.

14   An exception is Caputo's 'The Absence of Monica: Heidegger, Derrida, and Augustine's Confessions,' in N.J. Holland and P. Huntington (eds) *Feminist Interpretations of Martin Heidegger*, University Park, PA: The Pennsylvania State University Press, 2001, pp. 149–164.

15   J.-L. Marion, *God Without Being*, trans. T.A. Carlson, Religion and Postmodernism Series, edited by M.C. Taylor, Chicago: University of Chicago Press, 1991.

16   M. Daly, *Beyond God the Father: Toward a Philosophy of Women's Liberation*, Boston, MA: Beacon Press, 1973, p. 19.

17   The Project on Lived Theology is housed at the University of Virginia, run by Dr. Charles Marsh, and funded by the Lilly Foundation. For information on the Project, see http://livedtheology.org/ (accessed 24 June 2003).

18   I develop this analysis in 'Interpreting Practices, Sustaining Differences.'

19   J. Derrida, *Positions*, trans. A. Bass, Chicago, IL: University of Chicago Press, 1981, p. 82.

20   L. Irigaray, *Sexes and Genealogies*, trans. G.C. Gill, New York, NY: Columbia University Press, 1993, pp. 23–54.

21   J. Derrida, 'Circumfession: Fifty-nine Periods and Periphrases,' in G. Bennington and J. Derrida, *Jacques Derrida*, Chicago, IL: University of Chicago Press, 1993.

22   L. Irigaray, *Éthique de la différence sexuelle*, Paris: Éditions Minuit, 1984, p. 124, my translation. See *An Ethics of Sexual Difference*, trans. C. Burke and G.C. Gill, Ithaca, NY: Cornell University Press, p. 129.

23   On Irigaray and the sensible transcendental, see my 'Questions of Proximity: Woman's "Place" in Derrida and Irigaray,' *Hypatia: A Journal of Feminist Philosophy*, 12: 1 (Winter 1997): 63–78. I draw out the implications of this concept for constructive theology in 'Divining Differences: Irigaray and Religion,' K. O'Grady, M. Joy, and J. Poxon (eds) *Religion in French Feminist Thought: Critical Perspectives*, London: Routledge, 2003, pp. 29–40.

24   'Through Flame or Ashes: Traces of Difference in *Geist*'s Return,' in N. Holland and P. Huntington (eds) *Feminist Interpretations of Martin Heidegger*, State College, PA: Penn State University Press, 2001.

Chapter 4

A POST-METAPHYSICAL APPROACH

Fionola Meredith

A POST-METAPHYSICAL APPROACH TO FEMALE
SUBJECTIVITY: BETWEEN DECONSTRUCTION AND
HERMENEUTICS

Fionola Meredith would seem to agree with Armour's post-metaphysical concern. Yet Meredith steps back from Derridean deconstruction in order to regain the singularity which, she contends, is lost by feminists who are overly reliant on post-structuralist methods. Meredith's philosophical argument aims to find a location for selfhood between hermeneutics and deconstruction. She seeks to re-introduce the singular nature of female subjectivity without forgetting the lessons of difference and otherness. She presents an especially strong challenge to feminist philosophers of religion who too quickly claim that all of their answers can be found in post-structuralism. Her counter-claim is that 'a radical disjuncture between the *referential* "I" who lives, speaks, laughs, weeps, gives birth and dies in the world, and the *textual* "I" which is a free-floating fiction' results in the deferral of female subjectivity to alterity and non-presence. She turns to Paul Ricoeur and Adriana Cavarero to elucidate a narrative account of selfhood, as an alternative to feminists who embrace multiplicity and risk female singularity. Although not writing explicitly about religion, Meredith explores the categories of textuality and referentiality, which remain fundamental to feminist interpretations of testimony, subjectivity/divinity, embodiment, autonomy, and ritual practice. In her words, 'the continuities and discontinuities between women's stories may be no more than glimpsed as potential lines of connection, brief vistas of different horizons, before they are submerged once more in the plethora of deictic coordinates which anchor each woman's story in a multiplicity of discourses' (p. 69).

there is no 'true' testimony without 'false' testimony.[1]

POST-STRUCTURALISM HAS transformed, inspired and invigorated feminist theory. As a critique, it is indeed a valuable tool in feminist hands. With post-structuralist or deconstructive approaches, we can trace the process of unravelling meaning within masculinist, unilinear, heterosexist discourses; we can explore the lacunae exposed by this process of hidden disintegration. These approaches illuminate denied ideological subtexts; oppose the sameness and stasis of monolithic thinking; demand that we lose the 'metaphysical comforts' of transparent identity, self-evident meaning and immediate self-reflection.

Yet I want to argue that the anti-representationalist aesthetic which post-structuralism offers feminist theory institutes a radical disjuncture between the *referential* 'I' who lives, speaks, laughs, weeps, gives birth and dies in the world, and the *textual* 'I' which is a free-floating fiction, so deeply scored by difference and deferral that it can only be signified by alterity and non-presence. It is this disjuncture that my chapter seeks to question.

Much post-structuralist ire is (rightly) reserved for the classical Western 'myth' of subjecthood, perhaps best summarised by Hegel's contention that 'consciousness of self is the birthplace of truth'.[2] Immobile and self-certain, the classical subject of Western philosophy is understood as

> a fixed, extralinguistic entity consciously pursuing its unique destiny . . . with its own sharp configuration . . . of well-defined, stable, impermeable boundaries around a singular, unified and atomic core . . .[3]

The masculinist myth of the self-contained subject transparently present-to-itself, with its privileged status as the origin and guarantor of meaning, knowledge and truth is countered by a (feminist) post-structuralist insistence on the fundamental *alterity* and *non*-presence of the subject. The female 'I' becomes fragmented, diffused and decentred in the play of textuality. Judith Butler describes this textual 'I' – the post-structuralist subject – as 'a linguistic category, a place-holder, a structure in formation'.[4]

Although there is a wealth of diversity within feminist post-structuralist criticism, there are many points of consensus on the deconstructionist continuum. Post-structuralist feminists often share a common suspicion of unity, coherence and synthesis; they stress the priority of difference (or *différance*), dislocation, antithesis and absence over sameness, continuity and identity. Many probe the relation between the (female) self and self-consciousness, and question the representativity of her self-image. In particular, female experience is regarded as slippery, duplicitous, a symbolic construction which reproduces rather than contests ideological systems. In the words of Joan Scott, it is 'always already an interpretation and something that needs to be interpreted'.[5]

I contend that there is a significant polarising tendency within (feminist) post-structuralist criticism, a noticeable proclivity to impose artificial either/or dualisms in ways which owe much more to the rigid binaries of structuralist thinking than to the fluidity of post-structuralist freeplay. In many instances, the 'either/or' of female subjectivity appears to take the form of a more or less submerged opposition between textuality and referentiality. *Either* the female subject must understand herself in the classical, masculinist sense, as a coherent, continuous self-same self *or* she must accept the primacy of the textual, celebrating the multiple forms of the discordant 'I'. It seems that the subject of enunciation – the referential 'I' – is implicitly tarred with all the negative associations of classical selfhood; the only hope is to abandon referentiality and take flight into 'fissures of female discontinuity'.[6] In post-structuralist eyes, the referential 'I' is radically incommensurable with the textual 'I'.

How would the anti-representationalist feminist aesthetic be challenged if we abandoned this dichotomous approach? What if decentring the self did not mean dissolving the self? What if the impossibility of the absolute coincidence of the self with itself did not mean pure absence? What if disjunctures and rifts did not preclude moments of partial coincidence? What if the positing of self did not imply an impossible escape from the differential movement of language, but an *interplay* of singularity and alterity, of particularity and discursivity, of appropriation and distanciation, of 'mineness' and 'otherness'? I argue that we need a framework which takes account of *both* the psycho-linguistic conditions of the production of subjectivities *and* the inexhaustible contingencies of our situated being. We need an approach that can accommodate an ambiguously representable female selfhood which is located in the space created by the disjunction of life and discourse, beyond the false alternatives of the subject and the anti-subject. We must ask – where can flesh-and-blood female bodies be situated *between* textuality and referentiality, between synchronicity and diachronicity, between surface and depth? If there is a point of intervention between the *material* experiences of women – what Liz Stanley calls 'the referential specificity of women's lives as distinctly female'[7] – and the *abstract* representation of women *sous-rature* or under erasure, then that may be the place where a post-metaphysical, rather than post-structuralist, analysis of women's subjectivity and experiences can begin.

The erasure of singularity by rhizomatic theory

Post-structuralism is centrally concerned with *system*, with *synchronicity*, with *surface*. It is a philosophy of horizontality, supplanting hierarchy with anarchy, centring with dispersal, semantics with rhetoric, origin with difference. Nowhere is this tendency more manifest than in the work of Gilles Deleuze,[8] in which the metaphor of the (vertical) 'tree' as origin and hierarchy is compared to the 'rhizome' of non-representational, 'radically horizontal' thought. The rhizomatic model emphasises 'lateral connectivity' as destratification, the permeability of all hierarchies and boundaries; it celebrates the Nietzschean demand that the vertical axis of objective truth be overturned by the horizontal axis of subjective values. It is precisely this insistence on 'rhizomatics' that denies the 'existential root' of the self, the particularity of the actual subject in her socio-historical context, the author as 'psycho-biographical signified'. The 'speaking/spoken' self[9] in the world and her attempts to bring her mediated experiences, her 'incipient story'[10] – however fragmented and displaced across the panoply of discourses – to language[11] are implicitly or explicitly denied, subordinated to the *surface* play of the Text.

Paul Ricoeur's philosophy serves as a timely reminder of the existential dimension of the speaking/spoken – or writing/written – subject. While linguisticality might be the most fundamental mode of realisation of our being-in-the world, and while consciousness does not occupy the position of absolute principle or radical origin – 'the ground that grounds itself'[12] – it is essential to acknowledge *the imprint of the subject on her words*:

> Language is not a world of its own. It is not even a world. But because we are in the world, because we are affected by situations, and because we orient ourselves comprehensively in those situations, we have something to say, we have experience to bring to language.[13]

Yet 'who' is speaking? 'Who' is writing? 'Who' is it that is making her imprint on her words? Where is

> That taste of myself, of *I* and *me* above and in all things, which is more distinctive than the taste of ale or alum, more distinctive than the smell of walnutleaf or camphor[?][14]

Above all, deconstructionist accounts of subjectivity – whether feminist or otherwise – erase *singularity*: 'I and me'. To believe oneself to be unique – an 'irreplaceable center of perspective on the world'[15] – is, in the post-structuralist world of discursively-constituted 'substitutable anyones', a rather naïve joke. Yet, as Jean-Luc Nancy observes, the notion of the subject, rather than focusing on traditional notions of 'being' or 'essence', can 'deliver an entirely different thought: that of the *one* and that of the some*one*, of the singular existent that the subject announces, promises, and at the same time conceals'.[16]

The idea of the unique is almost always included in deconstructionist accounts of the Western 'myth of universal selfhood'. The following passage by the feminist critic Sidonie Smith is representative:

> [A] certain ideology of language accompanies the notion of universal selfhood. The self so understood is both prelinguistic and extralinguistic . . . [this] self [has] a singular, unified and atomic core. . . . Unique, unitary, unencumbered, the self escapes all forms of embodiment. . . . Autonomous and free, . . . the self comes to . . . know the world in a monological engagement that establishes individual consciousness as the center and origin of meaning. . . . All 'I's are ontologically identical rational beings – but all 'I's are also unique. This is the stuff of myth, imperious and contradictory.[17]

In a similar way, in *Gender Trouble: Feminism and the Subversion of Identity*, Judith Butler questions the singularity and the continuity of individual identity:

> What can be meant by 'identity' then, and what grounds the presumption that identities are self-identical, persisting through time as the same, unified and internally coherent?[18]

For Butler, identity operates as an effect of discourse, a 'normative ideal rather than a descriptive feature of experience'; indeed, Butler calls the very notion of 'the person' into question, contending that 'the 'coherence' and 'continuity' of 'the person' are not logical or analytical features of personhood, but, rather, 'socially instituted and maintained norms of intelligibility'.[19] Moreover, in *The Psychic Life of Power*, Butler cautions against conflating this suspect category of 'the person' or 'the individual' with subjectivity, which she considers the condition for the intelligibility of individual persons:

> 'The subject' is sometimes bandied about as if it were interchangeable with 'the person' or 'the individual'. The genealogy of the subject as a critical category, however, suggests that the subject, rather than be identified strictly with the individual, ought to be designated as a linguistic category, a place-holder, a structure in formation. . . . The subject is the linguistic occasion for the individual to achieve and reproduce intelligibility, the linguistic condition of its existence and agency.[20]

Coherence, continuity, stability and self-sameness of 'the person' are apparently derived from the 'illusion of substantial identity', which Butler would replace with the non-substantive 'I': a linguistic category which is no more than 'a consequence of certain rule-governed discourses that govern the intelligible invocation of identity'.[21]

Both Smith's and Butler's accounts contain the implicit assumption that, if a subject is understood as unique or singular, it follows that it must also be extra-linguistic, self-same, unified, autonomous, monological and originary.[22] Yet, we may ask, must a diffuse selfhood imply non-identifiability? Must a non-autonomous, non-originary self be denied singularity? Can the unique exist in a subjectivity which avoids both the 'atomic core' of the cogito and the dissipative non-identity of the anticogito? Refusing the submerged structuralist dualisms which remain within post-structuralist thought means challenging these implicit assumptions, adopting theoretical frameworks which are non-oppositional yet resist totalization.

I contend that a re-evaluation of the status of the unique, the singular, the particular within our discursive modes of being may provide a point of opening for a post-metaphysical hermeneutic/deconstructive approach to the representation of the (sexed) 'I' which can acknowledge both the 'flesh and blood existent'[23] and the discursive terms through which she is shaped, thus superseding both the horizontal 'rhizomatics' of pure textualism and the vertical 'hierarchy' of objective truth. My analysis of the category of the singular will be based on an exploration of sameness and otherness, and their relationship to identity.

'Working-through': narrative identity beyond the immediacy of reflection

In his Introduction to the collection of essays, '*Who Comes After the Subject?*', Jean-Luc Nancy asks:

> But what existence? It is not an essence, it is the essence whose essence it is to exist, actually and in fact, in experience, 'hic et nunc.' It is the *existent* (and not the existence *of* the existent). With this in mind, the question asks 'who?' Which means that the question of essence – 'What, existence?' – calls forth a 'who' in response.[24]

For Nancy, 'who' someone is denotes 'that actual, existent "what", as it exists, a factual (even material) punctuation of Being',[25] this 'who' could be said to exist both before and after 'the subject'. Nancy stresses that, for him, the question 'who is "who"?' is not a question of essence, but one of identity or of the presence of the existent, understood in the sense of 'that which occupies a place':

> as when one asks before a group of people whose names you know but not the faces: 'Who is who?' – is this one Kant, is that one Heidegger, and this other one beside him? . . . That is to say, a question of presence: Who is *there*? Who is present there?[26]

Thus, where there was nothing, some*one* comes. This 'one' who comes never stops arriving, in the sense that the subject is never the subject of itself, or entirely self-identical with itself: it is

> 'one' because it 'comes', not because of its substantial unity: the she, he or it that comes can be one and unique in its coming but multiple and repeated 'in itself'.[27]

In coming into the world, then, the unique existent engenders a 'presence-to [the world] that is not to-itself'.[28] The philosophical tenor of Nancy's short essay on the singular existent is echoed by Ricoeur's collection of essays, *Oneself as Another*.

If there is a way of approaching identity that does not dissolve singularity in the 'identi-fictions' of the non-substantive self, it must involve a conceptual distinction between self-sameness and identity in such a way that, in rejecting the homogeneity and stasis of sameness, the unique existent who 'possesses' her identity is not effaced. A different modality of identity is called for. In *Oneself as Another*, Ricoeur acknowledges the pressing need for rethinking subjectivity beyond the alternative of the cogito and the anti-cogito, observing the

> amazing oscillations that the philosophies of the subject appear to present, as though the cogito out of which they arise were unavoidably caught up in an alternating sequence of overevaluation and underevaluation. . . . Exalted subject, humiliated subject: it seems that it is always through a complete reversal of this sort that one approaches the subject.[29]

In this series of studies, Ricoeur distinguishes two major meanings of the concept 'identity', based on the Latin terms *ipse* and *idem*. The distinction between *ipse* and *idem* distinguishes 'the person as some*one* in contrast to the fixed permanence of sameness'.[30] Identity in the sense of *idem* denotes stasis, immutability, permanence in time, as opposed to 'that which differs': namely, 'diversity, variability, discontinuity and instability'.[31] Ricoeur notes that

> in its diverse uses, 'same' (*meme*) is used in the context of comparison; its contraries are 'other', 'contrary', 'distinct', 'diverse', 'unequal', 'inverse'. The weight of this comparative use of the term 'same' seems so great to me that I shall henceforth take sameness as synonymous with *idem*-identity and shall oppose to it selfhood (*ipseity*), understood as *ipse*-identity.[32]

According to Ricoeur, identity in the sense of *ipse* implies 'no assertion concerning some unchanging core of the personality'.[33] Rather, *ipse*-identity denotes less a category of *being* than a category of *doing*: it is concerned with questions of agency and authorship, with the 'who' that is doing, speaking, writing, acting in the world. *Ipseity* encapsulates self-constancy; however, unlike *idem*-identity, it refers not to static, inflexible, substantive identity, but to a dynamic, diachronic and incomplete identity always under construction.

If the identity of the self is understood within the framework of *ipseity*, which acknowledges the 'fragmentation that follows from the polysemy of the question "who?"',[34] will the singularity, or the unrepeatable uniqueness of the individual person not be lost amid this chaotic multiplicity? Ricoeur's answer lies in a shift of focus from the *category* of the 'individual' to the individual that each of us actually *is*: a unique existent, an 'irreplaceable center of perspective on the world'.[35] How then does one respond to the question ' "Who" says "I"?':

> We first answer this question by naming someone, that is, by designating them with a proper name. But what is the basis for this proper name? What justifies our taking the subject of an action, so designated by his, her, or its proper name, as the same throughout a life that stretches from birth to death? The answer has to be narrative. To answer the question 'Who?' as Hannah Arendt so forcefully put it, is to tell the story of a life. The story tells about the action of the 'who'. And the identity of this 'who' therefore itself must be a *narrative identity*.[36]

The philosophy of Hannah Arendt also provides an important point of departure for Adriana Cavarero's concept of the narratable self. Arendt argues that philosophical discourse, directed as it is towards determining 'what' rather than 'who' 'Man' is by searching for qualities that he could possibly share with other living beings, is inherently incapable of capturing the individual uniqueness of a human being. She writes that 'who' someone is 'retains a curious intangibility that confounds all efforts towards unequivocal verbal expression'.[37] Taking up Arendt, Cavarero distinguishes two registers, philosophy and narration, which manifest opposite characteristics:

> Philosophy . . . has the form of a definite knowledge which regards the universality of Man. . . . Narration . . . has the form of a biographical knowledge which regards the unrepeatable identity of someone. The questions which sustain the two discursive styles are equally diverse. The first asks *'what* is Man?' The second asks instead of someone *'who* he or she is'.[38]

Cavarero's concern is with the 'unrepeatable existence' of each human being 'which – however they run disoriented in the dark, mixing accidents with intentions – neither follows in the footsteps of another life, nor repeats the very same course, nor leaves behind the same story'.[39] She is interested in the singularity beyond the 'what', in the means by which 'narration reveals the finite in its fragile uniqueness, and sings its glory'.[40] In her thinking, she seeks to prevent the 'inevitable sacrifice' of the 'fragility of each one . . . to the philosophical glories of the One'.[41]

Although Ricoeur does not participate in Cavarero's theoretical promotion of the register of narration over that of philosophy, he does recognise the possibilities which narrativity, or more particularly, the notion of narrative identity, offers in terms of approaching personal identity without recourse to polarised 'either/or' positions. Ricoeur is aware of the drawbacks of these analyses:

> Without the recourse to narration, the problem of personal identity would in fact be condemned to an antimony with no solution. Either we must posit a subject identical with itself through the diversity of its different states, or, following Hume and Nietzsche, we must hold that this identical subject is nothing more than a substantialist illusion, whose elimination merely brings to light a pure manifold of cognitions, emotions and volitions.[42]

Indeed, in *Life: a Story in Search of a Narrator*, Ricoeur argues that only a narrative understanding of ourselves can escape the 'pseudo-alternative' of pure change – 'an incoherent succession of occurrences' – or absolute identity – 'an immutable substance incapable of becoming'.[43]

Thus another layer is added to the difference between *idem* and *ipse*, namely between *idem* as formal or substantial identity and *ipse* as narrative identity: that is, a 'model of dynamic identity arising from the poetic composition of a narrative text'.[44] For Ricoeur, this narrative identity is constitutive of self-constancy, a sense of 'oneself' which can accommodate mutability within the cohesion of one lifetime. Far from embracing the stasis of the 'abstract identity of the Same', this model recognises the provisional quality of narrative selfhood; for Ricoeur, the story of a life is continuously 'on the wing', ceaselessly refigured by all the (truthful or fictive) stories a subject relates about her or himself: 'this refiguration makes this life itself a cloth woven of stories told'.[45] The process of refiguration is potentially infinite and thus inexhaustible: indeed, it is this 'endless rectification of a previous narrative by a subsequent one . . . and . . . the chain of refigurations that results from this' that leads Ricoeur to conclude that 'narrative identity is the poetic resolution of the hermeneutic circle'.[46] Moreover, for Ricoeur, the notion of narrative identity can be applied to the self-constancy of a community as well as to an individual: 'Individual and community are constituted in their identity by taking up narratives that become for them their actual history.'[47] Thus the story of a life is constituted through

> a series of rectifications applied to previous narratives, just as the history of a people, or a collectivity, or an institution proceeds from the series of corrections that new historians bring to their predecessors' descriptions and explanations . . .[48]

Cavarero's model of the narratable self places less emphasis on the process of dynamic configuration and refiguration characteristic of Ricoeur's notion of ipseity and more on the *pre*-reflective, expositive dimensions of unique selfhood. Indeed, she argues that memory need not be an 'active remembering'; it is not only in the conscious act of remembering, but more particularly in the 'spontaneous narrating structure of memory itself'[49] that Cavarero locates the narratable self. Thus the horizons of the terms 'subject' and 'object' coalesce and become indistinguishable: 'the narratable self is at once the transcendental subject and the elusive object of all the autobiographical exercises of memory.'[50] For Cavarero, each one of us *lives* himself or herself as his or her own story, without distinguishing the 'I' who narrates from the 'self' who is narrated. The familiar 'sense of self' which is derived from this process of circular memory is, for Cavarero,

> not the fruit of an intimate and separated existence, or the *product* of our memory. It is neither the fantasmatic outcome of a project, nor the imaginary protagonist of the story that we want to have. It is not a *fiction* that we can distinguish from reality. It is rather the familiar sense of every self, in the temporal extension of a life-story that is this and not another.[51]

The narratable self, for Cavarero, 'makes her home' in the narrating memory: 'the inalienable dwelling of her living her/himself, remembering herself.'[52] It is this spontaneous process, this 'sense of being narratable', and the awareness that the others whom we encounter are also narratable selves with unique life-stories, which, I contend, enables us to refer to a singular existent irreducible to her discursively-produced subjectivity.

Thus, for Cavarero, the

> particular contents – the pieces of story that the memory narrates with its typical and unmasterable process of intermittence and forgetting – are inessential.[53]

The narratable self consists in the pre-reflective sense that my life-story belongs to me alone; it coincides with the 'uncontrollable narrative impulse of memory that produces the text'.[54] Thus considered, the contents of the text itself are indeed superfluous; the narratable self is neither the product of the life-story recounted by memory, nor a construction of the text, nor an effect of the performative power of narration. For Cavarero, 'the self-sensing of the self as narratable' is 'irremediably mixed up with [her text]'[55] but is not *derived* from it. The narratable self is ontologically *anterior* to her text:

> Put simply, through the unreflecting knowledge of my 'sense of self' [*dell'assaporarmi*], I know that I have a story and that I consist in this story – even when I do not pause to recount it to myself.[56]

Moreover, as Cavarero remarks, someone's life-story always results from an existence which has *exposed* her to the world: 'the one who is exposed generates and is generated by this life-story – this and not another – which results from such an exposition.'[57] The inevitability of our 'nakedness' (to adapt Ricoeur's term) or exposure to the world – 'the constitutive coinciding of appearing and being'[58] – defines, for Cavarero, the non-substantive, expressive, exhibitive character of identity. Indeed, for Cavarero, the existent *is* the exposable and the narratable: 'neither exposability nor narratability, which together constitute this peculiarly human uniqueness, can be taken away.'[59]

'It's me here!': the 'story' of my singularity

What light does our exploration of narrative existence in the work of Cavarero and Ricoeur cast on our understanding of the category of singularity? It seems that my singularity, if I can be said to possess such a thing, is completely contingent; it is without beginning or end; it is relational and expositive – inextricably entangled in the life-stories of others, the 'living, continuous overlap of all the life-stories'.[60] Furthermore, if my experience is prereflectively colonised by the psycho-linguistic workings of hegemony, then we might conclude here that our sense of uniqueness – derived as it is from our experiences – is equally enabled and delimited by our discursive positionings.

These objections do indeed hold considerable weight if applied to a notion of singularity based on a substantive conception of uniqueness as grounded in a permanent, pre-given essence. But if we regard singularity neither as a substantialist[61] illusion nor, with Butler, as merely a 'socially instituted and maintained norm of intelligibility',[62] but as an interpretation indefinitely pursued by an embodied, finite existent, we move closer to a sustainable anti-foundationalist conception of uniqueness. Bearing in mind 'the constitutive unmasterability'[63] of the 'who' emphasized by Cavarero, we acknowledge that alterity permeates my singularity at every level, whether through the discontinuities and contingencies of the (re)configured narrative self, through the diffusion of my uniqueness in and through other narrative selves, through my 'topped and tailed' life-story, lacking beginning or end, or, perhaps most significantly, through the otherness of the discursively-mediated nature of my subjectivity. The paradox of this theoretical standpoint is that it reveals a 'me and no other' that is nonetheless predicated on otherness. The play of difference or dispossession which disrupts the (transitional and relational) construction of my unity and singularity is also the *condition* for my fragile uniqueness: that which both anchors my ipseity and casts it adrift. Hence Ricoeur's comment that 'there is no true testimony without false testimony'.[64]

Developing the notions of uniqueness contained in the narrative theory of Cavarero and Ricoeur, I contend that singularity itself operates in two distinguishable yet intersecting registers. At the *pre-reflective* level, by virtue of the irreducible insubstitutability I assume by being born 'unique and one', and thereafter corporeally anchored as I live until I die, 'I' and all other 'I's possess a luminous, existential singularity which is derived from our being-as-existents; it is the very 'thereness' of my 'who'. It is the acknowledgement – and no more[65] – that I am some*one*. I derive this understanding of pre-reflective singularity primarily from Nancy's assertion that 'existence is the essence of the subject to the extent that it *is*, prior to any predication'.[66]

At the *reflective* level, singularity, understood in the sense of *ipseity* or narrative identity, is an opaque and vulnerable *construct*: the product of a continuous (and arguably spontaneous) process of discursively-mediated figuration and refiguration undertaken by an individual existent. It is fragile in that it is quasi-fictional: it is an ongoing but retrospective organisation of life, an attempt to 'fix the outline of these provisional ends',[67] a 'consolation' in the face of nothingness. Yet the (semi)fictionality of my singularity is not conferred, as the post-structuralists would have it, by the non-individuated play of difference, which, through the process of 'auto-affection', creates the illusion of my identity. Rather, developing the standpoints of both Ricoeur and Cavarero, it is (notwithstanding the alterity which saturates the conditions of my acting, speaking, writing) an *affirmation* – both a desire *for*, and a *choice* in favour *of* meaning – conferred by the self-stories related by 'me', a finite, contextually-located flesh-and-blood existent, a constitutionally-incomplete yet reflective self.[68]

Singularity, thus considered, is a dynamic, diachronic yet disrupted process, traced through and through with difference and alterity: insubstitutably 'there' (or 'here') at a pre-reflective, existential level; more or less deferred and dispersed in a non-totalisable plurality of interpretations; alienated by the hegemonic conditions of discursively mediated existence; yet partially recovered/created in the 'insubstantial unity' which my (conscious and unconscious) imagination and desire weaves from the disparate and contingent experiences of my embodied existence.

Connecting specificity to system: the female 'I' between text and reference

We can incorporate these insights into a post-metaphysical model of the experiential based on the interpenetration of post-structuralist thinking and hermeneutic phenomenology. This model of the experiential neither posits an essential, 'true' or extra-linguistic subject of experience nor a purely textual, intrinsically discursive self thus alienated from her experiences. The either/or of transcendental subjectivism/linguistic determinism becomes the both/and of an opaque self who posits but does not possess her experiences.

Why is this framework particularly appropriate for theorising female subjectivities? First, because it offers an account of both experience and selfhood that not only acknowledges but *incorporates* the negativity and alienation generated by our insurmountably hegemonic being-in-the-world. Feminist post-structuralists have demonstrated this central fact of our existence as sexed beings over and over again: that positing (sexed) selfhood or identity as cause or origin of our being masks the fact that these supposed origins are actually '*effects* of institutions, practices, discourses with multiple and diffuse points of origin'.[69] Thus, argue these critics,[70] our experience of 'being-women' itself must be regarded with the utmost suspicion, due to its capacity to reproduce, rather than contest, ideological systems. This thorough-going suspicion is well-justified from a feminist perspective; it should not be elided in a cosy understanding of female experience as unproblematically predicated on universalising connections and similarities derived from some form of female 'essence'. It is right that women's experiences should not be interpreted as ideologically innocent; rather, they should indeed be subject to theoretical interrogation and critique. But, as we know, the critique which some feminist post-structuralists apply to the category of female experience is so all-consuming that it disappears as a positive concept. The implication is that displacement of transparent experience by textuality *can only* result in the negativity of 'what is not'; the process is apparently inexorable.

The deconstructive moment of *distanciation*, operating in dialectic-without-synthesis with the positive, interpretive hermeneutic element of our theoretical framework allows scope for the incisive critique offered by feminist post-structuralists. This 'moment' recognises that experience, if it is to be understood at all, must be understood *in and through* distance or difference.[71] Applied to the notion of women's experiences, it disallows the possibility of categorising that experience as purely the conscious relationship of an ontologically stable, coherent, essentially female subject to an immediately encountered world. The 'authenticity' of female experience, thus conceived, is continuously displaced. The deconstructive moment could be read as *decontextualising* women's experiences, stripping away the historical, sociological, ethnological, psychological and physiological elements of our experiences. This post-structuralist intervention temporarily holds in suspension the very deictic coordinates of sex, class, ethnicity, age, sexual preference and so on that locate and situate individual women and exposes the non-individuated play of difference, absence and distortion that permeates women's experiences at the deepest levels. The decontextualisation of women's experiences thus acts as a mode of *reduction* (*epoche*) and explanation, a (necessarily partial) exposure to the uncomfortable fact that one's experience is both enabled and delimited by 'the epistemological, ontological, and logical structures of a masculinist signifying economy'.[72] Moreover, the multiple significations of my 'gender' cannot be extracted from the political or cultural 'intersections' which produce and maintain it:

> If one 'is' a woman, that is surely not all one is; the term fails to be exhaustive, not because a pregendered 'person' transcends the specific paraphernalia of its gender, but because gender is not always constituted coherently or consistently in different historical contexts, and because gender intersects with racial, class, ethnic, sexual, and regional modalities of discursively constituted identities.[73]

In short, the moment of the deconstructive *epoche* alerts us to the feminist implications of the post-Saussurean observation that what we can experience consciously is determined by a system which always escapes consciousness.

The potentially inexorable progression towards the dissolution of female experience in pure textualism (which is implicit in the deconstructive element of our integrative post-Saussurean/hermeneutic framework) is ceaselessly held in check by the moment of *appropriation* which allows a reconnection with the specificity of the diverse and contradictory experiences of individual women.

Appropriation is the moment when the 'undecidability' of deconstruction becomes the 'inexhaustibility' of hermeneutic phenomenology; it is the moment when the linguistic closure of the post-Saussurean *epoche* is lifted, and *Sprachlichkeit* (linguisticality) becomes open to the innovative unpredictability of experience. From the admission that *Sprachlichkeit* is the ontological condition of my experience-in-the-world it need not follow that my experience is merely an alienated function of *Sprachlichkeit*, which, at most, can only reiterate negativities: 'what/where/who I am not.'

I contend that the moment of appropriation is as essential to the internal dynamic of a post-metaphysical account of women's experiences as the inclusion of the critical element of distanciation. From the point of view of feminist analysis, the appropriation of the 'mineness' of the experiential is necessary in order to hold the deconstructive slide in check. The reactivation of the deictic coordinates that were suspended by the deconstructive *epoche* – from my own sexed body, my class, my ethnicity, my age, through to my lifestyle preferences, my education, my work, my geographical location and so on – reopens the multiple, contradictory and shifting axes of identity along which my experiences flow; the fluctuating, contingent points of conjuncture where these myriad coordinates intersect are the 'punctuations' where 'I' am momentarily (ambiguously) present or, better, anchored. Appropriation, then, cannot be inter-preted as a simple statement of my being-as-a-woman (which, after all, is ensnared in conceptual and discursive tangles); rather, it is a complex affirmation – which continues to be haunted by the 'hermeneutics of suspicion' in the form of post-structuralist critique – of the 'mineness' of my experiences, of the non-self-identical yet partially-present self which both possesses and is dispossessed of these experiences; it acknow-ledges my being-as-a-woman as one contextual strand among many, and one which may be only partially disentangled and interpreted. Nonetheless, following my commitment to the phenomenological/ hermeneutic 'choice in favour of meaning', I believe that it is important for feminist theorists of the experiential to *lay claim* to these experiences – in the face of deconstructive opposition – rather than allowing the threads to tangle endlessly upon themselves in confusion and discontinuity. Seeking out and affirming continuities and similarities in women's experiences from within an anti-foundationalist deconstructive/hermeneutic framework which simultaneously imposes a series of deconstructive interventions to prevent the attribution of these experiences to a female essence – conceived as an irreducible 'fixed and static "real"'[74] – may allow the female subject (whoever 'she' is/was/may become) to engage in what Sean Burke terms 'the productive reconciliation of the subject and alterity'.[75] Total interpretive *possession* of my experiences 'as a woman' is impossible; yet the aporia generated by this dispossession can be temporarily traversed and inhabited by the acts of appropriation which posit and affirm the 'ownness'[76] of my deictically-coordinated experiences, as belonging (and also not-belonging) to a decentred but quasi-present self occupying a series of particular historical/cultural/political spaces.

Let us return to the experience of pregnancy and the act of giving birth by way of example. We can begin with two affirmations: 'I live in a female rather than a male body; my female body has the (perceived) potential to give birth.' Immediately, however, these statements plunge us into post-structuralist doubt.[77] The perceived 'naturalness' of the act of giving birth is inevitably compromised – and indeed arguably constructed – by the discourses of sexuality, reproduction, maternity, techno-logy and so on that inhabit childbirth at the deepest social and political levels. The capacity to give birth cannot be read as purely biologically defined, nor as a given to which all women bear the same relationship. As the feminist critic Michelle Stanworth notes:

> While it is the case that the lives of all women are shaped by their biological selves, and by their assumed or actual capacity to bear children, our bodies do not impose upon us a common experience of reproduction; on the contrary, our bodies stand as powerful reminders of the differentiating effects of age, health, disability, strength and fertility history. There is, moreover, little reason to assume that the biological potential to give birth has an identical meaning for women, regardless of their social circumstances or their wishes with regard to childbearing.[78]

The differentiating elements which fracture and disconnect women's experiences of birth are taken to even further lengths by thinkers such as Judith Butler. Butler is uncomfortable with the discourse of female 'sameness' implied in the relationship of childbirth to the female body; indeed, she doubts whether the question of reproduction is, or ought to be, what is absolutely salient or primary in the sexing of the body. If it is, I think it's the imposition of a norm, not a neutral description of biological constraints.[79]

If we characterise these viewpoints of alienated maternal function as the *distancia-tive* element in our model – the 'not-mineness' of experience – then where can the *appropriative* claim to 'what is mine' re-enter?

The existential phenomenologist Erwin Straus, writing on the subject of 'mine-ness', observes that

> The meaning of 'mine' is determined in relation to, and in contraposition to, the world . . . to which I am nevertheless a party. The meaning of 'mine' is not comprehensible in the unmediated antithesis of 'I' and 'not-I', own and strange, subject and object. . . . Everything points to the fact that separateness and union originate in the same ground.[80]

Adrienne Rich speaks of the experience of pregnancy in a way which might indi-cate affirmative intervention:

> In early pregnancy the stirring of the fetus felt like ghostly tremors of my own body, later like the movements of a being imprisoned in me; but both sensations were *my* sensations, contributing to my own sense of physical and psychic space.[81]

In parallel with Straus's account of the dialectics of mineness, the 'strange' 'not-mineness' of the movements of the growing foetus are nonetheless experienced here as belonging to *me*: a phenomenological fact which the feminist philosopher Iris Marion Young terms 'myself in the mode of not being myself'.[82] Young's qualification of this phraseology is illuminating:

> The pregnant subject is not simply a splitting in which the two halves lie open and still, but a dialectic. The pregnant woman experiences herself as a source and participant in a creative process. Though she does not plan and direct it, neither does it wash over her; rather, she *is* this process, this change.[83]

Thus the pregnant subject is an apt metaphor for the 'productive reconciliation of the subject and alterity': she appropriates her experiences, lays claim to them as her own, yet acknowledges that she is neither the sole radical origin of the changes happen-ing to her body nor is she detached from the discursive underpinnings which situate and partially constitute her: the polarities of textuality/referentiality, inner/outer, subject/object, passivity/creativity, discursivity/intentionality are blurred.

Rapprochement

We have seen that Ricoeur's call to move 'beyond the false alternatives of the cogito and the anti-cogito' can be transposed as a move beyond the false alternatives of the experience-as-ideological-construct and experience-as-origin to an understanding of women's experiences as simultaneously receptive and agential, meaningful and duplicitous. In restoring the significance of the experiential self as more than a mode of textuality but less than unmediated referentiality, I believe that this model of the experiential provides a productive point of departure for a post-metaphysical analysis of the female subject.

If the reincorporation of the experiential provides a place for the (ambiguously) *referential* in theories of women's selfhoods, I believe that the notion of *ipseity* or narrative identity – which posits a dynamic, continuous and incomplete identity always under construction – can provide the purely synchronic play of 'textual' identity with a much-needed vertical or *diachronic* dimension. The diachronic or 'depth' element is provided by the affirmation that the singularity of one's life-story is an interpretation both lived and indefinitely pursued over time by an embodied, finite existent.

Virginia Woolf's observation is pertinent here:

> Here I come to one of the memoir writer's difficulties. . . . They leave out the person to whom things happened. The reason is that it is so difficult to describe any human being. So they say: 'this is what happened'; but they do not say what the person was like to whom it happened. And the events mean very little unless we know first to whom it happened. Who was I then?[84]

Reintroducing the 'unique, unrepeatable, personal identity'[85] of the woman to whom the events of her life-story happened is, I argue, a vital move for feminist theorists of subjectivity. It is vital because if women's selves are so radically dispersed and fragmented across the panoply of discourses as to make their representations nothing more than pure performance (*pace* Butler) something is lost: the psycho-biographical signified, the 'woman to whom things happened', and her 'li[f]e-with-meaning'.[86]

The reluctance of feminist post-structuralists to engage with the idea of the unique is understandable, given its associations with masculinist notions of autonomy, transcendence, transparency. Yet, as we have seen, it is possible to theorise singularity without committing oneself to any of these notions. We recall that singularity, thus considered, may be read as a dynamic, diachronic yet disrupted process, traced through and through with difference and alterity. It is insubstitutably 'there' (or 'here') at a pre-reflective, existential level yet deferred and dispersed in a non-totalisable plurality of interpretations. It is alienated by the hegemonic conditions of discursively-mediated existence; yet partially recovered/created in the 'insubstantial unity' which my (conscious and unconscious) imagination and desire[87] weaves from the disparate and contingent experiences of my embodied existence. Moreover, my singularity is not understood as the unified and atomic core of consciousness which is the guarantor of all meaning but is found *relationally* and *expositively* in the diffusion of my uniqueness in and through other narrative selves: my 'life-story is different from all others precisely because it is constitutively interwoven with all others'.[88]

Understanding singularity as a non-substantive, expressive, exhibitive mode of identity which continually makes and unmakes itself may help to avoid the either/ors of the feminist post-structuralist position by positing 'me' not as a purely *textual* creation, predicated on absence, nor as a directly representable *referent*, predicated on absolute presence, but as a sexed existent, a contextually-located, constitutionally-incomplete yet reflective self. Thus conceived, the singular self is not a stable, self-same entity with a coherent, univocal story. Indeed, as we have seen, the play of difference or dispossession which disrupts the (transitional and relational) construction of my unity and singularity is also the *condition* for my fragile uniqueness: that which both anchors my ipseity and casts it adrift. Thus a constitutively-sexed but ontologically-incomplete 'I' may be posited *between* textuality and referentiality: an insubstitutability 'not necessarily a lie but certainly a highly complex truth'.[89] In affirming the particularity, the specificity, the singularity of 'my' story that is mine and no other's yet is predicated on otherness, each woman, in all the contingencies of her finitude, demonstrates her 'diverse ways of understanding and inhabiting the subject-position of "woman"'.[90]

Yet, as we know, 'speaking as a woman' risks erasing the many profound differences between women beneath a false representativity: 'the super-personal paradigm of Woman.'[91] Rich observes that

> there is no neutral place to stand free and clear in which one's words do not prescriptively affect or mediate the experience of others, nor is there a way to decisively demarcate a boundary between one's location and all others. . . . We are collectively caught in an intricate, delicate web in which each action I take, discursive or otherwise pulls on, breaks off, or maintains the tension in many strands of a web in which others find themselves moving also.[92]

The deconstructive dimension of our model insists upon the radical historical and cultural variability which marks the 'volatile collectivity'[93] of the social group 'women'.

This distanciating moment resists a reconciliation or assimilation of the insubstitutability of each woman with the collectivity 'women'. Yet the interpretive, hermeneutic element of our framework seeks provisional meanings, tenuous continuities (always arrested by the intervention of deconstructive discontinuities) between women's stories; it in turn arrests the extremity of 'hyper-individualism'[94] which is the ultimate logic of the assertion of radical differences between women.[95] Starting not from 'the authority/authenticity of experience' nor from 'the illusion of experience', but from the uncertain and shifting ground-without-a-ground between textuality and referentiality that we have characterised as the domain of the female subject, the continuities and discontinuities between women's stories may be no more than glimpsed as potential lines of connection, brief vistas of different horizons, before they are submerged once more in the plethora of deictic coordinates which anchor each woman's story in a multiplicity of discourses. The *rapprochement* between hermeneutics and deconstruction thus demonstrates that at the level of reference, at the level of textuality, at the level of singularity, at the level of collectivity, 'distanciation is the condition of understanding'.[96] As Merleau-Ponty observes, 'that which permits us to centre our existence is also that which prevents us from centring it absolutely'.[97]

Notes

1   P. Ricoeur, *Oneself as Another*, trans. Kathleen Blamey, Chicago, IL: University of Chicago Press, 1992, p. 22.
2   G.W.F. Hegel, quoted in Georges Gusdorf, 'Conditions and Limits of Autobiography', in J. Olney (ed.) *Autobiography: Essays Theoretical and Critical*, Princeton, NJ: Princeton University Press, 1980, p. 38.

3   S. Smith, *Subjectivity, Identity and the Body: Women's Autobiographical Practices in the Twentieth Century*, Bloomington, IN: Indiana University Press, 1993, p. 5.

4   J. Butler, *The Psychic Life of Power*, Stanford, CA: Stanford University Press, 1997, p. 10.

5   J.W. Scott, 'The Evidence of Experience', *Critical Enquiry*, 17 (1991): 773–797.

6   S. Benstock, 'Authorizing the Autobiographical', in S. Benstock (ed.) *The Private Self: Theory and Practice of Women's Autobiographical Writings*, Chapel Hill, NC and London: University of North Carolina Press, 1988, p. 29.

7   L. Stanley, *The Auto/biographical I: the Theory and Practice of Feminist Auto/biography*, Manchester: Manchester University Press, 1992, p. 97.

8   The notion of 'arborescence' (tree-likeness) is examined in G. Deleuze and F. Guattari, *A Thousand Plateaus*, trans. B. Massumi, Minneapolis, MN: University of Minnesota Press, 1987.

9   The term 'speaking/spoken' self is coined by the hermeneutic theorist G.B. Madison; it refers to the fact that the self-presence of the hermeneutic subject is always mediated by signs. Madison writes, 'to the degree that [the subject] exists self-understandingly it does so only as the result of the constitutive and critical play of signs, symbols and texts' (Madison, 'Ricoeur and the Hermeneutics of the Subject', in L. Hahn (ed.) *The Philosophy of Paul Ricoeur*, Chicago, IL: Open Court, 1995, p. 80).

10   P. Ricoeur, 'Life: a Story in Search of a Narrator', in M.J. Valdes (ed.) *The Ricoeur Reader*, New York, NY/London: Harvester Wheatsheaf, 1991, p. 435.

11   It will be noted that we have once more entered the boundaries of the hermeneutic circle with this assertion. If the experiences of the self are always already linguistically mediated, how can she 'bring' her experiences to language? Subject and object are indeed mutually implicated by this statement; there can be no response to demands for empirical verification. Nonetheless, I believe that vicious circularity is avoided by the 'theoretical equi-primordiality' of the existentially-situated speaking subject and language.

12   Ricoeur, *Oneself as Another*, p. 11.

13   P. Ricoeur, *Interpretation Theory: Discourse and the Surplus of Meaning*, Fort Worth, TX: Texas Christian University Press, 1976, pp. 20–21.

14   G.M. Hopkins, quoted in J. Olney, 'Autobiography and the Cultural Moment: a Thematic, Historical and Bibliographical Introduction', in J. Olney (ed.) *Autobiography: Essays Theoretical and Critical*, Princeton, NJ: Princeton University Press, 1980, p. 23.

15   Ricoeur, *Oneself as Another*, p. 55.

16   J.-L. Nancy, 'Introduction', in E. Cadava, P. Connor and J.-L, Nancy (eds) *Who Comes After the Subject?* London: Routledge, 1991, p. 4.

17   Smith, *Subjectivity, Identity and the Body*, pp. 5–8.

18   J. Butler, *Gender Trouble: Feminism and the Subversion of Identity*, New York, NY: Routledge, 1990, p. 16.

19   Butler, *Gender Trouble*, p. 17.

20   J. Butler, *The Psychic Life of Power*, Stanford, CA: Stanford University Press, 1997, pp. 10–11.

21   Butler, *Gender Trouble*, p. 145.

22   A marked example of this blurring of conceptual boundaries can be found in Butler's discussion of the unrepresentability of women in *Gender Trouble*. Here Butler refers to women as 'linguistic absence and opacity' (p. 9). Yet opacity is far from synonymous with absence; for a subjectivity to be opaque, it has to be in some sense 'there' or present, however decentred or discursively-mediated it may be.

23   P.A. Kottman, 'Translator's Introduction' , A. Cavarero, *Relating Narratives: Storytelling and Selfhood*, trans. P.A. Kottman, London and New York, NY: Routledge, 2000, p. xiii.

24   Nancy, *Who Comes After the Subject?* pp. 6–7.

25   Ibid., p. 7.

26   Ibid.

27   Ibid.

28   Ibid., p. 8.

29   Ricoeur, *Oneself as Another*, pp. 4, 16.

30   K. Blamey, 'From the Ego to the Self: a Philosophical Itinerary', in L.E. Hahn (ed.) *The Philosophy of Paul Ricoeur*, Chicago, IL: Open Court, 1995, p. 577.

31   Ricoeur, *Oneself as Another*, p. 140.

32   Ibid., pp. 2–3.

33   Ibid., p. 2.

34   Ibid., p. 22.

35   Ibid., p. 55.

36 P. Ricoeur, *Time and Narrative*, vol. 3, trans. Kathleen Blamey and David Pellauer, Chicago, IL: University of Chicago Press, 1988, p. 246 (emphasis added).

37 H. Arendt, *The Human Condition*, Chicago, IL: University of Chicago Press, 1957, p. 181.

38 Cavarero, *Relating Narratives*, p. 13.

39 Ibid., p. 2.

40 Ibid., p. 3.

41 Ibid., p. 38.

42 Ricoeur, *Time and Narrative*, p. 246.

43 Ricoeur, 'Life: a Story in Search of a Narrator', *The Ricoeur Reader*, p. 437.

44 Ricoeur, *Time and Narrative*, p. 246.

45 Ibid.

46 Ibid., p. 248.

47 Ibid., p. 247.

48 Ibid.

49 Cavarero, *Relating Narratives*, p. 34.

50 Ibid.

51 Ibid.

52 Ibid.

53 Ibid.

54 Ibid., p. 35.

55 Ibid.

56 Ibid.

57 Ibid., p. 36.

58 Ibid., p. 23.

59 Ibid., p. 36.

60 Ricoeur, 'Life: A Story in Search of a Narrator', p. 435.

61 It is important to stress here that the anti-foundationalist notion of singularity which I propose is *not* predicated upon a coherent, stable 'core-self', but operates as a series of interpretations indefinitely pursued by a finite existent whose selfhood is understood as a 'teleology without telos'.

62 Butler, *Gender Trouble*, p. 17.

63 Cavarero, *Relating Narratives*, p. 23.

64 Ricoeur, *Oneself as Another*, p. 22.

65 Although this theoretical standpoint posits the ontic level as prior to the discursive and reflective levels, it remains anti-foundationalist in the sense that pre-reflective singularity cannot be represented as a radical origin since it is simply a 'thereness': an exposed existence without interiority, not a 'self'.

66 Nancy, *Who Comes After the Subject?* p. 6.

67 Ricoeur, *Oneself as Another*, p. 162.

68 Moreover, it is only the affirmation or attestation that 'it's me here!' that protects my precarious singularity against the erosion of alterity; this attestation, which Ricoeur also refers to as 'credence' is 'a trust in the power to say, in the power to do, in the power to recognise oneself as a character in a narrative' (*Oneself as Another*, p. 22). Attestation is unable to entirely overcome what Ricoeur terms 'suspicion' and what we, in our hermeneutic/deconstructive model of the experiential, termed the deconstructive moment of distanciation, where the insurmountability of hegemony's prereflective inhabitation of experience is acknowledged.

69 Butler, *Gender Trouble*, p. xi.

70 See, for example, Butler, *Gender Trouble*.

71 In particular, the work of Julia Kristeva focuses on the difference and alterity operative within the concept of 'identity'. For instance, as we have seen, in *Revolution in Poetic Language* (trans. M. Waller, New York, Columbia University Press, 1984) she considers how, in poetic language, identity is subverted by alterity, with particular reference to maternity as a paradigm model of alterity within identity. As Kelly Oliver notes, for Kristeva, 'the other is always within and originary to the subject, who is always in process' (Oliver, *Reading Kristeva*, p. 188).

72 Butler, *Gender Trouble*, p. 13.

73 Ibid., p. 3.

74 C. Battersby, *The Phenomenal Woman: Feminist Metaphysics and the Patterns of Identity*, Cambridge: Polity Press, 1998, p. 22.

75 S. Burke (ed.) *Authorship from Plato to the Postmodern: a Reader*, Edinburgh: Edinburgh University Press, 1995, p. xxi.

76   Interestingly, in *New Maladies of the Soul*, Julia Kristeva notes that discourse has been standardised to the extent that it becomes meaningless, unable to account for 'my own' experience. She contends that 'modern man' [sic] is unable to represent himself; thus, argues Kristeva, the role of the psycho-analyst is 'to restore psychic life and to enable the speaking entity to live life to the fullest' (Kristeva, *New Maladies of the Soul*, trans. R. Guberman, New York, NY: Columbia University Press, 1995, p. 9).

77   Post-structuralism has provided us with many insights into the discourses at work within the experiences of pregnancy, birth and motherhood. In particular, '*Stabat Mater*', Julia Kristeva's study of the Virgin Mother, explores the psycho-social functions of the 'cult of the virgin' on contemporary women's experiences of motherhood. Kristeva calls for a new, 'post-virginal' discourse on maternity, a 'herethics'; she asks, 'what are the aspects of the feminine psyche for which the representation of motherhood does not provide a solution or else provides one that is felt as too coercive by twentieth-century women?' (Kristeva, '*Stabat Mater*,' in Toril Moi (ed.) *The Kristeva Reader*, Oxford: Basil Blackwell, p. 182). Moreover, in *Powers of Horror*, Kristeva explores the way in which the bodily secretions – blood and milk – of the abject maternal body represent the forces of nature, and thus operate as a threat to the boundaries of the social subject's identity. She remarks that 'the abject confronts us . . . with our earliest attempts to release the hold of maternal entity. . . . It is a violent, clumsy breaking away, with the constant risk of falling back under a power as securing as it is stifling' (Kristeva, *Powers of Horror: An Essay on Abjection*, trans. Leon S. Roudiez, New York, NY: Columbia University Press, 1982, p. 13).

78   M. Stanworth, 'Reproductive Technologies: Tampering with Nature?', in S. Kemp and J. Squires (eds) *Feminisms*, Oxford: Oxford University Press, 1997, p. 485.

79   J. Butler, 'Gender as Performance', interview with P. Osborne and L. Segal, *Radical Philosophy* (September/October 1994) 67: 33.

80   E. Straus, *Psychiatry and Philosophy*, New York, NY: Springer Verlag, 1969, p. 29.

81   A. Rich, *Of Woman Born: Motherhood as Experience and Institution*, New York, NY: Norton, 1976, p. 63.

82   I.M. Young, 'Pregnant Embodiment', in D. Welton (ed.) *Body and Flesh: a Philosophical Reader*, Oxford: Blackwell, 1998, p. 276.

83   Young, 'Pregnant Embodiment', p. 280.

84   V. Woolf, 'A Sketch of the Past', in J. Schulkind (ed.) *Moments of Being*, 2nd edn, London: Hogarth Press, 1985, p. 65.

85   Cavarero, *Relating Narratives*, p. 74.

86   Stanley, *The Auto/biographical I*, p. 20.

87   'Desire' here refers to the desire for truth, for possible meaning.

88   Cavarero, *Relating Narratives*, p. 71.

89   Stanley, *The Auto/biographical I*, pp. 242–243.

90   R. Braidotti, *Nomadic Subjects: Embodiment and Sexual Difference in Contemporary Feminist Theory*, New York, NY: Columbia University Press, 1994, p. 115.

91   Cavarero, *Relating Narratives*, p. 60.

92   A. Rich, 'The Problem of Speaking for Others', *Cultural Critique*, 30 (1991–1992): 20–21.

93   D. Riley, 'Does Sex have a History?' *New Formations* 1 (Spring 1987): 35.

94   K. Soper, 'Feminism, Humanism, Postmodernism', in *Feminisms*, p. 289.

95   This stance also reinvokes in a new form the self as 'isolato': this self may lack the coherence and autonomy of the unified, transcendental subject, but it remains closely associated with the notion of individual consciousness.

96   P. Ricoeur, 'The Hermeneutic Function of Distanciation', in K. Blamey and J.B. Thompson (eds) *From Text to Action: Essays in Hermeneutics, II*, London: Athlone, 1991, p. 88.

97   M. Merleau-Ponty, *The Phenomenology of Perception*, London/New York, NY: Routledge Humanities Press, 1962, p. 85.

Chapter 5

A THEOLOGICAL APPROACH

Harriet A. Harris

STRUGGLING FOR TRUTH

■ From **STRUGGLING FOR TRUTH**, *Feminist Theology*, 28 (September 2001): 40–56.

Harriet Harris, like Meredith, responds to the dangers of anti-realism inherent in feminist post-structuralism. Yet, unlike Jantzen, Armour and Meredith, Harris does not offer a Continental alternative. Instead Harris returns the reader to the critical tools of analytic philosophy of religion. While postmodernity may celebrate difference and multiplicity, Harris revives the realist search for truth and unity. Her philosophically precise method is given content by her honest struggles as a female Christian cleric and academic. At home in analytic philosophy of religion, Harris appeals to feminists who reject it: her own struggle for truth tackles the lies and loss suffered by feminists who move too easily beyond any sense of truth as simple, coherent and real. Attention and honesty are virtues of Harris's theological approach to feminist philosophy of religion. If sexism in religion (e.g. in the Anglican church) is to be recognised and defeated there cannot be more than one truth of the matter.

MUCH FEMINIST ENGAGEMENT WITH theology and philosophy has resulted in wariness about the quest for truth, because claims to truth are frequently repressive. Here I illustrate and respond to the challenge to truth, particularly as it is raised by Grace Jantzen in her feminist critique of philosophy of religion.[1] I make the plea that we must not give up on truth, but that we should work to disclose truth, particularly by exposing unacknowledged partiality and dishonesty. The struggle for truth should be understood as a moral and spiritual task, rather than rejected as a narrow and mistaken preoccupation of epistemologists. We should resist moves within the feminist philosophy of religion that would divert us from that struggle.

Should philosophy concern itself with truth?

Feminists who work in philosophy of religion are questioning the very goals and principles of philosophical reasoning, and so are redefining the philosopher's tasks. Influenced by developments in the sociology of knowledge, critical theory, and recent
Franco-phone philosophy, they inquire into the complex ways that power-relations
affect the construction of reason. This has a crucial effect on the practice of philosophy,
the consequences of which are still being worked out. The effect is this: that we ask
how beliefs are formed before we can ask whether those beliefs are justified. Feminist
philosophers are joining with a range of other thinkers who want to know 'whose
beliefs' are occupying the philosophers' attention, and who is supplying the criteria of
justification. Who decides, for example, that linguistic analysis is a good way, even the
normative way, to understand what is going on in religious belief? Who decides that the
existence of God or the problem of evil should be debated as though these matters
were theologically and morally neutral, or as though the debate should not be affected
until some quite advanced stage by how theological traditions conceive God's relation
to the world or divine responses to suffering? Who is controlling the discipline and
setting its norms? These are the crucial questions currently predominating in feminist
scrutiny of philosophy of religion.

But what happens to philosophy when these questions take centre-stage? These are
empirical questions, answerable by social–scientific investigation into the relation
between power and reason. Does this mean that by prioritising questions about
the formation of belief and the construction of rationality, we are no longer doing
philosophy? If so, does this matter? Such questions undermine epistemology in particular, which is that area of philosophy focusing on criteria for rationality and justified
belief.[2] Epistemologists are interested in the relation between justified belief and knowledge, and between knowledge and truth. Their work is severely relativised by
social–scientific inquiry into the processes behind selecting criteria for rationality and
justification.

Jantzen, in her provocative book *Becoming Divine,* challenges the plausibility and
relevance of epistemology, and the moral rectitude of devoting time to it. She proposes
that philosophers should sideline questions of truth, belief and rationality, and attend
instead to ethical matters. She justly scorns philosophers who think that the rest of
humanity shares their fascination with the rationality of beliefs about God. She has in
mind those whose focus has become so refined that they regard not the existence of
God, nor even belief in that existence, but the rationality of belief in that existence as
'one of the most important of human concerns'.[3] Such thinking not only distorts the
activity of religious believing, but fails to comprehend that practical and moral struggles
are more concerning for most people. So Jantzen argues:

> The struggle against suffering and injustice and towards flourishing takes prece-
> dence, beyond comparison, to the resolution of intellectual problems; and
> although it is important that the struggle is an intelligent one, there is no excuse
> for theory ever becoming a distraction from the struggle for justice itself.[4]

Should anyone say that her project is not philosophical, she would want to know
why:

That a feminist philosophy of religion which seeks a new symbolic and social order requires an altered demarcation of the boundaries of the philosophy of religion is not an objection, it is part of the point. Philosophy of religion more intent on preserving the boundaries of the discipline than in engaging with issues of how particular religious beliefs perpetuate or alleviate suffering is in urgent need of exactly such radical revision.[5]

The challenge to revise what we mean by philosophy is one philosophers should rise to because their discipline, particularly under the analytical tradition, has ceased to advance wisdom for living. But Jantzen asks us to stretch the boundaries in ways that dichotomise belief and practice. She says that religion has gone adrift when people put ontology and epistemology before ethics.[6] She therefore refuses to write about whether reasoning is sound or whether a belief may be true. She gives no guidance on how feminist critical reasoning might proceed. Therefore I find it hard to recognise what she is doing as philosophy, although I know that thereby I am begging the question: who decides what counts as philosophy? Who is setting the boundaries?

Classically, philosophy has been in pursuit of truth and justice as though the two were intimately related. We might say that Jantzen continues the quest for the 'Good' without seeking the 'True', though this begs the further question of 'What is truth?' The minimal convictions underlying the argument in this chapter are: that we can train ourselves to recognise falsehood;[7] that we do recognise moments of truth, which we can experience as times of enlightenment; and that our understanding of the nature of truth develops with our attempts to disclose truth and overcome falsehood.[8]

Feminist philosophers are ambivalent and sceptical about the quest for truth in so far as they conceive of subjects as multiple, heterogeneous, contradictory or incoherent.[9] If this is how we are, then one might argue that, at most, we can aim for ways of improving people's lives; that we cannot make any pretension to aim at truth, and ought never to claim to have arrived at truth, because any such claim will do violence to those who fall outside the 'truth' so defined.

This dilemma cuts out the heart of philosophy as we have known it. Classically philosophy has been driven by the very idea of getting nearer to truth and goodness, and has presupposed unity: truth is one, truth is simple.[10] But if it is the case that we speak more truly when we point out heterogeneity and complexity, thereby exposing the myth of universal, unifying rationality, how can we pursue the goal of unified truth? Would we not be deceiving ourselves if we aimed at something called 'truth', and would not our own attempts at truth-telling be oppressive to others?

Attending to belief

Jantzen finds it a travesty that people engage in intense critical thought about religious beliefs, when we should be attending to the promotion of human flourishing.[11] But unless we are careful about belief (including belief about God, ourselves and our circumstances), we can fall into, or fall subject to, bad or abusive practice. Put positively, in being careful about belief (especially belief about God, ourselves and our circumstances) we can move into powerfully enriching understanding. Some examples given later in the chapter should help to bear out these claims. Admittedly, as they stand, these claims are a pragmatic response about the efficacy of careful believing, as able to enhance flourishing. A more confessional response might proceed with the conviction that God is our creator and has made things such that we should use our minds to try to understand God's works, God's will and Godself. However, philosophers of religion do not usually proceed confessionally (at least, not explicitly), so let us work with Jantzen on her own grounds. Even if we stay with her concern for pragmatic effects, we can see that she obscures the interaction between belief and efficacy by promoting a pragmatic concern for flourishing over an intellectual concern with beliefs. This seems to be a strong binary opposition in her work, despite her protests against such dichotomies.[12]

An irony is that to oppose belief and practice, or epistemology and ethics, is to play into the hands of analytical philosophers. Further back in our philosophical heritage, the ability to think virtuously was understood to go hand-in-hand with a virtuous disposition and hence a virtuous life. Conversely, vices such as dishonesty, pride and laziness were understood to undermine our ability to think well and pursue truth.[13] Even throughout Enlightenment thought, so often the bogey in people's minds today, right thinking was understood to be a moral matter. John Locke, for example, was well aware that temptation could lead people into error:

> If we could but see the secret motives that influenced the men of name and learning in the world, and the leaders of parties, we should not always find that it was the embracing of truth for its own sake, that made them espouse the doctrines they owned and maintained.[14]

I can quite imagine turning these words from Locke to the advantage of feminist critique and, keeping the exclusive language, exposing the 'secret motives' that lead men to espouse the doctrines they own. At the same time, the direction in which the Enlightenment eventually took philosophy was away from the idea of intellectual virtue and towards the idea of 'pure reason'; reason that was devoid of emotion so that it would not be subject to the sorts of abuses Locke fears.

We need to recover the notion of educating our emotions and holding our reasoning to moral account. Jantzen may in fact agree with me on this point, given her vision of reason being interrogated by passion for the good.[15] However, she says almost nothing about the process of struggling for truth. If we think in terms of intellectual virtues, we can see that this process is not just an epistemological matter, but is a moral and spiritual matter.

Aiming at truth is a moral matter

In indicating the moral dimension of the search for truth, I will begin by drawing on Pamela Sue Anderson's account of strong objectivity.[16] Anderson is the first philosopher to have written a monograph in feminist philosophy of religion, and the only one besides Jantzen to have done so. It is therefore interesting to see how she differs from Jantzen in giving credence to the quest for knowledge and truth (which she would express as a quest for fuller knowledge and less-partial truth).[17] Anderson rejects many principles of formal reasoning as used by analytical philosophers, including simplicity, consistency and coherence. But she retains the principle of objectivity, and is able significantly to transform it in the light of feminist standpoint epistemology.

Strong objectivity is formed by working with insights from multiple standpoints, including, most significantly, standpoints from the margins rather than the centre of power. It differs from weak objectivity, in which 'certain biases allow subjects to claim knowledge of the world as it is while excluding from that world the lives of women, of nondominant races, of nonprivileged classes'.[18] The feminist contention, Anderson says, 'is that this privileged perspective narrows and distorts the subject's knowledge not only of social life but of scientific "facts"'.[19] What counts as fact is shaped by the knowers and their processes of coming to knowledge.

Anderson's argument is that we move into fuller knowledge when we become aware of the limits of our own thinking, and are prompted by the experience of others to reflect critically on our outlook. Anderson's account of standpoint is very much one that reaches out to others: to practise standpoint is to be in solidarity, working with others towards a stronger objectivity. Empathy is crucial to this task. It is not just a moral virtue but an intellectual one. Empathy informs our thinking, and drives us towards greater understanding.[20] Do we not then see that the line between reason and practice, belief and ethics is transgressed?

What feminist standpoint epistemologists call strong objectivity is a quest for fuller knowledge. I see this as an attempt at truth-telling. Jantzen rejects this whole way of thinking because she finds the quest for knowledge or truth oppressive. It can easily be so: where certain 'norms' are made true, all sorts of people and experiences are rendered 'abnormal'. Human beings are very practised at screening one another out, or making one another strange. We do it by not noticing those who are different, or by wilfully ignoring or under-representing them. It is crucial that we recognise when claims to knowledge and truth operate oppressively in these ways.

Many of us will have both experienced and perpetrated such oppressive practices, borne by an over-confidence about representing the truth. We might consider an example from a church community, before going on to look at the community of philosophers of religion. CH is a mother of young children and has a part-time job. This is not shocking, but within her church community it is not the truest or best way to raise a family. It is abnormal and regarded as slightly deviant. This has the effect of silencing her, because she cannot describe her day without getting this sort of reaction: 'You must be mad, going out to work. I don't know how you cope.' She feels unable to say when she feels tired, let alone when she would appreciate help, without inviting an implicitly censorious response. Not surprisingly, she now avoids talking much there. She looks elsewhere to have personally engaging conversations. The community has a norm for family life, and is not operating from the perspective of working mothers. Therefore she cannot be fully herself there, because much of who she is falls outside the community's legitimated norms.

Now, an example from philosophy of religion. Jantzen notes how Paul Helm, in his book *Belief Policies*, has criteria of adequate belief that conform to what Helm calls 'overarching principles of rationality': coherence, consistency, non-contradiction and entailment. She says, 'Helm proceeds as though the challenges to that gesture by Continental philosophers or feminists can be ignored without affecting his case.'[21] Indeed, Helm flatly says, without apology, that he makes no mention of Continental thinkers. Jantzen comments that if he had taken Continental thought on board, his book could not have been written. 'What is going on,' she asks, 'when a philosopher of religion concerning himself with rationality and belief policies deliberately ignores central thinkers whose work is well known to challenge the position he wishes to maintain?'[22]

These examples might be taken to justify Jantzen's fears about the quest for truth and knowledge, but arguably they should not be used to undermine that quest. They are instances where the principles of standpoint, notably empathy and self-reflective criticism, are not practised. Staying with our second example, we quickly see that feminist and Continental philosophers fall outside the legitimated norms of Anglo-American philosophy of religion. They cannot really exist in that territory, and are in exile. The people they represent are in exile too. If philosophers of religion do not care for exiles, if they are inhospitable to exiles, then these are ethical and not just epistemological matters. This lack of hospitality silences people and shuts them out. The community carries on as though these strange people do not exist. To this extent, the philosophy of religion bolsters those tendencies within Christianity that have made it an oppressive religion. Sharon Welch condemns the way that intellectual resources are used to bolster shaken credulity in a system of doctrine and practice that has in fact been highly oppressive, when these resources could be directed instead to deepening moral commitment to relieve oppression.[23]

So Jantzen is justifiably worried by attempts to achieve final knowledge, and by the setting of norms. However, whilst standpoint epistemology aims to develop fuller knowledge, its best practitioners will not expect to arrive at final knowledge. Rather, they will understand themselves to be always in a process. If they should forget this, they can at least be called to task according to their own principles. Anderson describes the aim of standpoint as the gaining of 'less partial knowledge . . . by scrutinising the credentials of knowledge-claimants and putting knowledge-claimants under communal criticism from the perspective of the outsider'.[24] Listening, empathising and self-evaluating are ongoing tasks, for as long as there are people on Earth. Even if all human beings became very good at these practices, the search for truth and knowledge could not come to an end because situations change. The need for understanding must continue so long as people are living and moving because the dynamism of life means that new liberative insights need to be found and articulated for new situations.

Attentiveness to others and willingness to re-evaluate one's own stance are moral components of the attempt to disclose truth. The work of relieving oppression need not require us to turn away from questions of truth. Rather, it could apply us to the struggle of exposing the partiality, and hence dishonesty, of supposedly impartial systems. That struggle takes place within and on the fringes of communities whose claims to truth appear plausible only because dissident voices are ignored or silenced. The struggle to expose partiality is a moral process with a moral goal, but does not on that count eclipse a concern for truth. Rather, the attempt to articulate truth more fully is part and parcel of working towards greater goodness.

Truth-telling as a spiritual practice

Meanwhile, as the exiles or the outsiders find ways to articulate their own experience, their understanding of their situation develops. This is so even if others ignore them.

Feminist standpoint epistemology is most often expressed from the point of view of relatively privileged subjects who aim to practice empathy. However, it could be expressed from the point of view of struggling exiles. Its practitioners know what it is to have been ignored or otherwise held outside of a community's norms. Struggling against alienation is spiritual work: growth in self-knowledge becomes a necessary part of the attempt to disclose truth, and to tell the truth. For, when we are made strange, our experiences are not legitimated. There are no readily available categories by which to make sense of them, and few willing listeners to credit them. It may therefore take a while to map our way through the disorientation, learn how to articulate our experiences and discern what needs to be said.

Part of this struggle is what we call metaphorically the attempt to see clearly. If you are a stranger in the land, you cannot quite make out how the people around you think. Their thoughts are not your thoughts, and you can wonder whether you are going mad.

> She never saw what was right before her eyes. She never told lies. So she could not see the lies they told her. . . . They told themselves it was better this way — better for them to pretend that they did not know what she was talking about. They did not care that it made the world seem like a nightmare to her, like a place where nothing made any sense. They did not care that it made her feel like a blind person, that she could not see things that were right before her eyes. . . . This is the way that they had lied about everything. . . . Everyone knew but me. Everyone could see but me. I was blind.[25]

If your perception and interpretation of your surroundings is at odds with the 'truth' being told by the larger community, your confidence in your own judgement is threatened. This is why you need to work through the fog and clouds to clear-sightedness. To speak of a multiplicity of 'truths', or to refuse to speak of truth at all will not help in this struggle to overcome blindness and disorientation, and may militate against it.

bell hooks writes that: 'Truth-telling has to be a spiritual practice for many of us because we live and work in settings where falseness is rewarded, where lies are the norm.'[26] When we come to recognise the falsehood and lies, we yearn for their opposite. We desire for our communities to live openly and truthfully. 'Deceit and betrayal,' hooks says, 'destroy the possibility of community.'[27] One of the key ways in which communities are deceitful and self-destructive is by failing to own up to their screening practices; practices that destroy the possibility of genuine community because those being screened out are simply not able to participate fully, and eventually do not will to do so. CH has little desire to continue as a member of her church community; feminist philosophers are losing the will to publish in mainstream philosophy journals, and so on. Persevering with certain communities means having a struggle on your hands, and the struggle takes spiritual and moral strength, and not only intellectual prowess.[28]

An illustration of spiritual struggle in the Church of England

A priest at a Church of England training college said, when I offered for discussion the bell hooks piece just cited, 'can't you see that deceit and betrayal hold a community together; honesty can destroy community?' He spoke openly, and thereby brought to light some of the compromises that parts of the Church of England are prepared to endure by knowingly living with dishonesty. The Church is trying to hold itself together and not alienate any of its members whilst maintaining two incompatible 'integrities': one in favour of the ordination of women, the other opposed.[29] The result is that women are ordained but their ordination need not be recognised. Sexism is officially institutionalised. For example, parishes can stipulate that they want only male priests. This is an inherently compromising situation, with each integrity being invalidated by the other, but both being validated by the one Church to which they belong. More particularly, women clergy and their supporters are paying the price for the Church's understanding of how not to cause offence.

Problems arise as to how honest and self-searching Church institutions are about their practice. Women priests find some areas of the country effectively closed to their ministry. Some work under bishops who do not recognise their vocation, or in teams where they are barred by colleagues from churches that officially come under their care (sometimes against the will or knowledge of the congregations). Bishops who ordain women can find themselves asked not to practice oversight of particular congregations, but instead to allow in an alternative episcopal visitor ('flying bishop'). Trainee women priests are sent to preach in parishes that have passed all the resolutions against association with women priests. They are sent on retreat to worshipping communities where people will not share the peace with them, and are prepared for ordination by retreat leaders who do not regard their call to priesthood as valid. There is nothing 'wrong' with these arrangements given the two integrities, although many would regard them as 'pastorally insensitive'! They are usually 'justified' on the grounds that all ordinands are made deacons before they are priested, and that most of the Church can now recognise women deacons. Women who have nevertheless been selected for priesthood are expected not to mind about this rationalisation. Such thoughtless and debilitating arrangements, repeated year after year and questioned by only a few, take on a veneer of normality so that any words of objection are made strange. The apparent normality of the situation only highlights the sense of disorientation suffered by those who cannot accept it as either good or true. The situation is not true in so far as the Church is perpetuating a partiality which it is not admitting. So before they complain, those who feel compromised have to question their judgement: are we over-reacting, given that everyone else regards things as reasonable? Why do we feel so disorientated? Are we going mad? They are calling their community to greater honesty and coherence, but are led painfully to question their perceptions by women and men who tell them that the battles have been won and that there are no issues to fight any more.

Feminist standpoint calls on all knowing subjects to practise empathy; to attempt imaginatively to see things as others see them. In this situation, it would question the perception of those who are comfortable and who do not want the boat to be rocked. Such people feel that they are eminently reasonable, because their stance leads to no reactionary behaviour. They will not enter into the feelings of injustice and shame that others feel and express. They are able to be complacent, partly because the lack of parity between the two integrities enables an array of practises to appear 'reasonable' within the Church. For example, the two integrities have instituted a situation whereby it is ecclesiologically legitimate for those opposed to women's ordination not to receive the sacraments from a woman priest, or from a man priest who has had sacramental contact with a woman priest. However, there is no parallel legitimacy running the other way. It is not legitimate to create a parallel distance between oneself and male priests who do not recognise a priestly vocation in women. All male priests are priests in the eyes of the whole Church. No woman priest is a priest in the eyes of the whole Church.

My point here is not to argue for 'fairness' between the two integrities; it is perhaps better that one integrity be inclusive of all people who are called to the priesthood by the Church, rather than that both be exclusive of each other. Rather my point is to allow the partiality, and the compromising and disorientating nature of the situation to emerge. The two integrities involve women in practises that undermine their very being. Women clergy and ordinands are shamed by the very nature of the situation. Most particularly, at a Eucharist celebrated by a priest opposed to their ordination, before they can even arrive at the altar they must choose between making one of two responses: honouring the priest who has been ordained by the Church, despite his refusal fully to acknowledge them; or not receiving from someone who at the very point of Eucharistic celebration holds women to be at a further remove from God than men. This second option involves putting oneself out of communion with the Church. Because the integrity in favour of the ordination of women is not denying or failing to recognise the vocation of any male priests, most women will receive communion and recognise the authority of men who do not recognise them. Yet by doing so, they engage in a practice that is undermining, that for many is psychically damaging, and that keeps alive an image of God they believe to be false. They are eating and drinking from a tradition that explicitly holds men as more in the image of God than women, even whilst they are ministering (in body, mind and spirit) with a different and contradictory message that stands out against the impoverishment of both God and humanity. Again my point is not that this puts a heavy burden on women (which it does), but that such an unhealthy situation can be allowed to seem reasonable. Challenging the power-structures that determine what is reasonable is part of the struggle for truth. It is not a different work that renders that struggle irrelevant or ill-founded.

The struggle is undertaken not only for the sake of those who remain in the church, but also for those who have found it impossible to stay. Penny Jameison, Anglican bishop of Dunedin, writes:

> We, in our life, our work and our commitments, contribute to the life and the health of the very church that has been responsible for sanctioning [abusive] behaviour. It has been a humiliating experience; we have had to realize that, despite our commitments, the church is still extraordinarily patriarchal and that we are not able to save it: only God can do that. We have wept for ourselves caught up in an institution with such a vile history, and we have wept at the loss of our friends who have found our continuing association with it quite incomprehensible. . . . But somewhere in the midst of all this pain, we have re-found and been re-found by the God who hung with us in all the pain of humankind, the God who was stretched and in that stretching found birth.[30]

This is spiritual work, and involves wrestling with our community and wrestling with God, to allow truth to emerge. Women clergy and ordinands carry a heavy burden, but even as we take up our cross we resist theological ideas that God abuses

'his' children, and intimations that the sacrifices made in the name of Christ are properly made by allowing the Church to crucify us. Both sets of ideas permit the Church to
persist in duplicitous (diabolical) practice, based on notions of God that need correcting
by critical scrutiny.

Disclosing truth

Despite her objections to feminist standpoint, Jantzen recognises the important point
that struggle and not simply marginalisation brings insight.[31] She seems to be saying that
there is something truthful about the struggle: 'Truth . . . is in the process,' she writes,
'as much as in the "truths" thereby produced.'[32] She speaks only of multiple 'truths',
and is not likely to relish a call to theorise the relationship between insight and truth
because that would be an epistemological endeavour, distracting us from the moral
tasks of relieving oppression. However, her own thinking practices suggest movement
towards fuller knowledge, or greater understanding, which I propose is related to the
emergence of truth. Some would perhaps prefer to speak of 'making truth',[33] since the
notion of truth as something we create does not tie us to potentially destructive, realist
claims. However, if all truth were of our own making, it is not clear how we could
bring our communities to judgement. They could claim to make their truth, and at best
we could claim to make a more liberative truth. I prefer to speak of 'disclosing truth'
because I understand the struggle for truth as the struggle to bring something into the
light. This is a realist position. If our communities are screening us out, we need to put
ourselves in the picture and reveal their partiality, which is a process of disclosure.

I read Jantzen as in fact engaging in this process – this struggle for truth – as she
works to gain insight into the way that women are oppressed in Western culture. In so
far as other women disagree with her, the insights that she has gained through painful
wrestling are called into question. The questioning concerns whether or not she gives a
true depiction, or has got to the truth of the matter. Exposing dishonesty and partiality
is a fraught business. It invites speculation as to whether you are disorientated, whether
your perceptions and interpretations have gone awry. We hold these suspicions against
others and also against ourselves. Not surprisingly, when people are oppressed they are
often divided against one another and against their own selves. We sometimes need
other people to tell us whether we are over-reacting, or under-reacting. Others can
hold a mirror up to us, and remind us of healthier realities than whatever distorted situations we find ourselves fighting. But we have to choose our advisers shrewdly. It is an
ethical and spiritual matter; poor advice can be compromising and damaging, as can
action that is either too weak or too strong. At the same time, we must not allow our
understanding to be wholly shaped by the pictures others have painted of us and our
situations. There are times when we need to turn those pictures to the wall and look
inside ourselves, trust our instincts and build up an understanding of what we have to
do.[34] The effort to disclose truth involves us at the core of our being and at the point of
our relationships to others. It goes far beyond an intellectual task of meeting epistemological criteria for justified belief!

But, contra Jantzen, I do want to stress the importance of critical reasoning, which
works hard at both exposing distortion and offering truer beliefs. It brings to light, for
example, the disparity between the two integrities and the resultant compromises that
people are asked to endure. So critical reasoning helps one to identify the problems in

one's situation. It also helps to modify or reformulate beliefs that have legitimated compromising practices. Through the tussles in the Church of England, many people have grown in the conviction that our understanding of God and the Gospel, and our dignifying of humanity, are undermined by a theology and practice that recognises only men at the altar. If we do not attend to contrary beliefs about God, such as that God is uniquely revealed as 'Father' and therefore as male, we will not eradicate convictions that are currently doing moral and spiritual harm. Where progress is made, it is made through critical reasoning that is spiritually and morally informed, and should reflect back on the beliefs being posited about God.

The issue of what philosophical principles we use to expose distortion and to claim a greater degree of truth desperately needs our attention. Can any good come from returning to a more classical practice of philosophy? After summarising my above argument, I will end by raising some questions to that effect.

Summing up

Feminists perform a service by practising philosophy of religion as a discipline that is concerned with truth. I use the term 'truth-telling' because that term holds the spiritual, the ethical and the epistemological together. Telling the truth is a spiritual task because it requires self-searching and the attempt to expose the lies that are doing us harm. It is also a moral good, and aiming for that good can be an arduous task. It requires empathy, which is not always practised in Christian communities that have a strong sense of what is normal or legitimate. Such communities live dishonestly if they practice a partiality that they are not admitting. And so they have victims, who are sacrificed to the lies that maintain the status quo. Naming the falsehood and disclosing the truth is moral work, but that is no reason to abandon epistemology. Truth-telling is an epistemological process because it concerns our knowledge and belief. Still, I hope I have gone some way in showing that it is not just an epistemological matter.

Should we return to classic philosophical principles? Some tentative questions

These reflections beg the all-important question about philosophical practice. What philosophical principles can we use in exposing distortion and aiming at truth? What about the principles of coherence, consistency and simplicity? Feminist philosophers are highly suspicious of these philosophical principles because they screen out our differences and repress diversity. The truth about a situation must reveal that situation in its complex and contradictory state. This is descriptive truth. But is there a place for prescriptive truth, which is goal-seeking and aims at coherence, consistency and simplicity? This is a shocking question in a feminist context, but I raise it because people are compromised by inconsistent systems, and thrown into confusion by structures that are not honest about power, and are left 'feeling complicated' where situations are complex and fragmented.

Part of what it means to criticise communities and institutions is to reveal incoherence and inconsistency. Wanting them to become better involves hoping that they will become more coherent and consistent in their thinking and policies. In so far as communities and institutions are twisted or arbitrary, they leave people feeling let down and unsafe, and allow people not to try to be honest. They permit a spiritual and moral laziness by letting people get away with not struggling for truth. This is especially disturbing in Christian communities where growth in self-knowledge and a willingness to be challenged and transformed are understood to be aspects of one's spiritual discipline. That said, we must also recognise that it can indeed be sinister when people act for the sake of coherence and consistency, because they may be attempting to cohere with bad practice or to be consistent with something that is itself problematic and harmful. There is little virtue, for example, in having a consistent policy to refuse freedom of information, when the policy itself should be overturned.[35] This begs the question, however, of whether bad practice could ever be fully consistent or coherent. Would not any bad practice ultimately be self-contradictory and self-defeating? Can we feel the lure of Kantian philosophy as we broach this issue and, behind that, the classical conviction of single unified truth? Are these temptations that feminists ought to resist, or that they can afford to resist?

Is simplicity, after all, a sign of the good and the true? Can we not aim for it, in the sense of overcoming duplicity? Half-truths and semi-concealed power-relations throw people into distraction, by holding them in 'diabolical' (which means duplicitous or distracted) circumstances. We may not know what truth is, in the sense of having arrived at final knowledge but we can come to recognise falsehood. We can embrace the effort to struggle against lies and to work hard at disclosing truth. I would venture that we also know when we glimpse truth: we recognise moments of truth. Are these moments of clarity and simplicity, and, if so, how might we represent that in our critical thinking?[36]

Notes

1   G. Jantzen, *Becoming Divine: Towards a Feminist Philosophy of Religion*, Manchester: Manchester University Press, 1998.

2   See S. Haack, *Evidence and Inquiry: Towards Reconstruction in Epistemology*, Oxford: Blackwell, 1993.

3   Jantzen, *Becoming Divine*, p. 79.

4   Ibid., p. 264.

5   Ibid., p. 264.

6   For example ibid., p. 257.

7   This conviction that we can expose falsehood even if we can never possess the truth in an absolute way resonates with the principle of negative dialectics in the work of Adorno and the Frankfurt school of critical theory, which has influenced liberation theologians writing about truth and justice. See especially the work of T.W. Adorno, *Negative Dialectics*, trans. E.B. Ashton, New York, NY: Seabury Press, 1973. For this point I am grateful to James Grenfell.

8   In her 'Response to Harriet Harris', *Feminist Theology* 23 (2000): 119–120, Jantzen explains that her intention is not to 'reject or even replace questions of truth so much as to reconstitute them'. She attributes the apparent neglect of truth and reason to her focus on recovering what has been repressed in the Western philosophical tradition. She tries to resuscitate passion, which should not be indifferent to reason, but should interrogate reason. It is helpful to have this clarification of her project, but Jantzen still gives no guidance on how we are to search for truth(s) in her re-envisioned philosophy. Nor does she reverse her rejection of feminist epistemologies in *Becoming Divine*, pp. 121–127, 213–219.

9   As expressed by P.S. Anderson, *A Feminist Philosophy of Religion*, Oxford: Blackwell, 1998, p. 86.

10 Cf. B. Almond, 'Philosophy and the Cult of Irrationalism', in A. Phillips Griffiths (ed.) *The Impulse to Philosophise*, Oxford: Oxford University Press, 1992, p. 215.

11 Similarly, though without the feminist critique, Michael McGhee proposes that 'it may be necessary to displace, not just familiar manoeuvres around "belief in the existence of God", but the very idea of *belief* as its central concern (we are not interested in what people *believe*, but in what *insights* are manifested in their lives)', in M. McGhee (ed.) *Philosophy, Religion and the Spiritual Life*, Cambridge: Cambridge University Press, 1992, p. 3. For McGhee's own, sustained attempt to re-envision philosophy of religion as a spiritual activity see *Transformations of the Mind: Philosophy as Spiritual Practice*, Cambridge: Cambridge University Press, 2000.

12 In Jantzen, *Becoming Divine*, e.g., pp. 64–68, 97, 128, 266–267.

13 See G. Axtell, 'Recent Work on Virtue Epistemology', in *American Philosophical Quarterly*, 34: 1 (1997): 1–26; J. Kvanvig, *Intellectual Virtues and the Life of the Mind: On the Place of Virtues in Contemporary Epistemology*, Savage, MD: Rowman & Littlefield, 1992; W.J. Wood, *Epistemology: Becoming Intellectually Virtuous*, Leicester: Apollos, 1998; L. Zagzebski, *Virtues of the Mind: An Inquiry into the Nature of Virtue and the Ethical Foundations of Knowledge*, Cambridge: Cambridge University Press, 1996; A. Fairweather and L. Zagzebski (eds) *Virtue Epistemology: Essays on Epistemic Virtue and Responsibility*, Oxford; New York, NY: Oxford University Press, 2001.

14 J. Locke, *An Essay Concerning Human Understanding*, 4: 20, 17.

15 In Jantzen, 'Response to Harriet Harris'.

16 Anderson, *A Feminist Philosophy of Religion*, Ch. 2.

17 For example, ibid., pp. 69, 130–134.

18 Ibid., p. 73. See also P.S. Anderson, 'Standpoint: Its Proper Place in a Realist Epistemology', *Journal of Philosophical Research* (2001): 131–153.

19 Anderson, *Feminist Philosophy of Religion*, p. 73.

20 For debate over the place of empathy in moral life see N.E. Snow, 'Empathy', *American Philosophical Quarterly*, 37: 1 (2000): 65–78. Snow argues that empathy is neither necessary nor sufficient for moral perception and responsiveness. At the same time she raises the possibility that 'perhaps we have moral duties to hone and refine our empathic skill so that we can be appropriately sensitive to the needs of others' (p. 75). My point is that a lack of empathy can blind us to the needs of others and therefore can impede our judgements about what would constitute a morally good response to a particular situation.

21 G. Jantzen, 'What Price Neutrality? A Reply to Paul Helm', *Religious Studies*, 37: 1 (2001): 83.

22 Ibid., p. 83. Paul Helm has responded to *Becoming Divine* in an article that professes to be 'not at all concerned with the issue of feminism, but only with the methodological turn that Jantzen makes'. He thereby separates Jantzen's methodology from her feminism in ways that she does not regard as valid, and so continues to evade feminist challenges to analytical philosophical methods. For example, he insists that 'a discipline is something which is essentially abstract'. See P. Helm, 'The Indispensability of Belief to Religion', and G. Jantzen, 'What Price Neutrality? A Reply to Paul Helm', *Religious Studies*, 37: 1 (2001): 75–86, 87–92.

23 S. Welch, *Communities of Resistance and Solidarity: A Feminist Theology of Liberation*, Maryknoll: Orbis, 1985, p. 4, cited in Jantzen, *Becoming Divine*, p. 220.

24 Anderson, *Feminist Philosophy of Religion*, p. 131.

25 b. hooks, *Wounds of Passion: A Writing Life*, London: The Women's Press, 1998, pp. 20–21.

26 b. hooks, *Remembered Rapture: The Writer at Work*, London: The Women's Press, 1999, pp. 120–121.

27 Ibid., p. 121.

28 The struggle is often a lonely one, and one where you cannot presume to speak for others because of the sheer complexity of feelings you and they experience, and the fearfulness produced by the distortion. Where that is the case, the attempt to show that you are being screened out involves the exhausting work of holding yourself up as an example by which to illuminate and convict the system. The perils of this work include the vulnerability of exposure, and the prospect that you will be made into a scapegoat for the problems that the community is being made to face, or that you will be perceived as a victim. By casting you in the role of victim, your community may continue to evade the truth about itself by becoming exercised in sympathy towards you.

29 The vote in the Church of England in 1992 to ordain women as priests was followed by a vast amount of legislation to enable the Church to hold two opposed theological positions with integrity. This contradictory state has come to be known unofficially as the 'two integrities'. It involves making provision at every level for those who do not recognise women's priestly orders, as well as for those who do.

30 P. Jamieson, *Living at the Edge: Sacrament and Solidarity in Leadership*, London: Mowbray, 1997, p. 163.

31 Jantzen, *Becoming Divine*, p. 215.

32 Ibid.
33 This was Professor Ursula King's suggestion when I read a version of this chapter at the University of Bristol.
34 Cf. Jamieson, *Living at the Edge*, p. 137.
35 For example, the theological college mentioned earlier in the chapter implemented a policy whereby neither supporters nor opponents of women priests could publicise information about events promoting their causes, believing that the best policy was to be consistent in suppressing information.
36 My thanks go to Dr Pamela Sue Anderson, Dr Beverley Clack, Revd Dr Joanne Woolway Grenfell and Revd James Grenfell for their comments on this chapter. Much of the work in this chapter was first given as a paper at the conference 'Whither Feminist Philosophy of Religion?', at the University of Bristol in March 2000, and I am most grateful for the comments received there.

Chapter 6

AN EPISTEMOLOGICAL–ETHICAL APPROACH

Pamela Sue Anderson

AN EPISTEMOLOGICAL–ETHICAL APPROACH TO
PHILOSOPHY OF RELIGION: LEARNING TO LISTEN

Pamela Sue Anderson picks up on Meredith's concern with selfhood and female testimony, as well as on Harris's concern with truth and realism. Both areas of concern need to be addressed, if truth and justice are to be distinguished from falsehood and injustice in ethical and religious practices. Anderson calls for collaborative thinking in feminist philosophy of religion, which is self-reflexive, imaginative and interactive. Collaboration is meant to replace the structures of opposition, which continue to characterize the more radical critiques of gender. A 'both-and' rather than an 'either/or' approach to feminist philosophy of religion is rendered possible with the cultivation of certain intellectual virtues. Reflective critical openness, care-knowing, strong objectivity and principled autonomy are explored as cognitive dispositions – the cultivation of which aims to redress the exclusion, from philosophy of religion, of credible witnesses, of ethical practices, of subjectivity by objectivity and of autonomous yet vulnerable agents.

Introduction

THE CONTENTION THAT MODERN philosophers have understood epistemology and ethics in oppositional terms is not new. Neither is it novel to present a feminist critique of binary oppositions, exposing a value hierarchy of terms such as fact/value, reason/emotion, hard/soft, male/female. Certain philosophers continue to give privilege to the hard, since durable, yet abstract nature of epistemology over and above the soft, since often less rigorous and less certain, yet more concrete nature of ethical theory. Arguments circulate against these binary oppositions, or dualisms of hierarchically valued terms, whether abstract/concrete or epistemology/ethics, in which the first term is given a (more) positive value. Yet often the critics of modern philosophy find themselves caught up in their own circular reasoning; accusations of oppositional thinking go round and round. It seems that as soon as one critic accuses another of opposing reason to emotion, the second turns around and accuses the first of giving greater value to emotion over reason. To give evidence of such oppositional thinking in feminist philosophy of religion, I need only mention that certain feminist philosophers have advocated giving priority to ethics over epistemology, and we can, then, recognize a pattern. That is, feminist philosophers of religion have followed suit, and insisted on rejecting the epistemology of (religious) belief for the more valuable ethical concerns of (religious) flourishing.[1]

However, in the face of these debates about hierarchies of valued terms, I would like to articulate another approach, strongly advocating collaboration rather than opposition.[2] When it comes to women in relation to both epistemology and ethics, they have been excluded, notably, from being credible witnesses or informants, from demonstrating knowledge of their ethical practices, from seeing reality objectively, and from acting autonomously as equally rational agents. Yet my proposal is that these exclusions can be avoided with the free cultivation of four intellectual virtues: *reflexive critical openness, care-knowing, strong objectivity* and *principled autonomy*. These virtues are meant to unite ethical and epistemological components in a form of virtue epistemology;[3] that is, our perspectives and practices would be shaped by the development of certain virtues with capacities for cognition.[4] Guided by reflexive, imaginative and interactive capacities for discerning truth, a feminist philosophy of religion would aim for practical wisdom.

To grasp the significance of this approach, we should recall certain reasons why women have been excluded from both epistemology and ethics. Basically, the associations of women with their bodies and bodily functions, with irrationality, passivity, lack, slime, abjection, deception and dependency rendered female persons ethically and politically inferior. These associations, then, rendered 'female philosopher' an oxymoron. Female epistemologist and female ethicist were equally suspect. Feminist philosophers of religion, such as those following Luce Irigaray's psychoanalytic, theological and political writings, aimed to revalue these female associations. In Grace Jantzen's terms, they sought to raise up – the repressed values of female becoming (divine).[5] Yet I have advocated – and still do – caution concerning this revaluation: we must not simply celebrate the revalued term, in this case, ethics. Feminist theorists are better off if they do not naïvely claim to reject the terms of dichotomies *tout court*, when rejecting the biased value hierarchy.[6] So passion, or 'female intuition', should not simply subvert reason.[7]

In *A Feminist Philosophy of Religion: the Rationality and Myths of Religious Belief*, I began the transformation of the philosophical domain and core concepts of philosophy of religion.[8] I advocated a reform and not a reversal of values. In the present chapter, I continue this process of transformation, addressing the need to uphold intellectual virtues. Let us assume initially that 'virtue' is essentially a disposition; and 'intellectual' refers to the motivation to know as the virtue's most basic component. To enhance understanding of this conception of intellectual virtue, I suggest that Eve in the Genesis story displays a motivation to know right and wrong. Let us, then, imagine this 'first' woman as the first moral philosopher in shaping the dispositions for both moral and practical reasoning. Like Eve, we would need to cultivate practical wisdom concerning our desires and dispositions. We can also imagine contemporary feminist approaches to philosophy of religion following Eve's lead: imagine this when feminist philosophers reflect upon their own religious practices and the cultivation of certain intellectual virtues. But we do not simply learn from our own religious perspectives and practices. For this reason, I will, for example, consider Vrinda Dalmiya's application of virtue epistemology[9] to certain Hindu ethical practices.[10]

In this light, my epistemological–ethical approach to feminist philosophy of religion urges an ethical engagement, especially with other female philosophers, in the struggle to transform philosophy on behalf of those women's beliefs and practices which have been excluded from traditional Western accounts of religion(s). It also urges an epistemological engagement, with other women and men, in imaginative thinking by, and with, those who have risked forming relationships bound by religious beliefs, yet on the margins of patriarchal societies. Dalmiya captures the spirit of this engagement:

> The particularity of the other ceases to be overwhelmingly exotic if we are required to struggle to adopt that point of view. . . . Merely allowing the other to speak need not ensure the . . . reciprocity . . . which is necessary for dialogue and moral respect.[11]

Philosophers of religion who actively engage in this struggle, to understand both other religious perspectives and other religious practices, will be made vulnerable[12] to having their own thinking and acting transformed.

Four intellectual virtues

Here I propose that the four intellectual virtues (named above) should shape a feminist philosophy of religion. Intellectual virtues would give norms, or standards, for discussion of general and particular issues, while also wedding reason and passion, thinking and acting into a definite shape.[13] Although motivating the ultimate search for practical wisdom, each intellectual virtue also has a distinctive motivational component for knowledge, which can be discovered in the response to a specific question, or line of questions. Such questions will guide my feminist epistemological–ethical approach to philosophy of religion.

Reflective critical openness

First of all, this feminist epistemological–ethical approach to philosophy of religion needs to address queries about knowledge and power. For each claim to knowledge, whether about the divine or about religious practices, we are compelled to ask, whose knowledge is it? In each case, who and what are excluded as subjects and objects of (divine) knowledge, respectively? More generally, who is a good informant? Is it someone able to give a reliable account of social and natural facts of the matter? These queries find a response in Miranda Fricker's account of *reflective critical openness*. As an intellectual virtue, reflective critical openness ensures against our unjustly giving either too much or too little credibility to certain people. It is characterized by a sensitivity to reasons for believing or not believing what we are told, preventing us from being indiscriminate *in whom* we believe. As a cognitive disposition, it is associated with testimonial sensibility which develops according to upbringing and education. If, despite clear evidence for the truth of her testimony, a witness is not believed because of certain social markers, whether these are sexual or racial features, ethnic manners or even a particular accent, our testimonial sensibility would seem to be unfairly biased. Reflective critical openness would, then, function to expose the ungrounded prejudice created by unfair stereotypes, especially those which make women untrustworthy witnesses and unreliable informants.[14] As such this intellectual virtue should have a pivotal role in any future philosophy of religion. In particular, philosophers of religion should learn from feminist critiques of social identity and power/powerlessness to develop less biased testimonial sensibilities, since testimony itself remains a significant source of religious knowledge and a model for our epistemic practices.[15]

Incorporation of reflective critical openness into philosophy of religion means thinking more effectively by shaping our epistemic practices with the help of the philosophical capacities for reflective, imaginative and interactive understanding. We seek to listen to the testimonies of those who are not merely trusted because of certain, largely exclusive social markers of rational authority, but because the informant genuinely acquires and offers a true account of the matter, whether of religious experience, practice or belief. The specific question guiding the development of this virtue is: are we motivated to bring about reflective critical openness towards the testimonies of women and those persons who lack the power necessary for rational authority due to their social location? Consider the injunction of Fricker:

> If you want the full story you had probably better *listen especially closely to* the accounts of experience that are given by people who are among *the least powerful in society*. Their hermeneutical disadvantage can become *a positive epistemic resource*, so long as one can *learn to listen*.[16]

To think effectively, and more openly, implies the crucial competence of listening to reasons for believing or not believing each female informant without fear of a conflict of points of view. This is not easy. And it will force the philosopher to confront 'the Cassandra problem'.[17]

Cassandra, the figure in Greek mythology whose prophecies are trustworthy, is not given the power – or rational authority – to be trusted. So no one believes her. Cassandra represents the problem of misplaced mistrust.[18] Here Christian philosophers of religion may think of the woman in the New Testament gospel story who saw and witnessed Christ after he rose from the dead on the third day, but none of the (male) disciples believed the female testimony.[19] Yet the problem is not merely one of a particular (sort of) woman being thought to be untrustworthy. It is also the more wide-ranging problem of the history of philosophy silencing, by mistrusting all women. Some contemporary philosophers still do not realize that centuries ago women such as Christine de Pisan (b. 1364/5) and Gabrielle Suchon (b. 1631; about whom more below) were lovers of wisdom, writing and formulating new ideas. For many, the concept 'female philosopher' has remained an oxymoron. After all, could women have had their own ideas?

Michèle Le Doeuff documents the history of male knowledge as built on the failure to recognize female philosophers, since 'only men produce ideas'.[20] However, as Le Doeuff demonstrates with more than a little irony, this is not because women had no ideas of their own! In particular, Suchon serves as Le Doeuff's 'veritable find' from the seventeenth century, a woman who produced new ideas concerning reason and (intellectual) freedom – ideas which in that time, and since, could not be attributed to a woman. Yet 'dis-inheritance' either eclipsed or wrongly attributed women's knowledge to male philosophers. Few, if any, objected since women simply lacked the authority of reason. I will suggest later how this dis-inheritance would exclude women from principled autonomy. Nevertheless, Le Doeuff uncovers evidence supporting the reflective power of women to make true judgements and formulate true ideas; hence, the ability of women to formulate general principles for thinking and acting.[21]

Consider the irony in a male-neutral idea of omniscience, playing an authoritative role in popular debates about omniscience. Charles Taliaferro offers the example of two male knowers, Dennis and Christopher, who both have knowledge of all true propositions.[22] Later Taliaferro slightly modifies his example by making the two knowers a man, Eric who takes the role of Dennis, and a woman, Miriam who takes the part of Christopher.[23] Each knower in both versions of the example has knowledge of all true propositions, where 'proposition' refers to a non-linguistic state of affairs, or abstract entity, which can be translated into any language.[24] In this sense, these propositions represent timeless truth. However, Dennis (Eric) acquires this knowledge from Christopher (Miriam), while the latter has acquired the omniscience for himself or herself. The difference, according to Taliaferro, is that Miriam (in place of Christopher) has greater cognitive power. Yet Taliaferro does not consider whether her power is shaped, or made possible, by the authority of the knower's social identity. Simply, Miriam's knowledge would be greater than Eric's, in so far as the former both possesses knowledge of all true propositions and knows how to acquire this knowledge.

Now, compare this knowledge to that which Suchon acquires from freely engaging with the biblical text, in particular, with the account of Eve's eating of the forbidden tree of knowledge of good and evil. Suchon concludes that far from a woman's desire for knowledge being the source of sin, this desire becomes the motivation for God-given reflective knowledge, recognizing the difference between the desire for earthly fruit and the desire for heavenly food. According to Suchon, the content of this knowledge is '*infuse*', i.e. inspired directly by God in highly specific details.[25] (In later centuries this sort of inspired knowledge will be read both as 'innate' and as 'intuited' ideas.) With such inspiration we would know, and be able to reflect upon the knowledge, that something would occur at a particular time and a particular place in a particular way. Suchon's ideal of divine knowledge and power is characterized by particularity and reflexivity. Whose account of knowledge – the one who knows all true propositions or the one who knows all the specificities making up the truth of what takes place – represents the greater knowledge? The former knowledge represents timeless truth, while the latter knowledge depends upon sensitivity to time, i.e. to listening to the other's intuition about what might or will take place.

In traditional theism, in which God is conceived to be omniscient and non-temporal, a problem arises concerning how this God could know the future, free acts of particular individuals in time. Can God have knowledge of indexicals? Whatever the answer, debating the attributes of the theistic God does not enhance practical wisdom. We would not uncover the unrecognized wisdom of Eve, or Cassandra, by debating the abstract question of an eternal God's foreknowledge. Taliaferro helpfully focuses on how knowledge is acquired rather than taking omniscience to mean strictly what is known. Yet, although incorporating the 'how?' with the 'what?' of knowledge is necessary, it is not sufficient, if gender is to be taken seriously in religious epistemology. It is necessary to assess the content (what?), acquisition (how?), context (when?) and possessor (who?) of knowledge. The cognitive power of beings with fallible and limited capacities may, ironically, be found in what has been called the 'weakness' of woman (as in Eve).

Once cognitive power includes the ability of the human knower to reflect critically upon what is known, how it is known, and who possesses it, then the reliable acquisition of knowledge – by both women and men – of particular things taking place at particular times in a particular location can become a gender-inclusive virtue, aiming at wisdom. Thus Suchon's *'connaissance infuse'* as a God-given capacity for knowledge gained by critical reflection represents a greater sort of truth and power than divine omniscience conceived as knowledge in timeless propositional form.[26] Yet the problem is women's ideas have not been recognized as reliable sorts of information – let alone knowledge. Think of the derogatory connotations attributed to 'women's intuition'! And yet pity the male philosopher who knows all true propositions, but fails to know that he should avoid a particular life-threatening situation, about which he could have learnt from the insight of a woman. Think of the King of Troy who would not listen to the trustworthy message of his own daughter, Cassandra, foretelling of the disaster awaiting him, if he went to war – hence, Troy fell! Granted this story assumes that Cassandra is infallibly informed by the god Apollo; yet the point is to trust the integrity of the knower.

Eve herself leads Adam to acquire knowledge of the difference between good and evil, and so to develop virtue through reflection, imagination and interaction. Such wisdom, then, becomes the superior sort of knowledge, while divine knowledge becomes a regulative idea, guiding open and critical reflection upon the trustworthiness of particular ideas and the particular knowers. As a gift (infused), divine knowledge emerges in the specificity and reflexivity of someone desiring wisdom. To recognize that the motivation to know is first represented by Eve – in whom we have personified a misplaced mistrust of all women – we need to imagine her social identity differently. And then, we need to develop a reflective critical openness to the testimonies of those who, like Eve symbolically and literally, have lacked rational authority.

Care-knowing

Dalmiya demonstrates the cognitive value of caring by linking the interactive dimension of what have often been traditionally women's practices (in the West) to the wider concerns of epistemologists and religious ethicists globally. She identifies 'care-knowing' as a *reliabilist* virtue which exhibits a distinctive sort of 'knowing how'. Reliable means here that the success of care-receiving is dependent as much on the one-caring as it is on the cared for.[27] This virtue involves critical self-reflection on the interactive practice of caring.[28] And this means an ability to listen to, and register, what the other says or, simply, needs. In externalist terms, beliefs about one's own and other's care-practices produced in a reliable way are likely to be true; so care-knowing can be achieved, according to a certain reliabilist method.[29] It is necessary to reject 'care' as a non-cognitive response or action, to embrace caring as a form of cognition. Like reflective critical openness, care-knowing is developed as a disposition for practical wisdom.

The question is, are we motivated to bring about the know-how of caring as a distinctive virtue for philosophy of religion today? This requires bringing about the state in which the interactive practice(s) of women and others who care are recognized and registered; these would exhibit reflective and imaginative competence. The proper understanding of our terminology is crucial. 'Care' is often employed to stand for much of what is today called 'care ethics', whose meaning is not at all clear; or if clear, it can have negative associations. Equally, the ideal of 'the carer' can have negative associations in the all-too-clear stereotype of a woman bound up with an oppressive construction of femininity. There is the self-destructive stereotype of the overly self-sacrificing woman whose 'care' allows her to be clearly exploited by her husband, or by other men with whom she may have a social or personal relationship. We cannot deny that religious ethics have often reinforced the exploitative, stereotypical case of the caring woman. Nevertheless, self-critical reflection, or what Dalmiya calls caring about caring, should ensure our crucial assessment of the relationships governing the lives of both the carer and the cared for.

As a cognitive disposition, care-knowing requires for its development a process of self-revelation and self-making. At the same time, this disposition is shaped intellectually by imaginatively listening to and reflexively registering the perspectives of others, especially as developed by one's interactive practices with these others. Dalmiya focuses on caring as a five-facet disposition, establishing the possibility of an interactive, cognitive practice between the one caring and the cared for.[30] The five-facets include *caring about*, *caring for*, *taking care*, *care reception* and *caring about caring*. Similar to care-knowing, the other intellectual virtues of reflexive critical openness, strong objectivity and principled autonomy also have their distinctive facets. Yet as acquired, cognitive dispositions of all of these virtues are suited to the feminist agenda of effectively challenging traditional stereotypes which have been oppressive to women.

Dalmiya's critical analysis of the nature and practice of caring aims to avoid the oppressive constructions of both feminine and religious care. Let us consider the way in which critical reflection upon the agent's rational principles shapes her knowledge of care. In 'Dogged Loyalties: A Classical Indian Intervention in Care Ethics', Dalmiya takes two examples from *Mahabharata*. She illustrates the way in which the carers – in one parable, a parrot, and in another, a male warrior – each resists following the instrumental reason of the ancient supreme Vedic god, Indra.[31] Indra is the 'self-styled opponent' to the voice of care in both parables.[32] In this context, the principle of loyalty has a categorical force. It is rationally compelling. This rationality is incompatible with ethical principles that strictly follow utilitarian rules or simply fulfil a social agreement. Yet its incompatibility with instrumental rationality does not make loyalty any less rational. The parrot in remaining loyal to 'its tree' (i.e. its shelter), even when that tree ceases to flourish, resists any utilitarian appeal to follow a rule for achieving its own health and preserving its own life. Similarly, the male-warrior, Yudhishthira, acts out of loyalty to a dog, even if the dog represents the most unworthy beast, because of a deeper debt to life, calling for repayment.

On a superficial reading, both parables may have suggested a potential for irrationality due to a self-destructive tendency inherent in caring for another – for a tree or a dog – at the apparent expense of human flourishing. Nevertheless, Dalmiya demonstrates the critical difference between an intellectually virtuous act and a self-destructive one.[33] She advocates both a re-enacting of, and a critical distancing from, the stories found in Indian scriptures, in order to recognize in precisely what sense the religious practice constitutes not a loss of self, but a creation of new relationships. An ethic of caring, as found in the parables of an Eastern religious tradition, involves both the creation of bounds through compassion (*anukrosha*) and the maintenance of bonds through loyalty (*bhakta*). This ethic, then, takes as its norm a fundamental aspect of social and inter-species relationships. The fundamental value of this norm gives a powerful reason for bringing about an inclusive sort of care-knowing, including even non-human species.

Thus Dalmiya demonstrates that practical wisdom is not limited by either the utilitarian idea of human flourishing or one's commitment to a social contract. Instead it emerges from a fundamental dimension of true being.[34] This is not to celebrate a one-sided, existential commitment to a personal project; so we should not read the desire to preserve a tree, or the whole eco-system, as blindly irrational. Instead this is to advocate the development of a virtue that (i) reflects upon the lives of oneself and others; that (ii) imagines what it is to need to care, to receive and to give the mutually right sort of compassion; and (iii) interacts with both one's own and others' lives, even when the other is completely unlike oneself. The depth of care-knowing, once acquired, becomes part of the unifying virtue of practical wisdom; that is, aiming quite literally at true philosophy, the care-knower develops a love of wisdom.

Strong objectivity

For the third intellectual virtue I modify Sandra Harding's notion of 'strong objectivity', which I discussed in *A Feminist Philosophy of Religion*. It is ten years since Harding herself rethought her original feminist conception of strong objectivity.[35] Previously, I followed Harding in associating strong objectivity with a certain self-reflexivity, exposing false ideals of neutrality. Harding exposed the weak objectivity of the male-neutral ideal of Enlightenment philosophy.[36] This ideal is assumed by men to be neutral but, in fact, exhibits male qualities exclusive to the men who assume neutrality. Today, if, with Nancy Hartsock and Harding, we again revisit what is meant by the situatedness of feminist standpoint epistemology, we can find an even stronger alternative to the modern ideal agent (observer) theory.[37] Other contemporary female and/or feminist philosophers support this alternative.

A guiding question for this virtue: are we (and if not, should we be) motivated to bring about strongly objective knowledge? By achieving knowledge of how others see us, we as privileged subjects are, in turn, transformed. The subjective is changed by what is, or has been thought to be, outside of it, i.e. the objective. The reflective and imaginative capacities of care-knowing are increased through self-revelation and self-remaking. To gain knowledge from another's perspective on one's own life, we need to 'assess the nooks and crannies in our subjectivities'.[38] In Harding's more recent terms, a 'robust reflexivity' is necessary, if we expect our listening to, and thinking from, the lives of others to transform our weakly objective perspectives. The goal of strong objectivity is, thus, less partial knowledge of our material and social reality, not absolute knowledge.[39]

The development of strong objectivity involves the cognitive social abilities implied in the virtue of reflective critical openness. And yet the latter, especially as presented by Fricker, is in tension with elements of Harding's strong objectivity. I would like to make this tension productive. Recall that Fricker finds the accounts of experience of the least powerful subjects in society an epistemic resource.[40] At the same time, Fricker is highly critical of (Harding's) feminist standpoint epistemologist's idea of locating epistemic privilege in the marginalized other of society. Fricker admits discovering the grain of truth in standpoint theory: 'Their hermeneutical disadvantage [i.e. that of the least powerful in society] can become a positive epistemic resource, so long as one can learn to listen.'[41] The challenge is to develop the capacities of reflexively and imaginatively listening, not just for ourselves, but for the other. In thinking from another's point of view about our own social location, we (i) recognize the injustice both of our epistemic practices and in our drive to become intellectually virtuous, (ii) eliminate this injustice; and, in this way, (iii) change how we see ourselves. The problem with this challenge is potentially a self-contradiction: be just and gain knowledge of the other for the cultivation of oneself.

Feminist philosophers have hugely disagreed concerning the very possibility of reversing standpoints.[42] Is it possible to hear the other without either exploiting the other for one's own sake, or imposing one's own view onto the other? The danger is seeing oneself only in the other. Iris Marion Young is a cogent critic of claims to imagine oneself in the position of another. She insists that we need not – and, in any case, it is an illusion to think we can – reverse points of view.[43] An 'asymmetrical reciprocity' prevents the more privileged knower, e.g. those of us who are privileged women philosophers, from gaining the necessary ground for understanding the particularity of the other. For Young, merely allowing the other to speak is the most we can do. To what degree would Fricker agree with Young? Dalmiya does not, and I would agree with the latter's critical query: 'What would prevent us from hearing only what we expect to hear in their voices?'[44] The answer given by feminist epistemologists such as Harding is that learning from others' lives necessarily involves struggle. I would urge us to acknowledge that *feminism* is *essentially* about *struggle*; not merely listening, but listening as essentially struggling. As Le Doeuff adds, patiently hoping is a virtue when we hope in an *active* sense; active hope is, in her words, like a religious person's praying that minds will be freely changed over time. Elsewhere I have argued that a feminist standpoint is the result of an epistemological struggle; it is not a spontaneous perspective which a woman possesses by virtue of being a woman.[45] Strong objectivity becomes the goal of this struggle – and hope – when the demand is for less partial knowledge of ourselves and for more justice in our interactive practices. However, neither feminist nor more traditional philosophers find it easy to work out how this sort of 'objectivity' can be coherent.

A distinction between two different sorts of objectivity helps: absolute objectivity and objectivity as a process.[46] Confusion of these two makes for tensions, if not contradictions. For example, Thomas Nagel seeks absolute objectivity as 'a view from nowhere'. Yet confusion comes in when, at times, Nagel also seeks to incorporate subjectivity, and so pursue the second sort of objectivity. The latter process of objectivity incorporates subjectivity rather than trying to eliminate it; objectivity, then, is achieved by understanding more and more about one's subjectivity and, especially, the limits of one's own perspective. The feminist standpoint theorist's strong objectivity is closer to this second conception. In contrast, the weakness of absolute objectivity is the drive to abstract more and more from any subjective elements in one's point of view, until no more subjectivity is left and absolute objectivity is reached: then, the goal is the view from nowhere. Ironically, this absolute objectivity is both weak and impossible to achieve.[47]

Consider this in context. We can recognize how the hermeneutical disadvantage of those women excluded from locations of social power in religious communities becomes a positive, epistemic resource for gaining greater objectivity. Not only by listening to the accounts of marginalized subjects, but by recognizing the views of women who 'fracture' the coherence of the dominant point of view, we begin to see the limitations of the privileged perspective on religious practices.[48] If successful, listening to the story given by the least powerful can become a positive epistemic resource, even though this may mean a radical disruption to the dominant interpretation of social reality. For instance, disruption of dominant interpretations of the ethics represented by stories in Indian or Hebrew scriptures, whether *Mahabharata* or *Genesis*, could lead to the transformation of certain ritual–ethical practices.[49] Disruption of the dominant interpretations of the confessional, or Eucharistic, roles of holy men and women in (Christian) religious ceremonies could transform liturgical–political practices. In a similar vein, the positive epistemic resource of hearing the stories of the least advantaged women could emerge at the level of the metaphors and symbols by which religious believers conceptualize the deity to whom they address praise, prayers and lament. Today these addresses would be shaped by ethically disruptive events such as legal or illegal abortions; death of an adolescent by an ecstasy overdose; death of a child of starvation in an underdeveloped country, and so on.

How, then, does a contemporary religious authority learn from the prayers or laments of women who struggle as a result of unsuccessful IVF treatment? Or what do we learn from women and men who live with untreated infertility because of lack of funds? The variety and complexity of ethical dilemmas increase as choice concerning reproduction increases. For another example, today a woman who objects to abortion on religious grounds can face the choice of giving birth to a baby who will not live; here medical knowledge and religious conviction place the pregnant woman in a situation which some would say is inevitably immoral. These ethical questions come more and more into the field of philosophy of religion as subjects of knowledge are no longer restricted to the interests of successful, white, European, Christian male philosophers.[50]

In addressing these ethical issues, we make an important shift to virtue theory. This moves us from the dominant, scientific methodology of traditional epistemology to an explicitly value-ladened methodology; we critically and imaginatively reflect these values in our interaction with other (feminist) subjects. Although the truth-claims of philosophers about reality tend to be formulated in scientific terms, or true propositions, philosophers of religion will (unwittingly) find that religious facts – in the sense of facts being shaped by the hermeneutic practices of a religious community or group – are more suitably construed as social facts which are variously interpreted. In Fricker's terms, social facts reflect the epistemic pluralism which results from no convergence on the truth of the matter. Instead there is bound to be more than one rational point of view on any social, or religious, fact of a matter. The crucial point for developing strong objectivity is to preserve the possibility of the full story. By listening closely to the accounts of religious experience that are given by people who are among the least powerful in society, we find that, far from advocating a view from nowhere – or the vantage of an ideal observer (see note 55) – we seek to incorporate the ever-greater understanding of our subjectivities in the pursuit of practical wisdom.

Principled autonomy

The fourth intellectual virtue is principled autonomy, which derives from Onora O'Neill's major rethinking of Kant's ethics.[51] Rejecting the popular, and unwittingly exclusive, idea of individual autonomy, O'Neill has promoted a principled autonomy, 'expressed in action whose maxims or *laws could be adopted by all others*'.[52] O'Neill draws an analogy between reasons for belief and reasons for action:

> We do not offer others reasons for believing if we communicate with them in ways that we know they will find unintelligible; we do not offer others reasons for acting if we present them with proposals for action that we know they will find unadoptable.[53]

By analogy, O'Neill's revised conception of principled autonomy can serve as an intellectual virtue for feminist philosophy of religion. It would enable the general intelligibility of our reasons for acting, and so enhance our interactive, religious practices.[54] This virtue is associated with the modal idea of seeking to recognize, and to know how to apply, principles that all *could* follow. Similar to strong objectivity, principled autonomy is a virtue which would make redundant any notion of an ideal agent/observer in ethical and epistemological theories. And yet this does not eliminate the functioning of certain limiting ideals or guiding principles.

The guiding question is, are we motivated to bring about reasons for believing which everyone could make intelligible, and reasons for acting which all could adopt or follow? This would be to achieve 'self-legislation' that puts the stress on legislation, not self. In other words, we would not advocate individual autonomy as represented by the male ideal of the detached agent who acts gratuitously. Self-legislation means a reflexive act which is free, not oppressive, in enabling each self-reflective agent to follow general principles. Legislative, or law-like, means according to principles that all could adopt. This would include principles such as supporting and assisting others. It would also include trust, which is the general principle behind what is its opposite, i.e. suspicion or deception. We could not will that deception becomes a universal law because it is only possible to deceive against a background of persons who trust; deception is the exception and not something which could become a general principle for all. Deception is not, as O'Neill demonstrates, a principle of reason, since it is not universalizable, i.e. it could not be adopted by all. Whatever principle is not adoptable by all would work against self-legislation and hence, principled autonomy.

I urge that principled autonomy become an intellectual virtue for feminist philosophers of religion, motivating an alternative to the ideal observer theory, which treats 'God' as the unmatchable ideal of cognition and morality.[55] In this alternative context, divine authority is antecedent to practical reason. The ideal observer theory would be decisively challenged by the reflexive, imaginative and interactive levels of principled autonomy. On a reflexive level, the ideal observer would, by definition (i.e. as perspective-less), necessarily fail to learn from a process of acknowledging one's own perspective, social location or the partiality of one's subjectivity. Thus the ideal agent would fail to offer reasons for believing or acting that all could follow. In fact, no-one could be this ideal agent, since no-one could follow the model of seeing the world from a God's-eye-view, as an 'omni-view', i.e. being omniscient, omnibenevolent, omnipotent, omnipercipient. On an imaginative level, the ideal observer would necessarily fail to grasp the particularities of the other, since the ideal agent, in claiming to be all-knowing, would have to maintain the opposite: a constant erasure of the limitations of any exclusively exotic, or subjective, perspective. The exotic would not be embraced, but excluded, by this ideal agent who, by definition, must exclude what is not all-knowing, not all-perceiving, so basically the distinctive particularity of any human moral agent. On an interactive level, it is difficult to see how there could be an interactive exchange between different subjects, since the ideal agent is meant to represent what would be the unlimited, universal ideal agent, not conflicting, limited views; hence, this ideal observer–agent would have to exclude the particularity of the other, which in being particular is limited to that particularity. This is precisely the opposite of principled autonomy, which seeks to make judgements taking into account the vulnerability of each agent. Ironically, the ideal observer theory seems to render the ideal agent someone who values only his own supposedly omniscient, individual self, since he is unable to reflect upon his own locatedness, to imagine the points of view of others or to interact through struggle and dialogue with each other. Thus the 'ideal' agent will fail to know not only the differences between subjects, but the practical wisdom which would unite us in true being.

Wisdom in the sense of *phronesis* becomes the unifying goal of virtue epistemology. Bringing together the more specific intellectual virtues, wisdom is not only the heart and head of Aristotle's philosophy, but the essence of Kant's intellectual virtue of autonomy. O'Neill directs us to Kant's assertion that 'the power to judge – autonomously, that is, freely (according to principles of thought in general) – is called reason'.[56] O'Neill's picture of Kantian autonomy paints a very different figure than the one portrayed by Iris Murdoch.[57] Murdoch's Kantian archetype is 'free, independent, lonely, powerful, rational, responsible and brave'.[58] Rather than Kant's own conception, Murdoch seems to give us an existentialist picture of autonomy, capturing the Sartrean character who bears the burden of a radically atomistic and gratuitous freedom. Murdoch rejects this conception of autonomy, but so would Kant!

I insist upon a strong connection between Aristotle and Kant on virtue and knowledge, but also a link between Suchon and Kant. Kant's assertion (quoted above) about autonomy's principles of thought and action links the power to judge – freely – and reason. Equally, Suchon links freedom and reason, as capacities that all men and women possess: we only need to discover this power for ourselves.[59]

Conclusion

To conclude, I urge thinking more openly with female philosophers such as Suchon about the nature of reason, autonomy and our norms or principles of thought and action. In the seventeenth-century, Suchon put her finger on what would become – and perhaps was already – the central weakness of traditional Western philosophy of religion. Her unwitting contribution to feminist philosophy of religion is the realization that our knowledge of the divine could not, without contradiction, be abstracted from a concrete, temporal context. Instead a more coherent view recognizes the divine in knowledge infused with the particularities of our everyday thinking and acting. Suchon's account retains the particular without giving up the guiding principle of the free and reflective use of reason by every human being. In this way, we also retain a certain dimension of the universal.

Reflective critical openness, care-knowing, strong objectivity and principled autonomy together motivate the feminist pursuit of the best possible shape for practices, relationships, thoughts and principles related to the divine. This grounding would link the rational authority and autonomy/vulnerability[60] of every woman and man with the accompanying virtues. This pursuit will not end until it achieves the practical wisdom, which is the very essence of *philosophia*, i.e. the love of wisdom. Thus the epistemological–ethical approach to feminist philosophy of religion promises to be expansive. We have yet to treat our insight on emotion as a fundamental component of epistemological–ethical pursuits.[61] Nevertheless, this affective component, inherent in our listening and talking with each other, is already accessible in our collaborative thinking. Such thinking enables us to cultivate intellectual virtues, reflecting both what makes us human, but not divine, and what is grasped as an intuition of the divine.

Notes

1   See G. Jantzen, *Becoming Divine: Towards a Feminist Philosophy of Religion*, Manchester: Manchester University Press, 1998; also see P. Anderson, 'Correspondence with Grace Jantzen', *Feminist Theology*, 25 (September 2000): 112–119; G. Jantzen, 'Feminist Philosopher of Religion: Open Discussion with Pamela Anderson', *Feminist Theology*, 26 (January 2001): 102–109. Unfortunately, this open correspondence was published in the wrong order; instead of Anderson's first letter appearing followed by Jantzen's first letter, and then, each of the replies to the other; the reader finds that Anderson's letter and reply to Jantzen were published together, even before Jantzen wrote to Anderson or replied. So these two issues of *Feminist Theology* should be read side-by-side, going from one issue to the other and back again. Anderson's first letter in issue 25 (pp. 112–118) should be read and then Jantzen's first letter in issue 26 (pp. 102–107); now, back to Anderson's second letter in issue 25 (pp. 118–119) and finally to Jantzen's second letter in issue 26 (pp. 107–109).

2   Fionola Meredith demonstrates the dangers of post-structuralist positions which polarize terms and impose artificial binaries, creating oppositional debates about the subject of philosophy; see Meredith, 'A Post-metaphysical Approach', Chapter 4.

3   For a brief account of the recent emergence of virtue epistemology, see L. Zagzebski and A. Fairweather, 'Introduction', in A. Fairweather and L. Zagzebski (eds) *Virtue Epistemology: Essays on Epistemic Virtue and Responsibility*, Oxford/New York, NY: Oxford University Press, 2001, pp. 3–14.

4   Amy Hollywood presents a critical alternative to the focus on belief found in *A Feminist Philosophy of Religion* (Chapter 15). And yet her alternative may be closer to Anderson's present concern with religious and epistemic practices in the formation of virtues as a shift away from more abstract approaches to epistemology.

5   Jantzen, *Becoming Divine*, pp. 11–28.

6   Anderson, 'Correspondence with Grace Jantzen', pp. 112–119; and P.S. Anderson, 'Feminist Theology as Philosophy of Religion', in S. Parsons (ed.) *Cambridge Companion to Feminist Theology,* Cambridge: Cambridge University Press, 2002, pp. 51–55.

7   For background on the mistrust of female intuition, see M. Le Doeuff, *Hipparchia's Choice: An Essay Concerning Women, Philosophy, etc.* trans. Trista Selous, Oxford: Blackwell, 1991; and *Le sexe du savoir*, Paris: Aubier, 1998, pp. 25–79.

8   P.S. Anderson, *A Feminist Philosophy of Religion: the Rationality and Myths of Religious Belief*, Oxford: Blackwell, 1998, and 'A Case for a Feminist Philosophy of Religion: Transforming Philosophy's Imagery and Myths', *Ars Disputandi: The Online Journal for Philosophy of Religion*, 1 (2000): 1–35.

9   L.T. Zagzebski, *Virtues of the Mind: An Inquiry into the Nature of Virtue and the Ethical Foundations of Knowledge*, Cambridge: Cambridge University Press, 1996, pp. 165f. Further on I will suggest that this cognitive motivation displays an affinity to the desire for knowledge, represented by Eve in Suchon's novel interpretation of the Genesis story.

10   Dalmiya also argues that the moral realm (or 'excellence in ethics') should be an integral part of

being spiritual; see V. Dalmiya, 'Loving Paradoxes: A Feminist Reclamation of the Goddess Kali', *Hypatia*, 15: 1 (2000): 146–147; cf. Chapter 16.

11 V. Dalmiya, 'Why Should A Knower Care?' *Hypatia*, 17: 1 (Winter 2002): 38–39.

12 See P.S. Anderson, 'Autonomy, Vulnerability and Gender', *Feminist Theory*, 4: 2 (2003): 149–164.

13 This shift from disputes about the 'justification' or 'warrant' of religious belief to the cultivation of intellectual virtues may render the disputes redundant. For a defence of this shift, see Zagzebski, *Virtues of the Mind*, pp. 176–184 and 258–299; cf. A. Plantinga, *Warrant: The Current Debate*, New York, NY: Oxford University Press, 1993; and *Warranted Christian Belief*, New York, NY: Oxford University Press, 2000; R. Swinburne, *Epistemic Justification*, Oxford: Oxford University Press, 2001, pp. 188–191.

14 M. Fricker, 'Epistemic Justice and a Role for Virtue in the Politics of Knowing', *Metaphilosophy*, 34: 1–2 (January 2003): 154–173.

15 False beliefs about female (mystical) experience as hysterical and 'female ideas' as in fact male, deriving from a male partner, priest or teacher, are critically exposed in Le Doeuff, *Le sexe du savoir*. In response to this history, less biased testimonial sensibility would not mean a neutral or completely impartial point of view – which, as we will see in the discussion of the third virtue of strong objectivity, is impossible (cf. S. Harding, 'Rethinking Standpoint Epistemology', in L. Alcoff and E. Potter (eds) *Feminist Epistemologies*, London: Routledge, 1993, pp. 49–82; S. Harding, *Is Science Multicultural? Postcolonialism, Feminisms and Epistemologies*. Bloomington, IN: Indiana University Press, 1998). For an alternative approach to female subjectivity, seeking to bring a woman's 'incipient story' into the words of testimony, see Meredith, 'A Post-metaphysical Approach'.

16 M. Fricker, 'Power, Knowledge and Injustice', in J. Baggini and J. Stangroom (eds) *New British Philosophy: The Interviews*, London: Routledge, 2002, p. 90 (emphasis added).

17 In Greek mythology, Cassandra is the daughter of Priam, King of Troy, who was given the power to foretell the future from the god Apollo (whose love for her went unrequited). Although her prophecies were trustworthy, no-one believed her, since she was not given the appropriate social marker, i.e. not the sort of power by which she would have been trusted. In particular, when she told her father what would be the outcome of the Trojan War, warning him of the fall of Troy, he did not believe her; the outcome of that war proved she should have been trusted.

18 Onora O'Neill refers to the Cassandra problem in her discussion of trustworthiness without trust, demonstrating that unlike misplaced trust, 'misplaced mistrust' cannot be simply eliminated by improving trustworthiness (O'Neill, *Autonomy and Trust in Bioethics*, Cambridge: Cambridge University Press, 2002, pp. 141–142 and 165f). We see this problem of the refusal to trust authority in ethics today.

19 See Luke 24:1–12; cf. John 20:1–18.

20 Le Doeuff, *Le sexe du savoir*; cf. M. Le Doeuff, 'Long Hair, Short Ideas', in *The Philosophical Imaginary*, trans. Colin Gordon, London: The Athlone Press, 1989, pp. 113–117.

21 Ibid., pp. 71–124; also see M. Le Doeuff, 'Feminism is Back in France – Or is it?', *Hypatia* Special Issue: Contemporary French Women Philosophers, edited by Penelope Deutscher, 15: 4 (2000): 253.

22 C. Taliaferro, 'Divine Cognitive Power', *International Journal for Philosophy of Religion*, 18 (1985): 133–140; and *Contemporary Philosophy of Religion*, Oxford: Blackwell, 1998, pp. 108–123.

23 Taliaferro, *Contemporary Philosophy*, pp. 122–123

24 Ibid., 108–109.

25 G. Suchon, *Traité de la morale et de la politique*, Lyon: B. Vignieu, 1693, II, pp. 1–7, 14, 32–34, 191 (this book is available in microfilm from Paris's Bibliothèque nationale).

26 Suchon, *Traité de la morale et de la politique*, II, pp. 139, 151–159.

27 For the terms of reliabilism, externalism and internalism, see Zagzebski and Fairweather, 'Introduction', *Virtue Epistemology*, pp. 3–6.

28 Dalmiya looks at practices of caring in religious texts, involving compassion and loyalty; cf. V. Dalmiya, 'Dogged Loyalties: A Classical Indian Intervention in Care Ethics', in J. Runzo and N. Martin (eds) *Ethics in the World Religions*. Volume III, in 'The Library of Global Ethics and Religion', General Editors, Runzo and Martin. Oxford: One World, 2001, pp. 293–308.

29 Dalmiya, 'Why Should A Knower Care?' pp. 34–52; cf. Annette Baier, 'The Importance of What We Care About: A Reply to Frankfurt', *Synthese*, 53 (1982): 274; E. Sosa, *Knowledge in Perspective*, Cambridge: Cambridge University Press, 1991; Zagzebski, *Virtues of the Mind*, pp. 8, 10–12 and 259f.

30 Dalmiya, 'Why Should A Knower Care?'

31   Dalmiya, 'Dogged Loyalties', pp. 294–297; cf. *Mahabharata* (third century BC) trans. Chakravarthi V. Narasimhan, New York, NY: Columbia University Press, 1965.

32   Dalmiya, 'Dogged Loyalties', p. 294.

33   This critical difference is illustrated by the powerful account of loyalty (*bhakti*) in the stories of Mirabai as presented by Parita Mukta; see Anderson, *A Feminist Philosophy of Religion*, pp. 171–174, 177–189; cf. P. Mukta, *Upholding the Common Life: The Community of Mirabai*, Delhi, India: Oxford University Press, 1994. Mukta's more recent writing creates a story from the narratives of the lives of members of her own family; her family's story is woven together with history, life-stories and songs such as those about Mirabai; see P. Mukta, *Shards of Memory: Woven Lives in Four Generations*, London: Weidenfeld & Nicolson, 2002. Compare Mukta's account with the philosophical argument in Dalmiya, 'Loving Paradoxes', Chapter 16.

34   Dalmiya, 'Dogged Loyalties' and 'Why Should A Knower Care?'.

35   Harding, 'Rethinking Standpoint Epistemology'; cf. S. Harding, 'Why Has the Sex/Gender Distinction Become Visible Only Now?', in S. Harding and M. Hintikka (eds) *Discovering Reality: Feminist Perspectives on Epistemology, Metaphysics, Methodology, and Philosophy of Science*, Dordrecht, the Netherlands: Reidel, 1983, pp. 311–324.

36   For her earlier account of strong objectivity, see Anderson, *A Feminist Philosophy of Religion*, pp. 18–19, 70–83.

37   N. Hartsock. 'Feminist Standpoint Revisited', in her *Feminist Standpoint Revisited and Other Essays*, Oxford: Westview Press, 1998, pp. 227–253; and Harding, *Is Science Multicultural?* especially, pp. 188–194. Also, see note 55.

38   Dalmiya, 'Why Should A Knower Care?', p. 43.

39   For robust reflexivity, see Harding, *Is Science Multicultural?* pp. 188–194; and Harding, 'Comment on Hekman's "Truth and Method: Feminist Standpoint Theory Revisited": Whose Standpoint Needs the Regimes of Truth and Reality?' in C. Allen and J. Howard (eds) *Provoking Feminisms*, Chicago, IL: University of Chicago Press, 2000, pp. 50–57.

40   Fricker, 'Power, Knowledge and Injustice', p. 90.

41   Ibid.

42   I.M. Young, 'Asymmetrical Reciprocity: On Moral Respect, Wonder and Enlarged Thought', in R. Beiner and J. Nedelsky (eds) *Imagination, Judgment and Politics: Themes from Kant and Arendt*, Oxford: Rowman and Littlefield Publishers, 2002, pp. 205–228. For the problems in trying to reverse standpoints, see M. Lugones and E.V. Spelman, 'Have We Got a Theory for You! Feminist Theory, Cultural Imperialism and the Demand for "The Woman's Voice"', *Women's Studies International Forum*, 6: 6 (1983): 573–581; and A. Seller, 'Should the Feminist Philosophy Stay at Home?', in Kathleen Lennon and Margaret Whitford (eds) *Knowing the Difference: Feminist Perspectives in Epistemology*, London: Routledge, 1994, pp. 230–248.

43   Young, 'Asymmetrical Reciprocity'.

44   Dalmiya, 'Why Should A Knower Care?', p. 38.

45   P.S. Anderson, 'Standpoint: Its Proper Place in a Realist Epistemology', *Journal of Philosophical Research*, xxvi (2001): 131–153; also see H. Harris, 'Struggling for Truth', *Feminist Theology*, 28 (September 2001): 40–56; a revised version of the latter is reprinted here, Chapter 5.

46   In a review of Thomas Nagel's *A View from Nowhere* (Oxford: Oxford University Press, 1986), Jonathan Dancy distinguishes absolute objectivity and a Hegelian form of objectivity; I describe the latter as a process; see J. Dancy, 'Contemplating One's Nagel', *Philosophical Books*, 29: 1 (1988): 1–16.

47   For an account of the possibility of the absolute conception, see A.W. Moore, *Points of View*, Oxford: Oxford University Press, 1997.

48   See Walton, 'Women Writing the Divine', Chapter 8.

49   See notes 28 and 29.

50   For instance, Philip Quinn employs an example of a Roman Catholic woman who is trying to work out her religious and secular reasoning on the topic of abortion. Quinn himself proposes to take the role of this woman and try to discover if there is any secular reasoning which the woman could employ to support her religious commitment against abortion (cf. P. Quinn, 'Religion, and Politics, Fear and Duty', in Jerald Wallulis and Jeremiah Hackett (eds) *Philosophy of Religion for a New Century*, Dordrecht, the Netherlands: Kluwer Academic Publishers, forthcoming 2003). Quinn's act of taking the standpoint of a woman, in thinking about abortion, raises the question of the possibility of reversing roles; for the problems with this, see Young, 'Asymmetrical Reciprocity', pp. 205–228.

51   O. O'Neill, *Constructions of Reason: Explorations of Kant's Practical Philosophy*, Cambridge: Cambridge

University Press, 1989; *Towards Justice and Virtue: A Constructive Account of Practical Reasoning*, Cambridge: Cambridge University Press, 1996; *Bounds of Justice*, Cambridge: Cambridge University Press, 2000, especially pp. 150–156. For her discussion of principled autonomy, see O. O'Neill, *Autonomy and Trust*, pp. 83–95.

52   O'Neill, *Autonomy and Trust*, p. 85.

53   O. O'Neill, *Autonomy and Trust*, p. 91.

54   Dalmiya, 'Dogged Loyalties', pp. 293–308; and 'Why Should A Knower Care?'.

55   See C. Taliaferro, 'The God's Eye Point of View: A Divine Ethic', in H. Harris and C. Insole (eds) *Faith and Philosophical Analysis: A Critical Look at the Impact of Analytical Philosophy on the Philosophy of Religion,* Aldershot, Hampshire: Ashgate Publishing Ltd, forthcoming; and P.S. Anderson, 'What's Wrong with the God's Eye Point of View: A Constructive Feminist Critique of the Ideal Observer Theory', in H. Harris and C. Insole (eds) *Faith and Philosophical Analysis*, forthcoming.

56   O'Neill, *Autonomy and Trust in Bioethics*, p. 90; cf. I. Kant, *The Conflict of Faculties* (1783), trans. M. Gregor and R. Anchor in Kant, *Religion and Rational Theology*, A. Wood and G. di Giovanni (eds), Cambridge: Cambridge University Press, 1996, 7: 27.

57   I. Murdoch, *The Sovereignty of the Good*, London: Routledge & Kegan Paul, 1970, p. 80.

58   Ibid.

59   G. Suchon, *Traite de la morale*; and Le Doeuff, 'Feminism is Back in France – Or Is It?', 243–255.

60   Anderson, 'Autonomy, Vulnerability and Gender', 149–164.

61   See, for example, M. Nussbaum, *Upheavals of Thought: The Intelligence of Emotions,* Cambridge: Cambridge University Press, 2001.

PART TWO

Philosophical topics in feminist philosophy of religion

TOPIC I

■ Divinity

Introduction

THE CONCEPT OF GOD constitutes one of the main themes for Anglo-American philosophy of religion. The three chapters that follow suggest something of the way in which feminists are engaging with a notion of divinity more broadly defined. Philosophers of religion have tended to focus upon formulating arguments for the existence of God and reflecting upon the character of 'the God of theism': a concept of God derived from perceived parallels between the monotheistic faiths, and divorced from any specific religious tradition. Feminist work in this area has challenged the masculinist bias of such accounts, whilst offering creative understandings of what constitutes 'divinity'. Early feminist analysis such as that conducted by Mary Daly focused on exposing the parallels between the construction of God and patriarchal values. Her own notion of divinity suggested a move from 'God' as noun to God as verb: divinity is thus understood as describing a way of acting in the world. Similarly, the work of Carol Christ, with whom Heather Walton engages, develops the idea that women need the Goddess if they are to fully realize their potential. Feminist thealogy thus takes on a creative approach to the notion of divinity that connects it with female self-awareness. In the work of Grace Jantzen this notion is further developed, and the desire to 'become divine' pervades her account of what a feminist philosophy of religion should look like.

Tina Beattie's chapter focuses on the significance of the maternal for feminist constructions of the divine. Writing from a Catholic perspective, she challenges the failure of feminist philosophers of religion to engage with the figure of Mary, Christ's mother. Mary is invariably seen as problematic for women, embodying as she does the paradoxical features of virginity and motherhood. Yet Beattie argues that such criticisms reflect the peculiarly Protestant character of Anglo-American philosophy of religion. There may be a desire to criticize what she calls 'modernity's God', but there is a singular failure to engage with Protestantism's own excluded female in a more creative way. Beattie shows the significance of considering Mary as a means of undercutting the abstract God of philosophical theism. She urges feminist philosophers of religion to move away from the generalized account of God that informs the method for philosophy of religion, towards a greater appreciation of the significance of religious context for the development of the divine. Such a move, she suggests, will lead to more subtle, and thus more effective, accounts of divinity.

Heather Walton's chapter grapples with the task of women writing the divine, and, in this way, reflects how feminist writers have begun to make significant interventions in the field of philosophy of religion. Walton focuses on the ways in which 'women's experience' has given content to women's theology; but she argues persuasively against any univocal claims about women and their experiences. Women are different from men, but they are also different from each other, and their relations to the divine accordingly offer a rich, but also disruptive, form of writing. Walton forces her readers to think and write about their own uniqueness that disturbs, but also binds them together. Women writing the divine will have to risk any form of comfort, for writing the divine means confronting reality in all its dangers and possibilities.

Melissa Raphael's approach to the divine derives from her engagement with her Jewish faith, and in offering a feminist response to the Holocaust challenges the patriarchal formation of the divine that she believes overly influences Orthodox responses to the *Shoah*. In such a context, human freedom becomes the key value, and she suggests that through engaging with the experiences of women in the death camps, a different set of values emerges. What mattered to these women was relationship, and Raphael employs this value to develop a relational account of the divine as the feminine *Shekinah*: the presence of God in the world.

Chapter 7

Tina Beattie

REDEEMING MARY: THE POTENTIAL OF MARIAN SYMBOLISM FOR FEMINIST PHILOSOPHY OF RELIGION

THERE WOULD SEEM TO BE A broad consensus among feminist philosophers and among many feminist theologians in Anglo-American academia that Marina Warner is correct when she says of the Virgin Mary, 'the reality her myth describes is over; the moral code she affirms has been exhausted.'[1] Even philosophers who are concerned with the symbolization and ethics of motherhood such as Christine Battersby, Grace Jantzen and Sarah Ruddick[2] accord no significance to Mary as a potential resource for the feminist reclamation of maternity and natality, even though, in Jantzen's case, she is specifically concerned with religious symbolism. Pamela Sue Anderson, in *A Feminist Philosophy of Religion*, also avoids any focused analysis of the cult of Mary, which she describes as the 'obvious dominant western myth stabilizing/retarding individual and communal identities of women, in relation to the divine.'[3] This elision of a Marian perspective is particularly interesting given that Battersby, Jantzen and Anderson all engage extensively with the work of Luce Irigaray, who accords considerable significance to Mary in her writings. While many English-speaking feminists represent Mary as an irredeemably patriarchal religious symbol, Continental theorists such as Irigaray and Julia Kristeva have a more nuanced approach that recognizes both the oppressive and the liberating potential of the Marian tradition for women.

In the first part of this chapter, I consider possible reasons for this, and I question the extent to which feminist philosophy of religion as represented by the pioneering work of Anderson and Jantzen, with their stated concern for contextuality, historicity and corporeality, risks perpetuating the failings of their masculine counterparts in adopting an ahistorical and decontextualized definition of religion. For example, in *Becoming Divine*, it is unclear whether Jantzen is criticizing 'The post-Enlightenment western cultural symbolic, especially as that has been informed by Protestantism',[4] or 'religion as it has been constituted in the west'.[5] If the former, then her position is obscured by too many references to Western religion in general. If the latter, she reifies religion and fails to acknowledge the complexity and fluidity of religious history, despite her stated intention to 'develop a gendered genealogy of religion'.[6] The genealogy of religion in the West has been shaped by intense conflict about the role of the Virgin Mary in the Christian faith, creating a polarity between Protestant and Catholic beliefs and practices. For a philosopher of religion concerned with maternal symbolism, such historical factors are hardly insignificant. Anderson observes that 'the empirical realist subject of conventional philosophy of religion is bound to be blind to historically specific beliefs surrounding the Western concepts of God',[7] but she too shows no real historical awareness of the circumstances in which Western concepts of God have been affected by changing philosophical and theological perceptions, not least with regard to the importance accorded to the Mother of God. So I begin by offering a brief outline of why I think feminist philosophers of religion need to be more contextualized in their analyses of religious narratives. Otherwise, they risk the colonisation of religious otherness through the elision of difference, because their homogenized and over-generalized accounts of Western religion (i.e. Protestant Christianity) leave the religious other – in this case, the Catholic other – no space from which to speak. In order to demonstrate that the Marian tradition can indeed provide a space of religious and gendered alterity from which a woman might speak differently of religion, subjectivity and God, in the second part of the chapter I offer a necessarily brief feminist refiguration of two core Marian symbols – 'virgin' and 'mother' – by reading early Christian writings in engagement with Irigaray and Jacques Derrida.

Marginality and religious otherness

Marginality and otherness are key themes in post-modern discourse, to such an extent that they have solidified into concepts that now themselves stand in need of deconstruction. In feminist religious studies, 'otherness' is usually associated with gender, but there is a tendency to overlook or minimize the ways in which religion also functions as a locus of alterity – the religious subject and the secular subject can be constituted as mutual 'others', but between and within religions, the politics of inclusion, exclusion, identity and otherness operate across a multitude of fluctuating historical and social boundaries. So if, as Anderson suggests, 'New thinking from the lives and beliefs of marginalized others, as well as new visions, become essential for the transformation of philosophy of religion',[8] then one has to recognize that 'marginalized others' is not a static category but a contingent term, whose meaning derives from what counts as normative in any particular context.[9]

In a 1996 article, Jantzen refers to 'the deep channel that separates England from France when it comes to conceptualizing what religion is'.[10] She argues that, whereas British and American philosophers of religion tend to be preoccupied with questions about the nature and existence of God within predominantly Christian paradigms of belief, terms such as 'God/Religion, the subject, and language'[11] are problematized in Continental thought, where 'the masters of suspicion' such as Freud, Marx and Nietzsche are taken more seriously. Thus, 'in French thinking, the force of the "masters of suspicion" is . . . in the ways in which they show Enlightenment assumptions about the rational subject, language, and religion to be radically destabilized by the combined factors of the unconscious and socially constructed ideology.'[12] She goes on to consider the resistance by British philosophers of religion to 'reading in the margins',[13] a practice that allows for the 'return of the repressed'[14] through the exploration of the literary and linguistic unconscious by Continental thinkers such as Derrida and Irigaray.

Interestingly, however, although she points to 'the prominence of religious themes in Continental thought',[15] neither in this article nor in her book, *Becoming Divine*, does Jantzen consider that religion might be a factor in the difference between British and Continental philosophy. Anglo-American philosophers of religion work in a context defined by white Protestant males whose identity as rational subjects of the Enlightenment remains secure because they conform to that philosophical worldview, including its privatization and individualization of Christianity. They do not read in the margins because they see themselves as unquestionably normative. In *Becoming Divine*, those who provide the resources for Jantzen's philosophical critique are either Jewish (Arendt, Derrida, Freud and Levinas), Catholic (Lacan and Irigaray) or Orthodox (Kristeva). Jantzen identifies women and non-Western religions as 'others' vis-à-vis the philosophy of religion, but Jews and Catholics are also marginalized others from the perspective of Protestantism in American and British academia. Only through sensitivity to the historical complexity of Western religious narratives, and through greater specificity in the use of religious terminology, is it possible to recognize sites of religious as well as gendered otherness from which to deconstruct the dominant Protestant tradition of the philosophy of religion.

In seeking to understand and hopefully overcome these ideological blindspots, I would argue for greater attentiveness to the ways in which religious symbols function in their historical, cultural and political contexts. Thus, if Anglo-American philosophy of religion is to be challenged for its exclusion of the rationality of female desire (Anderson), or of birth, maternity and materiality (Jantzen), then it is necessary to look not across traditions but within the tradition of Western religious thought, to ask when and why particular patterns of belief have emerged and how they have been shaped by the politics of power and gender. By recognizing the ways in which Kantian philosophy and Protestant theism are situated on this side of a violent symbolic rupture, amounting to a collective Oedipal crisis within Christianity that denied access to the maternal body and reinstated the man of reason as the subject of Western philosophy and politics, it becomes possible to undertake a historically and socially contextual analysis that might allow for a return of the repressed, through the recognition of what has been sacrificed in order to create modernity's God and modernity's man.

Christian matricide

The Western man of reason is modelled on the virile and virtuous male citizen of the ancient Greek and Roman worlds. *In Speculum of the Other Woman*, Irigaray traces the genealogy of this masculine construct, with its repression and denial of the mother, matter and the female body, from Freud's theory of the Oedipus complex back to Plato's allegory of the cave. She refers to Freud as 'a prisoner of a certain economy of the logos, of a certain logic, notably of "desire", whose link to classic philosophy he fails to see'.[16] Yet Irigaray herself is constructing a metanarrative, a theory of female non-subjectivity that runs the same risks of abstraction, universalization and homogenization that she criticizes in her male philosophical counterparts and predecessors. Contrary to Irigaray's uni-dimensional survey of Western philosophy, the tradition that links Derrida and Lacan to Freud, Kant, Descartes and Plato is one of discontinuity, because for the first 1,500 years of the Christian tradition, it was interrupted if not entirely overwhelmed by a different concept of subjectivity. This was premised upon Christian beliefs about personhood, understood not solely in terms of the rational and autonomous male individual but more importantly in terms of an interdependent community organically related to one another, to nature and to God through its incorporation into the sacramental, maternal body of the Church.

Jean Bethke Elshtain, in her book *Public Man, Private Woman*, argues that

> The prevailing image of the Divine Father and Christian king in medieval Christendom had been considerably softened in belief and practice, in part through devotion to the Holy Mother. The Church itself was conceived as a 'feminine' institution (Holy Mother Church) despite the fact that Church governance, though not all religious orders, consisted of male hierarchies. Christianity is also a religion in which the Son of God, though sacrificed, is ultimately triumphant and who himself embodies such 'feminine' qualities as mercy, forgiveness, and compassion.
>
> With the breakup of the medieval synthesis and the demise of the power of the spiritual 'sword' over the secular, lines of division hardened within Christian Europe along vectors of nationalism sanctioned, in some instances, by a state church governed by a lordly father. A more stern and forbidding image of the patriarchal God emerged.[17]

There have been few feminist attempts to examine the impact of the Reformation on the Western understanding of God, subjectivity and society, despite the fact that this was a religious revolution that focused its most destructive energies on the figure of the mother. The faceless Madonnas and empty niches in churches and cathedrals across Britain attest to the ferocity with which the maternal dimension of Catholic Christianity was expunged from Protestant religious consciousness. This was not an organic process, but the violent repression of a dimension of religious thought and practice that suffused daily life, in contexts that were often of particular significance for women. For example, Eamon Duffy gives details from a catalogue of monastic reliquaries compiled prior to their destruction by Cromwell's commissioners in 1535, many of which were frequented by pregnant women and women in labour. Duffy comments, 'In attacking monastic "superstition", . . . Cromwell's men were striking at institutions with a central place in popular religious practice, perhaps most unexpectedly in the domestic intimacies of pregnancy and childbirth.'[18]

Sarah Jane Boss, in her book *Empress and Handmaid*, traces the relationship between Marian theology and iconography and changing attitudes towards nature and the female body in Western culture. Using the Frankfurt School of critical theory as a resource, she argues that the history of Marian devotion reflects the West's increasing domination of nature, so that

> the development of Marian devotion in Western Europe provides an index of humanity's increasing mastery over the natural and social orders, and its aspiration to ever greater domination. The high medieval perception of Mary as the powerful Queen of Heaven was produced by a society in which people experienced themselves as dependent upon their physical environment, and in which that environment was the bearer of sacred power, as Mary herself was the bearer

of God incarnate. The modern image of the Madonna as a humble young girl at prayer signifies on the one hand a Christian culture in which the created order is seen as very distant from its Maker, and on the other hand a wider society in which 'nature' is supposed to be ever more subordinate to control by human invention.[19]

These historical examples attest to my argument that the figure of the Virgin Mary is of profound significance for feminist research into Western religious traditions and symbols. The Reformation and its aftermath saw a widespread transformation in attitudes towards the maternal body and the material world, which has significance not only for the role and representation of women, but for the Christian understanding of the relationship between nature, humanity and God. Roger Horrocks writes that 'The history of Mary is . . . a history of our civilization and its dislocation'.[20] With this suggestion in mind, I turn now to consider ways in which psycholinguistic philosophy makes possible the feminist reappropriation of Christian maternal feminine symbolism associated with the Virgin Mary, as a rich resource for the development of a Western feminist religious consciousness.

Redeeming symbols – the archaeology of Marian symbolism[21]

In his early work, Paul Ricoeur argues that reflection on symbolic meanings 'must embrace both an archaeology and an eschatology'.[22] This is because symbols have 'a double intentionality'[23] which serves to conceal as well as to reveal meanings. Freud's theory of psychoanalysis allows for the disclosure of the revelatory potential of symbols which, arising as they do out of the primal levels of human consciousness, are also invested with irrational fears and phantasms that distort and conceal the truths they are ultimately capable of revealing.

I find Ricoeur's theory of the archaeology of symbols helpful in explaining why Irigaray, through the psycholinguistic analysis of Marian symbolism, is able to suggest meanings and refigurations that resonate with some of the insights of the early Church, although I suspect that she is unaware of such resonances. In order to demonstrate what I mean by this, I am going to give a brief summary of the context in which Christianity's earliest beliefs about Mary were formulated, and I shall then look at the symbolic possibilities of Mary's virginal motherhood.

Christianity's foundational beliefs about Mary were not peripheral to reflection on the nature of Christ, but lay at its very heart. If Christians wanted to say something about the God-man Jesus, and if they wanted to find a language that suggested both the continuity and transformation of the human condition in the incarnation, then they believed that they had to do so in the context of motherhood. Had patristic theologians been willing to bow to Docetism and posit belief in a divine avatar who only appeared to be human, or had they agreed with the Manichees and Gnostics that God could not possibly become fully identified with the corruption of the material world, they would more easily have won their battle for the hearts and minds of the ancient world. But they knew that the uniqueness and mystery of the incarnation lay in its capacity to overcome dualism through the reconciliation of God and creation, word and flesh, time and eternity, and those who eventually came to be included in the canon of Christian orthodoxy regarded this as a non-negotiable aspect of their faith. Olivier Clément refers to the emphasis that the second-century apostolic fathers laid on the 'dignity of the body' which is 'at the very opposite pole from any ontological dualism, either the dualism of a degenerate Platonism . . . or that of Manicheism and Gnosticism'.[24]

Elizabeth Grosz writes:

> Western metaphysics is structured in terms of binary oppositions or dichotomies. Within this structure the opposed terms are not equally valued: one term occupies the structurally dominant position and takes on the power of defining its opposite or other. The dominant and subordinated terms are simply positive and negative versions of each other, the dominant term defining its other by negation. Binary pairs such as good/bad, presence/absence, mind/matter, being/non-being, identity/difference, culture/nature, signifier/signified, speech/writing and man/woman mark virtually all the texts of philosophy, and provide a methodological validation for knowledges in the West.[25]

It was this philosophical structure that the early Church sought to challenge, and it did so through insisting upon the pairing of opposites to form a reconciling whole. Thus the claim that Christ was born of a virgin mother has threefold significance – theological, anthropological and philosophical. Theologically, Mary's virginity is the vertical or transcendent dimension of the incarnation. It affirms that Christ is fully God, because, to quote Ambrose of Milan (c. 339–397), 'That a virgin should give birth is a sign of no human, but of divine mystery.'[26] Anthropologically, Mary's motherhood is the horizontal or immanent dimension of the incarnation. It affirms that Christ is fully human, and thus challenges those who denied the possibility of the humanity of God. In the second century, Ignatius wrote: 'Be deaf, then, to any talk that ignores Jesus Christ, of David's lineage, of Mary; who was really born, ate, and drank; was really persecuted under Pontius Pilate; was really crucified and died.'[27] Mary's motherhood not only identifies Christ fully with the human flesh, it also incorporates him into human history from the beginning. Thus by the second century, she was already being referred to as the New Eve, in a prismatic series of analogies with Genesis that compared her to the virgin earth from which the New Adam was born and to the first woman of the new creation.

Philosophically, in referring to the virginal motherhood of Mary, the early Church was searching for a language that might express the inexpressible mystery of the incarnation. Maximus the Confessor (580–662), writes, 'For the same person is both virgin and mother, instituting nature afresh by bringing together what is opposed, since virginity and giving birth are opposed, and no-one would have thought that naturally they could be combined.'[28] The combination of 'virgin' and 'mother' was seen as a challenge to established meanings that, from the perspective of contemporary psycholinguistics, was intentionally deconstructive in its approach. Referring to Derrida's idea of the chiasmus, Jantzen describes it as

> a figure which symbolizes both that we cannot start from nowhere – we are always already situated in relation to a dominant text/discourse and culture and must take it seriously – and also that we need to look for ways in which that dominant reading is intersected by its own undoing, thus opening a gap for thinking differently.[29]

The virginal motherhood of Mary signifies such a chiasmus: her motherhood affirms that Christ did not 'start from nowhere' but was born of a woman into the context of human culture and history, while her virginity is the point at which the divine intersects with that history, undoing it and 'opening a gap for thinking differently'.

With these suggestions in mind, I turn now to explore the implications of Mary's virginal motherhood for the Christian understanding of God, of human personhood and of redeemed womanhood. This necessarily entails the summarization of complex and multi-faceted symbolic meanings, but I hope that I can at least give a sense of the ways in which a feminist refiguration of Marian theology can provide as potent a challenge to contemporary philosophical theism as the earliest claims about Mary provided to Greek philosophy.

Mother of God

For the early Church, Mary's humanity was the counterpoint to God's divinity, and it was the chiasmus, the point of intersection between the two, that constituted the space of the incarnation. From a critical perspective, one could argue that this symbolics perpetuates the association of femininity with matter, immanence and the body, and the association of masculinity with the spirit, transcendence and God. The early Church never entirely broke free of these associations, and Janet Martin Soskice argues that the influence of Neoplatonism led early Christian thinkers to revive Platonic and Aristotelian 'generative metaphors in their idea of the One as first principle, fertile power, and source of all life'.[30] Nevertheless, as long as Mary occupied a central position in the doctrine of the incarnation, her motherhood was a potent reminder that the Christian God was not reducible to the omnipotence, omniscience and aseity of Greek philosophical concepts of the divine. In her study of motherhood in the Christian tradition, Clarissa Atkinson writes:

> The One of Greek philosophy required no mother and was not subject to pain and suffering and humiliation: Hellenized intellectuals objected not to the oneness of the Christian God but to the humanity of Christ. Their conversion, like that of the gnostics, demanded that they be persuaded of the reality and necessity of the Incarnation, and thus of the birth of Christ to Mary.[31]

The first Christians shared with some modern feminists the recognition that the most effective way to challenge philosophical dualism was through an appeal to the maternal body and its relationship to the incarnate Christ. Perhaps the most robust example of this is in Tertullian's description of the birth of Christ, in which he responds to Marcion's contempt for the human flesh. Tertullian writes:

> Come now, beginning from the nativity itself, declaim against the uncleanness of the generative elements within the womb, the filthy concretion of fluid and blood, of the growth of the flesh for nine months long out of that very mire. . . . Inveigh now likewise against the shame itself of a woman in travail, which, however, ought rather to be honoured in consideration of that peril, or to be

held sacred in respect of [the mystery of] nature. . . . This revered course of nature, you, O Marcion [are pleased to] spit upon; and yet, in what way were you born? You detest a human being at his birth; then after what fashion do you love anybody? . . . Well, then, loving man [Christ] loved his nativity also, and his flesh as well.[32]

Irigaray argues that

The womb is never thought of as the primal place in which we become body. Therefore for many men it is variously phantasized as a devouring mouth, as a sewer in which anal and urethral waste is poured, as a threat to the phallus or, at best, as a reproductive organ.[33]

Tertullian invokes these male phantasms by confronting the philosophical subject with the bloody process of his own birth. He suggests that the incarnation redeems the carnality of childbirth and restores it to its rightful place as the natural origin of human life.[34] Tertullian's graphic description is unique as far as I know in its visceral affirmation of the processes of pregnancy and childbirth, and it was not long before Christianity succumbed to a dualistic symbolics that purged Christ's birth of any hint of blood or body fluids. Nevertheless, patristic writers persistently defended the birth of Christ against those who argued that the maternal body could have no association with the incarnation of God because of the polluting power of the female flesh. Augustine challenges his opponents by saying: 'Suppose I am not able to show why he should be born of a woman; you must still show me what he ought to avoid in a woman.'[35] The incarnation refutes those who would present self-actualization as an ascent from the body to the soul, from the material to the immaterial, from the sensible to the transcendental, from the mother's body to the father's word. The human flesh that unites Christ with Mary is as intrinsic to his identity as the divinity that unites him with God, for without her there can be no true salvation of the flesh.

Irigaray argues that Freud's failure to attribute significance to the mother's role in the origins of life and the formation of language and culture exposes the hidden dynamic at work in the Western social order: 'The entire male economy demonstrates a forgetting of life, a lack of recognition of debt to the mother, of maternal ancestry, of the women who do the work of producing and maintaining life.'[36] Margaret Whitford summarizes Irigaray's interpretation of Plato's allegory of the cave as follows:

Truth has come to mean leaving behind the Mother (the cavern) and her role in reproduction. Truth becomes linked to the paternal metaphor, the Idea/Father engendering copies and reflections without apparent need for the other partner normally required in processes of reproduction. The Platonic myth stages a primal scene in which Plato gradually manages to turn his back, like the pupil/prisoner, on the role of the Mother altogether.[37]

The extent to which the early Christians implicitly shared this insight and sought to challenge established philosophical concepts of divinity and truth through an appeal to the maternal body is expressed in one of Augustine's Christmas Day Sermons based on

Psalm 85:11: 'Truth has sprung from the earth, and Justice has looked forth from heaven.' The tone of the sermon is one of jubilant rejoicing:

> Truth, which is in the bosom of the Father (Jn 1:18), has sprung from the earth, in order also to be in the bosom of his mother. Truth, by which the world is held together, has sprung from the earth, in order to be carried in a woman's arms. Truth, on which the bliss of the angels is incorruptibly nourished, has sprung from the earth, in order to be suckled at breasts of flesh. Truth, which heaven is not big enough to hold, has sprung from the earth, in order to be placed in a manger.[38]

Some of the radical implications of these patristic insights have long been neglected or repressed in the development of the Christian tradition, in Catholicism as well as in Protestantism. However, Mary remains a central figure of considerable potency in the Catholic tradition, and perhaps that is why Catholic Christianity has never succumbed to the kind of abstract metaphysics that feminist philosophers such as Jantzen and Anderson criticize in Anglo-American philosophy of religion. The precondition for Protestant theism, which allows it to posit a rationalised and disincarnate God akin to that of Greek philosophy, is the matricide of the sixteenth and seventeenth centuries, and only a historically contextualized and culturally specific philosophy of religion can ask what this means for women.

However, if the maternal body of Mary is a potential resource for feminist philosophy, her virginity is a more problematic proposition, having become a potent symbol of men's fear of female sexuality, and representing as it does an impossible double bind for women who are confronted with an ideal of virginal motherhood as the ultimate model of holiness. Nevertheless, in what follows I suggest ways in which this too has its origins in a theological vision that affirms rather than negates the personhood of woman, so that the Virgin Mary can be interpreted as a radical symbol of female subjectivity with a different symbolic configuration from that of the masculine subject of philosophical discourse.

Ever virgin

The title 'ever virgin', which refers to the Catholic doctrine that Mary was a virgin before, during and after Christ's birth, is one of the earliest Marian titles. In a culture preoccupied with scientific facts, this has become one of the most contested of all Catholic beliefs about Mary. However, in what follows I suggest that Patristic writers used the language of virginity and sexuality in a highly metaphorical sense, not unlike the way in which Irigaray uses the imagery of sexual intercourse to explore the symbolic possibilities of the sexuation of language and culture. This means that the patristic understanding of language has more in common with contemporary psycholinguistic theory than with the various forms of realism, literalism and nominalism that later came to be associated with Christian theological and Western philosophical discourse. In what follows, therefore, I propose the symbolic refiguration of perpetual virginity, not as a literal description of the state of Mary's hymen, but as a figurative statement about the redemption of woman. In arguing this, it needs to be borne in mind that, in the early Church, Mary was understood as the generic woman – in her, all womankind was redeemed, including Eve.[39]

Lacan argues that the symbolic phallus is the primary signifier, the symbol which stabilises meaning and holds the social order in place, since the language of socialization begins with the Oedipal crisis when an awareness of sexual difference first assigns us to our place in the social order in relation to our possession or lack of the phallus. However, representing as it does the prohibition of the father associated with the incest taboo, the phallus conceals its symbolic function, which is to control the space between the speaking subject and the maternal body through the displacement of desire, serving as a substitute for the mother while at the same time forbidding access to her. As Irigaray argues in her subversive appropriation of Lacan, his theory exposes a social order constructed around the denial of desire, the linguistic negation of the body and nature, the repression of the maternal relationship through the privileging of the paternal law, and the non-symbolization of the woman as subject. If women are to be liberated from the position of non-subjectivity and absence to which this phallocentric scenario consigns them, the phallus itself has to be removed from the scene of representation in order for a more fluid and life-enhancing exchange to become possible.

This leads Irigaray to suggest that the Christian story of the annunciation implies the potential displacement of the symbolic phallus by appealing to the angel as an alternative symbol of mediation. While from a Lacanian perspective the phallus bars access to the forbidden body of the mother, the angel opens the way to a more fertile form of exchange which allows for the expression of desire. Language thus functions no longer in terms of repression and concealment, but rather in terms of fecundity and celebration. The angel initiates a new relationship between language and the body, through the restoration of symbolic significance to the maternal body. Irigaray describes Mary as

> A virgin in the eyes of the traditional order. Receptive to the whole of the world – to all that is forgotten and all that is to come. Listening to the breath of the spirit? That overcomes walls dividing property. Seed that goes beyond and stops short of any word ever written, any land ever conquered. That might perhaps give birth to a new figure of history? Arriving from beyond the sky, by the mediation of an angel? . . . The patriarchal machine locks, clogs.[40]

From the time of the earliest Marian writings of Justin and Irenaeus in the second century, the mutual virginity of Eve and Mary has been a prominent feature in the interpretation of woman's role in the fall and redemption, despite the fact that Genesis makes no specific reference to Eve's virginity. The recapitulation of Eve in Mary requires that Mary, like Eve, is a virgin, but Mary remains a virgin while Eve loses her virginity after the fall. Irenaeus refers to the virgin Eve being 'seduced by evil'.[41] Tertullian, in suggestively sexual imagery, writes:

> For it was whilst Eve was yet a virgin that the word crept in, which was the framer of death. Into a Virgin, in like manner, must be introduced the Word of God who was the builder up of life: so that by that same sex whence had come our ruin, might also come our recovery to salvation. Eve had believed the serpent, Mary believed Gabriel. The fault which the one committed by believing,

the other by believing blotted out. But it might be said, Eve conceived nothing in her womb from the devil's word. Nay, but she did conceive; for the devil's word became to her as seed, that she might conceive as an outcast, and bring forth in sorrow.[42]

Tertullian gives graphic expression to ideas that are widespread in patristic texts, with his emphasis on the word as the impregnating source, and the ear as the site of penetration. It is not the serpent but the word that penetrates Eve, just as in Lacanian psycholinguistics power lies not in the penis but in the linguistic function of the symbolic phallus. Ephraem writes that 'as death entered and infused itself by the small winding aperture of the ear, so did life penetrate and pour itself into the new ear of Mary'.[43]

The Christian doctrine of original sin derives from the Book of Genesis, Chapter 3, with its themes of verbal seduction and the acquisition of moral knowledge (the knowledge of good and evil) as precursors to the loss of sexual and social innocence. It is interesting that in an age when psychoanalysis has given an authenticating twist to the idea of original sin with its Oedipal narrative of separation, shame and concealment, the doctrine is being called into question by many Catholics. To suggest that the association between sex and sin derives primarily not from physical intercourse but from the perpetuation in language of the consequences of the fall through the operation of forbidden desire might be to recover some of the original meaning of Genesis, retaining the symbolic relevance of the idea of original sin while liberating it from its Augustinian biological literalism.

With this in mind, I want to consider how virginity becomes a symbol which has particular significance for the redemption of women, when the symbolic significance of the hymen is interpreted in engagement with Derrida. Derrida uses the word 'hymen' as an unstable concept which has the potential to disrupt established relationships between binary opposites, and I would suggest that this opens creative doors in the feminist imagination with regard to the resymbolization of Mary's virginity.

In Greek and Latin mythology, Hymen is the god of marriage and of the laws governing family relationships. Derrida plays with the ambivalence inherent in the word as a signifier of both virginity and marriage, to expose the unstable position of the subject in relation to the alliance with language and the social contract. He writes:

> At the edge of being, the medium of the hymen never becomes a mere mediation or work of the negative; it outwits and undoes all ontologies, all philosophemes, all manner of dialectics. It outwits them and – as a cloth, a tissue, a medium again – it envelops them, turns them over, and inscribes them.[44]

In Derridean terminology, hymen belongs with other words such as trace, *différance*, supplement, *pharmakon*, dissemination and woman, as a sign of ambiguity and irresolution. Grosz refers to Derrida's use of hymen as signifying 'rupture and totality', such that it is 'poised over both binary categories, revealing that they are impossible or untenable'.[45] Kelly Oliver writes that 'Within the economy of Derrida's corpus the hymen is a marriage and an undecidable "concept" that calls any alliance into question . . . "hymen" becomes associated with an economy that operates outside of the economy of the proper.'[46]

Neither inside nor outside, the hymen occupies a site of symbolic mediation. Traditionally, it represents an exchange of property between men – the unruptured hymen allows the father to hand his daughter over as unspoiled property to her husband, whose rupturing of the hymen seals the marriage alliance and perpetuates the social contract. But the unruptured hymen also symbolizes the space between the two, the ambiguity of that which has not yet established its proper place. It is prior to and outside the symbolic order, and its meaning is uncertain. Its symbolic significance is established only in absence – the unruptured hymen is only socially determinative when ruptured, and therefore it is a conceptual impossibility which defers meaning. The virgin is a woman whose place in relation to the laws governing the patriarchal economy has not been finally determined.

However, for virginity to be a sign of woman's freedom from the law, it must be perpetual if one accepts Derrida's understanding of the ambivalence of the unruptured hymen. Virginity acquires patriarchal significance when it is lost. The ruptured hymen becomes retrospectively a sign not of the woman's integrity and independence, but of her commodification. The virgin daughter has been preserved intact by her father, in anticipation of the transaction by which her body will pass into her husband's possession. So only perpetual virginity symbolizes the recreation of woman in a way which is outside the control of phallic signification. If Mary is a virgin only for as long as it takes to produce God's son, and after that she becomes Joseph's wife in a sexual relationship, then retrospectively Mary will be seen to have been nothing more than an object of exchange between God the father and Joseph her husband. Her virginity does not have intrinsic value for her own personhood but only in functional terms as part of the necessary apparatus of the incarnation. Mary's perpetual virginity affirms woman's eternal liberation from the power of the phallus/serpent. The virgin birth is a Christological symbol relating to the incarnation, but Mary's virginity is also an anthropological symbol relating to the redemption of women from the consequences of the Fall. In Mary's case, the potential ambivalence of the unruptured hymen resolves itself into an affirmation of woman's integrity and freedom from the laws of patriarchy.

The attribution of virginity to Eve and Mary exploits this ambivalence through developing a dialectic between virginity as sign of fallenness in Eve and virginity as sign of redemption in Mary. In Eve's case, the ambivalence resolves itself in the other direction, and her virginity becomes associated with sexual subjugation and incorporation into the law of patriarchy. The loss of Eve's virginity is a sign of marital domination, but this functions in such a way that her original freedom before God is also lost and the patriarchal mind sees only her subordination and her inferiority. In other words, when Christianity forgets the subtlety of its own dialectic, it falls prey to the patriarchal view of Eve as the one who has always been subordinate to Adam. So although Genesis clearly states that woman becomes subordinate to her husband as a consequence of the fall, Christian interpreters have tended to see this as already implied in the order of creation.[47] The hymen, once ruptured, loses its potency and becomes a retrospective sign of the woman's place in the patriarchal social order, from the beginning.

Conclusion

The foregoing has been an attempt to sketch some of the possibilities of the Marian tradition for feminist philosophy and theology, inviting readings that challenge the androcentrism both of traditional Catholic Mariology and of Protestant philosophy of religion. Space precludes a discussion of the implications of this for the viability of a feminist philosophy of religion dissociated from any religious tradition or practising community of interpretation, but I shall conclude by identifying the questions which I think my own work poses to Anderson and Jantzen respectively. I focus on them because together their work opens new frontiers in the philosophy of religion, with the potential for critical and creative dialogue with feminist theology.

With regard to Anderson, her quest to articulate a philosophy of religion in general leads her to adopt a *sui generis* model of religion, with an expressed concern to avoid focusing only on Western myths and traditions. This means using a modified Kantian epistemology as a basis for analysing the coherence and rationality of women's beliefs across a range of cultural and historical contexts, as is illustrated by her choice of the Greek myth of Antigone and the medieval Hindu cult of Mirabai. However, a number of postmodern philosophers and theologians argue for a narrative approach, which recognises that the rationality and coherence of religious beliefs must be assessed within rather than between traditions.[48] In other words, each religious tradition has its own rules of grammar, and it is only by understanding these that one is able to assess whether or not any particular doctrine or practice is rational within that tradition. Although so far these arguments have been produced by scholars who by and large ignore the challenge of feminism and who also sometimes seem to have a barely concealed agenda to reassert the hegemony of Christian theology in the academy, nevertheless I think they pose a challenge to philosophers such as Anderson who would insist upon the applicability of Western philosophical analysis to non-Western religions. Hinduism is a vast and complex set of beliefs with its own philosophies and theologies, and its own historical narrative. Given that it has never postulated the kind of deity that preoccupies Protestant theistic philosophy, it is hard to see how the story of Mirabai can provide a coherent basis from which to pose a feminist challenge to such philosophy. Protestantism and Kantian philosophy share the same historical and religious context as the cult of Mary, and I have suggested that it is more fruitful and more rational to interrogate philosophy of religion from that perspective, even though it means that feminist philosophy of religion might have to understand itself more modestly as feminist Christian philosophy. To argue this does not entail confessionalism, nor does it necessarily dissolve altogether the boundary between philosophy and theology. However, it does call into question why that boundary is so zealously defended even by feminist thinkers in English-speaking academia, when, as Jantzen argues, it barely exists in the work of Continental philosophers such as Derrida and Irigaray, who provide such a rich resource for feminist thought.

Turning to Jantzen, the logic of my own position makes me more sympathetic to her radical feminist assault on philosophy of religion. Yet Jantzen has, I believe, argued herself into an impossible and indeed self-defeating position. In postulating an immanentist, pantheistic religious imaginary without doctrines, beliefs or truth claims, she does not say how such a revolution in religious thought and practice is to be brought about. Who is to mediate between the academy and the lives of ordinary women and men seeking this more life-affirming religion? Jantzen's book is a highly theoretical argument, abstracted from any religious context that would give it meaning outside the academic environment. Apart from the ethical problems of a Western philosopher proposing the wholesale demolition, not only of philosophy of religion but of religious beliefs and practices that have sustained, inspired and consoled countless millions, Jantzen's ideas have nowhere to go unless (a) she proposes to found a new religion, or (b) she makes a transition from philosophy to theology, and commits herself to realising her work within the beliefs and practices of an existing tradition. If the former, then she will have to adopt some rather extreme disciplinary practices, to root out the near-universal heresies of truth and belief that she condemns. If the latter, then perhaps only Catholic Christianity can provide a viable religious framework for what she proposes, because from the perspective of feminist Marian theology, her philosophy reads like a Mariology *in absentia* – a graceful, complex and persuasive critique of Protestant theism that has been inexplicably evacuated of its core Christian referent. This would be a Catholicism revitalised and transformed almost beyond recognition by feminism. Yet as questions about the body, nature, motherhood and God press with ever more urgency upon Western consciousness, English-speaking feminists might need to recognise that the ideological barriers of the Reformation and the Enlightenment must be dissolved in the quest for a more holistic way of being and living in the world. 'With the drawing of this Love and the voice of this Calling,' we might, with T.S. Eliot, 'arrive where we started/And know the place for the first time'.[49]

Notes

1   M. Warner, *Alone of All Her Sex: The Myth and the Cult of the Virgin Mary*, London: Picador, 1990 [1976], p. 338.
2   See C. Battersby, *The Phenomenal Woman: Feminist Metaphysics and the Patterns of Identity*, Cambridge: Polity Press, 1998; G.M. Jantzen, *Becoming Divine: Towards a Feminist Philosophy of Religion*, Manchester: Manchester University Press, 1998; S. Ruddick, *Maternal Thinking: Towards a Politics of Peace*, London: The Women's Press, 1990.
3   P.S. Anderson, *A Feminist Philosophy of Religion*, Oxford: Blackwell, 1998, p. 149.
4   Jantzen, *Becoming Divine*, p. 21.
5   Ibid., p. 11.
6   Ibid., p. 78.
7   Anderson, *A Feminist Philosophy*, p. 86.
8   Ibid., p. 119.
9   I do not want to under-estimate the complexity and subtlety of Anderson's philosophical arguments, and her appeal to feminist standpoint epistemology in theory recognises this contingency and the demands it makes upon the scholar in terms of identity and otherness. However, I do not think she applies this with sufficient rigour to her own positioning in terms of religious subjectivity, and her analysis of religion therefore risks presenting itself as 'the objective view-from-nowhere, understood in the sense of the God's-eye view' (Anderson, *A Feminist Philosophy of Religion*, p. 36) that she criticises in the male philosophical subject.
10   Jantzen, 'What's the Difference? Knowledge and Gender in (Post)modern Philosophy of Religion', *Religious Studies*, 32 (1996): 431–438, 432; reprinted in Part One of this volume.
11   Ibid., p. 435.
12   Ibid., p. 436.
13   Ibid., p. 439.
14   Ibid., p. 438.
15   Ibid., p. 446.

16   L. Irigaray, *Speculum of the Other Woman*, trans. G.C. Gill, Ithaca, NY: Cornell University Press, 1985, p. 28.

17   J.B. Elshtain, *Public Man, Private Woman: Women in Social and Political Thought*, 2nd edn, Princeton, NJ: Princeton University Press, 1993, p. 105.

18   E. Duffy, *The Stripping of the Altars: Traditional Religion in England 1400–1580*, New Haven, CT and London: Yale University Press, 1992, p. 385.

19   S.J. Boss, *Empress and Handmaid: On Nature and Gender in the Cult of the Virgin Mary*, London and New York, NY: Cassell, 2000, p. 15.

20   R. Horrocks, 'The Divine Woman in Christianity', in A. Pirani (ed.) *The Absent Mother: Restoring the Goddess to Judaism and Christianity,* London: Mandala, 1991, pp. 100–135, 121.

21   The ideas in the rest of this chapter are developed in more detail in T. Beattie, *God's Mother, Eve's Advocate: A Marian Narrative of Woman's Salvation*, London and New York, NY: Continuum, 2002.

22   P. Ricoeur, 'The Hermeneutics of Symbols and Philosophical Reflection: II', trans. C. Freilich, in D. Ihde (ed.) *The Conflict of Interpretations: Essays in Hermeneutics*, Evanston, IL: Northwestern University Press, 1974, pp. 315–334, 333. It should be noted that in Ricoeur's later work he changed his emphasis from focusing on individual symbols to a narrative approach that considers the linguistic relationship between symbols (see Ricoeur, 'On Interpretation', in *From Text to Action: Essays in Hermeneutics, II*, trans. K. Blamey and J.B. Thompson, London: The Athlone Press, 1991, pp. 1–20, 16). However, for the purposes of this chapter, his earlier theories on the interpretation of symbols remain a useful resource.

23   P. Ricoeur, *The Symbolism of Evil*, trans. E. Buchanan, Boston, MA: Beacon Press, 1969, p. 15.

24   O. Clément, *The Roots of Christian Mysticism*, trans. T. Berkeley, O.C.S.O., London, Dublin, Edinburgh: New City, 1997, p. 69.

25   E. Grosz, *Sexual Subversions: Three French Feminists*, London: Allen & Unwin, 1989, p. 27.

26   Ambrose, *Expos. Ev. sec. Luc.*, Lib. ii.2,3 in T. Livius, *The Blessed Virgin in the Fathers of the First Six Centuries*, London: Burns and Oates Ltd., 1893, p. 131.

27   Ignatius, Letter of Ignatius to the Trallians in *Library of the Christian Classics*, Vol. 1, *Early Christian Fathers*, ed. and trans. C.C. Richardson, London: SCM Press, 1953, pp. 98–101, 100.

28   Maximus the Confessor, *Difficulty, 5* 1052D-1053A, quoted in A. Louth, *Maximus the Confessor*, London: Routledge, 1996, p. 175.

29   Jantzen, *Becoming Divine*, pp. 74–75.

30   J.M. Soskice, 'Trinity and the "Feminine Other"', *New Blackfriars* (January 1993): 2–17, 7.

31   C.W. Atkinson, *The Oldest Vocation: Christian Motherhood in the Middle Ages*, Ithaca, NY and London: Cornell University Press, 1991, p. 108.

32   Tertullian, *The Writings of Tertullian*, Vol. 2, Ante-Nicene Christian Library, Vol. 15, Edinburgh: T & T Clark, 1870, pp. 170–171.

33   L. Irigaray, *Sexes and Genealogies*, trans. G.C. Gill, New York, NY: Columbia University Press, 1993, p. 16.

34   There are interesting resonances between Tertullian's description and Kristeva's maternal subversion of Marian theological discourse in her essay, 'Stabat Mater'. See J. Kristeva, 'Stabat Mater' in *Tales of Love*, trans. L.S. Roudiez, New York, NY: Columbia University Press, 1987, pp. 234–263.

35   Augustine, 'Sermon 51', in J.E. Rotelle O.S.A. under the auspices of the Augustinian Heritage Institute, *Sermons 51–94 on the New Testament*, *The Works of St. Augustine – a Translation for the 21st Century*, III, trans. and notes E. Hill, O.P., 1991, p. 21.

36   L. Irigaray, *Thinking the Difference*, trans. Karen Montin, London: The Athlone Press, 1994, p. 7.

37   M. Whitford, *Luce Irigaray: Philosophy in the Feminine*, London: Routledge, 1991, p. 110.

38   Augustine, 'Sermon 185', n. 1 in *Sermons III/6 (184–229Z) on the Liturgical Seasons*, *The Works of St. Augustine III*, under the auspices of the Augustinian Heritage Institute, 1993, p. 21.

39   See Beattie, *God's Mother, Eve's Advocate*, Chapters 6 and 7.

40   L. Irigaray, *Marine Lover of Friedrich Nietzsche*, trans. G.C. Gill, New York, NY: Columbia University Press, 1991, p. 180.

41   Irenaeus, *Against Heresies*, Books 1–5 in *The Writings of Irenaeus*, Volume 1, Ante-Nicene Christian Library, Edinburgh: T & T Clark, 1868, Book 5, 19, 1.

42   Tertullian, 'On the Flesh of Christ', in *The Writings of Tertullian*, Volume 1, Ante-Nicene Christian Library, Edinburgh: T & T Clark, 1869, p. 17.

43   Ephraem of Syria, Serm. in loc., Opp. Syr. T. ii in Livius, *The Blessed Virgin*, p. 66.

44   J. Derrida, *Dissemination*, trans. B. Johnson, London: The Athlone Press, 1993, p. 215.

45   Grosz, *Sexual Subversions*, p. 30.

46   K. Oliver, 'The Maternal Operation – Circumscribing the Alliance', in E.K. Feder, M.C. Rawlinson

and E. Zakin (eds) *Derrida and Feminism: Recasting the Question of Woman*, London and New York, NY: Routledge, 1997, p. 63.

47 In this connection, see M. Bal, 'Sexuality, Sin, and Sorrow: The Emergence of Female Character (A Reading of Genesis 1–3)', in S.R. Suleiman (ed.) *The Female Body in Western Culture: Contemporary Perspectives*, London, UK and Cambridge, MA: Harvard University Press, 1986, pp. 317–338. Bal explores the tendency in Christian exegetes to interpret the story of creation retrospectively from the account of the fall, thus reading into the account of creation an interpretation of Eve's subordination to Adam which is not in the text.

48 See G. Lindbeck, *The Nature of Doctrine: Religion and Theology in a Postliberal Age*, Philadelphia, PA: Westminster Press, 1984; G. Loughlin, *Telling God's Story – Bible, Church and Narrative Theology*, Cambridge: Cambridge University Press, 1996; A. MacIntyre, *Whose Justice? Which Rationality?*, London: Gerard Duckworth & Co. Ltd, 1988; J. Milbank, *Theology and Social Theory*, Oxford: Blackwell, 1990.

49 T.S. Eliot, 'Little Gidding', in *Collected Poems*, London and Boston, MA: Faber and Faber, 1974, p. 222.

Chapter 8

Heather Walton

WOMEN WRITING THE DIVINE

IN HIS ACCESSIBLE AND ENGAGING text *What is a Story*,[1] Don Cupitt identifies an alliance between philosophy and theology in opposition to the creative and imaginative arts. Theology, he maintains, has accepted the security and power offered by the dominant discourse of non-narrative reason and concealed its own origins in story and drama.[2] As a consequence theology, described as 'Platonism with a biblical vocabulary'[3] now faces, alongside philosophy, a crisis that has been generated by its own deep antipathy to the ambiguous, emotive, embodied and aesthetic aspects of existence.

For Cupitt this aversion to narrative is also a rejection of the feminine and the maintenance of this gynophobia is profoundly dangerous in the current context. He argues that if we are to survive at all, human beings must embrace a feminisation of knowledge. Narrative, as an ancient feminine art, structures experience in such a way as it enables us to inhabit it safely. Just as children draw a house in the style of a human face, 'with a central doorway representing the mouth . . . a little above it windows representing the eyes, the roof – especially when it is thatched – is like a head of hair',[4] so narrative makes inhabitable a formless and potentially unfriendly world,

> [a]nd keeps darkness and death at bay – at least for a while. We are listening to Scheherezade again. Putting off death by telling tales through the night. Narrative, only narrative conquers darkness and the void.[5]

Cupitt's work abounds with celebratory feminine imagery extolling the virtues of narrative. In contrast philosophy and theology are imaged as impotent, inadequate and male.

> [Hume remained] an unmarried male contemplative like virtually every other philosopher from Plato to Kant. He still felt the need to look for philosophical happiness in the same direction as all his predecessors had done, namely towards a timeless and universal, objective order of Reason. This order of Reason had always been a kind of exalted and spiritualised and generalised masculinity, phallogocentrism.[6]

In making an elision between the logocentric discourses of theology/philosophy and gendering these as masculine, in opposition to the exotic femininity of literature, Cupitt is employing the rhetoric of gender in a manner that has become conventional when debating the relation between these disciplines. Indeed current debates on this topic have an extended genealogy going back at least as far as discussions concerning the relations between philosophy and poetry in the work of Plato and Aristotle.[7] Cupitt's intentions when employing these gendered rhetorical codes appear entirely progressive, but more conservative scholars have used gendered distinctions in a manner which is much less favourable to the 'feminine' arts.

T.S. Eliot is frequently taken as representative of a tradition in which literature is perceived as harmoniously complementing philosophical/theological thinking – providing it is clear that paternal authority remains unchallenged. He is particularly concerned to warn against the dangers that ensue when literature abandons its appointed place and seeks to usurp the authority of theology. He opposed those 'who would make literature a substitute for a definitive theology or philosophy' and dedicated himself to 'try and keep the old distinctions clear'.[8] Literature in her own place is worthy of honour but unrestrained she has the potential to corrupt the common cultural home.[9]

Whilst Eliot's concerns may sound anachronistic, the terms of the relation between these distinctive (gendered) spheres is still fiercely contested today. Martha Nussbaum is perhaps the best-known contemporary philosopher who has drawn upon this familiar rhetorical schema in her project to revive philosophical discourse through an accommodation with what has previously been excluded. She argues that philosophical thinking can be enriched through engaging with literary texts that testify to the mystery and beauty of human life and emotion into the world of practical reason. Emotion is another way of knowing the world that has its own genius, and narratives contain emotion in their very structure.

On an initial reading it might appear that Nussbaum is a defender of the genius of literature and adamant in her insistence that 'literature cannot be reduced to philosophical example'.[10] However, a critical consideration of her work reveals that literature is seen as a necessary supplement to philosophy rather than an equal partner. Literature does not change the agenda of philosophy but facilitates a fuller enquiry into the great themes that philosophers have always debated. The emotions that literature supposedly embody are ones that are harnessed to facilitate more effective intellectual enquiry into these issues. And literature is not merely a worthy helpmeet for philosophical thinking; she is also good in bed. Novels seduce with 'mysterious and romantic charms', they lure into 'a more shadowy and passionate world'. They require the reader 'to assent, to succumb'.[11]

In a devastating critique of Nussbaum's project, Robert Eaglestone concludes that she reinscribes traditional conventions through which the relations between logocentric discourse and literature have always been debated. For Nussbaum, 'Philosophy is rational, abstract, universal, fully present on the page as argument. Literature is emotional, specific, contingent, not present as text, but as "real life" situations.'[12] He concludes that Nussbaum reinstates 'binary oppositions, which can no longer have any value for argument when one side is subsumed in the other'.[13]

Affinity and appropriation

This brief discussion of the way in which theology/philosophy and literature are gendered in contemporary debate is intended to make clear some of the conventions which are operative, and which should be acknowledged, when feminist theologians and philosophers of religion approach women's writing. This is particularly important as we too have absorbed the discourse of distinctively gendered fields and continue to employ it because it is so evidently useful to us in our attempts to rewrite the philosophical tradition.

In the vigorous and exciting assault that women are making upon the philosophical/theological regime, 'literary forms'[14] are already playing a very significant role. Pamela Sue Anderson makes the configuration of cultural myths and traditions a priority for the feminist philosopher of religion[15] and Grace Jantzen prophesies that the philosophical discourse which will emerge from a new female symbolic will look 'more like literature that science'.[16] In these and other feminist texts an 'affinity' is implicitly assumed between this feminist project and the work of creative artists – particularly women writers. They are not only taken to be constructing cultural forms which are less oppressive than those claiming the authority of abstract rationality but are also seen as bringing the specific insights of women's embodied experience to bear upon their work.

Clearly feminist philosophers and theologians have much to gain from an engagement with women's writing. The existence of a body of work created by women, many of whom have already emerged as spiritual deviants, provides our own project with an impressive prehistory. We can demonstrate the significance of our own concerns through showing how women have wrestled with similar issues in the past. Furthermore, women's writing abounds in vivid and unorthodox namings of the divine. Some feminist critics have gone as far as to claim that a 'distinctive female sublime' can be identified in women's literature[17] which employs the symbolism of female embodiment to articulate religious yearning and emancipatory visions. If our aim is to generate religious understandings from a female imaginary[18] clearly it would be foolish not to relate to this rich and beautiful material. However, not all women writers have been enthusiastic about the uses that have been made of their work by religious feminists.[19] We have rarely debated amongst ourselves the distinctions between *claiming affinity* and *appropriating* the energies of literature for our own ends. As we stand at a significant moment in the development of a feminist philosophy of religion, it is important to ask what are the uses of literature for us? How can we allow our own project to be challenged and reimagined through an encounter with women's writing? In order to begin to explore these questions I shall examine three differing models of engagement between religious feminism and women's writing as they are presented in the work of Carol Christ, Alicia Ostriker and Kathleen Sands.[20]

Carol Christ and 'women's experience'

Carol Christ began her work in the early days of feminist scholarship and, to the present day, texts which explore the relation between women's writing and theology continue to engage with her thinking.[21] In the 1960s and early 1970s, women scholars and researchers lacked mentors and colleagues. Just as significantly they also lacked authoritative academic sources from which to construct a gendered critique of their disciplines. The works of Simone de Beauvoir and Margaret Mead were frequently quoted because of their recognised status within academic circles. However, a great leap forward occurred when women began to claim that the justification for their dissatisfaction with male-centred thinking came not from borrowed sources considered acceptable to the academy but from something much more immediate and accessible – 'women's experience'.

The activist and egalitarian ethos of feminist circles at this time, coupled with the power of the 'consciousness raising group', served to create an understanding of experience as a source of shared knowledge and political power. The conviction that this knowledge could be translated into an academic resource stimulated women researchers to open up debate on a whole range of issues that had previously been judged unworthy of serious attention. Many questions have since been raised as to whether sufficient commonality exists between women to employ experience as a foundation for feminist politics. However, when arguments based on experience were first rehearsed they had a profound impact and inspired a creative flowering of feminist thinking. What was particularly significant in the work of Christ was the use she made of women's literature as a privileged medium of access to women's experience. This important step was provoked by her encounter with the fiction of Doris Lessing.

In the early 1970s, Lessing was exerting an extraordinary influence upon her feminist readers[22] and her five novel series *Children of Violence* spoke so powerfully to Christ that she 'dreamed about it for weeks'.[23] She felt that her own personal struggles and yearning for change were being given voice through Lessing's central character, Martha Quest. In the course of her studies at Yale, Christ had come to believe that the historical traditions of theology did not reflect women's experience and that the concerns of male theologians within the Faculty appeared far removed from the everyday lives of contemporary women. However, if women were starved of access to resources that enabled them to derive religious meaning from their lives, then literature provided a means to satisfy their hunger. Christ recommended that women 'devour literature which reflects our experience'.[24] Not only will this be personally affirming but, Christ came to believe, in women's writing can be discerned the structure of a spiritual quest described 'from the perspective of women's experience which strikes a chord with many women'.[25] Literature was the vital resource which women could use to generate a new religious consciousness now that they were no longer content to 'read themselves sideways' into theological discourses in which 'the daughters do not exist'.[26]

From a contemporary perspective, Christ's optimistic belief that women could construct a new spiritual tradition, based on their common experience as expressed in literature, appears naïve. Many of the critiques of her work have focused upon the implicit racism that enables her to draw upon literature written by black women to support her own perspectives without acknowledging the very different 'experiences' upon which it draws. The idea that women from entirely different ethnic and social backgrounds can be envisioned as all pursuing a similar spiritual quest, the features of which are archetypal, is one that would no longer find approval amongst religious feminists. But what about the reading practices employed by Christ in the construction of her 'spiritual quest'?

An important thing to note is Christ's requirement that literature be 'realistic'. It should both mirror life in a creditable fashion and provide believable representations of women achieving their emancipatory goals. Feminism is taken as the key to demystifying women's lives and Christ appears to believe that it also gives her the keys to demythologise the literary texts she studies. At times she seems to claim more insights into these than those possessed by the authors themselves and appears to stand in judgement over the women whose work she employs. Her verdicts are not based upon the literary merits of the texts but upon the political requirements of the women's movement. She states that feminists readers require that women authors

> write stories in which the spiritual and social quests can be combined in the life of a *realistic* women. And also one of the tasks facing readers is not to be satisfied with women's literature until it does so.[27]

Christ's commitment to realism as a literary genre is not in itself a problem. Poststructuralist theory has made feminists more alert to the subversive dynamics of non-realist literary forms[28] and for a time it was fashionable to argue that realism as a literary genre was complicit in logocentric thinking. However, articulate defences of the role that realist fiction plays in provoking attitude shifts, particularly in periods of radical change, have led to revisions of this simplistic judgement.[29] What is disturbing, however, is that Christ's influence has encouraged religious feminists to view some forms of women's literature and not others as alternative sacred texts and, when literature is read in this way, interpretative possibilities are restricted and forms of critical orthodoxy ensue.

One of Christ's severest critics, Annelies van Heijst, has argued that commitment to identity politics based upon women's experience and realistic readings of women's literature are inextricably linked in Christ's work. She accuses Christ of inaugurating a tradition of highly restrictive reading practices and being influential in the construction of a canon of realist literature deemed appropriate for theological reflection. Van Heijst contends that this has resulted in a situation in which theology, albeit now feminist theology, is placed in a position of dominance over literature: 'the literary text is an aid for another better type of theology. In that sense Christ is a far more faithful follower of the theological tradition of reading than she herself acknowledges.'[30]

Whilst there are some justifications for van Heijst's criticisms, it is also the case that feminism remains dependent upon conceptualisations of women's experiences and it is difficult to imagine how concrete political objectives can be pursued without this resource. Feminist philosophers of religion like Anderson and Jantzen implicitly acknowledge this fact in their dependence upon such concepts as embodied understanding, situated knowledge and standpoint epistemology – which are the more nuanced and politically accountable means of drawing upon experience today. Nor is it unreasonable to claim that women's literature is one vehicle through which women's ways of knowing the world can be mediated – providing literary texts are not sifted for small chunks of empirical data whilst the other treasures they contain are discarded.

In this frame Christ's legacy is ambivalent. Her work freed women to turn with confidence to their own lives as authoritative sources of understanding and also to enrol women's literature as a resource in the struggle to achieve radical social change. She has encouraged religious feminists to see women's writing as a powerful text capable of challenging male-centred theological discourse. However, she has obscured the vital differences between literature and life which may be precisely those which enable literary forms to challenge feminist politics and practice.

Alicia Ostriker and the feminist revision of tradition

Alicia Ostriker is best known in feminist circles as a literary critic and poet. It is only recently that her deep concern for religious traditions has assumed prominence. Ostriker was formed as a literary theorist by the gynocritical movement which emerged in the 1970s through the pioneering work of a number of North American feminists.[31] Gynocriticism reads literary texts written by women with a number of key concerns in mind. The first of these is the distinct role of the woman author in a culture in which women's literary contributions have been continually obscured and denied. Gynocritics focused attention upon the dynamics of 'writing as a woman' within a male-centred culture and raised for the first time questions concerning the relation of women writers and readers to textual production. Through this scholarly work they achieved a remarkable renewal of interest in the work of significant women authors whose work had been neglected both by the publishing houses and by the critical establishment. This provoked a new recognition that women have always been active and influential in the vanguard of literary movements.

A second focus of interest is the identification of similarities in the work of women authors which gynocritics have claimed can be described as a 'women's tradition' in which 'female culture is center. . . . Beyond fantasy, beyond androgyny, beyond assimilation'.[32] They argued that women have brought their own distinctive concerns into the public arena progressively more confidently as they have secured other emancipatory goals. Gynocritics cherished the hope that women's literature was moving into a new phase in which it would be possible for female authors to draw directly upon women's culture in a manner that was only possible obliquely in the past.[33]

Third, gynocriticism is concerned to demonstrate the impact that women authors and women's traditions have made upon dominant cultural forms. The woman writer is envisioned as engaged in a forensic examination of the tradition which have forged her consciousness *in order* to engage in the painstaking work of claiming her inheritance and revisioning a transformed future. This famous passage from Adrienne Rich's essay 'When We Dead Awaken: Writing as Revision' gives a good indication of the scope of this revisionist project:

> To question everything. To remember what it has been forbidden even to mention. To come together telling our stories, to look afresh at, and then to describe for ourselves, the frescoes of the Ice Age, the nudes of 'high art', the Minoan seals and figurines, the moon landscape embossed with the booted print of a male foot, the microscopic virus, the scarred and tortured body of the planet Earth. To do this kind of work takes a capacity for constant active presence, a naturalist's attention to minute phenomena, for reading between the lines, watching closely for symbolic arrangements, decoding difficult and complex messages left for us by women of the past.[34]

In her most famous work to date, *Stealing the Language: The Emergence of Women's Poetry in America*,[35] Ostriker sets out to test the convictions of gynocriticism concerning

the cultural intervention of women authors. Claiming her method to be radically inductive she analyses over 300 volumes of women's poetry published since the 1960s. She
argues it is possible to discern in these the clear features of a shared tradition amongst
women poets engaged in radical revisionary work. In the concluding chapter of this
book, Ostriker argues that those very aspects of women's experience which have been
portrayed as inimical to spiritual understanding in the past are now being used by
women to point to new ways of understanding the divine. Furthermore, she states that
when such understandings are given figurative expression through the introduction of
transgressive metaphors into authoritative stories, the effect is to promote change,
'the figure or tale will be appropriated for altered ends, the old vessel filled with new
wine, initially satisfying the thirst of the individual poet but ultimately making change
possible'.[36]

The ways in which women are engaging with myths as a means of promoting social
and spiritual change is explored further in Ostriker's later text, *Feminist Revision and the
Bible*.[37] In this she claims that women writers are not merely engaged in an adversarial
relation with male-centred traditions but they also enjoy an 'erotic relation' with the
dominant culture.[38] In reflecting upon her own Jewish tradition she argues that it is too
precious to be simply discarded or replaced by new religious identities more friendly to
women. What is looked for is a process of amorous interpenetration of 'male' and
'female' spheres:

> I argue that the woman writer can write from a stance of pleasure and can inter-
> vene in the creation of culture. . . . We assume that the language, the culture,
> one's own experience are always already so capacious as to make room for female
> pleasure and female reality.[39]

In claiming that the tradition invites the revisioning process that women are currently engaged in Ostriker locates herself within the Jewish midrashic tradition of
plural readings and multiple re-imaginings. In the sacred dynamic of midrash, which
Ostriker has called the hermeneutics of desire, everything is put into play. Because all is
in motion, the static presentations of logocentric authority in theology and philosophy
are revealed as childish impersonations of divine power.[40]

This is a very positive way of framing the relation between women writers and the
male-centred tradition. It is one that is obviously attractive to religious feminists who
wish to remain within the boundaries of their inherited faiths. However, in placing
women's writing in the role of consort to the male tradition Ostriker, like Christ, is
using women's writing to support her particular strategic ends. Leaving aside the question of whether gynocriticism's invention of a women's tradition is any less of a universalising process than Christ's depiction of an archetypal spiritual quest, the question
remains as to how to approach women's writing which resists such a coupling. Much of
women's writing is perverse, angry and even conventionally unintelligible. It expresses
mourning and grief as much as pleasure in creative construction. Madness is present
alongside ecstasy and there are many strange tongues which do not actively revision
dominant forms but, rather, haunt daytime communication with night-time horrors.

Whereas Ostriker uses many positive erotic metaphors to refer to the intervention
of women in cultural practice, the poet Adrienne Rich uses far more chilling images to
refer to the violence which has made normal cultural 'intercourse' so painful for

women. For Rich, revisioning is close to agony. It involves uncovering old wounds, returning to the wreck to uncover the dead and being painfully honest about all that has been lost in the long years of women's marginality and exclusion. In her poem 'The Wild Child', Rich employs the image of a child who has somehow survived the appalling wounds of attempted infanticide and grown up in the dangerous protection of the wilderness. The marks of the first violence are over-scored with other scars which have been received as a consequence of inhabiting a place beyond the boundaries. On being brought back into human culture normal speech is impossible for this outsider but the face is writing:

> A cave of scars!
> ancient, archaic wallpaper
> built up, layer on layer
> from the earliest, dream-white
> to yesterdays, a red black scrawl
> a red mouth slowly closing . . .
> these scars bear witness
> but whether to repair
> or to destruction
> I no longer know.[41]

Kathleen Sands and thinking through the tragic

The work of Kathleen Sands[42] represents a decidedly new turn in religious feminism's engagement with women's writing. Although she is keen to acknowledge the debt she owes to Carol Christ and others, her thinking reflects the theoretical shift from 'women's experience' to 'situated knowledge', acknowledges the racism implicit in the suppression of difference and displays a cautious engagement with some aspects of post-structuralist theory – an approach to literary texts which challenges many of the core values of the gynocritical movement.

In like Cupitt, Sands is keen to explore why theology has become so closely inter-twined with philosophy. In particular she claims that theodicy stands at the heart of theological thinking, relying upon abstract arguments to deflect the questions raised by concrete experiences of human suffering. If theodical defences are breached, then the theological edifice itself will crumble and, Sands maintains, this is exactly what is taking place in this 'post age'.[43]

In Cupitt's work, the alliance between philosophy/theology is linked to the cultural manifestations of political power, a power which has resisted the contingent, the embodied, the aesthetic and the feminine aspects of experience. However, Sands is far more bold in her analysis of the material reasons why theological discourse functions in this way. She argues that the tragic dimensions of human life are excluded from theological thinking because it would provoke a fundamental reassessment of the basis upon which the social order is founded.

> The challenge of tragedy is not merely that the fullness of human experience has not been acknowledged by theology. There is also a fundamental link

between repressing certain knowledges and the process of political domination by particular groups over others, the rationale for suppressing resistance is still the assumption that fundamental contradictions or conflicting orders do not really exist.[44]

If the tragic is excluded from theology it is manifest in the struggles, rituals and narratives of subjugated groups which are frequently nurtured and sustained by women. All these are theological sources upon which religious feminists can draw. However, literature written by women is particularly valuable because it reveals a process of narrative formation through which women from diverse backgrounds attempt to knit together the tragic aspects of life into useful (if provisional) knowledge on the basis of which they can generate shared identity and pursue political ends. Literary texts are sites where meaning is negotiated and invented. The theological dynamic Sands employs consists in placing these literary narratives next to her own life story and reflecting upon the familiarity and strangeness this intertextuality reveals:

> In that spirit I turn to literature by women though without presupposing that other women's stories are in fact my stories. My model, rather, is one of dialogue with these novels, putting my story next to theirs. . . . For in fact the stories of women have been woven next to each other, and it is a task of religious feminists to inquire what this has meant and might be made to mean.[45]

Sands offers readings of four novels to illustrate her feminist reading strategy or 'tragic hermeneutics'. The texts she chooses to use are multi-vocal and non-hegemonic. They contain the subjugated knowledge of marginalised people in which Sands seeks to identify some hope for the future. Her reading is a very concrete process and involves achieving a dialogue between the concerns of these texts and the plot of her own life. She is empowered by the accounts she reads of endurance in the face of tragedy. These enable her both to face the personal tragedies she has experienced and nurture a commitment to the political struggles of suffering communities whose texts have touched her deeply. These reading encounters point her towards an emerging new theology she believes religious feminists should cherish. This is a theology fully dialogical, immersed in and emerging from living communities. It is a theology that will acknowledge contradiction, listen for what has been silenced and 'cross more worlds . . . searching for what is absent'.[46]

Sands's vision of literature as a means through which women weave the threads of their painful experience into a beautiful and useful garment is one which is appealing to many feminists today. Once again gendered distinctions are brought into play as this narrative creativity is contrasted with the male propensity for abstract reasoning. Adriana Cavarero, for example, argues that 'the discourse of the universal ... is always a matter for men only'.[47] In contrast women have survived extreme hardships through their story-telling activities:

> Cornered in weaving rooms, like Penelope, they have, since ancient times woven plots with the thread of storytelling. . . . Whether ancient or modern, their art aspires to a wise repudiation of the abstract universal and follows an everyday practice where the tale is existence, relation and attention.[48]

Sands has brought a greater sophistication to the feminist religious reader of women's writing. However, her work continues to demonstrate the strong investment we have maintained in our claims that these texts (gendered female) are ours by natural right and can be relied upon to support feminist reconstructive work. Sands frequently employs the word tragedy but perhaps this is a misleading term in the context of her vision of regenerative communal forms emerging from contexts of extreme pain and suffering. Tragedy implies an encounter with the unassimilable, the uncanny, that which cannot be borne yet cannot be avoided, the dread force of the divine. This sense of an awful encounter with alterity is quite lacking from Sands's impressive work. Her text reveals the recurring dilemma of feminist religious thinking. We desire a god who will affirm us in our difficult process of self becoming but not trouble us by writing strange words on the wall at our banquets. Literature can certainly be used to express our pain and inspire our hope – but it can also play a quite different and potentially more challenging role.

In his passionate and eclectic text, *Telling Stories: Postmodernism and the Invalidation of Traditional Narrative*,[49] Michael Roemer argues that the power of literature is not to establish a fragile mastery over circumstances but rather to enable us to live with the deep unresolvement in human affairs and to receive a vision not of the fulfilment of our own best selves, but of the unutterable other. This other 'is necessity, the sacred'.[50] An ungovernable other is present to use as a dark epiphany that undoes our delicately woven threads of meaning and appalls us with what we cannot contain. Fiction may become strangely redemptive because,

> unlike theology it does not comfort us with an all-knowing, all powerful deity – who very likely is fashioned from our own needs and who in turn often serves for a model of domination and control. Story insists on the utter alterity of the 'other'.[51]

Feminist religious reading

In reflecting upon the work of Carol Christ, Sands states that, despite the criticisms ranged against her, Christ had established women's literature as 'a theological source that while still largely ignored by androcentric religious studies has become vital to most religious feminists'.[52] I hope that it is clear from my brief overview of Christ, Ostriker and Sands that there is much to be admired in their creative work. They have adopted the gendered discourses of literature and theology and used these strategically to open up new forms of theological reflection which have contributed significantly to feminist religious thought and political action. However, as we seize this significant moment in the development of a feminist philosophy of religion, it is important to ask what weakness can be discerned in our current reading practices.

Annelies van Heijst has argued that 'until now feminist theologians have read for recognition. They wish to see their meanings (theological or feminist themes) endorsed in the literary texts.'[53] This is a harsh judgement but one which I believe is justified. What has been sought in women's writing is a home, a place of meeting and affirmation, a place where our genealogy is recognised and the wisdom of women affirmed.

And literature can provide all these things – but it can offer much more. Whilst religious feminists have been eager to use literature to establish our dwelling places, many women writers have deliberately 'left home', wandering far beyond familiar and charted territories in order to construct new forms of writing and create new metaphors and symbols which bring the inexpressible to form. It is an underestimation of the terror and the passion of their creative work if we use its energy only for domestic purposes.

In her poetic manifesto 'Notes on Thought and Vision' the poet H.D. sought to express her thoughts on artistic creativity. These reflections were set out shortly after the blight of the First World War and her own near-death in pregnancy. As well as making audacious connections between artistic creativity and the body, she also made the scandalous assertion that artistic vision had the power to regenerate this 'murky, dead, old, thousand-times explored old world'[54] but only at the cost of great risk.

Human beings, she observes, are frequently content to dwell safely in their dull little houses.

> Each comfortable little home shelters a comfortable little soul – and a wall at the back shuts out completely any communication with the world beyond.

> Man's [sic] chief concern is keeping his little house warm and making his little wall strong . . .

> Outside is a great vineyard and grapes and rioting and madness and dangers. It is very dangerous.[55]

Rioting, madness and danger. What is missing from our readings but what we might need to revive our murky old world in the future. Feminist theology and philosophy of religion are now moving in an era in which women can express their insights with confidence. We will continue to struggle with centuries of authoritative reasoning on the divine from which women's perspectives have been excluded. However, as we do so we will be aware that we are constructing the strong walls of our own disciplinary conventions and academic traditions. Women's writing can help us to retain the vital awareness of what it is like to stand unsteadily with stained lips in the wild vineyard. But only if it remains dangerous for us.

Notes

1   D. Cupitt, *What is a Story?* London: SCM Press, 1991.
2   Ibid., p. x.
3   Ibid., p. 40.
4   Ibid., p. 58.
5   Ibid., p. 80.
6   Ibid., p. 75.
7   See ibid., p. 40.
8   R. Kojecky, *T.S. Eliot's Social Criticism*, London: Faber and Faber, 1971, p. 76.
9   T.S. Eliot's views on the proper relations between literature and theology have their counterpart in his views concerning the proper relations between women and men. Commenting upon the Nazi determination to locate the energies of women in the kitchen, childcare and church he argued that this idea could not be dismissed simply because of its fascist origins. 'Might one suggest that the kitchen, children and church could be considered to have a claim upon the attention of married

women? Or that no normal married woman would prefer to be a wage earner if she could help it?'
(T.S. Eliot, *The Idea of A Christian Society*, Glasgow: Glasgow University Press, 1951, p. 70).

10   M. Nussbaum, *The Fragility of Goodness: Luck and Ethics in Greek Tragedy and Philosophy*, Cambridge: Cambridge University Press, 1986, p. 14.

11   M. Nussbaum, *Love's Knowledge: Essays on Philosophy and Literature*, Oxford: Oxford University Press, 1990, p. 258.

12   R. Eaglestone, *Ethical Criticism: Reading After Levinas*, Edinburgh: Edinburgh University Press, 1997, p. 57.

13   Ibid., p. 58.

14   I use the term 'literary forms' to indicate that I make no decisive separation between literature and narrative. In the work of some Christian theologians a distinction is made between narrative, a neutral and natural category, and the fictional devices of literature. Narrative belongs with Christian doctrine but literature is a culturally contaminated category. I follow Stephen Crites in the conviction that narrative is always cultural artifice and that literary categories are the ones through which narratives continue to be structured and performed. See S. Crites, 'The Narrative Quality of Experience', *Journal of the American Academy of Religion*, XXXIX: 3 (1971): 291–311.

15   P.S. Anderson, *A Feminist Philosophy of Religion: The Rationality and Myths of Religious Belief*, Oxford: Blackwell, 1998.

16   G. Jantzen, *Becoming Divine: Towards a Feminist Philosophy of Religion*, Manchester: Manchester University Press, 1998, p. 22.

17   See P. Yaeger's classic text on this subject, *Honey Mad Women: Emancipatory Strategies in Women's Writing*, New York, NY: Columbia University Press, 1988.

18   See, for example, Anderson, *A Feminist Philosophy of Religion*, pp. 209–216.

19   For a discussion of Margaret Atwood's response to theological interpretations of her work, see A. van Heijst, *Longing for the Fall*, Kampen: Kok Pharos Publishing House, 1995, p. 258.

20   It has been necessary to limit my reflections to these three women because of the constraints of this context. Other women such as Katie Cannon and Susan Thistlethwaite have also made considerable contributions to debates in this area.

21   See, for example, S. Thistlethwaite, *Sex, Race and God: Christian Feminism in Black and White*, London: Geoffrey Chapman, 1989 and K. Sands, *Escape from Paradise: Evil and Tragedy in Feminist Theology*, Minneapolis, MN: Fortress Press, 1994.

22   See G. Greene, *Changing the Story: Feminist Fiction and the Tradition*, Chicago, IL: University of Chicago Press, 1991, p. 106.

23   C. Christ, 'Spiritual Quest and Women's Experience', in C. Christ and J. Plaskow (eds) *Womanspirit Rising*, San Francisco, CA: Harper and Row, 1979, pp. 228–245, p. 231.

24   Ibid., p. 231.

25   Ibid., p. 238.

26   Ibid., p. 230

27   C. Christ, *Diving Deep and Surfacing: Women Writers on the Spiritual Quest*, Boston, IL: Beacon Press, 1980, p. 40, my emphasis.

28   See, for example, J. Kristeva, *Revolution in Poetic Language*, trans. M. Waller, New York, NY: Columbia University Press, 1984.

29   See, for example, M. Lauret, *Liberating Literature: Feminist Fiction in America*, London: Routledge, 1994.

30   Van Heijst, *Longing for the Fall*, p. 226

31   For an overview of the concerns of gynocriticism, see E. Showalter (ed.) *The New Feminist Criticism: Essays on Women, Literature and Theory*, London: Virago, 1986.

32   E. Showalter, *A Literature of Their Own: From Charlotte Bronte to Doris Lessing*, London: The Women's Press, 1977, p. 319.

33   See, for example, S. Gilbert and S. Gubar, *The Madwoman in the Attic: The Woman Writer and the Nineteenth Century Literary Imagination*, New Haven, CT: Yale University Press, 1979.

34   A. Rich, 'When We Dead Awaken: Writing as Revision', in Adrienne Rich, *On Lies, Secrets and Silences: Selected Prose 1966–1978*, New York, NY: W.W. Norton, 1978, p. 13.

35   A. Ostriker, *Stealing the Language: The Emergence of Women's Poetry in America*, London: The Women's Press, 1987.

36   Ibid., p. 213.

37   A. Ostriker, *Feminist Revision and the Bible*, Oxford: Blackwell, 1993.

38   Ibid., p. 116.

39   Ibid.

40 Ostriker's early passion for the poetry of William Blake is evident here. See A. Ostriker, *Vision and Verse in William Blake*, Madison, WI: University of Wisconsin Press, 1965.

41 A. Rich, 'The Wild Child', in A. Rich, *Diving Into the Wreck: Poems 1971–1972*, London, New York, NY: W.W. Norton, 1973, pp. 57–58.

42 Sands, *Escape from Paradise*.

43 An evocative term which Sands uses in preference to terms such postmodernism which are deeply embedded in cultural analyses that take little cognisance of the historical agency of some dominant groups.

44 Sands, *Escape from Paradise*, p. 3.

45 Ibid., p. 138.

46 Ibid., p. 116.

47 A. Cavarero, *Relating Narratives: Storytelling and Selfhood*, London: Routledge, 2000, p. 53.

48 Ibid., p. 53.

49 M. Roemer, *Telling Stories: Postmodernism and the Invalidation of Traditional Narrative*, Landam, MD: Rowman and Littlefield, 1995.

50 Roemer, *Telling Stories*, p. 25.

51 Ibid., p. 151.

52 Sands, *Escape from Paradise*, p. 124.

53 van Heijst, *Longing for the Fall*, p. 256.

54 H.D. 'Notes on Thoughts and Vision', in B. Kime Scott (ed.) *The Gender of Modernism*, Bloomington, IN: Indiana University Press, pp. 93–106, 96

55 Ibid., pp. 104–105.

Chapter 9

Melissa Raphael

THE PRICE OF (MASCULINE) FREEDOM AND BECOMING: A JEWISH FEMINIST RESPONSE TO ELIEZER BERKOVITS'S POST-HOLOCAUST FREE-WILL DEFENCE OF GOD'S NON-INTERVENTION IN AUSCHWITZ

Taking bets on history

JEWISH PHILOSOPHICAL REFLECTION ON the Holocaust has devoted much of its intellectual energy to establishing how the catastrophe was a result of two causally related factors: the abuse of human freedom and the exile or hiddenness of God's presence from history. Human evil banishes God from the world and, conversely, God's mysterious self-hiding permits, but does not sanction, the abuse of human freedom. It has been this circular causal relation between human freedom and the hiddenness of God that seems at once to acknowledge the abyssal reality of Auschwitz and to justify continued faith in the reality of God and in human possibility. By appealing to a free-will defence that is widespread in Western theodical discourse, Jewish philosophy can defend the perfect God's having created an imperfect world, holding that God can only judge history, rewarding the good and punishing the evil, because human beings are also fully responsible for their own imperfection. However, God and 'man' (the gender-specific referent is accurate here) must both take responsibility for evil: 'man' because he has freely abused his power; God because he has permitted that abuse by withholding his power to intervene and by creating a world in which such evils could occur.

Using the free-will defence of God's apparent countenance of evil, it is argued that human freedom can only be secured if God does not selectively intervene to avert its consequences. But while freedom is the condition of human becoming, the freedom to do evil as well as good is a contingency of choice. Jewish philosophy is broadly resigned to this possibility because it accepts that logically contradictory demands cannot be made upon the God of classical theism it holds more or less in common with that of Western philosophy of religion:

For the world to be an arena for the emergence of moral worth and value requires a world in which there is evil to overcome that this value might emerge.

Thus, even God cannot create such a world without evil, not because there are limits to His powers but because a contradiction would be involved.[1]

However, Jewish philosophy is not only concerned with the justification of faith by the operations of reason.[2] Revelation, not reason, takes precedence, and therefore Jewish philosophers can resolve the ethical and philosophical problems of the free-will defence by affirming that God is not finally an absent God but a providential God whose love and justice is revealed in law, study, prayer and the historical fulfilment of his promise of the land of Israel. Indeed, it is in the founding of the Jewish State that most Jewish commentators declare God to have the historical process at his ultimate command. The plea of suffering which appears to go unanswered must therefore be situated within the collective, namely Israel as an assembly and as a territory, and understood within the terms of the tradition rather than those of individual experience or merit.

Essentially, God and men take a gamble on freedom's chances. Auschwitz represents a bet both tragically lost and tragically won. Although 'man' has suffered and died unspeakably, his humanity has ceded nothing to God's divinity. But if 'man' has also lost heavily, it was a risk worth taking for, since humanity is made in the image of God, there is a strong probability that freedom will be exercised beneficiently. Though Jewish history rarely justifies its confidence, Jewish philosophical anthropology would suggest that the odds are generally good that men will make the right choices. Biblical and rabbinic tradition do not question 'man's' free will to choose the good (Deut. 30:19). So too, against Christian doctrines of original sin, Jewish philosophers from the medieval to the contemporary period propose that 'man', guided by revealed law, can freely perfect his moral self.

Zachary Braiterman's book (God) After Auschwitz rightly observes that post-Holocaust theological reflection, other than that of Ultra-Orthodox rabbis, has abandoned those older Jewish theodicies which tend to exonerate God and castigate Jewry for its sins. Jewish thought has made a variety of responses to the Holocaust rather than account for its divine cause. But that post-Holocaust theology is therefore what he calls 'antitheodical' is not, I think, the case. Given that so much of this corpus assumes the silence, eclipse or absence of God from Auschwitz (though not his non-existence), the corollary of a theodical free-will defence is also usually implied even where it is not stated if only because Jewish theology accepts as self-evidently true that freedom has its price.[3] Although the post-Holocaust free-will defence was to be forcefully challenged (though not altogether rejected) by Steven Katz,[4] numerous Jewish thinkers of the post-Holocaust period have invoked the free-will defence of God. Even Emmanuel Levinas, a prophet of heteronomous obligation, follows Western philosophical convention and argues that absolute morality requires absolute freedom and it is this which allows the possibility of absolute immorality.[5]

For Arthur Cohen, God has benevolently created the world and given us the Torah; beyond that (following Maimonides) God does not intervene and therefore cannot be held responsible for those who ignore its prohibitions. Prayer for intervention is in this sense meaningless (despite its undoubted prevalence in Jewish tradition). In the name of freedom, God lets the *tremendum* of human Godlessness take its most terrifying course. Cohen's theme is one with which we will become familiar: God's love entails that he cannot intervene in history because that would curtail humanity's capacity to be human, that is, independent and free, just as it would curtail God's capacity to be God who must be that which goes indefinitely before: 'the mystery of our futurity.'[6] Cohen's thinking is in the Judaeo-Hellenic philosophical tradition of Maimonides, Halevi and Spinoza who regard passion as a weakness foreign to God and which would curtail his absolute freedom. For Philo too, the apathetic man – free, self-sufficient and unmoved – is akin to God who, in his own *apatheia*, is unchangeable and unmoved by the passions that are associated with the finite life of the flesh. Despite some biblical stories suggesting otherwise, for God to be God he must both act in history and be unconditioned by finitude and change. Cohen's is just such a removed God who, in giving 'man' his freedom, is freeing him to become as God himself is, divinely free. God could not, then, avert the Holocaust only because he found himself, after all, unable to countenance its actual agonies.

Eliezer Berkovits's free-will defence of God's holocaustal absence has, however, been the most normative of all such proposals, even though he himself realized that it does not entirely exonerate God whose debt to us must be redeemed in the hereafter.[7] In *Faith After the Holocaust* he argues that had God exercised his power in preventing the Holocaust he would have impeded 'man's' becoming: the project to which even divine justice is subordinate. The good is only the good because of the possibility of evil. 'Man' would have had no opportunity to exercise and demonstrate his morally good will – indeed, could not *be* 'man' if God had not curbed and hidden his power (and, for the meantime, his justice).[8] That is, 'while God waits for the sinner to turn to him, there is oppression and persecution and violence among men. Yet there seems to be no alternative. If "man" is to be, God must be long-suffering with him; he must suffer man.'[9] Weeping for his exiled children (as the Talmudic text Berakhot 59a expresses it), God must not only suffer 'man's' choice, he must also suffer on 'man's' behalf. God's face is turned away (*hester panim*) and he is powerless 'until man becomes what he ought to be' even to the extent of God becoming an exile in his own world.[10]

Berkovits' argument is structured by penalty and compensation. That man may be, God must absent himself; his interventionary power is withheld from us (an injustice that Berkovits is at least once moved to rebuke). But that humanity may not perish entirely, God must remain present. The God of history must be at once present and absent, or present in his absence: his being there but not there is expressed by Berkovits in the biblical and rabbinic trope of hiddenness.[11] God's mightiness, then, consists paradoxically in his 'self-restraint'. So that 'while He shows forbearance with the wicked, He must turn a deaf ear to the anguished cries of the violated'. Both 'man's' freedom and, significantly, his suffering become an index of God's love for him: 'God's very mercy and forebearance, his very love for man, necessitates the abandonment of some men to a fate that they may well experience as indifference to justice and human suffering.'[12] 'Man' must have his freedom in order to be 'man' even though the historical record of his abuse of freedom suggests that his freedom will destroy him. But because God cannot entirely divest himself of his responsibility to 'man' he cannot finally withdraw his providential presence.[13] Hence he has hidden himself, but has not departed from us.

A competition of wills

There is always the risk that interpreting a set of arguments with a single category of analysis – here, that of gender – will reduce their complexity to a single element. Bearing in mind that there is always much else to be said, this chapter will argue that the post-Holocaust free-will defence can be rebutted on feminist historical and ethical grounds. First, its appeal to providence privileges masculine Jewish religious and military interests and therefore inadequately addresses the resolution of innocent female suffering. Second, reading Jewish women's (largely secular)[14] memoirs of survival in the death and concentration camps may not resolve the problem of innocent suffering theodically, but it does demonstrate that, in the holocaustal context, Jewish women typically invested their dignity as subjects less in freedom than in the degree to which they were needed and bound to others by ties of love and obligation. In so far as that was the case, God may, in fact, have been present in Auschwitz without precluding human freedom. The gamble was not only reckless, but unnecessary. Third, this chapter will argue that Jewish philosophical discourse on freedom of the will is not only a philosophical argument but also a modern religio-political discourse on the distribution of masculine power, human and divine – on who, to put it crudely, has the historical upper hand.

To take this last point first: that the basic validity of the post-Holocaust free-will defence has been assumed even by those who do not make a direct appeal to it owes much to its capacity to bridge ancient and modern elements of the quintessentially patriarchal struggle for the supremacies that are in freedom's gift. In post-Holocaust Jewish thought, history as well as the historical vanquishment of evil are typically construed as being subject to competing drives for power and ontological fulfilment: that of men and of the masculine God. In so far as the Jewish God's power underwrites male Jewish power which is an index to his own, the Jewish free-will defence is a political, that is, historically contingent rather than philosophically necessary, resolution of the problem of evil. The post-Holocaust free-will defence of God negotiates the (re)distribution of power between a male God, male Jewish subjects, and Nazi Germany as itself a locus of hyper-masculine and apparently absolute power; it replays a struggle between men and God over who at any one time is to be the sovereign L/lord of history. I want to suggest that the post-Holocaust free-will defence (especially Eliezer Berkovits's) is primarily concerned with the ways that masculine agents' wills, both human and divine, are imposed upon history; so that their wills might condition history but not be conditioned by it. It is only secondarily concerned with the suffering of which that agency is the cause. In fact, the post-Holocaust free-will defence rewards both divine and Jewish masculine agency. It asserts that 'man's' general freedom has prevailed over particular evils and even over God's will that his creation should flourish. Nonetheless, since these are religious arguments, the exercise of human freedom does not finally override God's will. God's will prevails because humanity (particularly men) become the autonomous subjects they were created to be (whether for good or ill) and men's good moral choices vindicate the goodness and glory of their creator. Above all, because God's omnipotence is not properly compatible with human autonomy, the free-will defence assumes God's omnipotence while permitting him to suspend it. The problem of innocent suffering is thereby set to one side.

But modernity does not always compensate God for his capitulation to the masculine human will. Despite the basically heteronomous nature of Jewish tradition as one of law and covenant, the post-Holocaust free-will defence draws not only on Jewish but also on Western Enlightenment discourses that tend to the displacement of God from history. Some Jewish commentators have suggested that the Holocaust was perpetrated so that (Western) 'man' could break free altogether from the Judaeo-Christian God whose towering will has constrained and humiliated his own.[15] This claim acknowledges that the Jewish God and modernity are fundamentally incompatible and in allowing that even God's happiness must be sacrificed to masculine becoming, makes Judaism a party to modernity's bid for freedom from heteronomous divine and human authority. That Orthodoxy can admit the possibility of autonomy by some form of separation from God or by the subjection of God to emotional pain is not wholly unexpected. The tradition anticipates modernity in rabbinic texts that, foreshadowing secularization, eliminate the biblical immediacy of God's presence from the halakhic (religio-legal) process, arguing that since God has given the Torah to 'man', no further interference from God can be allowed (Baba Metzia 59b). God's law becomes an object of study and now 'man' (as scholar) interprets the law and decides what is the law, for the law is now his.[16] (On occasion) Jewish patriarchy asserts its sovereignty by an abstraction of God from history by, effectively, using divine law against God.

While Ignaz Maybaum's God limits Jewish freedom on account of Israel's election ('Again it was demonstrated that to be chosen means to have no choice. God chooses'),[17] Irving Greenberg is more representative in arguing that after God allowed the Holocaust and withheld his protection from Jewry he can have no moral claim on Jews' covenantal allegiance; it must now be voluntary. The covenant can no longer be commanded or enforced by reward and punishment.[18] Berkovits's free-will defence similarly marks the confluence of tradition and modernity. His view is close to that of Kant who argued that were God's awful majesty to be 'before our eyes' (that is, were God to be present) this would deprive us of the opportunity of good will – an unqualified good – and we would act from fear and hope rather than duty. Our acts would be the mere gestures of puppets without life in their figures.[19] Like so many Jewish thinkers of his period, Berkovits also draws on the existentialist philosophy of his period. He is impressed by Sartre's notion that autonomous choice defines our relation to being; that the meaning of a situation is conferred by one's taking responsibility for it and that to be a person is to be one who chooses.[20] In Berkovits's use of the free-will defence, even God recognizes that his existence constrains our own and he must therefore disappear or hide (just as Jews all over occupied Europe were trying to do). The consequences of God's disappearance will be terrifying, but modern 'man' is willed by God to be master of his destiny, whatever its cost to those unfortunates who are not.[21]

Autonomy and gender

Characteristic of its period, the post-Holocaust free-will defence is articulated wholly without reference to gender difference in Jewry's suffering and without reference to the gendered nature of autonomy. Nonetheless, an account of human dignity that makes freedom its first priority is, in fact, gendered and particular to the masculine posture. This is demonstrated by the women's memoirs of Auschwitz–Birkenau and other death and labour camps which suggest precisely the contrary argument to that of the free-will defence: in these texts freedom is not secured by divine absence. Freedom as such and autonomy in particular are not the *sine qua non* of women's dignity; dignity is a function of being in relation to others. Of course, the memoir literature, like any record of the past, does not give unmediated access to historical truth(es). Both author and reader are participant in an interpretive process governed by public and private narratives that shape experience and its reading. Even so, it would be apparent to any reader and whatever their interest in the text, that women's ethical 'choosing' (to the degree it could be called that in a death camp) was not an arbitrary, individualistic, cerebral matter of free choice but a response strongly determined by familial, national, political and other bonds.

Those women who were not wholly broken by the regime sought (like men) to remain human by resistance to the gross dehumanization of sadism and absolute deprivation of every kind. But they did so not because they sought freedom but because the obligations of the common ties of family, friendship, politics, nationality and Jewishness, to feed, warm and comfort the other were what constituted their humanity.[22] Of course, the memoirs would never have been written if armies (of men) had not defeated Germany and its allies and liberated the camps. Women are, like anyone else, dependent for their happiness on basic freedom of thought and action. But this latter is political liberty and it is not to be identified with an ontological state. Redemption from degradation and erasure (though not death) is not, finally, secured by a military operation but in the continuous restorative labour of relational care.

For the purposes of physical, emotional and spiritual survival, women in the death and labour camps generally formed cooperative familial and quasi-familial groups, the latter composed of women known to each other as *Lagerschwestern* (camp sisters).[23] The non-Jewish Auschwitz survivor Charlotte Delbo summarizes the camp sisterhood common to non-Jewish and Jewish women alike: 'my friends never left me alone'; 'only surrounded by the others is one able to hold out.'[24] Or again, when mothers with very young children were not selected for labour and it was apparent that they faced imminent death, it was common for daughters and sisters, at or before the point of separation from their mothers, to promise their mothers that they would do everything in their power to keep what was left of the family together.[25] The outworking of this quasi-covenantal motif then becomes both structure and substance of the biographical narrative.

Judith Tydor Baumel's research on Jewish women's structures of mutual support in pre-war Nazi Germany and during the Holocaust is historical confirmation that an emphasis on autonomy as the necessary safeguard of human dignity and personhood is skewed to the masculine interest, not necessarily true to women's holocaustal experience and, in any case, morally problematic. Tydor Baumel has shown that, by necessity and priority, the crisis situation strengthened 'women's spheres' of influence: their traditional philanthropic welfare and educational endeavours. Persecution and the deportation of men from communities reinforced patterns of female leadership that had been developing since the nineteenth century. These activities were no longer means of middle-class women's self-expression, but survival strategies of a cooperative, interdependent, 'horizontally oriented', adaptive, practical nature that was profoundly gendered. Within the sexually segregated environments imposed by the Nazis, women's ethical practice fostered sisterhood and solidarity. Tydor Baumel concludes that 'long-term crisis situations may strengthen women's communal identities and power by negating the masculine ideal of the autonomous individual'.[26]

By contrast, Berkovits is struck by Victor Frankl's biographical account of his determination to be a free inmate of Auschwitz.[27] But Frankl's *Man in Search of Meaning* precisely illustrates our problem. Frankl wrote of Auschwitz:

> We who lived in concentration camps can remember the men who walked through the huts comforting others, giving away their last piece of bread. They may have been few in number, but they offer sufficient proof that everything can be taken from a man but one thing: the last of the human freedoms – to choose one's attitude in any given set of circumstances, to choose one's own way.[28]

Of course, this text about men who chose to exercise 'the last of the human freedoms', to retain their human dignity, yields multiple readings. If the text is one more instance of the masculinist valorization of autonomy as a guarantor of dignity, this is perhaps understandable at a time when (as Fackenheim points out) Jews in Auschwitz did not even enjoy that most basic and animal freedom – that of emptying their bowels at the time of need.[29] Frankl can also be read as arguing that the care of others – here comforting and feeding them – are themselves the occasion and mark of freedom (which would be closer to my own position). More congruent, though, with Frankl's individualist psychology of survival, the text indicates that, for him, the dignity of bodies and of selves is separable: to be a man is to be one who bows down to no (other) man; whatever the abjection of the body, redemption lies in the triumph of the unbroken will long before it lies in love for the broken body.

The problem with Frankl's making power and dignity a function of autonomy is that autonomous freedom can also be exercised as the choice to be free by constraining others' freedom to limit your own. Nazism – a hyper-masculine philosophy – assumed its God-given demonic freedom to deprive Jewry of any arena for ethical choice. Divine self-restraint in the name of human becoming, does not, by and large, create morality. It can hardly do so where it was experienced by countless Jews as a divine desertion of post and by their murderers as a permission and vindication of their acts. This God seriously underestimated how the silence left by his absence would be taken as licence for some men to be as absolutely powerful as they chose to be. When Nazi Germany adopted the posture of absolute power, God paid the price for men's autonomy in his anguish at the Nazi's degradation of his creation; men themselves paid a very high price for their autonomy in suffering, but women also paid that price for an autonomy that they could not or did not wish to exercise. Feminist philosophy has questioned how it can be fair or necessary for men to, as Pamela Sue Anderson puts it, 'learn about the consequences of their free will at the expense of women'. No free-will defence can justify 'this masculine God allowing so much more suffering and such long histories of oppression for women'.[30] Anderson's point is heavily underscored by feminist historians of the Holocaust who have demonstrated how gender difference placed women under different, and in many cases, more acute pressures than men: they were both the primary targets and the carers of the very young, the old and the sick under a regime that sought the biological eradication of a people.[31]

A much less well-known sense in which Eliezer Berkovits preserves masculine autonomy is by the anaesthetic effect of the transcendental religious will whose apathetic posture recalls the ideal represented in classical Jewish philosophy. In *With God in Hell* Berkovits describes observant Jewish males whose 'contemptuous indifference to the [Nazi] enemy [was] the ultimate of human autonomy'.[32] In a passage that could only have been written of men like those in Rabbi Avreimele Weinberg's study group in the Warsw ghetto who hid themselves away to study Torah – who had, for reasons good in themselves, chosen to detach themselves from their immediate moral obligation to the world of familial dependencies and relationships – Berkovits writes:

> To be unconcerned about what others may do to you, even when your life is at stake, because you are committed to the truth of your own life, is the supreme act of personal autonomy. . . . We are thinking of those who showed that radical indifference to the external reality that had been imposed on them. . . . It was the same indifference, the same contempt for the might of the oppressor that Rabbi Akiva showed so many centuries earlier to the Roman Empire.[33]

In practical religious terms, (Orthodox) Jewish law and worship must withstand all practical and emotional obstructions to its observance. For it is freedom of study and prayer that, above all, defines Jewish humanity (actually, manhood). Masculine study and observance is also the paradigmatic sanctification of God's name and is therefore the telos of God's creation. If, as Berkovits sets out to demonstrate, observance can continue with apathetic indifference to the interruptive agency of powerful oppressors then, however great the suffering, such interruptions are of negligible religious significance because Israel – and through Israel, the world – remains under God's command, not that of any other masculine authority. As God's regent, acting in God's name, Israel remains the subject, not the object, of the historical process. Logically, if not emotionally, this position removes the theodical sting of the Holocaust altogether. The Jewish family exists to support the study and observance of fathers and sons. In that Berkovits's account of male observance in the ghettos and camps shows that study and worship can survive irrespective of mass murder, the destruction of the family and whatever women might experience or do in that crisis situation is a problem of only second order importance as the purpose of creation continues to unfold – even under the conditions of genocide.

There is no doubt that the transcendence of evil by spiritual autonomy is a moving testament to the power of the human spirit. But few who loved another absolutely, or, as parents, were also absolutely obligated to care for their starving, desperately thirsty, ill and terrified children, could adopt a religio-heroic posture of sublime indifference to those oppressors who more than jeopardized the future of those relationships.[34] And why should they wish to do so? From a Jewish feminist perspective, the covenant not only produces a textual inheritance to study, but is also the sacred canopy or *chuppah* under which commitments to actual and particular relationships are sustained. If Baumel and others are right that cooperation, solidarity and relational bonding were broadly characteristic of women's practical, moral and emotional experience during the Holocaust, then what Baumel describes as the historical 'negat[ion] of the masculine ideal of the autonomous individual' should inform a post-Holocaust philosophical theology that is true both to women's experience and to Jewish tradition.

Feminist philosophers' sustained critical scrutiny of freedom and its individualist correlate, autonomy, also equips the argument that the free-will defence of God's inaction during the Holocaust is not as neutral and objective a philosophical argument as it appears to be, but has been socially and historically conditioned. Feminist philosophers and theologians have wanted to say that when the liberal tradition speaks of freedom as a right and function of full moral and rational agency, that is, full humanity, it primarily and normatively means that of men. Freedom is not the quality and telos of human becoming (as liberal individualism would have had us believe) but, like subjecthood itself, is a privilege of historical and political power. And very often this freedom is a function of alienated power where the powerful have bought freedoms or prevailed upon others so as to be free of ordinary constraints and dependencies. The free elite are those who can grant but no longer ask permission. Patriarchal, that is, hierarchical, freedom is therefore a function and cause of the alienation of relationality, not only a precondition of its choosing.

Feminist philosophers have exposed the implicit and explicit misogyny of the Western philosophical tradition from which much of the discourse on autonomy derives. Here women do not merit autonomy: they are, it is claimed, childlike creatures, rationally ill-equipped to vote or legislate, whose autonomy would endanger the social order.[35] Alongside religious teaching paradoxically combining a biblical distrust of women as the embodiment of Eve with trust in their maternal self-sacrificial care for the vulnerable, such ideologies of femininity have underpinned women's economic dependencies and familial responsibilities of primary care. In prosperous, educated Western circles where women can, at least in theory, attain the status of men, such ideologies now appear antiquated, unscientific and morally unpersuasive. Even so, the social and ideological obligations of female care, for so long regarded as natural or divinely ordained, have continued to produce a relative lack of the ego-differentiation long considered prerequisite by both feminist and patriarchal commentators to the dignity and privileges of autonomy.

From the mid-1960s to the mid-1980s, Second Wave reformist feminism attacked the social order as one they believed to have grossly limited female autonomy (and therefore fulfilment) by imposing a cramped daily round of domestic and intra-familial duties. To escape these drudgeries, liberal feminists sought self-actualization in the attainment of a freedom and independence that had previously been enjoyed by a white male elite alone. On these grounds it would have seemed self-contradictory for a feminist to criticize theologies dependent on the notion of freedom and autonomy. After all, liberal feminism has shared modernity's own masculinist drive towards self-legislated experience, and reformist religious feminists have argued (and continue to argue) that the full humanity of women is a function of their becoming the agents, not objects, of law and tradition. But by the late 1980s, still under the influence of cultural feminism and coming under that of the postmodern celebration of difference, feminist ethicists such as Sara Ruddick and Nel Noddings were revisiting patriarchal ideologies of femininity, arguing that they could themselves develop and own a maternalist ethic of care that – as a matter of ethical choice – valorized the particular virtues of biological difference.[36]

While maternalist philosophies will inform any critique of liberal individualism, more recently, postmodern feminist philosophy has questioned the notion of a true, free, unified essential self (male or female) of the sort the free-will defence intends to realize, and has instead posited multiple and fluid identities performed or constructed within given social frames. The postmodern decentring of authority and self, coupled with the relational turn in philosophy, theology and ethics, has yielded a different construal of freedom within the academy where to become the subject of one's own experience may not mean the attainment of autonomy for its own sake. If the free, unified self does not subsist in abstraction from the relations that produce a self, then becoming is manifest in the authority to articulate and sacralize values, knowledges and histories produced and named out of women's own experiences. In short, while liberal feminism might have some qualified sympathy with the free-will defence, it is postmodern feminism, more than cultural feminism, which finally exposes the vacuity of this defence.

Heteronomy and the Jewish God of covenant and exile

Where Berkovits's use of the free-will defence can be rebutted on a number of feminist philosophical and historical grounds, it can also be rebutted on Jewish ones. Despite the tradition's susceptibility to modernity in so far as it is a discursively and practically self-sufficient dispensation, Jewish freedom is not the absence of constraint. The Jewish agent is freely subject to divine commandments; social freedoms are secured by divinely ordained covenantal and legal restraints. Since the nineteenth century, Reform Judaism has modified Jewish law so as to secure an a priori autonomy of belief and religious practice. But from an Orthodox perspective – the Hegelian analogy is Michael Wyschogrod's – 'man' must be both slave and free. God's mastery is only real if he has enslaved 'man's' freedom, but 'man' must be not only slave. He must also be free because God's mastery is not real if it is over a mere beast; hence the biblical God's tenderness to our vulnerability and fury at our rebellion.[37] To Orthodoxy, freedom is secured through the acceptance of heteronomy as a willing submission to God. An observant Jewish male is free but not autonomous in that his will is not the author, judge or final authority of his choices; he has not decided which moral principles he will abide by or which are binding upon him. Where Judaism postulates a God of law who has foreknowledge as a function of his omniscience and omnipotence, its ethic cannot know autonomy in the full sense of the term. This was why twentieth-century Jewish philosophers and intellectuals – most notably Martin Buber – raised Kantian objections to Judaism's halakhic observance. Buber insisted that God was not a law-giver but that (anticipating feminism) obligations arose through dialogical relation with the divine and human Thou. Law represented the fading of religious experience; the cooling embers of the fire of revelation.[38]

Of course, in (mis)casting halakhah and Torah as *Gesetz* – the iron hand of statutory law – Buber may have missed the sacramental point of the performance of *mitzvot* which flow from a personal as well as collective experience of divine love and the divine commandment to love.[39] But whether or not Buber was right, Berkovits's notion that Auschwitz is the price of free will is antithetical to the spirit of Judaism either as a consensual but heteronomous system of law, or as it is envisaged by Jewish feminism: that is, as a nexus of relationships halakhically regulated by men and women. Rachel Adler's Jewish feminist ethic assists us here. In refusing to define Jewish law as a 'closed system of obsolete and unjust rules, but as a way for communities of Jews to generate and embody their Jewish moral visions', Adler understands halakhah as that which steers orthopraxis but does not enforce it. As Adler points out, the etymological root of the word halakhah is 'the act of going forward, of making one's way. A halakhah, a pathmaking, translates the stories and values of Judaism into ongoing action.'[40] In which case, Jewish becoming is the narrative of a community that turns together in its historical situation and goes out with God to meet its future.

What we have seen to be questionable from a Jewish feminist perspective is not the basic logical assumption that at any one time human beings are presented with a number of options from which they must choose a single course of action, but the patriarchal ontological prioritizing of free will over any of its historical consequences and over the freely chosen constraints that constitute the covenantal relationship that is the form and substance of Judaism. Here, both the covenant, and women, children and men feminized by their powerlessness, pay the price for masculine becoming. A covenantal theology in which Jewish history constitutes the inter-generational nurture of persons in a trans-temporal, trans-national family must question Berkovits's prioritizing of supererogatory religious virtue and its ontological correlate: the equation of humanity with its freedom. The purpose of Jewish law is not merely to yield opportunities for the right choices. The redeemed world envisaged by prophetic Judaism is not one in which personhood is liberated as an individuated abstraction from all other persons, but one of liberation and healing (*tikkun*) from the coercive and exploitative powers of elite others, including their gods.

From a post-Holocaust Jewish feminist prophetic perspective, women's relational obligations to the oppressed and vulnerable other (quite literally, here, the widow and the orphan) yield rather than occlude divine presence, especially where God's relation to Israel is figured parentally rather than as a lonely monarch in whose gift liberty or subjection lies. Whether parenthood is innate or learned and performed, mothers (and usually in less immediately practical ways, fathers) are not, in fact, autonomous in relation to their duties and responsibilities to children or elderly parents. True, they can choose to ignore their responsibilities and desert their families, but most choose more or less freely to be unfree: to act heteronomously, or more precisely, co-onomously, because it is in the discharge of their covenantal promise to stand by the other that they know and situate their humanity. Divine presence could not obstruct Jewish women's autonomy because they are not, in fact, the authors of their choices but are subject to the binding and more or less mutual responsibilities of marital and biological care of those they live among. If the patriarchal aspiration of omnipotence is not attributed to God, she can be present to humanity without disabling their humanity. Rather, God can be figured as one who laboured by humanity's side to keep her own covenantal promise of a love that would sanctify both God and Israel. If the immanence of God is figured by the Shekhinah – the traditionally female image for the indwelling presence of God in our exile that has been reclaimed by Jewish feminism – then there was no logical or theological necessity for this God in mourning to be absent from Auschwitz, exile's last stop.

It is not the purpose of this chapter to elaborate a theology of divine presence in Auschwitz.[41] Suffice it to say that, contra Berkovits, a Jewish God's presence, far from impeding moral choice, would sustain and empower it within a matrix of interdependent relationships. And since the presence of God is invited by the practical and ethical purification of space and time, God's presence would be welcomed by moral acts which were less a haphazard matter of ethical choice per se, than the necessary acts of practical love. The post-Holocaust deployment of the free-will defence has cast God in the modern guise of a transcendental guarantor of autonomous choice. But this establishes a moral atomism that is alien to Judaism and to the interconnected character of the created world whose salvation history is not that of particular individuals but a dynamic ecology of relationships between all its inhabitants. God immanent as Shekhinah – a God whose (suffering) face is imaged in that of Israel – is known in and by the relationships that produce the human(e) even while Israel is in bondage and in ways that continually redefine its freedom. For as all relational philosophers have wanted to say, true freedom is found in (what Hegel would call) the 'substantial ties': the profound solidarities and affiliations of love where, within a covenantal framework, each freely relinquishes the freedom to be free of obligations to the other, thereby breaking the modern equation of freedom and autonomy. This is especially significant in the traditional Jewish context where freedom does not entail autonomy and both are qualified by revelation.

In Auschwitz, God appears as a woman at a moment where patriarchal power is exceeding even its own limits and where women, with the sick, the very old and the very young, are the powerless of the powerless – those who would be the last to come to be; who will, indeed, very soon cease to be. This is the face of the immanent God seen and seeing; who is fully God but not free because she is with Israel in her exile, just as Israel is not free but is fully human because she too is there with the suffering other. The moral and existential freedom of persons in their response to suffering could not, therefore, as Berkovits fears, be constrained by God's presence in Auschwitz. For the God characterized by qualities that might be described as female is not a God of miraculous deliverance or the suspension of historical causality. And the relational gift of human and divine presence to the suffering other is one that is offered and, it is hoped, received; it cannot by its nature be coerced. The (deported) assembly of Israel, by virtue of being such, always marks the presence of God; on account of a love manifest precisely in her being there, she suffers alongside us.[42] The God immanent in Auschwitz could not overwhelm human freedom because to be immanent where we are she must come as we are, at the crisis of two Jewish narratives: that of holocaustal dying and that of redemption from slavery, when God and Israel are both subjected to history and liberated by it.

Notes

1   L. Jacobs, *A Jewish Theology*, London: Darton, Longman & Todd, 1973, pp. 126–127.

2   Not all Jewish commentators accept that philosophy is a properly Jewish intellectual activity. It is often regarded as alien to the biblical spirit of Judaism, imported through cross-cultural exchange in diaspora communities influenced by Greek, Islamic and modern European thought. See Julius Guttmann's argument to this effect in *The Philosophy of Judaism: The History of Jewish Philosophy from Biblical Times to Franz Rosenzweig*, trans. D.W. Silverman, Northvale, NJ: Jason Aaronson, 1988, esp. pp. 3–4.

3   Z. Braiterman, *(God) After Auschwitz: Tradition and Change in Post-Holocaust Jewish Thought*, Princeton, NJ: Princeton University Press, 1998. It should be noted that not all post-Holocaust philosophers have deployed the free-will defence of God, not least because they do not all regard God as holocaustally hidden or silent. See, for example, Emil Fackenheim's heteronomous theology of the 'Commanding Voice of Auschwitz' who commands Jewry to withstand the Nazi assault by remaining Jews (E. Fackenheim, *God's Presence in History: Jewish Affirmations and Philosophical Reflections*, New York, NY: Harper & Row, 1972, esp. pp. 84–95).

4   In particular, Steven Katz has criticized Eliezer Berkovits's position, arguing that God could have created persons with a weaker *yetzer ha'ra* (inclination to evil) and a world which produced fewer challenges to moral choice. Katz also asks (much as feminist philosophers would) whether it is morally acceptable to suggest that Jewish children should suffer starvation and horrific forms of death in order that others might have an opportunity to demonstrate their moral goodness in comforting them. The evil of Auschwitz exceeds the good of moral heroism. As Katz notes, there is surely a

moral and logical flaw in Berkovits' argument if God's 'care for Nazis and for their freedom meant a total absence of solicitude for their victims' (S. Katz, *Post-Holocaust Dialogues: Critical Studies in Modern Jewish Thought*, New York, NY: New York University Press, 1983, p. 277. See also pp. 270–279).

5   E. Levinas, *Difficile Liberté: Essais sur le Judaisme*, Paris: Albin Michel, 1963, pp. 106–107.

6   A. Cohen, *The Tremendum: a Theological Interpretation of the Holocaust*, New York, NY: Continuum, 1993, p. 97.

7   E. Berkovits, *Faith After the Holocaust*, New York, NY, Ktav, 1973, p. 136.

8   Ibid., pp. 102–107. See also E. Berkovits, *With God in Hell: Judaism in the Ghettos and Deathcamps*, New York, NY and London: Sanhedrin, 1979, p. 62.

9   Berkovits, *Faith After the Holocaust*, p. 106.

10   Ibid., p. 124.

11   Ibid., p. 107. Susan Shapiro reminds us that in Jewish philosophy rhetorical tropes bear a constitutive rather than secondary relation to the logic of texts (S. Shapiro, 'A Matter of Discipline: Reading for Gender in Jewish Philosophy', in M. Peskovitz and L. Levitt (eds) *Judaism Since Gender*, New York, NY and London: Routledge, 1997, pp. 158–159).

12   Berkovits, *Faith After the Holocaust*, pp. 109, 106.

13   Ibid., p. 107.

14   Divine providence plays little or no role in the women's Auschwitz memoir literature other than in the few memoirs of ultra-Orthodox women. Broadly speaking, it is women's relationships – both actual and remembered – which are the source of consolation, not the idea of God or a sense of his presence.

15   Katz understands the *Endlösung* not only as a political phenomenon but as 'a recreation of humankind and a restructuring of the cosmos' whose precondition was the annihilation of Jewry (S. Katz, 'Holocaust, the Jewish Theological Responses', in M. Eliade (ed.) *The Encyclopedia of Religion*, New York, NY: Macmillan, 1987, vol. 6, p. 423. In *In Bluebeard's Castle: Some Notes Towards the Re-definition of Culture*, London: Faber & Faber, 1971, pp. 37–38, George Steiner argues that the 'requirements of absolute monotheism [had] proved all but intolerable'. Jewry had to be destroyed because it had 'invented' the unattainable ideal and impossible demand of ethical monotheism. Similarly, Berkovits claims that, despite its secular ideology, Nazism knew that it would fail to conquer the world if it failed to eliminate the 'Jewish influence' on history, in whose processes Nazism sensed the presence of God (Berkovits, *With God in Hell*, pp. 79–80, 83–84). See also, E. Fackenheim, *To Mend the World: Foundations of Future Jewish Thought*, New York, NY: Schocken, 1982, p. 323; I. Greenberg, 'Cloud of Smoke, Pillar of Fire: Judaism, Christianity, and Modernity after the Holocaust', in E. Fleischner (ed.) *Auschwitz: Beginning of a New Era?: Reflections on the Holocaust*, New York, NY: Ktav, 1977, p. 29; M. Wyschogrod, *The Body of Faith: Judaism as Corporeal Election*, New York, NY: Seabury Press, 1983, pp. 103, 223.

16   Wyschogrod, *The Body of Faith*, p. 36. See also p. 189.

17   I. Maybaum, *The Face of God After Auschwitz*, Amsterdam: Polak and Van Gennep, 1965, p. 25.

18   'Voluntary Covenant', in S.L. Jacobs (ed.) *Contemporary Jewish Religious Responses to the Holocaust*, Lanham, TX, New York, NY and London: University Press of America, 1993, pp. 92–93.

19   T.K. Abbott, trans., *Kant's Critique of Practical Reason and Other Works on the Theory of Ethics*, London: Longmans, 1909, pp. 245–246. A Kantian notion of autonomy is not to be confused with the license of passion. Autonomy is the basis for rational, responsible choice and respects the moral autonomy of others who are never ends to others' means. Governed by conscience, autonomy is, for Kant, precisely what makes us moral agents.

20   Berkovits, *With God in Hell*, pp. 61–63. It should be noted that, for Sartre, but not for Berkovits, an Orthodox Jew, individuals define their own moral universe.

21   Berkovits's argument has particular poignancy in that his mother, two sisters and brother were killed by the Nazis in 1944.

22   See further, M. Raphael, *The Female Face of God in Auschwitz: A Jewish Feminist Theology of the Holocaust*, London and New York, NY: Routledge, 2003, Chs 3–5.

23   The literature is too extensive to list here. See, for example, J.T. Baumel, 'Social Interaction Among Jewish Women in Crisis During the Holocaust', in *Gender and History*, 7 (1995): 64–84; Charlotte Delbo, *Auschwitz and After*, trans. R.C. Lamont, New Haven, CT: Yale University Press, 1995; B. Ferderber-Salz, *And the Sun Kept Shining...*, New York, NY: Holocaust Library, 1980; S. Rabinovici, M. Pressler and J. Skofield, trans. S. Rabinovits, *Thanks to My Mother*, London: Puffin, 2000; G. Tedeschi, trans. T. Parks, *There Is a Place on Earth: A Woman in Birkenau*, London: Minerva, 1994.

24   Delbo, *Auschwitz and After*, pp. 72–73, 104.

25 See, for example, R. Kornriech Gelissen with H.D. MacAdam, *Rena's Promise: A Story of Sisters in Auschwitz*, Boston, MA: Beacon Press, 1996; I. Leitner and I.A. Leitner (eds) *Fragments of Isabella: A Memoir of Auschwitz*, New York, NY: T.Y. Crowell, 1978.

26 J.T. Baumel, 'Women's Agency and Survival Strategies During the Holocaust', *Women's Studies International Forum*, 22 (1999): 333–334, 343, 344.

27 E. Berkovits, *With God in Hell*, pp. 61–62.

28 V. Frankl, *Man's Search for Meaning: An Introduction to Logotherapy*, trans. I. Lasch, Boston, MA: Beacon Press, 1962, pp. 65, 66.

29 E. Fackenheim, *To Mend the World*, p. 298.

30 P.S. Anderson, 'Philosophy of Religion', in S. Young (ed.) *Encyclopedia of Women and World Religion*, vol. 2, New York, NY: Macmillan, 1999, p. 776.

31 See, for example M. Gillis-Carlbach, 'Jewish Mothers and Their Children During the Holocaust: Changing Tasks of the Motherly Role', in J.K. Roth and E. Maxwell (eds) *Remembering for the Future: The Holocaust in an Age of Genocide*, Basingstoke: Palgrave, 2001, pp. 230, 237–238; M. Goldenberg, 'Different Horrors, Same Hell: Women Remembering the Holocaust', in R.S. Gottlieb (ed.) *Thinking the Unthinkable: Meanings of the Holocaust*, New York, NY: Paulist Press, 1990, pp. 150–166; M.A. Kaplan, *Between Dignity and Despair: Jewish Life in Nazi Germany*, Oxford: Oxford University Press, 1999; esp. pp. 50–73; C. Rittner and J.K. Roth (eds) *Different Voices: Women and the Holocaust*, New York: Paragon Press, 1993.

32 E. Berkovits, *With God in Hell*, p. 76.

33 Ibid., pp. 7, 74f. Orthodoxy generally maintains that the Holocaust presents no new theodical challenge to a faith that has been severely tested throughout the course of Jewish history. However, sufficient evidence of God's providential love is the survival of Jewry and its observances against all odds and, most particularly in the events of the Exodus and the Establishment of the State of Israel. Emil Fackenheim denies that Berkovits's *With God in Hell* suggests that, to faith, 'nothing has happened at all'. For Berkovits, faith has been shaken by the Holocaust, but not altered (Berkovits, *To Mend the World*, p. 309).

34 It is notable that Etty Hillesum's transcendence of her incarceration in the Dutch transit camp of Westerbork was the exercise of a (quasi-Christian) spiritual freedom more readily available to those who, like herself, were childless. (See her *Etty: A Diary 1941–43*, trans. A.J. Pomerans, London, Grafton Books, 1985 and *Letters from Westerbork*, trans. A.J. Pomerans, London, Grafton Books, 1988.)

35 Two ground-breaking studies of the representation of women in Western philosophy have been J. Grimshaw, *Feminist Philosophers: Women's Perspectives on Philosophical Traditions*, Hemel Hempstead: Harvester Wheatsheaf, 1986, and, more recently, B. Clack, *Misogyny in the Western Philosophical Tradition: A Reader*, Basingstoke: Macmillan, 1999.

36 S. Ruddick, *Maternal Thinking: Towards a Politics of Peace*, London: The Women's Press, 1990, N. Noddings, *Caring: A Feminine Approach to Ethics and Moral Education*, Berkeley, CA and London: University of California Press, 1986. The temper and content of this approach has been congenial to many Jewish feminists who have sought their liberation through predominantly intra-Jewish sources and values which themselves inscribe gender difference.

37 M. Wyschogrod, *The Body of Faith*, p. 108. In his *Renewing the Covenant: A Theology for the Postmodern Jew*, Philadelphia, PA: The Jewish Publication Society, 1991, Eugene Borowitz steers a *via media* between traditionalist and liberal conceptions of Jewish autonomy with his dialectical account of the freedom of the self as properly exercised within the social and historical structures and constraints of universal moral norms and those of the covenantal community. Kenneth Seeskin has recently argued that the tradition presents the Jew as an autonomous agent because he or she has reason and conscience and can choose to do good or evil. Within the consensual framework of covenant or partnership, Jews bear moral responsibility for their choices, God's self-revelation not withstanding (K. Seeskin, *Autonomy in Jewish Philosophy*, Cambridge: Cambridge University Press, 2001).

38 M. Buber, *The Eclipse of God: Studies in the Relation Between Religion and Philosophy*, New York, NY: Harper & Brothers, 1952, p. 175.

39 See further, P. Mendes-Flohr, 'Law and Sacrament: Ritual Observance in Twentieth Century Religious Thought', in A. Green (ed.) *Jewish Spirituality from the Sixteenth Century Revival to the Present*, London: SCM Press, 1989, pp. 317–345, esp. pp. 318–332.

40 R. Adler, *Engendering Judaism: An Inclusive Theology and Ethics*, Philadelphia, PA: The Jewish Publication Society, 1988, p. 21.

41 The purpose of my *The Female Face of God in Auschwitz* is to elaborate a theology of divine holocaustal presence.

42 Post-Holocaust Jewish theology has generally found the static God of classic Jewish philosophy morally and affectively wanting. Models of a God who is engaged with human suffering, if not actually suffering himself, now prevail. Existentialism has deeply influenced twentieth-century Jewish philosophy and produced a vibrant theology of encounter best known in the work of Martin Buber. Differently again, Elie Wiesel and David Blumenthal's post-Holocaust theologies of protest assume that God is susceptible to human argument and judgement. (That God is moved, completed or otherwise mutable is, in any case, characteristic of the biblical, rabbinic and mystical traditions.) Michael Wyschogrod has rejected Maimonides' Aristotelian suprapersonal Unmoved Mover in no uncertain terms as unbiblical and 'dangerous to Jewish faith' (Wyschogrod, *The Body of Faith*, p. xiv). While not repudiating God's freedom and transcendence, A.J. Heschel argued that the biblical prophets were very far from apathetic in their theology. They proclaimed an affective, relational God who suffers with the suffering of his beloved people in whom he enters into history. Moreover, a function of God's suffering and injured love is his wrath. And without the involved passion of wrath there would be no divine or human justice. The *pathos* of God shapes human *pathos*; 'man' is *homo sympatheticus* (A.J. Heschel, *The Prophets*, vol. 2, New York, NY: Harper Collins, 1975).

Embodiment

Introduction

ANGLO-AMERICAN PHILOSOPHY of religion has tended to avoid direct discussion of the body. This apparent lack of interest in physical exist-ence is reflected in the account given of God. God has been defined as incorporeal: according to Richard Swinburne, God is 'something like a "person without a body (i.e. a spirit) who is eternal, free, able to do anything, knows everything, is perfectly good, is the proper object of human worship and obedience, the creator and sus-tainer of the universe"'.[1] This reification of disembodiment, not surprisingly, influ-ences the extent to which philosophers of religion are able to see the realm of the body as of any real philosophical interest. Only when discussing death and suffering does the fact that we are embodied creatures enter the discussions of philosophers of religion, and then there is a tendency to neglect the actual experience of being creatures with bodies in order to write about more abstract ideas of immortality, or why God might have allowed suffering in the first place. Philosophers of religion influenced by contemporary Continental philosophy have tended to engage more directly with issues arising from the physical body, and this willingness to engage with neglected aspects of being human has profoundly influenced the work of femin-ists in this area: not least because, historically, women have been associated with the body and all its ills, men with the mind and the spiritual life which has been based upon its perceived qualities of rationality and detachment.

The writers in this section are concerned with specific issues surrounding embodiment, and are particularly concerned to relate these issues to their religious context. In some ways, fairly traditional themes inspire them: so, Kathleen O'Grady is concerned with exploring the meaning of the Eucharist; Alison Jasper relates her work to the incarnation; while Beverley Clack is concerned with issues of mortality. Yet here the similarities with traditional engagements end. The body is used not as a starting point for *metaphysical* discussions, but rather provides the arena in which key religious issues can be discussed.

Kathleen O'Grady's chapter uses the ideas of Julia Kristeva to explore the relationship between love and the Christian ritual of the Eucharist. O'Grady is concerned to explore the embodied nature of religious practice. As such, she considers Kristeva's claim that 'transubstantiation' should be understood as a metaphor which offers the possibility that the Eucharist might become 'a vehicle for psychic renewal'. O'Grady juxtaposes Kristeva's sensual reading of this ritual with Umberto Eco's focus on a formalist faith expressed through binary oppositions. For Kristeva, the Eucharist is best understood as a consummation with the maternal body, and thus O'Grady shows how a specific religious ritual is intimately connected with issues of human embodiment.

Continuing this engagement with central Christian themes, Alison Jasper narrates a self-reflexive interpretation of the ambivalent meanings given to the Christian doctrine of incarnation in the tradition understood in its broadest sense: so she engages not only with the Christian canon, but also with religious relics. Her aim is to recollect religion in the realm of the body, which for her is bound up with incarnation. Her task is more than metaphorical; she confronts the traditional canon, its language and its representation in art and artefacts, finding traces of the feminine in even the most Orthodox efforts to exclude the messy side of embodiment. Relating her ideas to key aspects of post-structuralist work on the self, Jasper employs figures as diverse as Mona Hatoum and Donna Haraway to argue that 'the narratives of Christian embodiment ... still have a part to play in naming a subversiveness that can be creative'.

Beverley Clack's approach is more self-consciously related to the analytic tradition. Her concern is similar to Jasper's in that she wishes to explore the relationship between the body and human spirituality by considering the connection often made between sex and death. She offers a critique of this habitual connection by figures as diverse as the Marquis de Sade and St Augustine, but is concerned to argue that it is by subverting this connection, rather than rejecting it, that death can be viewed not as an aberration, but as part of life.

Note

1   R. Swinburne, *The Coherence of Theism*, Oxford: Clarendon Press, 1977, p. 1.

Chapter 10

Kathleen O'Grady

SACRED METAPHOR: JULIA KRISTEVA AND UMBERTO ECO[1]

Of love and technology: metaphor

IN A BURST OF CONFIDENCE for technological advancement, Umberto Eco, in his *The Role of the Reader*, declares that the possibility now exists for a computer to comprehend the basic structure of metaphor, conceivably cognizant not only of its semantic formation, but also of metaphor's creative potentialities.[2] This metaphor-machine would be capable of systematically generating the progeny of poetic imagination, as well as the conceptual metaphors that frame our everyday thought processes – Zarathustra's 'worn soles' – and even the monotony of catachresis ('foot' of the mountain, 'head' of the class), through a computer program that dictates the grammatical rules of substitution and contiguity in the signifying chain.[3]

Eco's understanding of metaphor could not be further from that of Julia Kristeva, who places 'transubstantiation' at the core of the metaphorical process, augmenting the linguistic model with affect, synaesthesia and the possibility for identification and subjectal renewal. In Kristeva's system, it would be impossible to dehumanize the metaphor, since metaphor is grounded in our physical being and lies at the base of our religious and cultural constructions. While Eco makes clear the combinatory activity of the metaphorical process, Kristeva focuses on the metaphor as a vehicle for psychic renewal. Kristeva examines the sensual lining from the merger between semantic features, characterized by the ritual of the Eucharist, while Eco's text is an apologia for a formalist faith in binarisms, illustrated by his examination of the production of the pun.

Both Kristeva and Eco locate much of their semiotic sensitivity in Jakobson, that prodigy of the Prague Circle, who thoroughly reformulated the metaphor–metonymy relationship. But where Eco adds Peirce, Kristeva adds Proust and, despite their shared linguistic framework, their fundamental understanding of metaphor becomes irreconcilable. Eco dreams of a Peircean unlimited semiosis, represented by a computer gushing metaphors from its rigid metonymic code; Kristeva talks of amatory idealization in linguistic osmosis, semantic units entwining, then metamorphosizing, a Proustian 'cool after warmth': that is, an understanding of metaphor based on love.[4]

Umberto Eco and the metaphor-machine

The very suggestion of a 'metaphor-machine' is surprising coming from a theorist who is not primarily interested in language as a fixed structure but in the point of intersection between the language code and the language user. Eco is not concerned with language in stasis, but has developed a theory that accounts for mobility within the linguistic system itself. His contribution to the study of semiotics aims to account for the ability of the language code to be renewed by those who use it and rejuvenated through the operations of the system. How is it possible, then, armed with a somewhat organic theory of language, for Eco to propose that a machine might be capable of producing the time-honoured material of poetry, prose and philosophy – the fulcrum of human creativity – the metaphor? Is the concept of the metaphor-machine not anathema to an Eco-based theory of semiotics?

Eco's understanding of the Peircean triadic activity of semiosis (the interchange between the sign, the *interpretant*, and the object) will elucidate his understanding of metaphor further:

> By semiosis I mean an action, an influence, which is, or involves, a cooperation of three subjects, such as a sign, its object and its *interpretant*, this tri-relative influence not being in any way resolvable into actions between pairs.[5]

This definition is notable primarily because of Peirce's insistence on the inclusion of the operations of the interpretant in any theory of signs. Eco augments and refines Peirce's interpretant in a non-anthropomorphic framework, indicating that it is that aspect of the sign which intends something other than itself. It is important not to mistake Peirce's interpretant for the *addressee*. The interpretant is both an element of the sign (its intention, idea) and the starting point for the establishment of a new sign (its production in the mind of the interpreter – its meaning – another representation).[6] That is, the interpretant is not simply the meaning or idea that a sign conveys but the creation of another sign, the moment where the understanding of one series of signs is produced only through another system of signs in an infinite 'textual matrix'.[7] The elaboration of the operations of the interpretant in the semiotic sphere becomes Eco's contribution to a Peircean *unlimited semiosis,* where language is defined as being equipped with self-referentially defining terms that augment, clarify and connect one to the other.

Perhaps Eco is not aspiring, in positing the metaphor-machine, to a regulative understanding of metaphor, but is presenting a means to discern the possibility for 'unlimited semiosis' as outlined by Peirce. The 'unlimited' in the Peircean expression does not literally indicate that a given text contains all possible meanings, but that the structural organization of the signification system provides the potential for a text to have a variety of meanings (for different readers or for the same reader). It accounts for the facility of a single sign to carry multiple meanings. It is not a 'free for all' theory of interpretation, where any and all renditions of the text are possible, but indicates the proclivity of signs to extend towards other signs, organized through contiguity in the semantic sphere. Eco's elucidation of Peirce's interpretant becomes the foundation for this theory of unlimited semiosis. It is an understanding of the linguistic system where each sign is part of a larger design of metonymic relations in the chain, permitting a multiplicity of meanings within a given text, 'each term is explained by other terms and where each one is, through an infinite chain of interpretants, potentially explainable by all others'.[8] This 'openness' to polyvalence, however, is not interminable but provides what Eco terms the 'field of *oriented* possibilities', where each reading is both open and yet bound by the contiguous structure of the semantic field.[9]

It is interesting to note that Eco borrows his main semiotic paradigm from the field of artificial intelligence (AI) in order to elucidate his organic theory of signification.[10] From Ross Quillian's work in AI, Eco assembles The Quillian Model (Model Q) to depict the polydimensional labyrinth of connected interpretants in any signifying system. This model is constructed very much like the Internet's World Wide Web, where from any point in the network every other point can be reached. Model Q demonstrates the operation of unlimited semiosis within the bounds of all possible reference, demonstrating the pre-determined relations of combination that underlie all linguistic construction. This is a graphic representation of Eco's ambitious aspiration to map out all of the contiguous relations in the language code:

> the model therefore anticipates the definition of every sign, thanks to its interconnection with the universe of all other signs that function as interpretants, each of which is ready to become the sign interpreted by all the others: the model, in its complexity, is based on a process of unlimited semiosis.[11]

Quite literally, Model Q is the assemblance of all possible signifiers connected to one another through bonds of association, begetting a massive web (infinite, perhaps) of signification. Model Q, by aggregating the sum of signifiers through relation, is able to foresee all possible uses of the code. Each sign in the linguistic system is structurally linked through the intending faculty of its interpretant (the idea and meaning of the sign), to all other signs in Model Q. It is a complex network of all possible meanings and interpretations – the ultimate fantasy of a formalist linguistics.

Eco, however, proposes to fashion this diagram to reflect the flexibility of the general community of language users to accommodate habitual alterations in the combinative field. The series of contiguous relations in the semantic code is perpetually evolving, responding to changes in cultural stimuli. Model Q demonstrates the ability of the linguistic system, structured through contiguity, to both generate and adapt to multiple shifting. Model Q allows for the inclusion of new components to the semantic field, yet every sign (and, by extension, its application – all acts of signification) is dependent upon pre-existing relations in the model. This flexible structure is not unlike Kristeva's theory of *intertextuality*, which chronologically precedes Eco's Model Q. Intertextuality demonstrates the ability of a sign system to permit an infinite number of conjunctions with another sign system, resulting in new meaning productions. And like Deleuze and Guattari's rhizomatic structures, Model Q imposes a logic without being limited or organized definitively by its own form. As Teresa de Lauretis states, the rhizome 'has no centre, no periphery, and no exit, and is virtually infinite'.[12] But where Kristeva and Deleuze and Guattari wish only to depict a pattern and organizing principle in certain semiotic operations, Eco wishes to definitively map out the entire semiotic sphere within his model. He must concede, however, that his rhizomatic Model Q can only ever be a 'regulative hypothesis', due to the proclivity of the relations in the code to shift and change.[13] Just as the construction for the model would be completed, it would already have to be altered to accommodate the modifications made to the established paths of connection between signifiers.

What then is the 'motive for metaphor' as Northrop Frye so aptly inquires?[14] Eco's response is clear: unlimited semiosis. The proposition of the metaphor-machine is the means through which Eco is able to theorize the metaphor as the vehicle for the process of unlimited semiosis. In Eco's vision, an automaton operating on binary logic would be capable of tracing all metaphors back to the chain of contiguity that is internal to the linguistic system. Eco appeals to the structural operations of the metaphorical process, demonstrating that the signifiers conjoined in metaphor have a relationship that is independent of the phenomenal world. That is, the metaphoric process is linguistic, an operation between signs in an ordered sign-system. Metaphor is not based on a similarity between things in the concrete world but is an example of 'infro-' or 'inter-semantic connections'.[15] The metaphoric process is determined by the code itself, structurally inscribed through the linking of interpretants delineated in Eco's Model Q.

Linguistic connection through mutual resemblance – the 'this is that' of the Frye-metaphor – is not created as such by an individual, but involves a drawing together of signifiers already associated in the metonymic chain.[16] Metaphor is first grounded in metonymy, the organizing principle of the semantic arena. Metonymy is generally defined as the substitution of one sign for another associated sign (commonly referred to as 'the part for the whole'). In 'The Semantics of Metaphor', however, Eco uses metonymy very much in the way Jakobson and Lacan employ the term, where metonymy is related to contiguity between signifiers, their linear sequence and 'semic interdependence'.[17] This metonymic relation is what Jane Gallop calls 'the forward push to finish signification'.[18] No signifier ever ends, as such, but perpetually extends towards its interpretant in the contiguous web of signs. The Model Q, with its interconnected, criss-crossing mass of associations is a mapping of the structural metonymic principles enmeshed in the total signifying arena.

Creativity exists, but only in a semiotic motility, finding resemblance in pre-existing linguistic relations. With Model Q as its program, the 'hypothetical automaton' need only map the available web of binary choices to create a series of meaningful metaphors.[19] Metonymy in Model Q is fixed by structure, and therefore, mechanistic, codifiable, capable of being programmed onto a computer chip. Or, as Eco would have it in his novel, *The Island of the Day Before*, Padre Emanuele's 'Aristotelian Machine' – an elaborate assemblage of card catalogues which create endless metaphors by fusing associated terms under the organization of Aristotle's ten categories.[20] Padre's machine, like Eco's Model Q, is an ambitious attempt to encompass all possible signification in a single model, providing metaphor-on-demand.

Eco's purpose, however, is not to develop a formally rigid model of the metaphoric process, but to elucidate further the flexibility of Model Q to respond to the operations of unlimited semiosis. In the Quillian model, Eco proposes to establish that the possibilities for metaphor, through combination and resemblance in the Q paradigm, are not limited by the structure, but incalculable because of the organizing pattern: that is, they are fixed but not finite. A metaphor is a metaphor because it discloses previously existing metonymic combinations, but culture provides the signifying system with its network of contiguous relations. Metaphor, therefore, is always the product of an ever-changing 'culturalized contiguity'.[21] These relations, determined by societal forces are not fixed signifiers, but connections established through language in use, in context.

The entire 'problem' of metaphoric creativity, as Eco calls it, is not eliminated by the establishment of Model Q, but merely becomes 'susceptible to translation in binary terms' and, consequently, easily transferable to a computer program.[22] Eco maintains that metaphoric creativity does not consist in generating new elements into the linguistic code but by making anterior bonds visible:

> Apparently, one entity is in the place of the other by virtue of a mutual resemblance. But the resemblance is due to the fact that in the code there exists already fixed relations of substitution which, in some way or other, link the substitute entities to those substituted for.[23]

A metaphor-wielding artist is not a deity, creating new forms, but an explorer, traversing the intricate pathways inscribed in the linguistic system. A 'creative metaphor' in Eco's vision is the recognition of identity between terms in the linguistic chain that have not yet been integrated by a community. The connection appears original, unprecedented, when it is a direct acknowledgement of what has always been latent in the sequential organization of the signifying system. The metaphoric process is not a simple recognition of metonymic links in Eco's Model Q but a revolutionary process of anticipating combinations not foreseen by the linguistic order. These are combinations which are inscribed within the system but not yet acknowledged by the culture. In a related essay, Eco states that 'epiphanies', which feel magical, fantastical and ground-breaking, follow this same pattern of exposing preceding linguistic relations that were not readily visible. It would seem that, by extension, Eco suggests that a computer is not only capable of providing the creative component of metaphor, but is also able to generate the mystical quality of the epiphany.[24]

Metaphor demonstrates the 'unlimited' semiotic potential depicted in Model Q. The metaphoric process is internal, residing within the signifying system, established through resemblance from terms within the metonymic code. The metaphorical process is therefore always semiotic and, by extension, makes statements about the nature of the signifying system itself. Eco delineates a theory of metaphor from within, a linguistic phenomena, bound by contiguous relations in the code, while self-referentially evaluating the code itself.

It is interesting that both Eco and Kristeva turn to Joyce to elucidate their theory of metaphor. Eco employs *Finnegans Wake* (which he designates a 'textual machine') with its miniature but intricate Model Q, to demonstrate that the *pun* is the most poignant example of the semiotic movement to occur in the metaphorical process.[25] Eco argues that the pun is a double-metaphor which flagrantly exhibits, rather than conceals, the contiguous arrangement that establishes similarity between signifiers. The terms conflated in a pun form a particular kind of metaphor where both the *vehicle* (the substituting word or words) and the *tenor* (the substituted word or words) are connected by phonic or semantic affinity.[26] A pun, more clearly than a metaphor, reveals the complex substratum of metonymy that binds the terms together in a single embrace. The 'ghost signifier(s)', implied but not explicit in the metaphor, are glaring in the pun and qualify the present signifiers in a reciprocal arrangement of both identity and difference. These reciprocally defining terms contribute to the multiplicity of meanings generated by the pun, making the pun both 'vehicle and tenor' and therefore a multiple metaphor.[27]

In any kind of metaphor, but in a pun particularly, there is a condensation of properties, a reciprocal transference of features between several terms. The conflation of terms affects the cultural network by either renewing or developing new associative links in the signifying chain. While the metaphor is constituted by the contiguity of terms, the pun makes this relationship most manifest. The contiguity is violently thrust upon two or more signifiers in a pun, resulting in an overt polyvalence that qualifies the metonymy which generates its existence. The metaphor-pun has the capacity to simultaneously temper the metonymic chain at the same time as the metonymic chain supports the metaphor–pun. The pun 'short-circuits' the signifying system by assimilating various connections that previously existed in the Quillian Model.[28] Instead of following the sequential metonymic connections in the Quillian web, the pun jumps rapidly in a 'leap of faith', a faith in the certainty of the contiguous chain that grounds its metaphorical operation.[29]

Eco's theory of metaphor, with the pun as a distinguished type, is quintessentially *semiotic*. He describes metaphor in purely linguistic terms, its systemic nature determined by societal norms and cultural practices that are reflected in the linguistic code. Eco's theory also allows for the possibility of metaphor, and pun specifically, to create 'metasemiotic judgments' that interrogate the validity of the semantic structure illustrated in the Quillian Model.[30] Metaphor not only demonstrates that the semantic system is capable of self-contradictions ('once we begin to substitute D for A by metonymic connections we discover that D has some semes in contradiction with those of A'), but it produces innovative semiotic information by demonstrating the before-unseen metonymic connections that inherently bind the two or more terms together.[31] Puns make visible the codification that was previously unrecognizable and in so doing, elucidates the very operations of the Quillian Model.

The question then becomes, not whether an automaton would be adept at generating metaphor, but whether a computer would be able to allow its program to be modified by both the continual influx of cultural information and the very metaphors it generates. It would be one feat to program a computer with the entire Q Model – the sum of culturally inscribed contiguous relations in the linguistic chain (which Eco indicates could only ever conceivably take place hypothetically) – but it would be quite another feat for a computer to be competent to fashion 'metasemiotic judgments' on the level of human metaphor.

It is not surprising to find that less than five years following the publication date of 'The Semantics of Metaphor', the essay in which Eco states that 'it would be possible . . . to construct an automaton capable of generating and understanding metaphors', he forcibly reverses his position and concludes an extensive chapter on metaphor in *Semiotics and the Philosophy of Language* with the following caution: 'No algorithm exists for the metaphor, nor can a metaphor be produced by means of a computer's precise instructions, no matter what the volume of organized information to be fed in.'[32] Of course, it is the right of every living philosopher to change his mind.

Julia Kristeva and the post-theological Eucharist

Eco's definition of the pun as a conflation of terms that do not eradicate one another but exist together in mutual modification is closer to Kristeva's definition of metaphor generally. While Eco provides a grand metanarrative for the operations of the metaphoric process, Kristeva examines the subjective effect of metaphor, the know-ledge granted from the interaction between linguistic elements, endowing metaphor with an archaic, prelinguistic quality that other theories do not (fully) account for. The Kristevan metaphor initiates a subjective process that transports identities by blurring boundaries without cancelling difference, resulting in a metamorphosis: the ideal representation for a forever-fragmented identity.

In a rejection of Lacanian psychoanalysis, with its emphasis on metonymy and desire, Kristeva returns to Freud (the 'original Father') to enrich her pre-Oedipal con-struct for understanding early subjective formation (primary identification). Unsatisfied with the descriptions of an autoeroticism that permeates the mother–child symbiosis prior to the mirror-stage of development, she seeks to augment the pre-specular rela-tionship by outlining the archaic foundations for the acquisition of language. She finds an undeveloped reference in Freud's *Moses and Monotheism* and *The Ego and the Id* to a third party that is capable of enriching her knowledge of primary identification: the 'father in individual prehistory'.[33] The symbiotic union between the child and the maternal container is disturbed by this third element, not a person, but a non-anthropomorphic, social and linguistic representation of the love that the archaic mother expresses for someone outside the mother–child dyad. Despite their names, neither the archaic mother nor the imaginary father are gendered subjects, since sexual awareness does not occur prior to the emergence of the Oedipal ego. Rather, the third party is someone for whom the mother expresses desire, someone other than the child and it is this ternary structure that diverts the homogeneity between the mother–child entity. Central to the operations of this tertiary economy is the understanding that the love expressed by the mother towards the imaginary father is communicated through language, a discourse that disturbs the undifferentiated body of the mother–child and propels the child towards 'a speaking other'.[34] Without this third element the subject would forever fall into abjection, unable to fully separate from the unity with the archaic mother and unable to completely cultivate an individual subjectivity.

Kristeva does not so much critique Lacan's mirror-stage as amplify the identifica-tion process. She asks: 'Does the "mirror stage" emerge out of nowhere?' and implies, *does the archaic mother have no role in language acquisition?*[35] Not satisfied with the over-bearing position that Lacan grants the Symbolic (the Law of the Father) in the develop-ment of the speaking subject, Kristeva describes an earlier identificatory process. This primary identification involves the heterogeneous conveyance of identity from maternal fusion towards the object of the mother's love – the imaginary father. It is not a full separation, a complete subjectivity (which Kristeva still believes only occurs during the mirror-stage) but a multiple identification that provides the substratum for the speaking subject.

This movement is not one of possession or need – I must have 'object a' – but a movement toward identification with a loved other. It is not a motion to 'have' but a gesture towards 'being like', that is, a *metaphoric* identification.[36] The imaginary father provides an early transference of drive energy towards the language of another. The identification, a conglomeration of the archaic trinity (mother–child–father), is drive-laden, bubbling with heterogeneous forces that simultaneously disperse and unify the (not-yet) subject. Kristeva's new triadic pattern restructures the psychoanalytic notion of primary narcissism, and places a metaphoric identification at the heart of the subject. This firm dismissal of Lacanian metonymy of desire allows Kristeva to remove the mother's body from the sphere of objectal relations, while simultaneously placing primary identification in the domain of love.

Critics (of which Eco is one) have mistakenly understood Kristeva's theory of language as regressive and her theory of metaphor overly ontological – ontological because it emphasizes the subject outside of language over the operations of signs in the signifying system. This view is based on a complete misreading of the Kristevan project. Though she undoubtedly emphasizes the power of metaphor on subjective formation, her concept implicitly remains linguistic. Metaphoricity is defined by Kristeva as an examination of 'a given number of specific states of the subject of the utterance act . . . who demonstrates by means of metaphors the complex process of identification'.[37] This definition highlights the operations of idealization in discourse, a replication of primary narcissism, a discursive echo of the pre-Oedipal triadic relationship. Yet tacitly manifest is Kristeva's concept of the 'subject' – not an external corporeal entity or a physiological internal process, but always already a speaking subject. The operations of subjectivity and intersubjectivity are linguistic, referential, encoded in and by the signifying system. In Kristevan analysis, there is no subject without language, and consequently there can be no analysis of language without the subject.

It is not surprising to find that both Kristeva's semiotic and psychoanalytic writings are motivated by an understanding of aesthetic textual productions. In linguistic creation Kristeva discovers the space where the subject plays with the ambiguity of the signifier, a 'place for excess and absurdity, ecstasy and death', a place for enacting the cacophony of pre-specular subjectivity.[38] Idealization is perpetually actualized in literary production, indicating the necessity for the continuous renewal of the linguistic subject. Metaphoric production, with its capacity to obscure the border between signifiers, best illustrates the operations of primary identification in the linguistic contract.

But the conflation of semantic features compressed in a single trope not only obscures the boundaries of the discursive subject but problematizes the univocity of the sign. The sign is dispersed, made ambivalent; a paradox, metaphor is both one and other, neither this, nor that. It is equivocally consolidated in difference yet bound by similitude, causing meaning to shift and open up, sliding towards 'an infinity of the signifier'.[39] The metaphor strains the signifying system to bursting: 'The "like" of the metaphorical conveyance both assumes and upsets that constraint and, to the extent that it probabilizes the identity of signs, questions the very probability of the reference.'[40] Nothing could be less ontological. The metaphoric movement refuses to allow the illusion of presence in the signifier. The terms conjoined in a single feature have no clear object of reference, but entertain a semantic slippage which takes place within the signifying system.

Is it possible that there is a meeting place, after all, between Eco and Kristeva? Is not Kristeva's understanding of metaphor, like Eco's, quintessentially semiotic? Kristeva delineates the metaphor in purely linguistic terms: semantic features thrust together in a marriage of identity and non-identity, where signification is confounded by this doubling, elaborated and augmented but ultimately dispersed and propelled forward. Metaphor designates not 'not an ontology, that is, something outside of discourse, but the constraint of discourse itself'.[41] Kristeva endows the metaphoric process with a self-reflective capacity, capable of initiating 'metasemiotic judgments' on the level of Eco-metaphor. The metaphoric process, by destroying the univocal identity (never truly present anyway) of the sign, exhibits openly all the perforations in the operations of the semantic arena, the slippage, the ambiguity, the movement forward implicit in any act of signification. Metaphor becomes the site where the referent and, by extension, the entire operations of the linguistic process both destroys and renews itself through its association with other semantic terms in the signifying arena.

Kristeva finds in poetic metaphor the best example of the conjunction between both semiotic and subjective metaphoric operations. The speaking subject, Kristeva demonstrates, is irredeemably linked to the discursive Other by means of metaphor. This sublime Other, however, is neither the identity of the originary term (vehicle) nor the identity of the second term (tenor), nor even the coupling of the two (metaphor), but 'the very space of metaphorical shifting', the place where meaning floats in gentle waves between loosely linked signifiers.[42] The identificatory process is motivated by the conglomeration of the terms fused in metaphor, while the heterogeneity of significance is simultaneously mimetic of the same (idealization) process. Metaphorization brings the subject to speech and to poetic and artistic representations particularly, with its multi-layered polyphonous and polysemic capering. It operates through a textual imaginary process, a reverberation of the first imaginary process (that longing for the pre-Oedipal father) which provides the originary ground for the subject of language and imagination. It is a reciprocal construction and deconstruction of the subject in language.

It is Proustian metaphor particularly that discloses, for Kristeva, a linguistic illustration of that flexible, plastic subjectivity that a metaphorical transaction not only allows but demands.[43] This polymorphic subjectivity, fuelled by the metaphoric process, is a merging not only of images or ideas, but of time, memory and space. It is a fusion of contradiction and paradox in a single term, assaulting the subject 'like a bolt of lightning'.[44] This amalgamation of sensations engenders a subjectal metamorphosis: a movement with the ability to transform, 'incarnate', 'transubstantiate'.[45] It is not incidental that Kristeva employs religious language to identify the Proustian trope. Proustian metaphor is elemental, pregnant with synaesthetic power, a 'complex abracadabra' that can transform the subject, drawing it back towards the archaic Other, that which is sacred and divine.[46] In Kristevan theory metaphor becomes the linguistic search for jouissance, for articulating that archaic Thing (that sublime space which cannot be articulated). It is a reaching towards the unnamable, the absent: 'Mamma is the starting mechanism [of metaphor] . . . a central erotic secret.'[47] The Kristevan metaphor is *mater-phor*. Kristeva inverts standard feminist theories of the Eucharist, like Naomi Goldenberg's, which depict the ritual as the consumption of the male body of Christ to displace the female body. Kristeva's understanding of the Eucharist necessarily links the metaphoric movement, and thus the Eucharist itself, to a consummation with the maternal body.[48]

Kristeva is one of those interesting hybrids, so common among contemporary French thinkers, who, having (re)discovered religion, discards God. In allegiance with this spiritual agnosticism, Kristeva in her essay, 'Identification and the Real', designates the Eucharist as the metaphoric rite 'par excellence', the 'fulcrum of all other identifications'.[49] In early Kristevan analysis, religious discourse was rejected, represented as the symbolic aspiration to homogenize difference. In her most recent works, however, Kristeva re-examines Christianity (Eastern Orthodox and Catholic traditions, specifically) as a dramatization of the internal strangeness (difference, otherness, foreignness) found at the base of every subject. As she states herself, 'I speak of religions because the question of the other is fundamentally, I think, a religious question.'[50]

The Eucharist becomes the perfect enactment of the Kristevan metaphorical process providing a succession of polymorphic states of subjectivity based especially in an identification with the body of an Other. As Cleo McNelly Kearns has noted, Kristeva's focus on the material aspect of the sacrament and its relation to the 'signifying word' are inspired by Aquinas.[51] The Eucharist, in Kristeva's vision, involves a crossing-over, a conflation of both physical nutrition (bread and wine) and the signifying body (the Word), an intersection between the physical and the psychic.[52] Kristeva scorns those who rationalize transubstantiation as a semblance of passage from bread to body. The Eucharistic rite is an actual assimilation of the Word, the body of Christ, a 'phantasmatic identification' that conflates both drives and verbal representations into a single moment.[53] In order to open oneself up to the other, it is necessary to renew the self through an identificatory process that allows for the internalization of foreignness. This subjective process is not a mimetic imitation of an other, not a comparison, but the actual absorption of other into self, a 'mystical metamorphosis' in the spirit of Baudelaire.[54] The Eucharist is the perfect combination of divine and human, a sacred movement encompassing the real, imaginary and symbolic. It is an identification from the body towards language and return. Clearly Kristeva is not interested in creating a Eucharistic theology, but in describing an identificatory process that is both natural and mystical, both of the body and language. And so it is to literature that she turns for her examples.

Proust's famous 'Petites Madeleines' comprise for Kristeva an excellent example of an aesthetic sacrament, which describes by means of metaphor an epiphanic transformation. In the cold of winter, Proust accepts the offering of tea and cake from his mother. The sensations of the warm liquid mixed with the plump cake summons an earlier impression; on Sundays before mass, Proust recalls his aunt Léonie dipping the 'little scallop-shell of pastry, so richly sensual under its severe, religious folds' in a lime tisane.[55] Sensations fuse – the fragrant lime, the scalloped shell heavy on the thick of the tongue, the warm body of mother, of aunt Léonie, body and blood ingested on a mass Sunday – in a Eucharistic movement, like love in all of its intensity, involving the transportation of the 'I' to the 'sublime Other'. Tea and cake, a domestic communion, as Proust's Madeleine, conjoined with the tisane, draws the subject towards the essence of an other. Proust describes his altered state:

> At once the vicissitudes of life had become indifferent to me, its disasters innocuous, its brevity illusory – this new sensation having had on me the effect which love has of filling me with a precious essence; or rather this was not in me, it was me.[56]

Both spiritual and corporeal, the invocation of the Petites Madeleines through memory is accompanied by an affective intensity, a transgression of bodily boundaries that divides the subject in order to grant it a fusion, but a fusion based on the heterogeneity within the subject. And this metaphoric unity, through difference, is what guarantees a healthy individual subjectivity.

The condensation of terms affords a jouissance. It is the result of a subjective merging: the I is both I and other, without being able to distinguish between them, a kind of possession, both imaginary and real, with an efficacy that impacts on the vitality and strength of subjectivity. The self has been wrenched from its stasis within the maternal container, 'leaves its resting-place and attempts to rise . . . I can feel it mounting slowly . . . I can hear the echo of great spaces traversed'.[57] This Eucharistic movement is an enactment of an imaginary relationship, in psychoanalytic terms, a transferential identification that provides the conditions for a dynamic psychic renewal.

James Joyce also affords an entrance into the Eucharistic movement for Kristeva.[58] But it is with Joycean prose that Kristeva focuses her attention, a prose style that incessantly spells out a series of multiple identifications. While Eco highlights the punning in Joyce, Kristeva points to the innumerable Eucharistic condensations throughout his work. 'Contrasmagnificandjewbangtantiality' is a word that aligns so many signs through phonic and semantic association that it threatens Eco's webbed Model Q with collapse, giving way to an infinite black hole. Kristeva notes that Joyce delights in challenging and transgressing the logic of language, what she terms the *symbolic*. This comprises the referential and communicative facet of language. The *semiotic*, on the other hand, is a linguistic expression of the drive force that disrupts the syntactic and semantic functions of language.

Some critics have mistakenly understood Kristeva's semiotic–symbolic as an elaboration of the binary computer model, but her theory is structured more on a mutual interaction of terms than on a 0–1 structure.[59] Kristeva herself indicates that the logic of the semiotic in dialogue with the symbolic ('poetic language') defies the 0–1 binarisms of the computer model.[60] Similarly she rejects the idea that her theory is in any way similar to the analogic–digital debate. She states: 'The heterogeneity between the semiotic and the symbolic cannot be reduced to the well known distinction between the analogical and digital. . . . [It] is analogical and digital at the same time.'[61] Very early in her semiotic work, Kristeva distanced herself from mechanistic and computer imagery generally and, even in her most recent works, continues to favour corporeal metaphors to explain the operations of the semiotic–symbolic exchange.

Joyce employs this 'semiotic' realm, a logic of rupture, rhythm and condensation in place of the referential and sequential logic of the 'symbolic'. He makes use of the dynamic, material component of language, its playfulness and illogicality. 'Contrasmagnificandjewbangtantiality' opens up the subject of language to ambiguity by supplanting linearity and univocity, and by interrogating the notion of a unified subject (either reader or writer). Kristeva provides a theory of language that endeavours to account for alterity at the base of the speaking subject. Joycean condensations (a type of metaphor–metonym conglomerate since they are joined by contiguity *and* association) incorporate the psychic identification process of Christian ritual not only through content (since Joyce talks incessantly of the Eucharist) but, more importantly, stylistically. The semiotic libidinal drives (expressed through affective language) transform and relativize the denotation of the symbolic realm, dissolving the fiction of a unified identity by creating a dynamic subject that is open to difference. Joyce becomes Kristeva's post-Christian, finding in discourse a place to communicate the operations of Eucharistic identification, the motivation for his literary style.[62]

But what stimulates this Eucharistic movement which is not comparison or mere analogy but the transport of both drives and signs? What gives the host-metaphor this sensory, affective power? *Agape*. Kristeva finds in Christian agape – a term she now interchanges synonymously with primary identification and primary narcissism[63] – an unconditional love which becomes the vehicle for the fusion of '*l'amour sublimé*' of the metaphoric process.[64] Agape provides a spiritual enactment of the loving that exists in the pre-Oedipal triad. I am never autonomous, but always structured by this gift of love from another. I am always already the 'subject of the other' and it is this love that makes me a subject and thus grants meaning to my speech. With such a privileging of the metaphoric–Eucharistic movement, it is perhaps not surprising to find Kristeva balancing her psychoanalytic notion of subjectivity on a theological understanding of love:

> Christian love: paternal, narcissistic, maternal, finds utterance in all fonts of individual lapses, and offers perhaps the richest mosaic of words that the human being, that precocious, possessed person, that lover, ever need hear.[65]

The Kristevan focus shifts from an exclusive examination of avant-garde aesthetic practices to a theory of subjectivity based on the triadic economy ('paternal, narcissistic, maternal') that grounds religious language. The Eucharist is the primary example of this metaphoric osmosis, this doubling, this becoming one in love: Kristeva quotes Jesus, 'He who eats my flesh and drinks my blood abides in me, and I in him'.[66] The Eucharistic rite is a dramatization of the metaphorical movement internal to primary narcissism, providing a symbolic replenishment for the individual, an epiphanic re-enactment of subjective formation, not just identification, but transubstantiation.

Her Proustian inspired understanding of metaphor, with the Eucharist as a distinguished type, provides Kristeva with a markedly Christian ethical model for the psychic functioning of a subject that both rejects and desires the other. The metaphor grants a means for identification with the other through condensation without the erasure of difference; it creates a subjective space for heterogeneity by uncovering internal foreignness at the site of the self.[67] Kristeva's understanding of metaphor offers up the possibility for a highly individualized subjectivist ethics (knowledge of the stranger within) as a foundation for intersubjective relations in the contemporary world.

Kristeva's theory of metaphoricity curiously, for a philosopher who was once so vehemently against any form of religion, aligns her directly with theological interests. It is the great 'eternal return to divinity' that appears contagious among her French philosophical contemporaries.[68] And yet Kristeva is careful to make clear that she is by no means reinscribing Christian theology. As she stated in an interview:

> People are puzzled by my interest in religious traditions and especially those of Catholicism. . . . The return to the theological texts or the texts of art that precede us is indispensable. With Freud as well as other theoreticians and philosophers, we find such an appropriation of traditions as a part of their revolutions, their revolt. We must, therefore, not allow ourselves to remain ignorant of this heritage. Instead, as before, we have to *question* it; as it were, to extract the rational kernels from the mystical shell, as Marx suggested vis-à-vis Hegel. . . .
>
> But we are still within the frame of the Bible and Gospels which poses the necessity of thinking of the Other as indispensable to the horizon of language.

Thus a tradition, stretching back two thousand years since its founding texts is still in debt to these texts and as such it cannot be abandoned or dissolved before we have interrogated it, lucidly, and without complacency.[69]

For Kristeva, an assessment of Western subjectivity necessitates a detailed understanding of religious texts and practices. She now includes in her exhaustive examinations of literary texts, a sympathetic account of the role religion plays in the development of subjectivity, indicating that both literature and religion offer a means to access the place of that 'sublime Other'.

Kristeva now regards atheism as the most severe form of repression. Atheism is depicted as a condition that is based solely on a repudiation of the 'father in individual prehistory' – a wistful reckoning back towards the undisturbed mother–child dyad of the pre-Oedipal state.[70] Atheism is a severe rejection of the metaphoric coupling that Kristeva believes is the foundation for a healthy, fully developed subjectivity. Furthermore, Kristeva also commonly aligns the position of the psychoanalyst with that of the priest, indicating that primary identification through metaphoricity can and should be replicated for the health of the subject, 'by the priest or by the therapist'.[71] A convoluted agreement arises between Eco and Kristeva on this point, as they both playfully depict themselves, semiotician and psychoanalyst, in priestly robes. As Eco finds his way through semiotics by means of Artificial Intelligence, Kristeva finds her way through psychoanalysis by means of theology, entitling her theory an 'esthetic religion', a 'religion of the imagination'.[72]

Conclusion: establishing the bounds of semiotic study

In this chapter, I have highlighted Eco's holistic search for unity in structure by means of the metaphor. A contemporary explorer of technology, he has all the faith in the conquest of the early explorers. But his triumph would be a total assimilation of all possible meaning, nothing less. Kristeva is also undertaking that search for the 'One', but her path leads to a resurrection of psychoanalysis, that most pious of faiths. Her metaphor, *grounded wholly in the body*, charts the corporeal suffering of division. Is it really so strange that the man thinks through the machine and the woman through the body?; the man through unity and the woman through division?

While I have examined in detail the different strategies used by Eco and Kristeva to delineate the metaphorical process, I have also provided an examination of the models that each employ to ground their respective semiotic systems. What becomes clear from this study is the fundamental divide between Eco and Kristeva on the boundary of semiotic study itself. Eco has developed an elaborately formal study of semiotics. Though his theory incorporates the ability of the code to shift and change to accommodate a community of users (both a synchronic and diachronic understanding of the sign), he refuses to accommodate the speaking subject in his analysis. Instead, he prefers to conserve its 'ghostly presence' and declares his opposition towards any study of the subject within the scope of semiotic theory: 'Any other attempt to introduce a consideration of the subject into the semiotic discourse would make semiotics trespass on one of its "natural boundaries".'[73]

Eco prefers to isolate the sign, to separate it from human contamination and understand the laws that engender its production. Subjective and inter-subjective semi-otic theories perpetuate an idealism. A semiotics can only be 'testable', he insists, if it is taken in isolation, in quarantine.[74] A properly scientific study would acknowledge the presence of an empirical subject, but contend only with the performance of signs them-selves in the signifying system.

Eco expresses a clear hostility towards those theories which prioritize the subject of signification. In particular, he targets Kristeva's theory as a 'degenerative notion of [the] linguistic sign' and suggests that this is a deviation from the 'most mature' philo-sophies of language.[75] However, as Vincent Colapietro has noted, Eco's rejection of subjectivity in signification is a curious departure from a Peircean conception of semi-otics. In fact, anticipating postmodern philosophy, Peirce not only acknowledged the subject of sign production and reception but was 'sensitive to the divided character of the human subject' in the discursive process.[76] Eco's dehumanizing movement is a firm rejection of the Peircean agenda. His attempt to formalize fully the linguistic process has culminated in the total effacement of the subject from the signifying system. Eco professes that this is purely a 'methodological' and not a 'metaphysical' presumption, but the claim is weak.[77] As both Colapietro and de Lauretis have noted, 'rather than avoiding idealism . . . he appears to lapse into it'.[78] By effacing subjectivity from the sig-nifying process, Eco reflexively replicates the pre-eminence granted to the transcen-dental ego of both structuralist and formalist linguistics; there could be no greater 'metaphysical' supposition. Eco's utopic vision of computer-generated metaphors is not haphazard or random but contingent upon this idealism. The mechanistic and computer terminology that saturates Eco's texts is a direct consequence of this refusal to accom-modate the subject in signification. The computer alone can provide Eco with that unified cogito, a synthesizing and totalizing, yet disem-*bodied* entity that can initiate programmable signification.

Nothing could be further from a Kristevan semiotics which places at its centre a critique of the transcendental ego inherited (most recently) from structural linguistics. In this ego's place, Kristeva puts a linguistic subject that is based on dialogism and alter-ity. She formulates a split-subject (semiotic–symbolic) that is marked by both physio-logical drives (that constitute part of the signifying process), as well as by the cultural structures that modify and motivate linguistic operations. As if addressing Eco directly (though it is likely that Chomsky and the Grammarians were her original targets), she states:

> The theory of meaning now stands at a crossroad: either it will remain an attempt at formalizing meaning-systems by increasing sophistication of the logico-mathematical tools which enable it to formulate models on the basis of a con-ception (already rather dated) of meaning as the act of a transcendental ego, cut off from its body, its unconscious and also its history; or else it will attune itself to the theory of the speaking subject as a divided subject (conscious/unconscious).[79]

Kristeva's project rejects the pseudo-mathematical formalism that threatens to topple linguistic study and instead works to unite the body with language, signification with physiological drives and historical–societal forces. Issues of gender, in particular, can enter the semiotic arena with the Kristevan framework, while they find no place in an Eco-based semiotics which substitutes a gendered speaking-subject with a computer (a contemporary version of philosophy's long tradition to escape from the corporeal body). Kristeva's 'transubstantiating metaphor' is a direct result of this insistence on the inclusion of the divided subject in any theory of language. The corporeal and religious language which suffuses her texts is consistent with her desire to reconcile the social and the physical, cultural constructions with libidinal drives, body with text. The Eucharist provides an ideal means to theorize the meeting place of drives and signs within a rich cultural practice.

Eco views Kristeva's theory as an example of what semiotic theory should reject; a proper semiotic study does not include the signifying subject. He insists that any study of the subject of signification is 'beyond the semiotic threshold' and that practitioners of semiotic studies should simply 'accept this limit'; Kristeva's work on subjectivity, Eco states, is a 'threshold-trespassing semiotics'.[80] Eco's use of territorial language is revealing. Kristeva's theory 'trespasses', it is 'beyond' and outside the confines of semiotics, it 'confuses' and mistakes; Kristeva does not 'accept the limit' that Eco himself outlines for semiotic theory. Eco aims to surgically separate the function of the sign from that of the subject. He wants no mixing or muddling of borders. He wants clean edges, clear spaces and neatly contained contents.[81] He does not invalidate the necessity for such work (in those lesser subjects such as psychology, sociology), but indicates that it is beyond the bound of the (real) semiotic frame.

We can, perhaps, attribute much of the blame to Saussure for initiating this marking of territory. Often great thinkers are not described as such for providing succinct and totalizing philosophical systems, but for simply asking the right questions. Saussure was one of these great 'enquiring minds'. The findings in *Cours de linguistique générale* have provided the foundation for much of contemporary semiotic and linguistic study and shaped the ensuing generation of the humanities and social sciences simply by asking: *what is the domain of semiology?*[82]

Eco and Kristeva have each taken up the Saussurian quest, though it may well be true, as Terry Eagleton has stated, that 'if Saussure could have foreseen what he started he might well have stuck to the genitive case in Sanskrit'.[83] Most of Eco's texts could be read as part of an encyclopaedic project to map out the scope of semiotic study. What this has sometimes resulted in has been the closing and protecting of self-imposed boundaries that privilege the form and structure of semiotic systems. Kristeva, on the other hand, has taken Saussure's project as an invitation to subsume new areas in the name of semiology. She continues to extend the domain of the semiotic inquiry to encompass subjectivity in all of its linguistic manifestations. What one sees as a confused mingling of the disciplines, the other sees as the central focus of any science of signs; what one rejects, the other embraces.

Notes

1   An earlier version of this chapter appeared as 'The Pun or the Eucharist? Eco and Kristeva on the Consummate Model for the Metaphoric Process', *Literature and Theology: An International Journal of Theory, Criticism and Culture* (Oxford University Press), 11: 1 (March 1997): 93–115. See original version for more comprehensive coverage of Eco's theory of metaphor.

2   U. Eco, *The Role of the Reader: Explorations in the Semiotics of Texts*, Bloomington, IN: Indiana University Press, 1979, pp. 67–89.

3   F. Nietzsche, *Thus Spoke Zarathustra*, trans. W. Kaufmann, Harmondsworth: Penguin, 1978, II.1.

4   J. Kristeva, *Proust and the Sense of Time*, trans. S. Bann, London: Faber and Faber, 1993, p. 57 (Kristeva quotes Proust here).

5   U. Eco, *A Theory of Semiotics*, Bloomington, IN: Indiana University Press, 1976, p. 15, quoting C.S. Peirce, *Collected Papers*, Cambridge: Harvard University Press, 1931–58, 5.484.

6   Eco, *A Theory of Semiotics*, 1.1–2.15, specifically pp. 15, 68–69; and *The Role of the Reader*, 7.2.

7   Eco, *The Role of the Reader*, p. 184.

8   Ibid., p. 74.

9   Ibid., p. 76.

10   U. Eco, *The Limits of Interpretation*, Bloomington, IN: Indiana University Press, 1990, p. 143.

11   Eco, *The Role of the Reader*, p. 89.

12   T. de Lauretis, *Technologies of Gender: Essays on Theory, Film, and Fiction*, Bloomington, IN: Indiana University Press, 1987, p. 61.

13   Eco, *A Theory of Semiotics*, p. 283.

14   N. Frye, *The Educated Imagination*, Toronto: CBC Massey Lecture Series, 1963, pp. 10–11.

15   Eco, *A Theory of Semiotics*, p. 283.

16   Frye, *The Educated Imagination*, p. 11.

17   Eco, *A Theory of Semiotics*, p. 281.

18   J. Gallop, *Feminism and Psychoanalysis: The Daughter's Seduction*, London: Macmillan, 1982, p. 30.

19   Eco, *The Role of the Reader*, p. 78.

20   U. Eco, *The Island of the Day Before*, trans. W. Weaver, London: Secker and Warburg, 1995, pp. 92–93.

21   Eco, *The Role of the Reader*, p. 78.

22   Ibid., p. 69.

23   Ibid., p. 79.

24   U. Eco, *The Aesthetics of Chaosmos: The Middle Ages of James Joyce*, trans. E. Esrock, Cambridge: Harvard University Press, 1982, pp. 23–32.

25   U. Eco, *Semiotics and the Philosophy of Language*, Bloomington, IN: Indiana University Press, 1984, p. 25; U. Eco, *The Role of the Reader*, p. 70.

26   Eco, *The Aesthetics of Chaosmos*, p. 65.

27   Eco, *The Role of the Reader*, p. 73.

28   Ibid., p. 77.

29   Ibid.

30   Ibid., p. 67.

31   Ibid., p. 88.

32   Ibid., p. 69; Eco, *Semiotics and the Philosophy of Language*, p. 127.

33   J. Kristeva, *Tales of Love*, trans. Léon S. Roudiez, New York, NY: Columbia University Press, 1987. *Histoires d'amour*, Paris: Denoël, 1983, pp. 21–56.

34   Ibid., p. 35.

35   Ibid., p. 22.

36   Ibid., p. 26.

37   Ibid., p. 268.

38   Ibid., p. 267.

39   Ibid., p. 277.

40   Ibid., p. 273.

41   Ibid.

42   Ibid., p. 38.

43   Kristeva, *Proust and the Sense of Time*; J. Kristeva, *Time and Sense: Proust and the Experience of Literature*, trans. Ross Guberman, New York, NY: Columbia University Press, 1986; *Le temps sensible: Proust et l'expérience littéraire*, Paris: Gallimard, 1994.

44   Kristeva, *Proust and the Sense of Time*, p. 64.

45   Ibid., pp. 56, 65ff.; Kristeva, *Time and Sense: Proust and the Experience of Literature*, pp. 262ff.

46   Kristeva, *Time and Sense*, p. 312.

47   Kristeva, *Proust and the Sense of Time*, p. 49.

48   N. Goldenberg, 'A Feminist Psychoanalytic Reading of the "Cat in the Hat Comes Back" ', presented at the *Women's Voices in Religion* speaker series, Faculty of Divinity, University of Cambridge, 1996.

49   J. Kristeva, 'Identification and the Real', in P. Collier and H. Geyer-Ryan (eds) *Literary Theory Today*, Ithaca, NY: Cornell University Press, 1990, p. 172.

50   S. Clark and K. Hulley, 'An Interview with Julia Kristeva: Cultural Strangeness and the Subject in Crisis', *Discourse: Journal for Theoretical Studies in Media and Culture*, 13: 1 (1990): 164.

51   C. McNelly Kearns, 'Kristeva and Feminist Theology', in C.W. Maggie Kim, S.M. St. Ville and S.M. Simonaitis (eds) *Transfigurations: Theology and the French Feminists*, Minneapolis, MN: Fortress Press, 1993, pp. 74–75.

52   J. Kristeva, in T. Moi (ed.) *The Kristeva Reader*, New York, NY: Columbia University Press, 1986, p. 233.

53   J. Kristeva, *New Maladies of the Soul*, trans. Ross Mitchell Guberman, New York, NY: Columbia University Press, 1995; *Les nouvelles maladies de l'âme*, Paris: Librairie Arthème Fayard, 1993, p. 131.

54   Ibid., p. 178.

55   M. Proust, *Remembrance of Things Past*, trans. C.K. Moncrieff and T. Kilmartin, London: Penguin, 1981, p. 50.

56   Ibid., p. 48.

57   Ibid., p. 49.

58   Kristeva, 'Identification and the Real'.

59   See D.C. Stanton, 'Difference on Trial: A Critique of the Maternal Metaphor in Cixous, Irigaray, and Kristeva', in N.K. Miller (ed.) *The Poetics of Gender*, New York, NY: Columbia University Press, 1986, pp. 157–182, 170.

60   J. Kristeva, *Sèméiotiké, recherches pour une sémanalyse*, Paris: Seuil, 1969, pp. 147–184.

61   J. Kristeva, *La révolution du langage poétique: l'avant-garde à la fin du XIXe siècle. Lautréamont et Mallarmé*, Paris: Seuil, 1974, pp. 65–67, my translation.

62   Kristeva, 'Identification and the Real', p. 173.

63   Kristeva, *Tales of Love*, p. 50.

64   Kristeva, *New Maladies of the Soul*, p. 197.

65   Kristeva, *Tales of Love*, p. 60.

66   Kristeva, *New Maladies of the Soul*, p. 131.

67   J. Kristeva, *Strangers to Ourselves*, trans. Léon S. Roudiez, New York: Columbia University Press, 1991; *Étrangers à nous-mêmes*, Paris: Librairie Arthème Fayard, 1988.

68   Kristeva, *New Maladies of the Soul*, p. 115.

69   K. O'Grady, 'Dialogue with Julia Kristeva', *Parallax*, Special Issue: 'Julia Kristeva 1966–96: Aesthetics, Politics, Ethics', 8 (July–September 1998): 8–11.

70   Kristeva, *Tales of Love*, p. 42.

71   Kristeva, *Strangers to Ourselves*, p. 28.

72   Kristeva, *Tales of Love*, p. 279.

73   Eco, *A Theory of Semiotics*, pp. 314, 315.

74   Ibid., p. 317.

75   Eco, *Semiotics and the Philosophy of Language*, p. 26; Eco, *A Theory of Semiotics*, pp. 315–318.

76   V.M. Colapietro, 'Semiosis and Subjectivity', in *Peirce's Approach to the Self: A Semiotic Perspective on Human Subjectivity*, New York, NY: SUNY, 1989, p. 39.

77   Eco, *A Theory of Semiotics*, p. 316.

78   Colapietro, 'Semiosis and Subjectivity', p. 43; T. de Lauretis, *Alice Doesn't: Feminism, Semiotics, Cinema*, Bloomington, IN: Indiana University Press, 1984, p. 171.

79   Kristeva, *The Kristeva Reader*, p. 28.

80   Eco, *A Theory of Semiotics*, p. 317.

81   In a satirical study of semiotic studies generally, Eco depicts Lacanian and Kristevan theory in the following humorous way:

>   *La parole dont je me leurre ne pourra que se taire dans l'éclatement de ce qu'elle cache. Et pourtant . . .* One hundred eighty minutes of silence followed while Dr. Lagache tried to extricate himself from a Borromeo knot, yelping constantly (cf. Julia Kristeva, 'Chora-Chora', in *Tell Quayle* 5 (1980), from pp. 70f.
>
>   U. Eco, 'Three Owls on a Chest of Drawers', in *How to Travel with a Salmon*, trans. W. Weaver, London: Minerva, 1995, p. 158.

82   F. de Saussure, *Course in General Linguistics*, edited by Charles Bally and Albert Sechehaye, New York, NY: McGraw-Hill Books, 1959, Chapter III.

83   T. Eagleton, *Literary Theory*, Oxford: Blackwell, 1983, p. 147.

Chapter 11

Alison Jasper

RECOLLECTING RELIGION IN THE REALM OF THE BODY (OR Body©)

Recollecting Yves – the incorruptible

A **FEW YEARS AGO**, I was in France with my family. In the small Breton town of Tréguier, we visited the cathedral dedicated to St Tudwal, a bishop of Welsh origin who had first set up a hermitage here in the sixth century. For me, the visit set in train a new reflection on how body and embodiment have been interpreted and understood according to what we could call the 'canon'. That term describes the work of the so-called 'authoritative' and very largely Christian (or Christianized) interpreters influential in forming a Western view on the subject.[1]

We see these canonical interpretations illustrated, for example, in the succession of commentaries on the incarnational 'infancy narratives' within the Gospels of Luke (Luke 1:5–2:52) and Matthew (Matthew 1:18–2:23) and on the Prologue of John's Gospel (John 1:1–18) or on the various texts concerning resurrection within the so-called 'New Testament'. These have tended to present body and soul, humankind and God, flesh and Word in antithetical, hierarchical, binary relationships. For example the Word – capitalized 'W' – became flesh – lower case 'f' – with all its baggage of gender, sexual desire and sensuality – and demonstrated His incomparable condescension and love for a human race, blinded by sin and ignorance, by being born of a woman. But the business is fraught with anxiety and tension for commentators, apparently desperate to demonstrate how Word was not contaminated or corrupted by this death-defying, divine risk-taking in the realm of the maternal, sexual body.[2]

In other words, canonical interpretation of the body and embodiment seems highly conflicted. It is sometimes galvanized by the awe-inspiring revelation of divine incarnation into reverence for the body and concern for embodied humanity in the here and now. On the other hand, it is sometimes overwhelmed by the disturbing implications this has for divine and human identity and the distinctions between them. My argument is that the Western canonical tradition has tended to underplay the revelation of divine incarnation as a vision of the divine possibilities for embodied humanity because the language and symbolism of embodiment themselves have belonged to a gendered system of meaning and significance – or epistemology if you like – based upon the normativity of the male/masculine and the unsettling invisibility of the female/feminine. But more than this, my argument would be that in spite of the conflicted and unsettled interpretative canon, formed on this basis to exclude – non-ethically – representation of that which is too disturbingly signified by the feminine, Christian texts and traditions never finally obliterate these traces.

In order to illustrate what I'm saying, consider, for example, St Yves, whose bodily remains are to be found in the Cathedral at Tréguier. St Yves was both a priest and also a civil and canon lawyer. He died at the beginning of the fourteenth century CE (1303) and was canonized by the Church and revered by the people of Brittany for his defence of the poor. In other words, he was concerned with the reality of embodied humanity. A prayer to St Yves celebrates him as *'l'Avocat des pauvres, le défenseur des veuves et des orphelins, la Providence de tous les nécessiteux...'* – advocate of the poor, defender of widows and orphans, Providence for all the needy. Inside the cathedral at Tréguier there are images of the saint, including one of him, dressed as a lawyer, flanked by two men. In the literature for visitors, this wooden carving in the south transept – perhaps early sixteenth century in origin – is called *'Saint-Yves entre le riche et le pauvre'* – St Yves between rich and poor. Yves is not swayed by the power and arrogance of the rich man – who wears his characteristically Breton hat proudly on his head – or tempted by lust for riches, to ignore the present needs of the poor man – who clutches his cap humbly in his hands. His rulings are just, taking the material needs of the poor man fully into consideration. And Yves' canonization – his adoption into a canonical view of embodied humanity – therefore recognizes this work as a point along the continuum of divine investment in the world of embodiment, suffering and corruption which finds its most extreme expression in the Incarnation of the Word.

But nevertheless represented in this tableau there is still an anxiety about Yves' prophetic involvement in the world. The prayer goes on to urge the saint to give the supplicant 'poverty of heart' so that they can resist the temptations of wealth. And he is himself commended for the modesty of his lifestyle. Although it is fitting for the divine to enter the realm of the body, to be concerned with it, the canonical interpreters, once again, register their nervousness. The solution to the dilemma here is, symbolically, to shore up the hierarchy and the primacy of the clergy over all laypeople. Yves' role as representative of the spiritual realm, uncorrupted by wealth or poverty, raises him onto the judgement seat where he gives form to the theoretical and ideal order of the masculine and spiritual over material bodily realms.

Augustine's 'original sin'

This illustration of the uneasy play between material and spiritual realms belongs to a historical tradition within Christianity which is particularly associated with Augustine. Of course without the formative tradition to which he was an heir and the agreement of many Christians, this one African bishop could not have imposed his ideas so firmly on the rest of the Church. I do not mean to demonize him. In many ways he was an exemplary pastor and teacher. But the role played by an 'Augustinian' tradition has been highly significant in the Western world. In spite of rejecting the dualistic Manichean philosophy of his youth – which regarded the lower half of the body as the disgusting work of the prince of darkness[3] – Augustine's hugely influential work still reflects the

Platonic chain of being that is described in the *Timaeus*. Plato's hierarchy of beings moves downwards in the scale of value from God and spirits to woman and matter, supporting a common identification of woman with body and passions that must be ruled by the masculine mind.

Augustine gave the Church the concept of *concupiscentia* – desire that is wilful and ultimately pointless, having nothing to do with God – estranging himself and many followers from what might otherwise be regarded as their home state of embodiment. And *concupiscentia* seemed particularly appropriate to Augustine as a description of sensual and sexual desire. For him, the image of God within humanity resided in its capacity to exercise a reason that was definitively disembodied and free from any concern with the body's sensuality.[4] Sexual desire was, from this point of view, a hiding to nowhere. He distrusted the original sexual sin – not the act itself which, without passion or excitement – or enjoyment presumably – he permitted for the continuation of the species, but the loss of reasonable control it implied.

Thus the gendered framework of a Christian metaphysics reflects a normatively male view of the female. And in consequence it becomes extremely difficult to find ways of giving expression to that other Christian tradition of – so to speak – incarnational celebration except in forms that strike us as perverse – pus-sucking,[5] holy starvation and the stigmata[6] are, for example, some of the ways in which, we might argue, we have maintained our hold on the bodily realm! There have been some less – for the modern mind – disquieting attempts too. During the medieval period, for example, Body becomes the Soul's beloved bride and by the early thirteenth century this trope was commonplace. The Soul's bride, Body would be received back at the end of time and endowed by her husband with four precious dowries.[7] Body is, with her husband Soul, one flesh, united – metaphorically at any rate – in sensual delight. But of course, she is, in this economy, still not the central social subject, but simply the desired object. Moreover, contemporary texts show that this metaphorical marriage was certainly not the only image available at the time for configuring our human condition of embodiment. Some paint a far darker picture. For example, the thirteenth-century *Ancrene Wisse*[8] talks about the flesh as a hobble or drag on the soul and describes it in terms of slime and stench and the privy hole.[9] The model of body as wife, though positive and celebratory in some ways, is clearly insufficiently subversive to short-circuit the whole hegemonic system.

When the dead won't stay buried

St Yves is interesting because his life and place in the tradition point instructively to the actually rather poor fit between ideas of divine involvement in the world and a constitutive spirit/body hierarchy. Even within the one cathedral at Tréguier, I could see that Christian views on the realm of the body were not singular or unequivocal – hardly even decently reconcilable. And perhaps something else was beginning to break out. In the Sacristy there were reliquaries containing saintly bones. The skull of St Yves minus his two front teeth is still displayed for the faithful and for the now not-so-faithful tourists. As I looked at the relic of the saintly body inside its casket of incorruptible gold (or at least gold plate!) it was not so hard to see a glimpse of an eternal realm of the spiritual that was not simply disembodied.

The earliest Christian images of the resurrection which were organic and suggested sometimes the very dramatic changes[10] we recognize in plant growth, gave way to images of a resistant and enduring bodily state[11] and a cult of relics, beginning in the fourth century, took off at the beginning of the fifth. Victricius of Rouen describes the relics he received from Ambrose as jewels – hard and whole.[12] Each part was still the saint complete in every bodily particle, a temple or building in which the saint resided. Admittedly, relics resist alteration in a way that is uncharacteristic of the body as a whole but nevertheless I could sense the excitement and awe in Saint Tudwal and Saint Yves' contemporaries who believed that the – Christian – truth was out there, made, so to speak, tangible through these very particular bodily remnants.

If we look carefully, then, we see that Christian traditions do sometimes appear inconsistent or even illogical. Christian saints do not always recommend us to accept our suffering in hopes of a heavenly escape from distressing and painful change. It isn't true that all Christians hated their own bodies or simply longed for release into a spiritual existence as we might sometimes unthinkingly make claim. For many medieval Christians, for example, the body was essential to self, and whatever the philosophical and theological problems this caused, they were not willing to abandon it in the resurrection. Resurrection of the body implied just that – the possibility of a glorious resurrection body, restored and beyond change to be sure, but in some important sense identical with the body on earth.[13] And many people – even Augustine himself[14] – have revered relics which appeared to guarantee miracles that could cheat death, decay and sickness in the soft and permeable context of changing, earthbound bodies. In other words, although the Christian Church has broadly taken the view that the possibility of knowledge rests on a gendered hierarchy between disembodied masculine reason and immersion in sensuality and emotion identified with the feminine, traditions – heretical and transgressive – leave their traces, always threatening to break up the coherence of canonical generalizations.

On not throwing out the baby with the bathwater

So what modern interpreters and theorists are beginning to do more confidently I believe is the work of decentring, of producing what the cultural critic Mieke Bal has called 'counter-coherences',[15] actually inviting us to confront some of the multiplicity or even the heterogeneity of our interpretative traditions and, of course, to begin to recognize that what any of us – feminist, queer or radically orthodox – chooses to foreground, our choices are never 'innocent'. So, for example, some feminist theorists have begun work on a revisioning of the relationship between body and culture asking questions about, for instance, representation – theological, philosophical, scientific and artistic – that classically reduce body and sexuality to the feminine but configure desire in masculine, heterosexist terms only. They have also asked questions about the sense in which canonical Christian interpretations have encouraged a view of the body of 'nature' in analogous terms as supremely desirable, exploitable and ultimately dispensable. They point out that the divinely painted canvas – in canonical interpretations – is sometimes rendered 'ethically non-suspect'.[16] But there is still plenty of which to be suspicious.

One 'counter-canonical' formation of this process of critique and revisioning, of course, is associated with the French writer, Luce Irigaray. In her first influential work, *Speculum of the Other Woman*,[17] Irigaray identified the 'imaginary' of our dominant culture – the images and dynamics that structure and support its most basic movements of thought[18] – as essentially masculine. In a movement that brings together psycho-analysis and philosophy, Irigaray saw that the *phallus*, a quasi-technical term which rep-resents – in terms of the French psychoanalyst and structuralist, Jacques Lacan – that which focuses our most intense desire, bears the morphological marks of the male body[19] most particularly in its singularity. Yet it requires an 'other' – the hand or another body – to know itself. But this other – necessary for attaining knowledge and definition – earns its identity only in so far as it serves the 'the central, unitary, and stable principle of identity'.[20] In this scheme, the woman becomes even less than the binary opposite of man,[21] playing the role of the flat reflecting mirror – an image also used by Virginia Woolf to similar effect in her ironical and 'counter-canonical' book of 1928, *A Room of One's Own*:

> Women have served all these centuries as looking-glasses possessing the magic and delicious power of reflecting the figure of man at twice its natural size. Without that power probably the earth would still be swamp and jungle. The glories of all our wars would be unknown.[22]

In other words, these commentators and readers have recognized the way in which a male-centred culture of masculine normativity sees woman – and the feminine – as nothing in herself or itself at all but as simply the ground of his identity, absolutely vital but also absolutely invisible in its own terms. In order to counter this, in *This Sex Which is Not One*, Irigaray put forward an alternative morphology to ground a different imagi-nary. She too uses the morphology of body but this time the distinctive and different body of desiring woman:

> In order to touch himself, man needs and instrument, his hand, a woman's body, language. . . . And this touching require at least a minimum of activity. As for woman, she touches herself without any need for mediation and before there is any need to distinguish activity from passivity. Woman 'touches herself' all the time . . . for her genitals are formed of two-lips in continuous contact. Thus, within herself, she is two but not divisible into one(s) – that caress each other.[23]

She is indefinitely other within herself.[24]

In the most general terms the 'imaginary' she proposes does not require singular solutions or a truth that must be defined by the exclusion of the 'other'. What she speaks about, then, are multiple Words and meanings and the both/and of male and female together. The morphology of the female body draws attention to an underlying multiplicity in our lived and embodied experiences. It points to the view, for example, that, even theologically speaking, without flesh there can be no Word.

Critiquing the singularity and ethical indifference of the canon: Mona Hatoum

How then to represent a new morphology of both/and, of male and female and of the possibility of female desire and pleasure? Perhaps one way is to be found in the realm of the creative artist and, by way of example, in the work of Mona Hatoum. Hatoum's work focuses a critique of Western canonical representations of the body that have been structured and supported by readings of Christian texts and traditions within a pre-modern culture based upon the normativity of the male and the centrality of the male gaze. But her work is also, in the choice she makes to represent body and embodiment, a celebration of embodied human knowledge and ethical practice. This is not to say that she would draw conclusions about re-collecting images or re-visioning religious identity in the same way as I attempt to do. Her work does, however, open up the possibility that representation of the body and embodiment may be achieved from a position that challenges the ethical indifference of the male-centred traditions of interpretation. Her 'readings' of body and embodiment indicate a particular context or place for witnessing the multiple and incarnational celebration I have also identified as an ineradicable aspect of the Christian tradition.

Mona Hatoum was born of a Palestinian, Muslim family living in Lebanon. She left her homeland to become a visiting art student in the UK, and settled in London in 1975 after war broke out at home. She has spent most of her adult life in England where she saw early on, she says, 'how divorced people were from their bodies'.[25] Many people have seen a parallel in her work between the unease of the exile and the stranger in a foreign land. But this parallel works well too as an image of our canonical unease, as exiles from embodied existence.[26]

Her artistic career began with performance art but, more recently, she has worked with installation, video, sculpture and photography. Of course, Hatoum hasn't worked in isolation from a contemporary artistic context which is highly conscious of the debates surrounding representation and the body. Artists as diverse as Gina Pane (1939–1990) who literally drew on her own body with razor blades, and Bill Viola (1951–) who works with video images of bodies, paint on this revitalized canvas in a dramatically different way from artists of the past. Hatoum's own work within this exciting area in contemporary art refuses, appropriately enough, to be limited to singular and exclusive interpretations. In an interview she says:

> I find it more exciting when a work reverberates with several meanings and paradoxes and contradictions. Explaining it as meaning this or that inevitably turns it into something fixed rather than something in a state of flux.[27]

Contemplating Hatoum's work as an expression, for example, of the way in which modern feminist theory challenges the singularity of the male imaginary, or of the way in which counter-canonical representation of the body can be celebratory are, then, only two ways to read its complexity. Nevertheless, thematic multiplicity (and even heterogeneity) is clearly an important aspect of her work, related to the ideas already noted of exile from the home state – or as I use her work to suggest, the home state of embodiment.

For example, Hatoum constructs a series of objects that are, formally speaking, pieces of furniture, very much designed with the context of embodiment as home in mind. In almost every case, however, Hatoum's 'furniture' is unwelcoming in some way. The form of the work is at odds with the experienced reality. She makes several baby cradles, but you wouldn't place a real baby in them. She makes a bed (*Divan Bed*, steel tread plate, 1996, Tate Modern Gallery, London), but since it is constructed out of the unyielding material that goes into the manufacture of heavy machinery, you wouldn't want to spend a night on it. The same theme is clearly illustrated in a welcome mat (*Doormat*, stainless steel pins, nickel-plated pins, glue, canvas, 1996) made of sharp stainless steel pins, points upwards, in which depressed pins form the word, 'welcome'. And she makes a wheelchair (*Untitled* (wheelchair), 1998, Tate Modern Art Gallery, London) that reminds me of school or hospital canteen trolleys, filled with discarded dishes and wasted food. The wheelchair, which is utilitarian and basic, supports the body but the handles of this trolley chair are stabbing knives. It represents, perhaps, how ill at ease we feel with our own bodily vulnerability.

Hatoum's works also draw attention to the scandal of representation that, in terms of canonical interpretations of body and embodiment, have failed to account for the diverse standpoints of race, ethnicity and gender. Hatoum herself features strongly – in her own work as a Palestinian woman. In *Negotiating Table* (three-hour performance, The Western Front, Vancouver, 1983), a 'tableau vivant', Hatoum herself lay for three hours on a table covered with entrails, bandages and blood and wrapped in a body bag. At the same time, tapes of speeches by Western leaders about peace played in the background. Hatoum recalls that she made the work right after the, for her, shattering experience of learning about how Israeli soldiers had invaded the Palestinian refugee camps of Sabra and Shatila in the Beirut area in September 1982 and massacred its inhabitants. The body, both non-white and female is, mimetically, torn open and apart, displayed to our view, a piece of meat. The disembodied 'Words' of peace become the rapacious discourse of power that fails to attend to the actual disintegration of the desiring female, culturally specific, flesh. And yet, of course, the artist/participant herself represents the refusal to be obliterated by those powerful words.

The work from which I took the title of this piece is *Recollection* (hair balls, strands of hair hung from the ceiling, wooden loom with woven hair, table. Installation, Beguinage St Elizabeth, Kortrijk, Belgium collection, De Vleeshal, Middelburg, the Netherlands, 1995). *Recollection* is my own favourite amongst Hatoum's works. Hatoum says she first made one of the hair balls that constitute a central element of the work at a friend's house. She was trying to remove the hair from the plug hole after she'd had a bath. Hair is a common cross-cultural symbol of beauty and femininity. But as a dark and wirey-haired woman myself, I know how it refuses to conform to standards of feminine beauty, how it refuses to be discrete and how, for example, it winds itself around the plug hole, collecting a coating of slime, the skin we daily slough off. Julia Kristeva's theoretical notion of abjection, set out first in her book, *Powers of Horror*, linking the ultimately heterogeneous elements of human subjectivity with an utterly alienating loss of the maternal and the transgressing of boundaries, signified for her personally by the gagging produced by the skin on warm milk,[28] is for me represented by the self/not self of the slimy hair clumps. But Hatoum gathers up this complex reflection making it – ironically perhaps – a beautiful thing, a light and airy ball, like a pearl produced by grit and irritation.[29] In *Recollection*, in an airy room, a hair loom turns bodily waste into artefact but still plays with our sense of embodied identity, troubled by multiplicity, heterogeneity or the problems of exile. The grid of the loom and the hair hung neatly from the ceiling at precise intervals form neat patterns but wiry hair curling into a tangle, hair balls randomly placed on the polished wooden floor, fail to conform.

Finally, Hatoum's work *Corps Etranger* (foreign body) (video installation with cylindrical wooden structure, video projector, video player amplifier, four speakers, collection Musée national d'art moderne, Centre George Pompidou, Paris, 1994) is a yet more uncomfortable work. I use it here in terms of Hatoum's sense of unease within the canons of Western embodiment, its forms of traditional representation and its ethical indifference to exploitation but also, of course, in terms of the artist's own mimetic/poetic[30] choice.

For *Corps Etranger*, Hatoum finally found an endoscopy specialist in 1992 who was prepared to help her film her own body. They had not been queuing up! The presentation of this film begins with a close sweep of her body surfaces followed by the camera's entry/penetration – as the 'foreign body' of the title – into various orifices and on into her stomach and intestines and vagina. The film is projected onto the floor inside a circular structure which Hatoum says she intended to be claustrophobic. This work would be intolerable had it not been focused by the artist on herself. All representations of human bodies are challenged as the images dissolve into a series of unfamiliar – to the non-medical observer – images that are beautiful in spite of the invasiveness required to achieve them. This too is troubling; the framing of the work is precisely a technology that mimes the ethical indifference to body and nature that the exploitative singularity of the masculine imaginary has supported.

Hatoum's work can be used as a tool to critique a tradition of interpretation that denigrates and devalues the categories of body and embodiment. Nevertheless, Hatoum herself is the poet, the maker in each case. Her work is not simply a critical lens but also offers us a prism to split the light into its constituent colours giving us, literally, a rainbow of possibilities. The method as well as the content of her work avoids singularities and stresses ethical non-indifference. And it is possible to see in her work some of the 'pleasures of exile', since, as Edward Said says of Hatoum's work – and his comments take the reader back, in some ways, to Irigaray's female imaginary – 'Seeing "the entire world as a foreign land" makes possible originality of vision. Most people are principally aware of one culture, one setting, one home; exiles are aware of at least two.'[31]

Walking on the moon – gazing down into the slime: Donna Haraway

The next image I want to consider is not by Mona Hatoum. But it functions in a similar way at least in so far as her works could be said to be representations of body or embodiment. This is a detail of the double helix DNA model (only the base plates are original) as built by Crick and Watson in 1953 to check their theory of the structure of DNA, the molecule that carries genetic information in living things (Chemistry Gallery, Science Museum, London). We could say the same, for example, of Neil Armstrong's photograph of Buzz Aldrin, the first and second men to walk on the Moon. Both images have a strongly encultured as well as a highly theoretical and technical context.

Both images participate within the myth-making and narrative discourse of our Western culture. But for such relatively contemporary images, they conform pretty well to the canonical interpretations of body and embodiment we've already considered with an important additional element. They represent a triumph over body or embodiment as a material problematic with commercial applications.

Modern journalism seems a little less triumphalist that it used to be when Pathe was producing its relentlessly up-beat news bulletins in the cinemas of my childhood, but what biologist and theorist Donna Haraway identifies as salvation history[32] still seems very much in evidence in newspaper reporting on the mapping of the human genome. The *Guardian*, in June 2000:

> Using awesome computing power and sophisticated robotics, teams in Britain, Europe and the US have deciphered the three-billion letter DNA alphabet that shapes and limits human existence. . . . Published on the internet the code has been posted in daily instalments so that the researchers worldwide can continue a new revolution in the understanding of life itself. It will be used to understand and eliminate the inherited diseases that have scarred families for generations: muscular dystrophy, Huntingdon's chorea, cystic fibrosis.[33]

God is not invoked directly but the language gives expression to what Haraway would undoubtedly call the 'overwhelmingly Christian signifiers of technoscience'.[34] What these signifiers do not do, of course, is to render visible levels of ethical indifference within such narrative interpretations of Christian scripture or tradition. If you, a relative or a friend suffer from one of these terrible inherited diseases you are entitled, I think, to be grateful for awesome computing power and sophisticated robotics. If your relatives and friends are suffering from cholera and dysentery due to dirty water, or from pneumonia because of malnutrition and lack of fuel or AIDS for lack of contraceptives and advice about how to use them, you are unlikely even to know about the mapping of the human genome.

It is notable that much of the so-called 'ethical' debate about the human genome project in the United Kingdom over the last few years has been related to the potential of this project for cloning human beings, following the success of researchers in Edinburgh who cloned a now-famous sheep called Dolly. The concern is undoubtedly related to the conundrum, dependent upon a more or less canonically dualistic way of thinking, of whether cloning human bodies amounts to cloning human beings. But, of course, while this debate consumes the media,[35] a more serious and pressing ethical issue in relation to biotechnological research – and one which Donna Haraway explores in detail – goes largely unmarked in the popular imagination.[36] This is the question of who will have access to the research facilities and any therapeutic or commercial outcomes. Who holds the patents? In whose interest is all this work taking place?

As a theorist and philosopher of science, Donna Haraway holds no truck with paranoid feminist science-haters and their conspiracy theories about masculinist scientists and philosophers.[37] Nevertheless she is herself highly critical of what might be called 'canonical' representations of the body and embodiment within a masculinist culture, and of the choices we all make in the light of these – scientists, philosophers and laypeople alike. She argues that in the apparently hard 'techno-scientific' realm, the way in which we regard the relationship between body and culture is still very dependent upon inherited Jewish and particularly Christian narratives which act to disguise the ethical indifference of many decisions and choices that are being made at the moment.

Alongside Irigaray and Hatoum in their diverse fields, Haraway is also concerned with the singularity that is the product of a fundamentally masculine imaginary but which affects us all, women, men and children. In her 1991 collection, *Simians, Cyborgs, and Women: The Reinvention of Nature*, Haraway first addressed the issue of singularity as it related to a definition of nature as merely the defining otherness of a racially and ethnically singular, masculine culture.

A particularly telling image that has been important for Haraway in developing her ideas along these lines is that of a Gorilla Group in the African Hall, in the American Museum of Natural History[38] dating from the 1920s. This is a dioramic recreation of nature starring, so to speak, a striking silverback male called the Giant of Karisimbi, with a younger male and a female sitting calmly in the foreground with her youngster. What this impressive and vibrant work represents every bit as much as the Age of Mammals, she suggests, is the story of Man. What this fundamentally religious narrative disguises or occludes is the non-innocent narrative of how the diorama was put together. It is a story she tells most dramatically and at length in *Primate Visions*.[39] It recurs later in her *Modest_Witness@Second_Millennium.FemaleMan©_Meets_OncoMouse*™. The ape in the jungle is the doppelganger and mirror to civilized white manhood in the city. The whole of nature is available, in fact and in terms of representation, for the exposition of a particular cultural formulation of the human patriarchal family. The 'family' of the diorama in its lush and Edenic setting relates much less to the groupings and aspirations of gorillas than to those of men in a broadly – and evidently non-ethically – religious sense:

> Dramatic stories about people, animals, tolls, journeys, diseases and money inhere in each precious corpse, from the chest-beating male . . . to the ape-child speared as it screamed in terror on the steep volcanic mountainside.[40]

Haraway identifies in this the 'Sacred Image of the Same',[41] something she sees as hegemonic and numbing and still evident in the technoscientific culture out of which she writes, consciously but conscientiously, however, as someone who does not want to be seen as merely negative:

> Biology is a political discourse, one in which we should engage at every level of the practice – technically, semiotically, morally, economically, institutionally. And besides all that, biology is a source of intense intellectual, emotional, social and physical pleasure. Nothing like that should be given up lightly – or approached only in a scolding mode.[42]

In an important earlier essay, 'A Cyborg Manifesto', included in the 1991 collection, she suggested that one way to subvert the canonical interpretations of body and embodiment with their natural and feminine signatures is in the contemplation of cyborgs – part organism, part machine – in reality or in science fiction – which actively transgress the boundaries between the categories of man-made and natural, culture and nature, masculine and feminine, self and other, making these underlying distinctions less and less tenable in fact or in imagination. The ultimate cause for celebration in this manifesto is perhaps that

> The cyborg incarnation is outside salvation history. Nor does it mark time on an oedipal calendar, attempting to heal the terrible cleavages of gender in an oral symbiotic utopia or post-oedipal apocalypse.[43]

Here then is another context for celebrating the incarnate nature of humankind 'in process', that canonical interpretations have tended to freeze, like the Giant of Karisimbi, in magnificent and impressive religious dioramas of divine or human progress: dioramas, moreover, that disguise their own ethical indifference to the standpoints and situated knowledges of communities marginalized by a succession of powerful, singular centres.

Haraway is not making the same deliberate attempt as I am to recollect the pieces, the waste in terms of multiply-invisible lives and devalued experiences in order to reconnect to a religious tradition or spirituality. She is perhaps too wary of the difficulties of revalorizing body and embodiment in terms of a tradition that has been built upon the subordination of women and the feminine as a metaphysical principle and a key element within our definition of knowledge as the exercise of a disembodied reason. However, as with Hatoum, her work is itself – I would argue – a work which celebrates the fully embodied human nature of the scientist and poet she is, stressing the ethical non-indifference of her choices.

Conclusions

What can I say then to round up these reflections? Haraway helps me to see that cultural myths – her definition of the canonical reflections of the Christian Churches on humankind, defined in hegemonic terms – persist into the realm of the body as it is understood today. However, in the realm of Body© – to borrow from Haraway the trope of defining using the commercial and non-innocent symbol of copyright[44] – we can see the work of Hatoum and Haraway as exemplars, making new counter-canonical and counter-coherent definitions that not only critique the definitions of the past but make a play for different poetic standpoints. Body© and Embodiment© are evidently less innocently exploitable.

Yet there may well still be a place for the sort of myth-making that Haraway and Hatoum have critiqued. Their own work, in very different ways, also recognizes the possibility of some form of incarnational celebration in terms of ethical 'non-indifference' in their own multilayered experiences of doing biology or of expressive art. In relation to both these cases, I would like to argue that the narratives of Christian embodiment – of incarnation and resurrection particularly – still have a part to play in naming a subversiveness that can be creative. This is not, I hope, to try one more turn at Western Christian colonialism, though some may well fear that it is. I am not suggesting that these narratives have any triumphalist or transcendent claim to authority but that they may still have authenticity in their attempts to name whatever it is that continually defies hegemonic attempts to entomb the realm of the Body – even in powerful Words – and define it out of existence.

Notes

1   The 'canon' as in the authoritative listing of books in the Bible we accept today is a term that came into general use in the fourth century CE, but there is disagreement about how and when the collections which constitute 'Old' and 'New' Christian Testaments were finalized. Modern scholars agree that the Hebrew canon was probably largely fixed before the Christian era but debate, for example, how far those texts usually included within the Apocrypha were or were not considered authoritative and for how long. The New Testament canon was virtually fixed in both East and Western Churches by the early fifth century. It was based on a listing of 27 books by Bishop Athanasius of Alexandria contained in a festal letter written in 367 CE and excluded a number of texts popular within the Christian Churches, for example, dating from the second century, 'The Shepherd' of Hermas and the 'Acts of Paul and Thecla'.

    'Canonical' interpretation of tradition and scriptural texts has a well documented history in the accounts of Oecumenical (accepted by East and Western Churches to be authoritative) Councils of the Church which attempted to deal with so-called heresies, from the council of Nicaea in 325 CE until at least the second Nicaean Council of 787 CE. and in the further Councils of the Western RC Church up to and including Vatican II, 1962–1965.

    My use of the term, then, notes the existence of the formal process within the Western Churches whereby 'orthodoxy' was defined but refers essentially to the way in which this process has informed and supported a less formal cultural consensus.

2   See discussion of this anxiety in relation to the Prologue of John's Gospel in A. Jasper, *The Shining Garment of the Text: Gendered Readings of John's Prologue*, Sheffield: Sheffield Academic Press, 1998, pp. 189–193.

3   H. Chadwick, *Augustine,* Oxford: Oxford University Press, 1986, pp. 11–15.

4   See Jasper, *The Shining Garment of the Text*, p. 51.

5   See C. Bynum, *Fragmentation and Redemption: Essays on Gender and the Human Body in Medieval Religion*, New York, NY: Zone Books, 1991, p. 211. Bynum makes reference, for example, to Catherine of Siena in a picture by M. Fiorini after E. Vanni, in which Saint Catherine drinks pus from the infected breast of a sick woman and then receives Christ's side to suck.

6   See, particularly, the treatment of these issues in C. Bynum, *Holy Feast and Holy Fast: The Religious Significance of Food to Medieval Women*, Berkeley, CA: University of California Press, 1987.

7   See C. Bynum, *The Resurrection of the Body in Western Christianity, 200–1336*, New York, NY: Columbia University Press, 1995, p. 132.

8   The *Ancrene Wisse* or *Riwle* is a guide or rule, written in a West Midlands dialect of English and was apparently originally composed for three well-born sisters. It was later revised for a larger group of recluses. It was copied and translated during the later Middle Ages and retained a place in English devotional literature until the early sixteenth century.

9   Quoted in Bynum, *The Resurrection of the Body*, p. 331.

10   See, for example, I Corinthians 15: 35–36.

11   Bynum, *The Resurrection of the Body*, p. 104. Bynum traces the development of ideas about resurrection away from complex organic images in some ways associated with Origen towards an idea of the reassemblage of bits and the beauty of wholeness and on the ending of change. This approach is associated with Tertullian in the second century and then taken up in the fourth and fifth centuries by Jerome and Augustine, who became interested in relics towards the end of his life.

12   Victricius of Rouen, in J. Mulders (ed.) *De laude sanctorum*, CCL 64, Turnhout: Brepols, 1985, pp. 69–93. This describes a shipment of body parts received from Ambrose, dated 396, constituting an early example of the trend away from the more organic images.

13   See Bynum, *The Resurrection of the Body*, pp. 120–122 and references to the *locus classicus* for the discussion of resurrection of the body during the late twelfth century; distinctions 43–50 of the fourth book of Peter Lombard's *Sentences*.

14   Bynum, *The Resurrection of the Body*, pp. 104–105.

15   M. Bal defines counter-coherences in *Death and Dissymmetry: The Politics of Coherence in the Book of Judges*, Chicago, IL: University of Chicago Press, 1988, p. 7.

16   The term was used by M. Bal in an as-yet unpublished paper on reading the story of Joseph and Potiphar's wife, given at the tenth annual conference of the Society for Literature and Religion, hosted by the Heyendaal Institute, Nijmegen, 7–9 September, 2000.

17   L. Irigaray, *Speculum de l'autre femme*, Paris: Minuit, 1974; *Speculum of the Other Woman*, trans. G. Gill, Ithaca, NY: Cornell University Press, 1985.

18   See S. Jones, 'This God which is not One: Irigaray and Barth on the Divine', in C.W. Maggie Kim, Susan M. St. Ville and Susan M. Simonaitis (eds) *Transfigurations: Theology and the French Feminists,* Minneapolis, MN: Fortress Press, 1993, pp. 111–116.

19   See Jones, 'This God which is not One', p. 115.

20   See ibid., p. 115.

21   Note the discussion of J. Butler on the distinctions between the position of S. de Beauvoir and L. Irigaray in *Gender Trouble,* London: Routledge, 1990.

22   V. Woolf, *A Room of One's Own,* London: Penguin Twentieth Century Classics, 1945, p. 37.

23   L. Irigaray, *Ce Sexe qui n'en est pas un,* Paris: Minuit, 1979; *This Sex which is Not One,* trans. C. Porter and C. Burke, Ithaca, NY: Cornell University Press, 1985, p. 24.

24   Irigaray, *This Sex,* p. 28.

25   M. Archer, G. Brett and C. Zegher (eds.) *Mona Hatoum,* London: Phaidon Press, 1996, p. 8.

26   See ibid., p. 34. Also, see *The Twentieth Century Art Book,* London: Phaidon Press, 2000, p. 191.

27   Archer, Brett and Zegher, *Mona Hatoum,* p. 25.

28   J. Kristeva, *Powers of Horror: An Essay on Abjection,* trans. L. Roudiez, New York, NY: Columbia University Press, 1982, pp. 2–3.

29   See, in reference to this, another work by M. Hatoum (human hair, wood and leather, collection of Eileen and Peter Norton, Santa Monica). In this work, Hatoum makes a necklace of human hair 'beads', displayed as pearls or other precious stones might be by a jeweller.

30   This is to relate the question of representation to – in particular – the discussion of mimesis in the light of Aristotelian theory, as a form of poesis, or making that is ethically directed, that was initiated by the theorist P. Ricoeur. See, for example, P. Ricoeur, *The Rule of Metaphor,* Toronto: University of Toronto Press, 1977, p. 39.

31   Edward Said in Archer, Brett and Zegher, *Mona Hatoum,* p. 113.

32   D. Haraway, *Modest_Witness@Second_Millennium.FemaleMan©_Meets_OncoMouse*™: *Feminism and Technoscience,* New York, NY: Routledge, 1997, p. 193.

33   The *Guardian,* June 26, 2000, 3.

34   Haraway, *Modest_Witness@Second_Millennium,* p. 193.

35   See, for example, the immensely popular TV sci-fi series *StarTrek Voyager* where there is an ongoing debate about the status of the holographic doctor as a non/person!

36   To be fair to the *Guardian,* their special supplement, *The Story of Life: The Mapping of the Human Genome,* 26 June 2000 did include some discussion of these issues. But their example is not generally followed in popular 'tabloid' journalism.

37   See D. Haraway, *Simians, Cyborgs, and Women: The Reinvention of Nature,* London: Free Association Books, 1991, p. 183.

38   Image reproduced in Haraway, *Modest_Witness@Second_Millennium,* p. 237.

39   D. Haraway, *Primate Visions: Gender, Race and Nature in the World of Modern Science,* New York, NY: Routledge, 1989.

40   Haraway, *Modest_Witness@Second_Millennium,* p. 237.

41   Ibid., p. 242

42   Ibid., pp. 104–105.

43   Haraway, *Simians, Cyborgs, and Women,* p. 150.

44   See, in particular, Haraway's discussion of her own concept of FemaleMan© as her "surrogate, agent and sister" although not in any Utopian sense, in Haraway, *Modest_Witness@Second_Millennium,* pp. 69–71.

Chapter 12

Beverley Clack

FEMINISM AND HUMAN MORTALITY

Introduction

A **SURVEY OF WESTERN PHILOSOPHICAL**, religious and literary thinking reveals a persistent – and, for the feminist, perplexing – connection between women and death. This connection takes many varied but interrelated forms. Woman, as the one who gives birth, is seen as responsible for introducing the child to the world of inevitable decay and death. Emergence from the womb leads inexorably to the tomb.[1] Identifying woman exclusively with the processes of reproduction leads to a more general connection between woman and the means of reproduction: sex. Thus, to equate woman with sex is also to equate her with death.

The work of feminists such as Sharon Welch has shown the importance of engaging with the masculinist construction of death in order to understand the forces which drive patriarchal thinking.[2] Death is the one thing that cannot be controlled; it is inevitable; and to reflect upon the gendered construction of death furthers Welch's analysis, for it suggests something of the convoluted thinking employed to overcome engaging with the reality of death.

The aim of this chapter is thus twofold. First, my intention is to continue the work of feminist criticism by exploring the masculinist attempt to control death by eroticizing it. Under such constructions, sex and death are seen as intimately connected: the ability to control the former – invariably associated with the female – gives an illusion of control over the latter. So far-reaching is this perceived solution to the problem of death that figures one would ordinarily hesitate about grouping together prove surprising bed-fellows: thus the case studies for this chapter, the Marquis de Sade and St Augustine, employ this connection (albeit in different ways) to suggest that the inevitability of death might be overcome. Connecting sex and death in this way has considerable ramifications for women's lives, and, having considered these, a feminist may well decide that it is crucial to resist eroticizing death. Subverting this connection, however, may provide a way forward for a feminist reappraisal of mortality: the object of the second section.

If the first section suggests something of the way in which death's reality has been evaded in the Western tradition, the second section is more concerned with how a feminist might engage with the existential issues death raises. What emerges from the first section is the temptation to avoid a proper engagement with the impact that death has upon our understanding of the nature of our own existence. What suggestions might a feminist make for how to live if we accept the fact that we are mortal and, thus, destined for death? Of crucial importance will be the rejection of a dualistic model of the relationship between life and death. Death is not an aberration, but part of the processes of life itself. To live meaningfully, I shall argue, death must be accepted as an aspect of life: an aspect that reminds us of our vulnerability, but also of our connection with others. It is no easy thing to arrive at such a conclusion, and integral to this section will be the attempt to provide a framework to support the considerable struggle necessary to come to an understanding with death.

Eroticizing death

The inability to adequately explore the relationship between life and death materializes in what appears to be one of the strangest connections in Western thought: that between sex and death.[3] Rather than see sexuality as something altogether different from death, linked with the processes of new life rather than its destruction, an explicit connection has been made between human sexuality and the inevitability of death. Some of the greatest poetry of the Western tradition reveals the power of this connection. When Hesiod in his *Theogony* describes Eros, the god of sexual love, he may describe him as 'the most handsome among the immortal gods', but he goes on to note that Eros is the 'dissolver of flesh, who overcomes reason and purpose in the breasts of all gods and all men'.[4] Sex might have the potential to bring about new life, but it is also potentially destructive. Reflection on the experience of sexual love suggests that in such acts there is a pre-empting of the dissolution of the flesh. Just as the body will inevitably be destroyed by death, so the experience of eros brings disruption to the life of the mind. Hesiod suggests that it is all too easy for Eros to destroy the order of life.

Linking sex with death in this way has a more seductively positive effect than these comments might at first suggest. If sex can be connected with death, there is the possibility that death might be something that can be ordered and controlled; death need not destroy us if we take charge of our lives. Very different accounts of what this might entail might develop, but at root the desire to control death through controlling sex remains the same. Consider the following case studies presented by the Marquis de Sade and St Augustine. The first could arguably be considered one of the greatest sinners in the Western canon,[5] while the second is probably the most important figure in the development of Christian doctrine.

Sade: women, sex and death

In Sade's work, sex is linked irrevocably with death, and women with both features of life. By making this connection, Sade attempts to control the inevitable – death – by identifying it with what can be controlled – women. The fear of death is sublimated at considerable cost to the women represented in his work.[6]

At the heart of Sade's account is an attempt to link women with the abyss of our inevitable destruction. Reflection on the nature of the female sex organs is used to suggest this connection. Hence the following exchange between two of Justine's tormentors:

> 'Look ye, friend,' said the younger, 'a girl's a pretty thing, eh? But what a shame there's that cavity there.'

> 'Oh!' cried the other, 'nothing nastier than that hole, I'd not touch a woman even were my fortune at stake.'[7]

Sade is not alone in describing the female sex as a hole – Jean-Paul Sartre's philosophy employs a similar account of what constitutes femininity.[8] In the writings of both men, the female sexual organs inspire both revulsion and fear. In Sade's work, this takes a specifically sexual turn: sodomy is preferred to vaginal intercourse. The reason for this preference is connected to a specific rejection of pregnancy and birthing. Pregnant women in Sade's universe serve no purpose other than to be mistreated and even murdered.[9] Even when not employed as a receptacle for the libertine's rage, the image of the womb is used to belittle the possibility of love between man and woman. The Comte de Belmor, in his speech against love, at one point uses the idea of birthing to diminish the possibility of any lasting affection for a woman:

> Picture her giving birth, this treasure of your heart; behold that shapeless mass of flesh squirm sticky and festering from the cavity where you believe felicity is to be found.[10]

The 'stickiness' of the newborn child resonates with Sartre's account of femininity.[11] There is no order attested to here; the infant is described as shapeless, formless. This may suggest something about the perceived 'chaos' associated with female sexuality; order has to be imposed from without, it is not an inherent aspect of the physical world.[12] Indeed, Sade's universe is one peculiarly concerned with the ordering of sexual desire: the pleasure of his libertines is invariably associated with the idea that order should be introduced to the sexual act. When the word 'festering' appears in the above passage we get an even clearer sense of the issues raised by the womb. Life, beginning in the womb, inexorably proceeds to the tomb. The mother might give the child life, but it is a life framed by death. Rather than resembling life, she represents the inevitability of death that comes with entering into the natural cycle of the physical world.

Indeed, Sade can be seen to give dramatic expression to such ideas in his descriptions of the murderous mothers, Olympia and Juliette. Reflecting upon the murder of her daughter, Olympia concludes: 'I restored to the elements an inert mass which had received life in my womb only in order to become the toy of my rage and my viciousness.'[13] There is an ambiguity about human existence that means that these words could be applied to any child born into the cycle of life and death. Against such a backdrop, the rage detailed by Sade against pregnant women can be understood as rage against the inevitability of death. The violence meted out to the female sex organs is simply a variation of the anger that knowledge of death brings. We are not immortal, and the realization of that fact leads to this outpouring of violence. To take on the mother and defeat her is to take on the chaotic and destructive forces of nature 'herself'.

Sade's presentation of female libertines goes some way to masking the fact that it is the female that represents death in his universe. Yet even Camille Paglia – who applauds his presentation of characters such as Juliette and Mme de Saint-Ange as 'high priestesses of savage nature'[14] – has to admit that he 'detests procreative women'.[15] It is by reflecting upon this fact that we arrive at what drives Sade's imagination: revenge on the female and the mother.[16]

It is at this point that we must turn our attention to the inseparable connection made by Sade between sex and death. One of the most noteworthy features of Sade's writings is the extent to which the pleasure of the sexual act is ultimately grounded in the death of the other. This structure is clearly present in the story of Juliette. Juliette's entry into libertinage begins with fairly standard sexual practices: mutual masturbation, oral sex, vaginal sex and anal sex. But basing the meaning of one's life purely upon sexual encounters means that there is a constant need for something different, something which will excite the sated senses with its innovation. The dissatisfaction inherent in libertinage is alluded to by Juliette when she comments: 'the effect of irregular desires [is that] the greater the height they arouse us to, the greater the emptiness we feel afterward.'[17] Rather than seek something outside such sexual acts to establish some kind of meaningful life, Juliette simply presses on with her attempts to find new and varied sexual acts. Soon, 'if there was not something exceptional or criminal in the frolics which were proposed to me, I could not even feign an interest in them'.[18] And it is this criminal element that necessitates the death of the other in order to secure ultimate pleasure in the sexual act. Sex and death quickly become linked in Sade's economy of desire. So Clairwil, while picking over the aftermath of one massacre, asks:

> think you one ever tires of the sight of death? Ever has enough of it? It was, to be sure, one of the most delicious horrors I've witnessed in all my days, but it is certain to leave me with an enduring sadness. For, alack, one cannot enjoy a massacre every fifteen minutes the whole length of one's life.[19]

What gives the representation of the death of the other its peculiar power to intrigue and excite? Sade portrays his libertines as unconcerned by the fact of their own mortality.[20] Yet reflection on the role of the mother suggests that the inevitability of death remains a problem, albeit a problem which is repressed, but which finds expression through rage against the mother. An equally strong response is to deproblematize death by eroticizing it. From being something that horrifies and repels, death is turned into something that has an artistic and sensual quality. So, Roland's torture chamber – while including human victims – also includes the waxen image of a crucified woman, whose beautiful hair and face, disfigured by tears, is described by Justine.[21] Creating an aesthetic of death in this way suggests a control over it that we do not, in fact, possess, and thus provides evidence to support Freud's comments on *The Merchant of Venice* and *King Lear,* where he argues that in both of these plays an attempt is made to control death by giving it the shape of a winnable woman.[22]

It is this issue of control that ultimately informs Sade's approach to death. Death is invariably introduced into Sade's stories as the result of a deliberate act perpetrated by the libertine. This gives the libertine a sense that death is under their control; that death is not as powerful as its inevitability might suggest. This point is emphasized by the way in which Juliette murders her closest 'friends' Olympia and Clairwil. There is a surprising suddenness in the way in which they are dispatched, which seems designed to replicate the unpredictability of death.[23] This literary conceit creates the false sense that even the randomness of death is under the libertine's control. A further example of this is provided by Roland's 'experiment' with hanging, which convinces him of the pleasure it is possible to feel when dying, and thus leaves him (as he claims) with no fear of death.[24] Even the libertine's own death will be pleasurable.

Despite his emphasis on cruel and violent deaths, Sade ultimately sidesteps the existential horror of death when it comes to considering the death of the subject. In noting Juliette's death, he does so in a vague and disingenuous way. Ten years after the events he details, he writes that: 'the death of Madame de Lorsange [Juliette] caused her *to disappear* from the world's scene, just as it is customary that all brilliant things on earth finally *fade away*.'[25] There is a peace, a tranquillity alluded to in her passing that was denied her victims, but which seems to represent the ideal for Sade. In seizing life by the throat, Juliette will find a similar control over her own death. Sade has effectively evaded the fear of death in a way that is not altogether convincing; especially when one thinks of the passage where Juliette, prisoner of the thief Brisatesta, fears that she will suffer the same fate as her own victims.[26] She quickly masters this fear, and, of course, comes out of the experience unscathed and better off. But this allusion to her fear suggests that death is not so easily confronted as Sade would have us believe.

Focusing on Sade's attempt to eroticize death in order to control its inevitability goes some way to explaining one of the more bizarre aspects of his work. Coprophagy, or the eating of faeces, is for some of his libertines an act of supreme pleasure.[27] Commentators have struggled to determine why such an act should be pleasurable. Andrea Dworkin suggests that the issue of control is again of paramount importance: in this case, the libertine is exercising control over every aspect of the victim's life. She argues that this act provides the final feature of 'a sexuality which is entirely cannibalistic'.[28] The victim has no control over their own life: power resides with the libertine who can make use of any part of the victim's body to attain their own pleasure.

There is much in Dworkin's analysis to commend it, but I would wish to contend that coprophagy makes more sense when placed alongside Sade's claim that meaning is to be based upon the death of the other. Defecation, like death, reminds us of the transience of human life. Contrary to what the phenomenon of thought suggests, we are not gods, but animals. The eating of faeces suggests defiance in the face of a mutable universe. That which marks us as animals – the need to defecate – need not horrify us, but can be responded to with pleasure; even, in this instance, can give us sustenance. Reflection on this phenomenon may even suggest that Sade is seeking to find a way in which we might transcend nature. Indeed, his emphasis on what might be considered 'unnatural' acts suggests that it is through shaping sexuality that human beings are able to transcend the apparently inescapable lot of being human.

Augustine: sex, sin and death

Sade's attempt to control death by eroticizing it finds surprising resonance in some aspects of the Christian tradition. The Apostle Paul dramatically connects sin with death,[29] while Augustine of Hippo extends this idea, connecting sex with sin and thus with death itself.[30] An analysis of Augustine's ideas shows that, like Sade, the desire to control death's reality underpins his connection of these two aspects of human existence. Tracing the development of this connection in his thought suggests something of the complexity of this connection. At the same time, it highlights the extent to which linking sex and death can avoid a more integrated understanding of the relationship between life and death.

Augustine uses the story of the Fall in Genesis 1–3 to shape his understanding of the human condition. According to his reading, the story of Adam and Eve presents us with the vision of a humanity lost in sin. Augustine's definition of sin focuses on the primeval act of disobedience instigated by the first human couple. In disobeying God, Adam and Eve lost paradise, and all humanity, as their heirs, share in this loss. Because they disobeyed God, humanity is condemned to live 'as the beasts do, subject to death: the slave of his own lust, destined to suffer eternal punishment after death'.[31] After this pivotal event, human beings are subject to the same laws as the animals who must reproduce through sexual intercourse and who are destined to die. In describing both sex and death as in some sense 'unnatural', Augustine develops what will become the orthodox Christian position. In contrast to those branded as heretics, who saw sex and death as part of the divinely ordained nature of things, Augustine sees both features as resulting from human sin.[32]

This 'unnatural' death is linked with the experience of the fallen, sexual body. A direct and immediate punishment for the Fall is that 'human beings' are no longer able to control what Augustine calls the 'shameful' parts of the body: the sexual organs. Adam and Eve's disobedience is thus 'the origin of death in us, and we bear in our members, and in our vitiated nature, the striving of the flesh, or, indeed, its victory'.[33] While this inability to control the sexual organs is viewed as a general punishment for both men and women, in point of fact Augustine seems more interested in how this judgement affects the *male* body, and returns again and again to the problematic issue of the male erection.[34]

The male orgasm reveals to Augustine the power that both sex and death have to affect the loss of the image of God, located in the mind.[35] In the act of sexual intercourse, the god-like capacity to reason is lost: 'when he achieves his climax, the alertness and, so to speak, vigilance of a man's mind is almost entirely overwhelmed.'[36] Similarly, the universality of death reveals the loss of the immortality that the first human beings shared with God. Natural, unredeemed human life is nothing but 'a progression towards death'.[37] The connection between sex and death is similarly clarified in *The Good of Marriage*, where Augustine claims that only after the Fall is sexual intercourse possible, for it 'can only take place between mortal bodies'.[38] Presumably there would have been no sexual intercourse in Eden: although in practice Augustine's response to this question is ambiguous.[39]

If the male body seems peculiarly open to feeling the punishment for the Fall, the female body is not immune from this judgement. After all, avoiding/excluding the female from one's life may be a good way of resisting such a temptation, and as Power shows, this is one of ways in which Augustine seeks to resolve the problems posed by his own sexual desires. Moreover, Augustine's formulation of the nature of sin has a particular impact on how the female body is viewed. Through sexual intercourse, the original sin of our primeval parents is passed on to each and every human being.[40] The womb is symbolized as the locus for death, and even the womb of Mary, the mother of Christ, is likened to a tomb from which Christ had to escape.[41] Sin is universal, and all stand in need of redemption. Only Christ, born of a Virgin Mother, is able to escape the universality of sin. In a shift that resonates with platonic philosophy, birth is associated with death, while death is seen as releasing us from this life.[42]

It is at this point that Augustine suggests a way out of this 'progression towards death' for the one prepared to pursue the spiritual path. To live as God intends us to live, we must learn to control the unruliness of the flesh. Such a lifestyle enables us to challenge the rule of death itself.

Augustine suggests that, in order to live the spiritual life, human (sexual) desire must be sublimated into the (spiritual) desire for God. It is notable that he describes his relationship with God in overtly sexual terms:

> You [God] shone upon me; your radiance enveloped me; you put my blindness to flight. You shed your fragrance about me; I drew breath and now I gasp for your sweet odour. I tasted you, and now I hunger and thirst for you. You touched me, and I am inflamed with love of your peace.[43]

Yet this desire is immune from the vulnerability implicit in sexual relationships: the divine lover will never let us down; the divine lover is eternal.[44] Moreover, by moving the sexual into the spiritual realm, Augustine sets up an opposition between the spiritual and the sexual. If one is to be spiritual, the sexual must be repressed: sublimated into the love of God. Of itself, sexuality is potentially destructive, and, as we have seen, it is the fruit of human sin. Sexual desire is thus linked with the curse of mortality.[45]

Controlling sexual desire for Augustine serves a broader purpose. Because sex is so linked with the curse of mortality, controlling sexual desire suggests the possibility of defeating death itself. Augustine appears to hold out the hope that sexuality might be controlled – 'our wish ought to be nothing less than the non-existence of these desires'[46] – that mind might subjugate body, and thus that we might be able to overcome the curse which fell upon humanity in the wake of the Fall. This is, however, something of a vain hope for Augustine: 'the accomplishment of such a wish [is] not possible in the body of this death',[47] and he tends to look forward to the next life where there will be no 'empty pleasure'.[48]

For the purposes of this chapter, what is interesting here is that Augustine, with Sade, seems to suggest that by controlling sexual desire, death itself can be defeated. Sade suggests that this can happen in this life: by challenging nature, by throwing ourselves into the life of pleasure, we can overcome our own fear of death. Augustine's focus is otherworldly: control sexual desire and one has an intimation of the delights of paradise. Despite their respective hopes, both are deeply pessimistic about human life. Sade's pessimism is grounded in a sense of the absurdity of human life: we are no different from vegetables and animals, and thus what happens to us is of little concern. As the Pope says to Juliette, 'what can it matter if of a man I make a cabbage, a lettuce, a butterfly, or a worm . . . ?'.[49] Augustine's focus is different: human life is lived under the sway of death, and only a transcendent God can rescue us from this perilous state of affairs. Yet despite this pessimistic feel, both men offer an illusion of control. Death is something which, when linked with sex, can be regulated; something which, perhaps, can even be avoided. Sade's work, in particular, suggests something of the implications of such an approach for women, whose bodies are to be controlled as a symbolic way of controlling nature and death. Given these ramifications it is not surprising that some feminist scholars have come to see the Western tradition as death-loving and misogynistic. But while the identification of a connection between sex and death may be open to such distortions, it may also be expressive of a deeper truth: albeit a truth that has been buried under centuries of misogyny. In perceiving a connection between these two features there is the suggestion that *life* and death cannot be separated, and it is this sense that death might be integrated into life that will inform the proposals that conclude this chapter.

A feminist approach to human mortality

The first part of this chapter revealed the destructive ramifications of failing to deal adequately with the sense of vulnerability felt in the face of death's inevitability. Linking death with sex gives the sense that, just as sexuality can be ordered, so death might be controlled. But because Augustine and Sade – and perhaps the tradition more generally – seek easy solutions to the issues death raises does not mean that a feminist should use their problematic accounts as an excuse to shirk addressing death.[50] Indeed, as Julia Kristeva shows, much fruitful and fascinating work can come from struggling with the existential issues death's reality raises.[51]

A first step in this engagement is to apply the feminist critique of dualism to the construction of death. A challenge needs to be made to the binary opposition of life with death. This ancient juxtaposition maintains its hold even in feminist writings that overtly challenge the dualistic construction of experience in Western thought. Plato in *Phaedo* offers a succinct account of this construction when he argues that the soul cannot die, for, as life, the soul cannot admit its opposite, death.[52] A similar opposition seems to inform the work of those feminists who reject the paradigm of mortality and argue that we should consider human being from the standpoint of birth. We have all been born, and, it is argued, the fact that we are 'natals' should determine our discussion of what makes us human. In taking this step, an opposition between life and death is implicitly accepted. So, Grace Jantzen talks of 'privileging' natality, which she views as the 'repressed other' of mortality.[53] This seems to suggest that death is something aberrant, something opposed to life: but I am not convinced that a feminist has to allow such a binary to dictate how she views death. Sade may symbolize death as violent; Augustine may see death as unnatural; but there is no reason why a feminist must accept such categorizations. Indeed, if we move from a discussion of how death works on the symbolic level to the realm of 'lived experience',[54] an altogether different view of death emerges. If we consider the nature of human growth and development, death is a necessary part of life. 'Dying' to the past is often necessary if we are to move on to what the future holds for us. And this poetic allusion is itself derived from a broader, natural pattern. There has to be death and decay in order that there might be new life and development: and it is interesting to note that it is not only ecofeminists who have made this point.[55] Marcus Aurelius, Roman Emperor and Stoic, notes that 'Nature's law is that all things change and turn, and pass away, so that in due order different things may come to be'.[56] Death is thus viewed as a necessary part of the cycles and processes of the natural world.

Feminists have been concerned to celebrate the wonder of being human in this world: quite rightly. They have also been concerned to expose the distorting nature of dualistic formulations. But neither position requires a simple reversal of binary opposi-tions. A more far-reaching and radical solution is needed: rather than rejecting the concept of mortality *in toto,* we need to revisit and remake it. My suggestion is that an account of mortality is needed which places death in the midst of life, rather than on its margins. To make such a move necessitates that we address the fear of death.

There seems to be an assumption in some feminist writing that women do not (or perhaps need not) fear death: perhaps because, as the life-givers, they are linked directly with the processes of creation.[57] Once this assertion is made, attention is then directed to the abstract, symbolic level at which death, it is claimed, feeds the Western imaginary. Having adopted this strategy, little reflection is given to the implications of death as a biological phenomenon. Edna St Vincent Millay's comment, 'I shall die, but that is all that I shall do for death', is used by Jantzen to suggest that the biological fact of death is not problematic: what is problematic is the way the West has incorporated death into its political, social and intellectual structures.[58]

Yet this easy dismissal of the biological fact of death seems to sidestep a proper engagement with the impact of such an acceptance. In many ways this is not surprising: to what extent do any of us adequately accept the inevitability of our own demise – or indeed the demise of those we love? Fear of death is a common response to its reality: and is not altogether absent in the work – or lives – of feminist philosophers of reli-gion. For example, Jantzen claims that analysis of the work of analytic philosophers of religion reveals the repression of desire.[59] An interesting – if debatable – point, but one that leaves her work open to a similar accusation: namely, that there are things which *she* is repressing, in this instance, the fear of death. Consider this comment: 'Of course it is no part of a feminist agenda to deny death: it will come, inevitably, and *all too soon.*'[60] Having made this point, there is little real engagement with how we might cope with such knowledge. Her concluding remarks to the chapter in *Becoming Divine* that deals explicitly with death suggest some ways of approaching death: 'we came into being at birth, before which we did not exist. There is nothing terrible in that recogni-tion';[61] 'the acceptance of life is an acceptance of limits.'[62] But what concerns me is that Jantzen tends to state these conclusions as if they were self-evident, or somehow easy to attain. Arriving at a concord with death, it seems to me, involves far more struggle that Jantzen will allow. Indeed, by emphasizing the symbolic rather than the existential form of death, she tends to deal rather abstractly with death's implications for the indi-vidual. Death is not an abstract problem, but an event that reminds us of the inevitable losses of human life: hence Tolstoy's analysis of the failure of abstract arguments when confronted with the existential horror of death.[63] While the history of Western think-ing may contain 'necrophilic' elements, it also offers examples of figures who grappled in a profound way with the problems death raises, and who provide possible models for how we might proceed. One such example is Marcus Aurelius, whose *Meditations* can be seen as a set of spiritual exercises designed to promote the kind of equilibrium that Jantzen advocates in the face of death.[64]

At the very least, Aurelius's need to collect aphorisms on death, amongst other things, suggests something of the struggle with mortality. We need to come to a recog-nition of our finitude. Yet this cannot be done unless we accept that we are mortals; that our lives will end. To come to such a conclusion we need exercises that refute the sense of our own permanence. The Western cultural context makes such a refutation especially difficult to achieve. It is not simply the case that death provides our culture with its last taboo; death *is* spoken of, but such discussions are invariably predicated upon the belief that it need not occur. Death is viewed as an accident that, if one adopts a suitably careful lifestyle, one might avoid. The prevalence of an insurance culture encourages such a view. This might seem an odd point to make: after all, insurance seems to be predicated upon a recognition that I could – indeed, I *will* – die, and therefore I need to ensure that my financial commitments can be fulfilled after my death. But the way in which insurance is sold suggests a different emphasis: by taking out a particular policy, it is implied that I can protect myself from the transience of life. Following precisely the mechanisms detailed in the first section, where death was eroticized in order that it might be controlled, in this context death is similarly objectified and placed in a category that makes it more manageable. In the process, it becomes distanced from me. Ultimately, an illusion of control over death itself is constructed. My existence seems permanent, even necessary.

The values promoted by Western consumerism reflect a similar, somewhat paradoxical, recognition of and denial of death. Surrounding oneself with desirable objects gives the impression that I am grounded in the world. The illusion of permanence derived from material objects is projected onto the self. The things I possess come not only to define who I am, but also mask the fact that I am a mutable creature who will one day die. Accepting such a conclusion is not easy, and it is not surprising that there has been a tendency for human beings to look to other worlds for their salvation from death. But reflection on death need not lead to such evasions; neither need it lead to a sense of alienation or loneliness. Indeed, employing the model of the spiritual exercise, engaging with writers who have grappled with death can lead precisely to the life-affirming stance that has informed the work of feminist philosophers of religion.[65]

Consider, for example, the way in which human beings have employed art as a way of wrestling with the issue of death and loss. Some of the most powerful passages from Shakespeare are those that reflect upon the death of loved ones, and the inevitability of one's own demise. In this passage, Macbeth has just learnt of his wife's death, and his sense of loss leads to this expression of the futility of human life:

> Tomorrow, and tomorrow, and tomorrow,
> Creeps in this petty pace from day to day,
> To the last syllable of recorded time;
> And all our yesterdays have lighted fools
> The way to dusty death. Out, out, brief candle,
> Life's but a walking shadow, a poor player
> That struts and frets his hour upon the stage,
> And then is heard no more; it is a tale
> Told by an idiot, full of sound and fury,
> Signifying nothing.[66]

Similarly the power of the last act of Verdi's opera *Rigoletto* is derived from the audience's engagement with the story of a misanthropic man who loses the one person whom he loves and who loves him. In part, his loss arises precisely from his futile attempt to protect this beloved daughter from the excesses of the Duke's court: in denying the existence of a daughter, he allows the courtiers to assume that the woman he visits is his mistress, and thus to conceive a plan to take her from him. Rigoletto is a fascinating character. We invariably feel that his callousness brings about his own doom. When intro-duced, he is far from sympathetic, acting as pander, jester and accomplice to the Duke. Yet it is difficult not to visualize one's own losses – both real and anticipated – in the trauma of his last words as his daughter dies in his arms. The sense that there is no moral value, no meaning in the universe, presents us starkly with the problems we face in coming to terms with mortality. A feminist cannot be immune to these challenges.

At the same time, accepting death's reality need not lead to nihilism, and it is perhaps here that a distinctive feminist voice can be heard. We might, for example, consider the feminist engagement with the figure of Antigone.[67] Dorothee Soelle analy-ses her defiant stand against Creon in developing her own response to human suffering. Courting the king's displeasure by attempting to bury her brother, a traitor to the city, Antigone is faced with a dilemma. Should she abide by the king's *diktat* that he should go unburied, or should she perform this last service of love for her dead brother? As Soelle represents it, Antigone's decision is to refuse to hate, to continue to love, even in the face of threatened death.[68] Relationship is the key to overcoming the destruction wrought by death.

A similar response is offered by May Sarton in the novel *A Reckoning*.[69] Her protag-onist, Laura, is dying, and the book catalogues her struggle to come to terms with this. At times, she sees her situation as an adventure: 'I am to have my own death.'[70] Death is not an alien, intrusive other, but part of 'a natural process'.[71] At other times, she expresses a fear of death which bears witness to the loneliness of the experience of dying: 'I'm not ready . . . I can't do it alone';[72] 'it's a lonely business, dying.'[73] Yet this sense of loneliness is not all that is conveyed: much of the novel concerns Laura's inter-actions with her dog, her nurse, her family and her friend Ella. Indeed, it is Ella's arrival that emphasizes the importance of human relationship:

> She didn't want to talk yet, there was fulfilment, such fulfilment simply in Ella's being there, sitting on the bed, touchable, real, not thousands of miles away, to be conjured up for comfort during the interminable nights of waiting for the dawn to come. She didn't want to talk yet, but she knew that she must summon herself back one last time. There were things she needed to say.[74]

The 'things she needed to say' concern their relationship, and her difficult relation-ship with her mother: reflections which lead her to stress the importance of 'joining with women',[75] of finding in each other a way to share the experience of living. What Sarton's writing suggests is that it is possible to face death in such a way that its inevitability is not evaded, and that through human connection we might find a way through the pain.

To engage, then, with such pieces does not foster a detached solipsism where all that matters is our own state of being. Rather, through such reflection we are con-nected with others who, like us, are struggling to find a way through the inevitable losses of human life. Writing or composing such pieces, or meditating upon them, creates empathic connections with others in similar situations. We recognize our selves and our own challenges in these works, and our relationships are strengthened through the recognition of a common humanity, that, like us, stands in the shadows of death and loss. And this recognition need not lead to alienation and depression. Rather, it can connect us more deeply with one another. Accepting, rather than resisting, the vulnerability that comes with our humanity may lead to a deeper, more profound engagement with life, and with each other, than that which resists such ideas. In this sense, to talk of human beings as 'mortal' is to locate human being firmly in this world. To be human is to be part of this world, its processes and cycles, its plants, and animals. There is no escape from this world, and to live meaningfully is to accept our limits and to celebrate them.

Conclusion

This chapter has attempted to offer a feminist approach to the existential issues raised by death. Evading death takes many forms. As the first section showed, connecting death with sex suggests a degree of control over its inevitability that we do not possess. Similarly, engaging with death only on the symbolic level allows an evasion of the existential problems it raises. Resisting such distortions, it is possible to see death differently. Placing death in the midst of life enables us to see ourselves as part of the greater cosmic cycles of life, death and renewal. Accepting that our life is defined by transience does not mean – or even necessitate – that we will not fear our own death or the deaths of those we love. Heartlessness or lack of feeling need not accompany the learning of this lesson. Early feminist work emphasized the connection between the personal and the political, and a similar commitment pervades the desire to address the existential problem of death. Learning to accept our finitude is fundamental to living well in this world: but such an acceptance is not attained without appropriate meditation. By reflecting on death it is possible to see things from a wider perspective, where we are connected more deeply with others and the world, finding in the very flux and change of life its meaning.

Notes

1   See S. Beckett, *The Complete Dramatic Works*, London: Faber & Faber, 1990, p. 83: '[Women] give birth astride a grave, the light gleams an instant, then it's night once more.'
2   S. Welch, *A Feminist Ethic of Risk*, Minneapolis, MN: Fortress Press, 1990.
3   For a fuller discussion of the various forms this connection takes, see B. Clack, *Sex and Death: A Reappraisal of Human Mortality*, Cambridge: Polity Press, 2002.
4   Hesiod, *Theogony and Works and Days*, trans. M.L. West, Oxford: Oxford University Press, 1988, p. 6.
5   A. Dworkin, *Pornography: Men Possessing Women*, London: Women's Press, 1981.
6   While it might be argued that Sade is not particularly misogynistic – after all, some of his greatest libertines are women – Angela Carter has effectively argued that his women are simply 'female impersonators' (A. Carter, *The Sadeian Woman*, London: Virago, 1979, p. 104).
7   D.A.F. Sade, *Justine, Or Good Conduct Well Chastised*, trans. R. Seaver and A. Wainhouse, New York, NY: Grove Press, 1990, p. 631.
8   See J.-P. Sartre, *Being and Nothingness*, trans. H.E. Barnes, London: Methuen, 1969, p. 614, where he states that 'sex is a hole'. For a feminist engagement with Sade's thought, see M.L. Collins and C. Pierce, 'Holes and Slime: Sexism in Sartre's Psychoanalysis', in C.C. Gould and M.W. Wartofsky (eds) *Women and Philosophy*, New York, NY: Pedigree, 1980, and Clack, *Sex and Death*, pp. 40–51.
9   Cf. D.A.F. Sade, *Juliette*, trans. A. Wainhouse, New York, NY: Grove Press, 1968, pp. 618–622.
10   Ibid., p. 510.
11   Sartre, *Being and Nothingness*, p. 600.
12   For a feminist, it is disturbing to note the extent to which Simone de Beauvoir accepts this view of

women in developing her own account of femininity (cf. S. Beauvoir, *The Second Sex*, Harmondsworth: Penguin, 1972; original French edition, 1949, p. 178; Clack, *Sex and Death*, pp. 51–57).

13   Sade, *Juliette*, p. 714.

14   C. Paglia, *Sexual Personae*, Harmondsworth: Penguin, 1991, p. 238.

15   Ibid., p. 244

16   For a fuller discussion of Sade's attitude to mothers, see J. Gallop, 'Sade, Mother and Other Women', in D.B. Allison, M.S. Roberts and A.S. Weiss (eds) *Sade and the Narrative of Transgression*, Cambridge: Cambridge University Press, 1995, pp. 122–141.

17   Sade, *Juliette*, p. 312.

18   Ibid., p. 548.

19   Ibid., p. 978.

20   Ibid., p. 1014.

21   Sade, *Justine*, p. 673.

22   Cf. S. Freud, 'The Theme of the Three Caskets', *Art and Literature*, Harmondsworth: Penguin Freud Library, 1985, pp. 238–240.

23   Sade, *Juliette*, p. 1017; pp. 1029–1030.

24   Ibid., pp. 687–688.

25   Ibid., p. 1193, my emphasis.

26   Ibid., p. 807.

27   Cf. D.A.F. Sade, *The 120 Days of Sodom*, trans. A Wainhouse and R. Seaver, London: Arrow Books, 1990, p. 371.

28   Dworkin, *Pornography*, p. 94.

29   Romans 6:23: 'the wages of sin is death.'

30   Augustine's work has been subjected to considerable feminist analysis: see, for example, K. Børresen, *Subordination and Equivalence: The Nature and Role of Women in Augustine and Thomas Aquinas*, Washington, DC: University Press of America, 1981; E. Pagels, *Adam, Eve, and the Serpent*, Harmondsworth: Penguin, 1988; U. Ranke-Heinemann, *Eunuchs for the Kingdom of Heaven*, Harmondsworth: Penguin, 1990; K. Power, *Veiled Desire: Augustine's Writing on Women*, London: Darton & Longman Todd, 1995.

31   Augustine, *City of God*, trans. R.W. Dyson, Cambridge: Cambridge University Press, 1998, p. 533.

32   For Pelagius (c. 354–after 418), death is part of the nature of God's world, while for Julian (386–454), sex and death were, from the very beginning, features of human life.

33   Augustine, *City of God*, p. 555.

34   Augustine, *Confessions*, trans. R.S. Pine-Coffin, Harmondsworth: Penguin, 1961, X, p. 30; *City of God* XIV, 16, 20, 23.

35   Augustine, *On the Trinity*, Book XII.

36   Augustine, *City of God*, p. 614. Cf. G. Lloyd, *The Man of Reason*, London: Methuen, 1984 for a discussion of the way in which such views lead to the conclusion that man is associated with reason, woman with nature.

37   Augustine, *City of God*, p. 550.

38   Augustine, *De bono coniugali*, trans. P.G. Walsh, Oxford: Clarendon Press, 2001, p. 3.

39   Cf. Power, *Veiled Desire*.

40   Augustine, *City of God*, p. 573.

41   Power, *Veiled Desire*, p. 180.

42   Plato, *Symposium*, 207–209; *Phaedo*, 64; also A. Cavarero, *In Spite of Plato*, Cambridge: Polity Press, 1998, for feminist appraisal of this platonic move.

43   Augustine, *Confessions*, p. 232.

44   Augustine, *De sancta uirginitate*, p. 56.

45   Cf. Augustine, *On Marriage and Concupiscence*, Book 1, Ch. 30.

46   Augustine, 'On Marriage and Concupiscence', in *The Works of Aurelius Augustine, Bishop of Hippo*, volume 12, edited by M. Dods, Edinburgh: T&T Clark, 1874, p. 128.

47   Ibid.

48   Augustine, *City of God*, p. 629.

49   Sade, *Juliette*, p. 773.

50   I am not convinced that such blanket conclusions about the Western tradition can be drawn. For example, as we shall see, Jantzen's own solution to the problem of death resonates with the arguments of the Epicureans.

51   It is interesting to note that Kristeva is often accused of masculinism because she focuses on death and

related issues such as melancholy and depression (cf. J. Kristeva, *Powers of Horror: An Essay on Abjection*, trans. L.-F. Celine, New York, NY: Columbia Press, 1982; *Black Sun: Depression and Melancholia*, trans. L.S. Roudiez, New York, NY: Columbia University Press, 1989, pp. 107–138): comments which suggest something of the difficulties feminists face when addressing such issues.

52 Plato, *Phaedo*, 105d-106e.

53 G. Jantzen, *Becoming Divine: Towards a Feminist Philosophy of Religion*, Manchester: Manchester University Press, 1998, p. 129.

54 P.S. Anderson, *A Feminist Philosophy of Religion: The Rationality and Myths of Religious Belief*, Oxford: Blackwell, 1998, p. 33.

55 See, for example, R. Ruether, *Gaia and God*, London: SCM, 1990.

56 M. Aurelius, *Meditations*, trans. A.S.L. Farquharson, Oxford: Oxford University Press, 1998, Book XII, 21, p. 114.

57 M. Raphael, *Thealogy and Embodiment*, Sheffield: Sheffield Academic Press, 1996, ch. 3, for a review of literature on women as life-givers.

58 Jantzen, *Becoming Divine*, p. 128; cf. E. Millay, 'Conscientious Objector', in *Collected Poems*, New York, NY: Harper Row, 1934.

59 Ibid., pp. 86, 97.

60 Ibid., p. 141, my emphasis.

61 Ibid., p. 154. See M. Nussbaum, *The Therapy of Desire*, Princeton, NJ: Princeton University Press, 1994, ch. 6, for discussion of these arguments. (Note the similarity of Jantzen's argument to those offered by the Epicureans and Stoics, suggesting that her categorization of the Western tradition as necrophilic is somewhat overstated.)

62 Jantzen, *Becoming Divine*, p. 154.

63 Cf. L. Tolstoy, *The Death of Ivan Ilyich*, trans. L. Solotaroff, New York, NY: Bantam Books, 1981; original Russian version, 1886.

64 See P. Hadot, *Philosophy as a Way of Life*, trans. M. Chase, Oxford: Blackwell, 1995, where this account of Aurelius' work is offered.

65 Even the most cursory of reviews shows the concern to ground feminist religious/spiritual praxis in an appreciation of this world: cf. N. Frankenberry (Chapter 1); M. Daly, *Beyond God the Father: Toward a Philosophy of Women's Liberation*, London: Women's Press, 1986; Ruether, *Gaia and God*; Jantzen, *Becoming Divine*; Anderson, *A Feminist Philosophy of Religion*.

66 *Macbeth* 5.5.

67 See, for example, Pamela Anderson, 'Re-Reading Myth in Philosophy: Hegel, Ricoeur and Irigaray Reading Antigone', in M. Joy (ed.) *Paul Ricoeur and Narrative*, Alberta: University of Calgary Press, 1997, pp. 51–68; Judith Butler, *Antigone's Claim: Kinship Between Life and Death*, New York, NY: Columbia University Press, 2000.

68 Cf. D. Soelle, *Suffering*, London: Darton, Longman and Todd, 1975.

69 See M. de Haardt, 'Transcending the Other-Self', in H. Walton and A.W. Hass (eds) *Self/Same/Other*, Sheffield: Sheffield Academic Press, 1999, for full discussion of this novel.

70 M. Sarton, *A Reckoning*, New York, NY: W.W. Norton, 1997, p. 7.

71 Ibid., p. 38.

72 Ibid., p. 10.

73 Ibid., p. 37.

74 Ibid., p. 250.

75 Ibid., p. 252.

Autonomy and spirituality

Introduction

THE RELATIONSHIP BETWEEN AUTONOMY and spirituality in the Western tradition has been well documented. The notion of freedom has been particularly significant for defining what constitutes the spiritual life, and the ideal of the free, rational and detached individual has dominated the way in which the spiritual life has been constructed. Feminist analysis has exposed the extent to which this ideal relates to patriarchal values: the detached individual pursuing the spiritual life could only be male, given the historical position of women. Appropriating Michele Le Doeuff's words on the philosophical life, the spiritual life requires a female 'other' to deal with the less noble, more mundane aspects of human experience.

Recent Western accounts of the spiritual life have promoted ideas of the connection between self-awareness and spirituality. Postmodernist thinkers have challenged such a vision by proclaiming the 'death of subject': a pronouncement that rejects the idea of an autonomous, free-floating self. In such a context, what does it mean to talk of 'the spiritual life'? The chapters that follow reflect some possible perspectives open to feminists engaging with this topic.

Janet Martin Soskice approaches this topic as a Catholic theologian. While coming from a particular faith perspective, she is critical of the dominant Western construction of spirituality, itself dependent on the rational, autonomous self for its expression. In particular, she highlights the incompatibility of this model with the traditional focus of women's lives (families and children) and suggests a different way of envisaging the spiritual life. Her concern is with employing 'attentiveness' as a way of shaping one's spirituality. By focusing on lived reality in all its varied aspects, a different picture of the universe emerges which suggests that the spiritual need not involve transcending the world, but can be found within it.

If Soskice's chapter is concerned largely with the issues confronting Western European women, Dorota Filipczak's piece suggests the different issues facing women in Eastern Europe. If Soskice is critical of the link between the autonomous self and the spiritual life, Filipczak reclaims the link in so far as the search for a 'composite self' becomes a spiritual quest of 'divining a self'. 'Divining' is her word for locating and reclaiming the autonomous female self in one's own political and religious context. Filipczak shows the importance in a woman's quest for autonomy by way of a re-creation of female spirituality. This is an important point, given the extent to which the 'death of the subject' has become an attractive proposition for Western intellectuals. As Daphne Hampson has pointed out, as soon as modern women are in a position to seek their own selves, they are told by the postmodernist that such a self does not exist! Moreover, Filipczak insists that women's quests must always be understood in the context of national and political cultures. Her chapter highlights the oppression women faced before and after communism in Poland. With Pamela Sue Anderson, Filipczak refuses to reject the Enlightenment project outright, and sees in the emphasis on human autonomy a way of advancing the sexual and spiritual liberation of women. A critical comparison of Filipczak and Fionola Meredith on women's struggle to write a narrative which is both singular and aware of the multiplicity of our discourses would be worth further exploration.

Chapter 13

Janet Martin Soskice

LOVE AND ATTENTION

■ From **LOVE AND ATTENTION**, in Michael McGhee (ed.) *Philosophy, Religion and the Spiritual Life*, Cambridge: Cambridge University Press, 1992, pp. 59–72.

I

THE MATCHED PAIR 'LOVE' and 'attention' is familiar to most of us from the essays in Iris Murdoch's *The Sovereignty of Good*. Although she tells us in that book that there is, in her view, no God in the traditional sense of that term, she provides accounts of art, prayer and morality that are religious. 'Morality', she tells us, 'has always been connected with religion and religion with mysticism.'[1] The connection here is love and attention: 'Virtue is *au fond* the same in the artist as in the good man in that it is a selfless attention to nature.'[2] Art and morals are two aspects of the same struggle; both involve attending, a task of attention which goes on all the time, efforts of imagination which are important cumulatively.[3] 'Prayer', she says, 'is properly not petition, but simply an attention to God which is a form of love.'[4]

Murdoch freely acknowledges her indebtedness to Simone Weil and the writings of both, in turn, have influenced many others – amongst whom, recently, is Charles Taylor in his book *Sources of the Self*. For Taylor, too, moral and spiritual intuitions go together. We must ask what we love, what we attend to, in order to know who we are and what we should do. He insists that 'orientation to the good is not . . . something we can engage in or abstain from at will, but a condition of our being selves with an identity'.[5]

So it seems that 'love' and 'attention' mark a place of confluence for the concerns to which the essays in this volume address themselves, Philosophy, Religion and the Spiritual Life, with the further desirable feature that, as they have been discussed and as I shall discuss them, the ethical too is central.

Weil, Murdoch and Taylor, but especially the two last, draw similar portraits of that which they admire and that which they eschew. Love is a central concept in morals. To be fully human and moral is to respond to that which demands or compels our response – the other attended to with love. It is this loving which both draws us out of ourselves and which constitutes us fully as selves. For Murdoch the best exemplar of the 'unselfing' by attention is our experience of beauty.

> I am looking out of my window in an anxious and resentful state of mind . . . suddenly I observe a hovering kestrel. In a moment everything is altered. The brooding self with its hurt vanity has disappeared. There is now nothing but kestrel.[6]

We respond to the 'Good' or the 'Beautiful'. There is a debt to Plato in the idea of a Good, the love of which empowers us to do good and be good. As Taylor says, this 'takes us far beyond the purview of the morals of obligatory action' with which much modern mainstream moral theory has contented itself.[7] Ancient philosophical accounts of practical reason both Platonic and Aristotelian, Taylor argues, were substantive and implied that 'practical wisdom is a matter of *seeing* an order which in some sense is in nature'.[8] And in the works of Weil, Murdoch and Taylor metaphors of vision and seeing are deliberately employed. Murdoch uses 'attention' 'to express the idea of a just and loving gaze directed upon an individual reality'. This she believes to be 'the characteristic and proper mark of the active moral agent'.[9] Attentive love is close to contemplation.

The indebtedness of this line of thought to Christian spirituality, as well as to ancient philosophy, is evident and acknowledged. But any note of self-congratulation on the part of the Christian must be short-lived when one realizes that what is criticized in these theories is also recognizably the product of a Christian tradition of spirituality. Neither Murdoch nor Taylor have much time for the 'man of reason' who in various guises trudges through the works of early modern philosophy, a disengaged self in the disenchanted universe. Although readers may be familiar, I cannot forbear quoting Murdoch's description of Rational Man,

> How recognizable, how familiar to us, is the man so beautifully portrayed in the *Grundlegung*, who confronted even with Christ turns away to consider the judgement of his own conscience and to hear the voice of his own reason . . . this man is with us still, free, independent, lonely, powerful, rational, responsible, brave, the hero of so many novels and books of moral philosophy. . . . He is the offspring of the age of science, confidently rational and yet increasingly aware of his alienation from the material universe which his discoveries reveal.[10]

This is he who, in Taylor's words, is 'capable of objectifying not only the surrounding world but also his own emotions and inclinations, fears and compulsions, and achieving thereby a kind of distance and self-possession which allows him to act "rationally".'[11]

This new agent of science gains control, even in his moral life, through 'disengagement' and objectification. Indeed Taylor argues it is only through a disengagement effected by radical subjectivity that the new radical objectivity is possible. Once confined securely within our selves we can manipulate and control a world of objects.[12] Even our affective responses come to have a value analogous in early modern philosophy and science to secondary properties such as 'red' and 'pain'. Accurate knowledge asks us to 'suspend the "intentional" dimension of experience, that is, what makes it an experience *of* something'.[13]

Taylor underlines the Augustinian ancestry of this disengaged self, and its radical reflexivity. Indeed this miracle of self-mastery is a familiar figure in the texts of spiritual theology. I am tempted to say that despite the criticisms the 'disengaged self' or 'Rational Man' has received in recent years from philosophers, his theological near-relation, Spiritual Man, has continued virtually unchallenged, especially in the area I shall call 'received spirituality'.

II

For each of us, no doubt, a vision is conjured by the phrase, 'the spiritual life' and for most, I'd wager, that in our personal lives at least this is an eschatological vision – something piously hoped for in the future but far from our daily lives where, spiritually, we just 'bump along'. I believe we can also speak of a 'received view' of spiritual life which in its Catholic Christian form might involve long periods of quiet, focused reflections, dark churches and dignified liturgies. In its higher reaches it involves time spent in contemplative prayer, guided or solitary retreats, and sometimes the painful wrestlings with God so beautifully portrayed by the Metaphysical Poets. Above all it involves solitude and collectedness. It does not involve looking after small children.

I have been in the past envious and in awe of colleagues (usually bachelors) who spend their holidays living with monks in the Egyptian desert or making long retreats on Mount Athos. They return refreshed and renewed and say such things as 'It was wonderful. I was able to reread the whole of *The City of God* in the Latin . . . something I've not done for three or four years now.' I then recall my own 'holiday' as entirely taken up with explaining why you can't swim in the river with an infected ear, why two ice creams before lunch is a bad idea, with trips to disgusting public conveniences with children who are 'desperate', with washing grubby clothes, pouring cooling drinks, and cooking large meals in inconvenient kitchens for children made cranky by too much sun and water. From such holidays one returns exhausted and wondering why people go on holidays. But middle-class family holidays are only memorable instances of a wider whole. Parents of small children find themselves looking enviously over the wall at their more spiritual brethren – are these not the true 'spiritual athletes' whose disciplined life of prayer brings them daily closer to God?

The 'received view' of the spiritual life seems to confirm this, as does a good deal of guidance from priests and pastors. One story will have to suffice. A devout Anglican woman of my acquaintance had her first baby. Like most new mothers she was exhausted, but she was also distraught to find her devotional life in ruins. She took advice from three priests. The first told her that if the baby woke at 6.00 a.m., she should rise at 5.00 a.m. for a quiet hour of prayer. The second asked if her husband could not arrange to come home early from work three times a week so that she could get to a Mass. This advice proved threatening to life and marriage. The third told her, 'Relax and just look after your baby. The rest of the Church is praying for you.'

The advice of the third was the best and shows, too, why one does not really resent the retreatant on Mount Athos, or the religious contemplatives. These people, on the Catholic model at least, are praying for us all. But still the priest's advice is not entirely consoling. Is the busy new mother a sort of Christian 'on idle'? Will others carry on seeking God's face while you spend six or eight or twelve years distracted by the cares of the home? Is this the 'Martha' phase of life when you run the creche and make the tea, while the real work of attending to God is elsewhere? Not surprisingly many new mothers feel slightly bitter about this state of affairs.

Despite markers that could lead elsewhere, Christian 'received spirituality' is still shaped by particular views of contemplation, contemplative prayer and religious ecstasy that disenfranchise many people, and perhaps especially women.[14]

The 'received view' has a noble ancestry. Consider Gregory of Nyssa's influential treatise 'On Virginity', written sometime around AD 368. It is not easy, says the author, to find quiet for Divine contemplation within secular life and, as he would create in his readers a passion for excellence he recommends as a 'necessary door of entrance to the holier life, the calling of Virginity'.[15] His praise of virginity takes an interesting tack. He does not, as might be expected by our prurient age, condemn sexual activity. Rather he reserves his disapprobation for marriage, even for an 'ideal' marriage. Consider a marriage in every way most happy – illustrious birth, competent means, deep affection. Beneath these blessings 'the fire of an inevitable pain is smouldering'.[16] The young wife will grow old and die, she may on the other hand die young in childbirth, and the child with her. Children born safely may be subject to accident, illness and disease. You (male) may die on a business trip. A young wife is soon a widow, friends desert her, families quarrel, finances fall to ruin. In short, family life is one damn thing after another. 'He whose life is contained in himself . . .', says Gregory, can easily bear these things, 'possessing a collected mind which is not distracted from itself; while he who shares himself with wife and child' is totally taken up with anxiety for his dear ones.[17]

The striking thing about Gregory's analysis is that it is so convincing. He is simply right, and while we in the affluent west may be spared many terrors of deaths in child-birth, we have no difficulty enumerating other vexations which erode time and energy and would take us from contemplative quiet in the way Gregory describes.

But what about the medicine he prescribes? There is only one way, he says, to escape from Nature's inevitable snares and

> it is, to be attached to none of these things, and to get as far away as possible from the society of this emotional and sensual world; or rather, for *a man to go outside the feelings which his own body gives rise to*. Then, as he does not live for the flesh, he will not be subject to the troubles of the flesh.[18]

He will not be disturbed then by the troubles of his own flesh, nor by the disturbing and demanding flesh of spouse and children. By this means, Gregory says, we may emulate the spirits who neither marry nor are given in marriage but rather 'contemplate the Father of all purity'.[19]

> How can the soul which is riveted to the pleasures of the flesh and busied with *merely human longings* turn a disengaged eye upon its kindred intellectual light? . . . The eyes of swine, turning naturally downwards, have no glimpse of the wonders of the sky; no more can the soul whose body drags it down look anymore upon the beauty above; it must pore perforce upon things which though natural are low and animal. To look with a free devoted gaze upon heavenly delights, the soul . . . will transfer all its power of affection from material objects to the intellectual contemplation of immaterial beauty.[20]

Once freed, the soul in its virgin state can emulate the God who is pure, free and changeless. Gregory takes seriously the idea that man is made in the image of God, but transcribes from an idealized 'Man' a picture of God as sovereign, rational and free, the very image of 'disengaged man'.

Even if we allow a little space for rhetorical excess it cannot be doubted that Gregory's Treatise invokes a spiritual ideal in which the demands of others, even of one's own babies and children, are not merely indifferent to the task of gazing on God, but in competition with it. The higher life is akin to that of Plato; reason, defined in terms of a vision of order, purity and immutability, governs desire. The 'good' man is 'master of himself'.[21]

A distinguished Latin counter-part to Gregory's essay may be found in the first book of *De Doctrina Christiana* where Augustine develops his famous distinction between things which we are to enjoy and things which we are to use. That which we enjoy makes us happy, we rest with satisfaction in it for its own sake. Those things which are objects of our use, on the other hand, help us attain to that which makes us happy. But should we set ourselves to 'enjoy' what should properly be 'used' we are hindered on our way.

Augustine illustrates this with a favoured simile of the voyage: suppose we were wanderers in a strange country and could not live happily away from home. We must use some mode of conveyance to return. But the beauty of the country through which we pass or the pleasure of travel may divert us from 'that home whose delights would make us truly happy. Such is a picture of our condition of this life of mortality. We have wandered far from God; and if we wish to return to our Father's home, this world must be used, not enjoyed. . . .'[22] It is our duty rather to 'enjoy the truth which lives unchangeably', for no one, according to Augustine, 'is so egregiously silly' as to doubt 'that a life of unchangeable wisdom is preferable to one of change'.[23] It is only the strength of evil habits that draws us to less valuable objects in preference to the more worthy. Human loves, as Augustine knew, bring bereavement and sorrow; 'those only are the true objects of enjoyment' which are 'eternal and unchangeable. The rest are for use. . . .'.[24] Even our neighbour, whom we are commanded to love, we love for the sake of something else – that is, in Augustine's terms, 'we use him'. The contrasts are between the eternal, changeless and Divine and the temporary and material. The latter – even one's own children – should only be used on our way to the former.

Few of us are likely to be attracted or convinced by Augustine's account of 'enjoyment' and 'use', an account which even he may have regarded as 'experimental and finally inconclusive'.[25] Neither Gregory nor Augustine was ultimately successful in stopping Christians from marrying and forming attachments to husbands, wives, and children. What they, or a complex tradition devolving directly and indirectly from them, may have been more successful in introducing is a particular idea of the 'spiritual life' still much present in 'received spirituality'. For there emerges between those wallowing in the vexations of secular life and the vision of God in which the blessed share, a distinctive account of an intermediate position of those who are *in via*. It is at this point that we may more readily be convinced by the Augustinian picture, for while none in this life is likely to reach the 'homeland', serious sojourners in the spiritual life may nonetheless establish themselves on the way. A hierarchy is established which privileges the detached life over that of affection and disruption and it is no coincidence that this spiritual hierarchy can be mapped onto other orderings. It is not simply a contrast between the cloistered life and the secular but is aligned with the distinction, common to ancient philosophy, which contrasts the demands and turmoil of ordinary domestic life with the excellences of the life of the polis – the life according to reason, the life of the philosopher, the citizen, and the lover of beauty. Such distinctions, in classical antiquity, ran along overt lines of sex and class. Women, children and slaves, as inhabitants of the rational demimonde, pursue life's necessities. Adult, male, free citizens pursue what Taylor calls the 'good life', 'men deliberate about moral excellence, they contemplate the order of things . . . decide how to shape and apply the laws'.[26] Cloister, academy and law court are judged more suited to the true ends and excellences of human beings than are kitchen and nursery.

The contrast of 'ordinary life' and higher calling is not without its philosophical representatives today – one case seems to be Hannah Arendt's distinction in *The Human Condition* between productive, artifact-generating *work* and repetitious, inconclusive *labour*. Most of what women and slaves have done is of course the latter – the endless cycle of making meals which will only be eaten and washing clothes which will only be soiled. But even our advocates of love and attention seem sometimes to prefer to illustrate their thesis with relatively fixed or 'pure' objects. For instance Iris Murdoch's preference for beauty as the best evidence for a transcendent principle of the good. Ordinary human love, she says, is normally 'too profoundly possessive and also too "mechanical" to be a place of vision'.[27]

It would be rash and inaccurate to suggest that exaltation of the spiritual life (so fashioned) has always in Christian history meant the denigration of family life (though sometimes it has).[28] You will be quick to point out the many places at which theologians and poets (even Metaphysical poets) have praised the daily round and trivial task. But for the most part such things as attending to a squalling baby are seen as honourable duties, consonant with God's purposes, rather than in themselves spiritually edifying. Most Christian women, for instance, think that what they do around the home is worthy in God's service – they do not think, they have not been *taught* to think, of it as spiritual. And here monastic figures who, apparently, found God over the washing up or floor sweeping will be called to mind, but these are not really to the point, since servile tasks were recommended because they left the mind free to contemplate. What we want is a monk who finds God while cooking a meal while one child is clamouring for a drink, another needs a bottom wiped, and a baby throws up over his shoulder.

III

It is not surprising that women philosophers, even when few in number, should have been prominent amongst those who have in recent years criticized that disengaged 'Man of Reason'.[29] Nor is it surprising that many Christian women find themselves little attracted to Augustine and Gregory of Nyssa's spiritual hero, who, going outside the feelings his body gives rise to and the vexations of secular life, turns to meet God. Women's lives are much given to attending to particulars; to small and repetitive tasks like the washing of clothes and the wiping of noses that leave no carved stone monuments behind them. Most women in general, if not every woman in particular, have been concerned with the management of ordinary life and the realm of necessity. And most mothers – and indeed attentive fathers – realize that there is something inchoately graced about these dealings.[30] They feel there is something unpalatable about the ancient suggestion that our affection for spouse and children is somehow in competition with a single-minded love of God. That something is unpalatable, of course, does not necessarily make it untrue. Maybe ours is just a spiritually lazy age. Perhaps Gregory is right in thinking the life according to excellence can only be sought via the autonomy he advocates. Mothers of large families would then need to rely on the prayers of these holy individuals bringing benefit to the whole communion of saints.

Certainly, and let me emphasize this now, there is an excellence to the monastic life, and the arguments I have used from Gregory and Augustine are not its only or its best defences. I am not trying to empty the cloisters, but rather to see what just one of many possible complementary accounts of the spiritual life (there could be many more) for those who do not take this path might be like.

It may be that ours is an unspiritual age, but it may also be that ours is just a different age. In the ancient wisdom of Gregory and Augustine there is a mixture of assumptions of a moral, philosophical and even a scientific nature which we might now want to call into question. For instance, do we think, as Augustine did, that it is 'egregiously silly' to doubt that the life of unchangeable wisdom is preferable to one of change? This no longer seems obvious to us, any more than it is a useful premise for science. We understand ourselves to be creatures of change in a universe that is changing. Cosmology, biology and the social sciences all give accounts of structures, creatures and societies that change. Scientists in general believe that our universe had a beginning and will have an end. Light, hydrogen, carbon, hydrocarbons and primitive life preceded our own human species in this world and made our existence possible. And we might do well to consider wisdom about human beings to be a wisdom about creatures of change.

And again, why should disengagement from the society of the emotional and sensual world be our path to spiritual excellence? Characteristically, as Charles Taylor points out, if we are trying to understand something we aim to be not disengaged but 'fully there', imaginatively present to that which concerns us. It is by this kind of attending that we are characteristically drawn out of ourselves (ecstasis) and come to understand ourselves fully as selves. Central to this are our physical bodies, with all their affective and passible characteristics. Common both to our belief that we are by nature changeable and changing and of necessity creatures of affections is the conviction, unproblematic for most moderns, that we are animals; rational and spiritual animals, perhaps, but for all that in recognizable continuity with other creatures in this universe.

IV

Let us return to the discussion of love and attention with which we began. To be fully human and to be fully moral is to respond to that which demands our response – the other, attended to with love. Morality, religion and mysticism are of a piece.

Let us complement these Platonic themes with an Aristotelian gloss more consonant with our present self-understanding. What we need attend to with love is a changing world full of creatures of change. We ourselves are such creatures.

Let us suppose that affective responses do not, or do not always, mislead and that describing the world as it appears to members of our kind is not inferior to an imagined 'value-neutral' observation of an ideal science but our best handle on the true, the good and the real. Let us suppose that our affections and even our animal responses, properly attended to, are not distractions but guides to what we are and to the love of God.

All life, even plant and protozoic life, is such as to be affected by the world it inhabits. The sunflower turns towards the sun. Attention is rewarded with reality. In his Colour Theory, Goethe makes the following reflection,

> The eye has light to thank for its being. Out of the indifferent animal frame Light has called an organ to be in its own image. And so the eye is built by Light for Light, so that the inner light may encounter the other. (my translation)

Stripped of its teleology this is a point modern biologists make. Not only does seeing 'give us' the world, the world in some real sense gives us seeing. Because of light, organisms have developed photosensitive capacities. (Goethe puts it more beautifully.)

To recapitulate, all life, even protozoic or plant life is such as to be affected by the world it inhabits. Attention is rewarded with reality. But is this a stage to the moral and the spiritual? Not if one thinks that moral and devotional acts are in some stark sense the product of a disengaged reason. Or if one believes that our affections and desires are delusions and snares on our path to the real. Nor yet if one follows what Martha Craven Nussbaum calls Plato's 'double story' with its split between *nous* on the one hand and brute necessity on the other, and the correlative split between human beings and the other animals. In this 'double story' the 'self-moving, purely active, self-sufficient intellect, generator of valuable acts' confronts 'bodily appetites, which are themselves passive and entirely unselective, simply pushed into existence by the world and pushing, in turn, the passive agent'.[31] A familiar scene but one in which, as it was Aristotle's genius to point out, it is difficult to explain animal motion. But what if, like Nussbaum, we follow Aristotle? Animals, even human animals, according to Aristotle, act on the basis of desires, and the study of animal motion may tell us something important about human ethical aspirations. As Nussbaum says, 'Both humans and other animals, in their rational and non-rational actions, have in common that they stretch forward, so to speak, towards pieces of the world which they then attain or appropriate.'[32] The dog leaps at the piece of meat, both because it desires meat *and* because it sees the object before it as meat. What the Aristotelian account with its focus on desire achieves, Nussbaum points out, is a restoration of the importance of intentionality. It enables us to focus on the intentionality of animal movement, both its 'object-directedness' and 'its responsiveness not to the world *simpliciter* but to the animal's view of it'.[33] This is not intended by Aristotle to rival the account of the deliberative but to provide 'an attractive account of the natural animal basis for the development of moral character.'[34] Rather than denigrating the animal appetites we should acknowledge that, 'It is our nature to be animal, the sort of animal that is rational. If we do not give a debased account of the animal or a puffed-up account of the rational, we will be in a position to see how well suited the one is to contribute to the flourishing of the other.'[35]

Returning to the spiritual life, once allow our physical natures into the picture as a good, or at least as a necessity, and the vexations of ordinary daily life may appear in a different light. Nothing convicts one more graphically of the implausibility of a sharp distinction between our rational and deliberate capacities, on the one hand, and the bodily appetites and responses on the other, than the experience of pregnancy and attending to an infant. Although it is not everyone's experience to be a mother, it is everyone's experience to have been an embryo and a baby, and it would be surprising if this did not have something to tell us about what it is to be a person. During pregnancy a series of changes take place to the mother's body which make it hospitable to the growing foetus and future child. These range from a suppression of the immune system (so that the foetus will not be rejected) to an increase in the flow of blood and preparation for lactation. None of these changes are voluntary. They are called into being by the presence of the embryo. But consider lactation; in the days following childbirth milk is produced involuntarily in response to the baby's cry. But the mother may be deceived, especially if she is sharing a ward with other mothers and new babies. Imagine this scene where the mother is deceived: the cry is heard, the milk gushes forth but examination reveals that it is not her baby who has cried. The milk stops. Or the reverse: cries are heard. The source is believed to be someone else's baby. No milk. A mistake is realized. The milk flows. The important thing to notice is that, in this example, the response of lactation is *both involuntary and rational*, dependent as it is on the mother's beliefs. And this rational component of the maternal response is not discontinuous with the other preparations her body has made. Whereas before birth the mother's body unreflectively attends to the needs of the embryo, after the birth the brain joins the other organs (kidneys, guts, lungs) in attending to the new other. Or better, the whole active being of the mother, in all her instinctual and reflective capacities, is brought to bear on the needs of the baby. Just as at this early stage simple beliefs, such as the belief that it is my baby that is crying, affect simple attentive response to the newborn, so beliefs will become more complex and result in more complex actions – belief that the baby is cold, that babies should get fresh air, that toddlers should be kept from fires, that small children should be courteous to their grandparents, say their prayers and so on. The child is introduced to a world of symbols, stories, goals and practices. By such means parents, even fairly mediocre parents, help babies to become 'selves'.

The process of attending to the child's needs on the basis of parental beliefs is continuous with the simple, involuntary response by which the mother produces milk when she believes her baby is crying. What we do is the result of what we believe about the child, the world, and about what it is good to have and to be. Our affections, though in Gregory's words 'low and animal', are continuous with our highest beliefs and values.

The parents – or those who attend in love – undergo changes as well. The biological reciprocity between mother and child in early infancy is continued in innumerable small acts of watchfulness, many almost as involuntary as lactation. For instance the scanning, native to parents of toddlers, of any new surrounding for steep steps, sharp, breakable or swallowable objects. Parents do not always think much about this, they simply do it as a few years further along in the child's life they will not. Other acts of attentiveness require the disciplined and conscious exercise of what Sara Ruddick calls 'humility'. To attend to the child properly is also to employ the proper passivity of 'letting the other be'. Ideally, as Ruddick says, 'Acts of attention strengthen a love that does not clutch at or cling to the beloved but lets her grow.'[36] By such means parents, at least once in a while, may be 'unselved', just as in Iris Murdoch's example we may be 'unselfed' by the beauty of the kestrel's flight.[37]

The child is, *par excellence*, the individual 'thought of as knowable by love'.[38] Attending to them is a work of imagination and moral effort by which parents try to 'see more' in Murdoch's sense, or to be 'more fully there', in Taylor's. This is not the moral and spiritual life of the needle-thin, disengaged, 'punctual' self. Rather, as Murdoch says, 'The task of attention goes on all the time and at apparently empty and everyday moments we are "looking", making those little peering efforts of the imagination which have such important cumulative results.'[39] The object of attention is not a changeless truth so much as a moving target. Children are creatures of change and chance, and an attentive gaze on the real in their case is a gaze on a changing reality.

Despite a certain advocacy for the changeless amongst spiritual writers, the points I have made above are not alien to Christian theology. God is after all portrayed in the Bible as creating a universe that endures for a time but will end. God is represented as attending to a chosen people involved, at God's behest, in seemingly ceaseless change. They are called out, established, exiled, freed. God is represented in the Prophetic writings as chivvying them along and unsettling their complacent accommodations. We seem far from Augustine's tale of the traveller who turns his back on what is material and temporary in order to seek that which is spiritual and eternal, but maybe not. Augustine elsewhere tells another story of a journey, his own journey as recounted in the *Confessions*. We know that Augustine as a young man was appalled by the crudeness of Christianity, his mother's religion, and indeed why should a cultivated man of his place and time have found the stories of an unimportant provincial people like the Jews edifying? But this seems to change once he believes that God became a man and had a human history. The story of the Jews then becomes not otiose and irrelevant but the locus of divine self-disclosure. The history of the Jews, and all human history is, so to speak, 'baptised'. All human history and each human history becomes the place where God meets women and men. Augustine can write his own history of divine encounter, the *Confessions*. For Augustine God's attentiveness does not derogate from God's qualities classically conceived. This is a philosophical leitmotif of the *Confessions*. It is because God is eternal that God is present to all and every time in Augustine's life. God need not be a creature of change to be attentive to changing creatures. God need not be a particular 'thing' to attend to particulars. Indeed for Augustine and for the mainstream of classical philosophical theology, God attends to everything, in particular.

Theologians must reach for analogies. Perhaps the gaze of God is like the gaze of the artist on the completed painting. Each mark of pigment is discrete, yet this green would not be present in its particular greenness were it not for this blue laid down next to it. Each mark has been laid down, one at a time, yet we apprehend the completed work in a single vision. The painting is thus a condensed temporality. We gaze on it as on a complete and consummated whole, bearing all the marks of its making. People might be like this under the attentive gaze of love. Perhaps creation is, too.

Notes

1   Iris Murdoch, *The Sovereignty of Good*, London: Routledge and Kegan Paul, 1970, p. 74.
2   Ibid., p. 41.
3   Ibid., p. 43.
4   Ibid., p. 55.

5   Charles Taylor, *Sources of the Self: The Making of Modern Identity*, Cambridge: Cambridge University Press, 1989, p. 68.

6   Murdoch, *The Sovereignty of Good*, p. 84.

7   Taylor, *Sources of the Self*, p. 93.

8   Ibid., p. 86.

9   Murdoch, *The Sovereignty of Good*, p. 34.

10   Ibid., p. 80.

11   Taylor, *Sources of the Self*, p. 21.

12   Ibid., pp. 173–174.

13   Ibid., p. 162.

14   'Received spirituality' is probably also a fantasy remote from the actual busy lives of many monks and nuns.

15   Gregory of Nyssa, 'On Virginity', trans. Moore and Wilson, *The Nicene and Post-Nicene Fathers*, Second Series, Vol. V. Grand Rapids, MI: Eerdmanns, 1979, p. 343.

16   Ibid., p. 345.

17   Ibid., p. 347.

18   Ibid., p. 350–351, my italics.

19   Ibid., p. 351.

20   Ibid., p. 351, my italics.

21   Taylor, *Sources of the Self*, p. 115.

22   Augustine, *St Augustine's Christian Doctrine*, trans. Rev. Prof. J.F. Shaw, *The Nicene and Post-Nicene Fathers*, First Series, Vol. II. Grand Rapids, MI: Eerdmanns, 1988, p. 523.

23   Ibid., p. 525.

24   Ibid., p. 527.

25   O. O'Donovan, *The Problem of Self-Love in Augustine*, New Haven, CT and London: Yale University Press: 1980, p. 26.

26   Taylor, *Sources of the Self*, pp. 211–212.

27   Murdoch, *The Sovereignty of Good*, p. 75.

28   It has been pointed out to me that I have paid no attention in this paper to the Lutheran and Reformed traditions of domestic holiness. This is largely deliberate, since I'm addressing a version of 'spiritual life' associated with the Catholic aspects of Christianity. Indeed the phrase 'spiritual life' is one which Catholic Christians (a category which includes more than Roman Catholics) are more likely to use than are Protestants. However, it is also the case that women friends of mine in the Reformed tradition tell me that, despite the positive signs, things are not much better for them in their own churches.

29   A recent work in this vein is Sara Ruddick's *Maternal Thinking* (1990) in which she attempts, on the basis of what she calls maternal practice, to construct an account of the practical reasoning appropriate to it. Love and attention figure large. The disengaged self, as one might imagine, fares badly as a paradigm of 'attentive parenting'.

30   I am not making an 'essentialist' case here. It is not that women or 'mothers' are 'born attentive', so to speak, but rather than those engaged in attending to the infant will learn from this. I am using the word 'mothers' for the attenders, pretty much throughout, because, as Ruddick points out, most people who look after children and home in this way are and have been women. This is not to say that they need be women.

31   Martha Nussbaum, *The Fragility of Goodness*, Cambridge: Cambridge University Press, 1986, p. 264.

32   Ibid., pp. 275–276.

33   Ibid., p. 270.

34   Ibid., p. 286.

35   Ibid., p. 287.

36   Sara Ruddick, *Maternal Thinking: Towards a Politics of Peace*, London: The Women's Press, 1990, p. 122.

37   It should be noted that this 'unselving' is not the destructive abnegation of self which, as Valerie Saiving Goldstein and others have pointed out, is, for many women, a kind of sin rather than a sort of sanctity. A remark of Julia Kristeva's comes to mind, 'The arrival of a child is, I believe, the first and often the only opportunity a woman has to experience the Other in its radical separation from herself, that is, as an object of love.'

38   Murdoch, *The Sovereignty of Good*, p. 40.

39   Ibid., p. 43.

Chapter 14

Dorota Filipczak

AUTONOMY AND FEMALE SPIRITUALITY IN A POLISH CONTEXT: DIVINING A SELF

IN HER NOVEL, *THE DIVINERS*, Margaret Laurence charts one woman's journey to autonomy through a re-creation of female spirituality.[1] Although Laurence's novel is set in a Canadian context, and so completely foreign to my own Polish setting, the goal of this chapter will be to demonstrate how this woman's creative pursuit of autonomy can be juxtaposed to alternative stories of spiritual quests for female identity in different cultural contexts. Unlike Margaret Atwood, whose novels have been translated into Polish, Laurence is only accessible to Polish students who choose to read works in the English of postcolonial literature. Yet Laurence's writings never fail to elicit an enthusiastic response from Polish readers, and this is not only from female students in Poland. One of the attractive characteristics of Laurence's fiction is that her heroines manage to integrate different aspects of the female self, which have been segregated into binary oppositions by patriarchal discourse. In *The Diviners*, female sexuality and spirituality come to form a harmonious union in the composition of the heroine's 'composite self'. Laurence's celebration of the physical redeems the body from the confinement of the profane, and allows it to feed into spiritual energies.

The distinctive reception of Laurence's message by Polish readers, whether in groups of women and men or individually, raises the question of what exactly a particular woman brings to her reading of a foreign text. The heroine's conscious retrieval of different aspects of her composite self can be juxtaposed against the discursive horizon of Polish women. In this chapter I intend to present the interaction between Laurence's story and stories from Polish literature. My interactive criticism seeks to guarantee a dialogic interpretation in which national particularity is respectfully represented. My method of reading is indebted to Lawrence Venuti's approach to translation.[2] The connections between criticism and translation are sometimes overlooked. Yet, as George Steiner reminds us, like the pianist performing a Beethoven sonata, the critic analysing and the translator translating the text are each concerned with interpretation.[3] In his *The Translator's Invisibility*, Venuti discusses two approaches to translation, i.e. domestication and foreignization.[4] Domestication, the method which seems to rule in the English and American markets, presupposes the 'translator's invisibility'. The translator erases herself or himself in what Venuti calls 'a weird act of self-annihilation'.[5] The text which she or he produces creates an illusion of being generated in the culture of the target language. In foreignization, the translator is present in her or his work, and the translation itself is not cut off from its source, but it is informed by echoes of cultural difference. Understandably, foreignization has been embraced by many postcolonial translators such as Gayatri Spivak. As for my own position in this chapter, it is not my aim to make myself and my tradition transparent by choosing a global discourse. On the contrary, I read Laurence without camouflaging my context and identity. My ethics of reading consists in making both the author and the reader visible. Interactive criticism can provide the author's message with a multiplicity of afterlives, much like the act of translation. Foreignizing translation tends to emphasize the trace of the other (in this case, the translator) rather than erase it. The same can be applied to interactive criticism. So I interact with Laurence's message not only as a gendered individual, but also as a foreigner who both welcomes and resists the mimicry of English at the very same time.

Divining a self

To grasp my central conception of 'divining a self', it is helpful to picture the protagonist of *The Diviners*. Morag Gunn is an orphan adopted by the garbage collector, Christie, and his wife, Prin, both from the prairie town. The 'nuisance grounds',[6] i.e. her stepfather's work place, represent her own marginal and impure status in the decent, mostly white prairie community. Morag tries to combat her second-class status with an inner strength fed by her stepfather's stories about her Gaelic origin. A powerful Celtic woman plays the crucial role in Christie's message. Salvaged from the nuisance grounds, the Bible in Gaelic stands for the world of roots that were discarded, buried or disseminated in order to survive. When Morag goes to university and falls in love with a professor of English literature, she cuts herself off from her past, symbolized by the nuisance grounds. She buries her impure origin, and finally purifies herself by marriage to both canon and order, represented by her husband professor.

Trapped in a stereotype associated with high heels, Morag still feels the urge to become a writer; this desire, though approved of when a student, now invites patronizing comments from her husband, who is teaching a course on the novel in Toronto, where the couple are residing. Only when Morag understands how she has distorted her true image will she be able to walk out of her restrictive marriage and reclaim her creative potential. Morag is rescued from conventions by a friend from her youth: Jules Tonnerre, a Métis, shares her experience of the nuisance grounds, because his origin is considered racially impure in the prairie community. The baby girl who Morag has by Tonnerre symbolizes the restored connection with her lost self. Morag comes to enjoy the creative resources, as both a writer and a mother, which were blocked for a long time by her authoritarian husband.

The title, *The Diviners*, refers to many things. It refers to the ability of the garbage collector, Christie, to read people's characters from the garbage they discard. The garbage is also a Freudian metaphor for what decent citizens try to forget, repress or relegate to inferior status because it inspires fear or disgust. Christie does not mind working on the collective subconscious in the nuisance grounds because the artificial boundaries between cleanliness and dirt, or reason and unreason, only make him laugh. His household is the result of a creative bricolage, or a collection of things, discarded by others and salvaged by him. His prophetic monologues, which conflate the sacred and the profane, come back to Morag and help her to find her own voice. Prin's death results in Morag's visit to her hometown. After this, she becomes aware of the potentially releasing desire to speak in the same way as Christie, to use his 'loony oratory', 'lean oaths with some protein in them', 'Protean oaths', as she calls them.[7] If Christie divined on the nuisance grounds, Morag divines on language grounds, the perilous territory of buried meanings, where the sacred commingles with the profane. Speech becomes protein, the source of nourishment, like the roll offered to the prophet Ezekiel.

Divining is also connected with another male character, Royland, Morag's neighbour and friend in the times of her maturity as writer and mother. His ability to locate the source of water is explained as a gift that came to him after he renounced the previous role of Bible puncher, the man whose family life fell apart under the pressure of ideological slogans. His ability to divine a hidden spring parallels the ability of Morag and Laurence to divine creative resources.

In my interpretation, divining is a metaphor for locating and reclaiming the autonomous female self, who has been fragmented, disseminated and buried in the patriarchal discourse. Before Morag gains strength to give up her secure but restrictive marriage, she goes back to her birthplace and thus establishes a connection with the past she has tried to erase. She descends into herself and regains access to her own anger, which proves liberating. It is significant that after their love-making, her Métis lover calls himself a shaman, i.e. the one who has exorcized the oppressive spirit of Morag's husband and helped her to embark on the quest for autonomy. Divining a self necessitates a quest beneath the surface of things. As a result, connections between previously segregated spaces are re-established and celebrated. Morag translates this quest for autonomy into spiritual terms. While talking to Jules about her sudden illumination, she mentions the hymn, *Jerusalem the Golden*, whose message is the revelation of things intuited much earlier.[8] Thus Morag's discovery of herself is framed by a religious context. Her quest takes her away from the centre into the forgotten peripheries of her past and self.

Marginalities

Laurence remains an iconic figure in Canadian literature. Yet, in spite of this status, her work has never been widely received in Britain. Even though her main novels were published in the United Kingdom, her appearance on the British market was ephemeral, and soon eclipsed by the more influential Canadian writer, Margaret Atwood. Stressing the fact that Laurence created most of her Canadian-based novels while in England, Coral Ann Howells finds it ironic that her fiction had to be reintroduced to British readers by the Virago Press in 1987.[9] Despite the earlier editions published in the 1960s and 1970s, as well as the Virago Press editions, the Manawaka novels are a rare sight in British libraries.

Ironically, such marginalization echoes Laurence's own choice to identify with the marginalized. Her characters are women from parochial, prairie backgrounds – which is her own origin. Their second-class status in the community brings to mind the position of the author, who started out as a Canadian, not American or British writer, and who, by empowering the characters from the Canadian prairie, also empowered Canadian literature.

What interests me in *The Diviners* are the ways in which Laurence empowers the marginalized voice: from Canada as opposed to the US, and from the prairie as opposed to a metropolis such as Toronto. This voice is removed from and at odds with the literary centre: Morag's husband Brooke Skelton identifies with the canonical standards of the British academic world. The marginalized voice is also cut off from the world of financial security and privilege: Morag's step-parents offer her a disadvantaged background. And, in each of these cases, the marginalized voice is enhanced by a focus on gender.

Having been born in Poland during the communist regime, I myself find Laurence's concern with the marginalized and oppressed particularly relevant. Laurence's feel for imperial oppression makes her writing more important to me than that of Atwood, whom I appreciate for other reasons, but whose women suffer much more from the mechanisms of consumerist society, completely removed from my own past and background. Atwood's message is more appealing for Polish readers now that we are inundated with the icons of American mass culture, and Polish glossies for ladies are marketing the woman as a product, a strategy deconstructed long ago in Atwood's *Edible Woman*.

In fact, oppressive gender stereotypes did not disappear with the communist regime. On the contrary, they are alive and well in hundreds of TV advertisements. For instance, there is the ad which shows a smiling, sexy housewife in the company of the latest scouring powder, while her husband is enjoying his beer in the male camaraderie of a pub. Unfortunately, the attitude of the church adds to this image of the new capitalist family. The Catholic church emphasizes the woman's maternal role (generally bypassing men's commitments as fathers) to the lesser or greater exclusion of her political role and intellectual potential. In a collection of essays, *Świat bez kobiet* (*The World Without Women*), Agnieszka Graff comments on the gradual exclusion of women from politics in the times of transformation.[10] The Solidarity movement did not imply solidarity with women's rights. The church that had been the refuge for political activists under communism now attempts to control female spirituality and physicality. Control over these latter elements is also exercised by the predominantly male Parliament.

Divining the divine

The creative gift in *The Diviners* is bestowed upon its recipients in a Christ-like fashion. The people who receive it (including Morag) are not connected with positions of social or political privilege. On the contrary, they are marginal figures without intellectual, social or financial advantage. The prescriptive authority of Morag's husband who condescendingly ministers to his flock in the field of English Literature is exposed as a sterile, colonial attitude, a Pharisaic abuse in contrast to Morag's moral and spiritual insight. By following her gift, i.e. the vocation to divine her creative resources, Morag saves her moral integrity and establishes her contact with the divine outside the masculine framework.

It is this aspect of Laurence's fiction that resonates with my own heritage. Polish culture lacks the secular interpretation of biblical and religious messages by women who want to see other dimensions in the Gospels than feminine self-effacement and self-sacrifice. Even though in the sixteenth century the Protestant movement gained many followers in Poland, the Catholic tradition ultimately prevailed. The result today is that all the entries into the sacred text are protected by the exclusively male authority of the church. Texts by Polish women often reject the biblical message as oppressive rather than open to transformation.

It is interesting to see how particular texts from Polish literature illustrate the dilemmas of the female condition. Here my choice of texts is influenced by Maria Janion.[11] In Janion's *Kobiety i duch inności* (*Women and the Spirit of Otherness*), the critic uses an extract from the play, *Nie-Boska komedia* (*The Non-Divine Comedy*) by a romantic poet, Zygmunt Krasiński. The connection between madness and female creativity which Janion explores also resurfaces in her analysis of the contemporary novel, *Absolutna amnezja* (*The Absolute Amnesia*), by a Polish feminist writer, Izabela Filipiak. I am concerned with the implications of both texts for the connection between women and the divine. In other words, I target the aspect that is strangely missing, not only from traditionalist, mostly masculine images of women, but also from a contemporary feminist analysis in Poland. The choice of Krasiński's play and Filipiak's fiction is not representative of Polish literature, but the presentation of the whole complexity of Polish perspectives is beyond the scope of this chapter.

Like most students in Polish secondary schools, I encountered *Nie-Boska komedia* as an obligatory canonical item on the reading list. Its protagonist, Count Henryk, is an aristocrat who feels estranged from his wife because, as a sensitive poet, he cannot really communicate with her. Instead, he pursues a disembodied muse. The wife, who loves him dearly, is overcome by great sadness and eventually committed to a mental asylum. When Henryk realizes that he has been chasing an illusion, he decides to ask for Maria's forgiveness, but now his wife makes a most interesting confession. She says she prayed to God and repented in order to be worthy of 'the spirit of poetry', and thus deserving of her husband's love. 'On the third day in the morning I became a poet,' she announces. The way she structures her confession brings to mind the crucial event that happened on the third day: Christ's resurrection. Metamorphosed by her mystical experience, the wife asks her husband: 'Haven't I become your equal?' And then she comes up with a sample of her own beautiful poetry. The husband is shocked. 'The curse, the curse,' he says. He obviously believes that she has been possessed by an evil spirit. The text clearly indicates that there is a discrepancy between the spirit of poetry and the female body. Prior to her confession the wife informs her husband that her soul has left her body and now resides in her head. The lack of connection between the body as the seat of instinct and the head as the intellectual citadel is a stereotypical echo of the manichean division which projected the physical onto the female, and the intellectual onto the male. The wife has ventured outside her gender territory and thus betrayed her own body. This is not the end of her extravagance, for now she embraces the religious code and comes up with an amazing, apocalyptic vision. The Count beseeches her to calm down. A doctor tries to examine her, but she dies.[12]

The incompatibility between creativity and femininity could not be expressed more explicitly. The irony of the text is that the poetic message of the Countess, while of the highest quality, is read by her husband as the sign of madness. This is not a far cry from Brooke's reaction to Morag's Protean speech. When the latter finally releases within herself the hidden gift of Christie's loony oratory, and shatters her façade, her husband accuses her of being hysterical, and asks if she is due to menstruate.[13] In both cases creativity in a woman is denied by the charge of madness and physiology. In fact, the Countess's creative gift in *Nie-Boska komedia* combines poetic and prophetic functions. She is not only a poet, but the one who proclaims the Apocalypse. In her vision, Christ is no longer able to save humanity and hurls his cross into the abyss where it shatters into smithereens. This is one of the most courageous acts of the seizure of the divine word by a woman in Polish literature. Interestingly, Krasiński associated the divine word with poetry. At the beginning of his play he draws a comparison between a person visited by the spirit of poetry and the world in which God was born. The Polish word for poetry, which is feminine, and the choice of masculine pronoun for the poet make the message gendered. Krasiński refers to poetry as the mother of beauty and salvation, which is not far from the language of Mariolatry.[14] While poetry is female, the poet is certainly male. This has significant implications for the seizure of the divine and poetic word by a woman.

What happens to the wife in *Nie-Boska komedia* is a powerful biblical experience on several levels. 'The spirit of poetry' brings to mind the well-known passage from the Book of Joel: 'And it shall come to pass afterward, that I will pour out my Spirit upon all flesh; and your sons and your daughters shall prophesy' (King James Version 2:28). Visited by 'the spirit of poetry', the wife begins to prophesy, and, just like in Joel's message, her prophecy concerns the Apocalypse. On a different level, the wife is in the situation of apostles on the Day of Pentecost. According to Acts 2:4 (King James Version) 'the Spirit gave them utterance' thus empowering Peter to start his speech with the passage from Joel. The wife's name is Maria, so she is a rendition of Virgin Mary, who was conspicuously absent from the passage about Pentecost. Yet it is Mary who crashed through the confines of Mariolatry and stereotype. Also, it is the female embodiment of the Spirit. Her death is the sign of interpretative closure. The encounter between the Spirit and the woman proves a lethal experience: her spiritual resurrection necessitates her physical death.

The wife continues to exist on the spiritual plane. She haunts her only son who claims he communicates with her. Before her death Maria confessed to Henryk that his son would also become a poet. This is how she tried to ensure his acceptance for their child. In her husband's thoughts Maria assumes a double identity. She is an angel who suffered because of him on the earth. At the same time she is a demon who relentlessly pursues him. The stereotypical binary opposition between angelic and demonic aspects in a woman is parallel to Krasiński's concept of poetry as female. In fact, Maria comes to personify poetry, but she is not supposed to create it.

The crucified woman

In her posthumously published memoir, *Dance on the Earth*, Laurence explores the connection between women and the divine. She ponders on the exclusion of women from the rituals and words of Christianity, which is evident in such popular forms as hymns.[15] The focus upon fathers and sons makes her ask a question about mothers and daughters. Quite significantly, her memoir is dedicated to the matrilinear genealogy in her family, that is, to women whose influence, however hidden, proved decisive in her own life. The women who she terms her 'three mothers' are connected with countless foremothers. Maternity, either as an actual or a potential experience, is very important in Laurence's approach to women. It is connected with a caring attitude not only to one's own children, but also to nature. Laurence insisted on the importance of the maternal, trying to combine it with the artistic in both herself and her creation of Morag Gunn. Interestingly, her heroines become strong women. Coral Ann Howells sees their 'hardy vitality' as a particularly attractive feature.[16] This is not typical in Polish culture, where the images of women in literature have been affected by the stereotypes of the disembodied maid and the suffering mother, both equally alienated from any life other than that which supports masculine society. But this is not the whole or true picture. Strong and autonomous women do exist in Polish history. Most of the information on them lingers in the nuisance grounds of useless historical data, like the Bible in Gaelic from *The Diviners*.

Pondering on the absence of a female principle in monotheisms, Laurence mentions her interest in polytheisms where the female element is easily identifiable.[17] Her interest in Akan religion dating back to her stay in Ghana alerted her to the identification of this element. She admits the influence of the Akan in a letter to Chinua Achebe and comments on the need to include a female element in the concept of the Holy Spirit.[18]

Laurence was a deeply religious person, though often unorthodox and at odds with her Presbyterian background. Her concern was to restore the communication between women and the divine by reclaiming the autonomy of the female self. Her interest in spirituality is particularly evident in the last years of her life, when her close friend was Lois Wilson, a woman moderator of the United Church of Canada. The theological comments on the feminine and the Holy Spirit are even more interesting in the light of Laurence's remarks on the statue of the Crucified Woman created by a Canadian sculptress, Almuth Lutkenhaus.[19] Laurence saw this statue as the image of the repressed female condition. It is interesting to see which aspects of the sculpture were particularly appealing to the writer. Among other things she stresses the fact that there is no cross, but it is the woman's body that is in cruciform. In other words, the woman is crucified by her own femininity, which turns her into an ever-renewing sacrifice. In Laurence's interpretation, female anguish is counterbalanced by a celebration of female autonomy. Describing the sculpted woman, Laurence sees her as the one who dances 'the life dance of pain and love'.[20] An interesting interpretation of this image emerges from the comparison of the crucified woman with the dancing woman from the materials for the novel which was never written by Laurence. In the passage quoted by James King in his biography of Laurence, the dancing woman is called 'a shawoman', which is said 'sha-womb-an',[21] to emphasize the life-giving powers, as well as the shamanic relation to the divine. Connecting heaven and earth in the *axis mundi* symbolism, the crucified woman is also a sha-womb-an, and the locus of hierophany.

The crucified doll

It is interesting to analyse the implications of female crucifixion in Laurence's text against the image of the crucified doll in a short story by Filipiak.[22] The story interpolates the voice of a small girl and that of the observer, exploring the woman she becomes. The small girl tells us about her mystical experiences at the age of six. Christ apparently visits her every evening and ushers her into a dream. In the morning she runs into the corner of the garden, thrusts a cross of sticks and grass into cucumber leaves and hangs a doll upon it. Only then is her control of the world returned to her.[23] In the light of what follows it seems that the girl is enacting a future scenario. The doll represents herself, and she can only connect with the world by the endless repetition of self-sacrifice. What does self-sacrifice imply in this context?

The story pushes the myth of Galatea to its limits. It describes the adult protagonist, Anna, whose wedding is followed by the delights of slavery. Anna takes pride in being the most precious jewel in her husband's collection. The ivory-coloured wedding dress and compliments become a prelude to her experiences in the torture chamber. The sadomasochistic relation between herself and her husband is couched in religious language. Anna knows she is guilty and desires punishment. She welcomes the physical and psychological maltreatment at the hands of her husband who is at the same time the Redeemer and Mr Rape. Her body is only beautiful and immaculate when it is tortured. She is Galatea, now that her torturer has created her again according to his canon. She is proud she can serve him. In the grotesque and surreal atmosphere of the torture chamber Anna undergoes the ultimate kenosis, the process she can watch and reflect upon, for part of the torture is that the victim must have the pleasure of observing her degradation in the mirror. Having become infinitely pliable and malleable, Anna ends up like the worm in Kafka's *Metamorphosis*. Only then can she learn to love herself.[24]

The crucified doll is the image of a woman reduced to an object. As pointed out by Kamila Budrowska, the doll is a frequent motif in Filipiak's fiction.[25] Examining different renditions of this motif, I was struck by Filipiak's interpretation of Krzysztof Kieślowski's film *Podwójne życie Weroniki (The Double Life of Veronique)*.[26] Kieślowski's film juxtaposes the lives of two identical women who were born at the same time in Poland and France, respectively. The Polish woman, Weronika, breaks up with her boyfriend and chooses the career of a vocalist, but she dies of a heart attack during the concert. Her French double, Veronique, subconsciously uses Weronika's experience in order to change her life. She abandons her career in music, and falls in love with a doll-maker who turns out to be a writer. The film ends with Veronique's boyfriend making two dolls which resemble her. In this way, she becomes aware of her identical twin. In Filipiak's interpretation, the doll-maker acquires a sinister meaning. He reduces Veronique to an object. Initially, he uses her to try out a dialogue from his book and find out if it is credible. He manipulates her as if she were a doll in his performance. Also, it is only due to him that she makes sense of her existence. In my view, this interpretation throws a different light on the first part of the film. Weronika, who dies during the concert, resembles Maria from *Nie-Boska komedia*. For both, death is the price they have to pay for their experience of art. Death is also a punishment for rejecting the stereotype of femininity geared to male order. Thus Kieślowski's film recycles a familiar romantic warning against female autonomy.

The ostensibly benign doll-maker has his malign counterpart in the character of the party secretary in *Absolutna amnezja*. When stripped of the remnants of political power, the secretary develops an odd hobby: he collects dolls which he finds in the garbage. The dolls are, then, brought to his garden where he plays at organizing a concentration camp with the ensuing pogrom.[27]

If Lutkenhaus's crucified woman is elevated to a sacred dimension in Laurence's interpretation, Filipiak's crucified doll is the female dimension profaned and degraded, emptied of any connection with divinity and therefore with personhood. In Filipiak's radical rejection of patriarchal tradition, the doll and the figurine of the Virgin Mary seem to come down to the same thing: the total obliteration of the female self, alienated from a woman whose life consists in following the model inherent in man-made icons of femininity. Is there any possibility for Filipiak's female character to write herself out of the man-made scenario as Morag does in *The Diviners?* This possibility is offered by *Absolutna amnezja*, the novel about a woman trying to divine.

Things buried and forgotten

In *Absolutna amnezja*, Filipiak depicts a teenage girl, Marianna, born into a reality which she finds hostile and unimaginative. The book follows Marianna's quest to slip beyond the scenario of her current situation and find a different world. Her alienation and imprisonment as a girl are offset by the portraits of her parents and grandparents who all reflect different aspects of Polish experience under the communist regime. Marianna's father is the secretary of the local party branch, and she always refers to him as the secretary, because he never makes any contact with her as a father. The secretary is a disciplinarian demagogue. His activity of pruning the trees in the garden is like eradicating the aspects of life he does not tolerate. He treats Marianna in a similar manner. He cuts her hair very short in the attempt to change her image, but the blemish of her sex is indelible. She remains a girl.[28]

The wife of the secretary is a caricature of some aspects of femininity in Polish tradition. Marianna calls her mother 'the Immaculate'. This description coheres with Mariolatry by caricaturing Polish images of the Virgin Mary, e.g. she is beautiful like the Queen of Poland, or, as in one of grotesque scenes, she is wearing a blue blouse, and awaiting Annunciation. As a mother, she is unable to protect her daughter from her secretary husband who is described as her own self-inflicted punishment. This mother apparently married the party activist in order to satisfy her masochistic inclinations. She also sought to alleviate the sense of guilt resulting from her rejection of the image of a housewife.[29] Like the secretary, her mind is on things higher than parenthood. She thinks that only the handicapped sex looks after children, and so despises the maternal role. The Immaculate distances herself from her daughter. She focuses, first, upon her career as a gynaecologist and obstetrician, and later, upon her political conspiracy of undermining the secretary's power behind his back. In spite of her everyday contact with physicality, she treats pregnant women and newborn babies as if they were vegetables. She is completely alienated from her own body and unable to usher her daughter into female experience. Marianna's first menstruation, described in a nightmarish and surreal way, provokes her hostility. The Immaculate accuses Marianna of trying to take her attention away from more important matters. Her only response to Marianna's newly acquired femininity is to warn her daughter against abortion. The Immaculate's lack of contact with herself and other people seems to have come from her own father, a lighthousekeeper whose job provided him with a pretext to live in a reverie of romantic poetry and pre-war Poland rather than relate to his family. As a result, Marianna is emotionally abandoned. She imagines that both parents collude in destroying her in favour of the fatherland. Thus the character of Marianna assumes the role of a new Iphigenia who has no chance for salvation, since the goddess Artemis arrives too late.

The secretary's mother, Aldona, completes the family portrait by representing excessive piety and mindless self-sacrifice. Her day boils down to peeling countless potatoes and cleaning the house to the rhythm of prayers. The self-degradation of Aldona is described in the religious language of ascetic renunciation. She readily takes any ill-treatment from her son and turns it into an occasion for suffering. While Marianna watches her grandmother in the kitchen, she realizes that a different world must exist somewhere, yet the knife for peeling potatoes cuts her off from it.

Marianna's own quest for a different reality is interpolated with her teacher's novel, *Absolutna amnezja*. This novel in turn incorporates Marianna's composition written for the Polish class. Both refer to the reality which has become distorted. Filipiak's text shows how school, family, church institution and political regime inculcate sexist stereotypes for women and men. Absolute amnesia is the social malaise resulting from the general suppression of sensitivity, difference and emotional intelligence. The quest of some characters in Filipiak's novel consists in defying the façade and searching for a better world, forgotten and buried as a result of sexist conditioning.

Marianna's Polish teacher, the author of the manuscript *Absolutna amnezja*, decides to shake the school staff and children out of their inertia by organizing a provocative performance on the eighth of March, which was celebrated as Women's Day under communism. The message of the play concerns the sexist evolution of the society, unforeseen in Darwin's theory.[30] Flaunting obscenities, the performance demonstrates how women's anatomy prevents them from aspiring to a better status. The Polish romantic tradition, with its emphasis on a masculine ethos, is invoked as the code that in fact justifies the reduction of women to sexual objects. At one point, an ambulance swiftly transports the Polish teacher to a psychiatric hospital, where she later remains of her own accord, finding refuge and camouflage in her alleged insanity.

Marianna and her teacher try to write themselves out of the oppressive scenario in which they find themselves. Another woman character, Izolda, wants to experience her femininity through motherhood envisaged as a mystical experience. Izolda happens to be Marianna's sister-in-law. Before giving birth to her baby, Izolda spends some time at the Immaculate's house, while her husband Antoni is at sea, thus confirming a stereotype of the absent father in Polish tradition. Marianna notices that Izolda does not feel guilty, so she does not have anything in common with the inhabitants of the house, specifically the Immaculate. Unlike Marianna and her mother, Izolda celebrates her physicality. She relates to her body rather than uses or watches it. She is compared to Mother Earth who awaits men's homage and veneration for her life-giving powers.[31] Yet Izolda's stay in hospital is a bitter disappointment. She finds out she is no longer in control, and people around her seem to know better than she does what is happening to her. The maternity ward turns out to be another instrument of women's oppression. Filipiak portrays childbirth as an experience completely stripped of dignity. Women in labour have to suffer as much as possible because pain is their major task. The only way for them to satisfy the doctors is to give birth quickly and efficiently. Yet women seem to accept their degradation in the maternity ward as a matter of course. Izolda learns that she will forget her humiliation sooner or later. Forgetting is the only effective coping strategy in the world of absolute amnesia.

Amnesia can only be defeated by anamnesis, the awakening and remembrance of one's divine and unique origin. This message is mediated by several characters in the novel. One of them is Marianna's boyfriend, Turek, a juvenile delinquent, whose activity springs from a rebellion against the adult world. At school, as Turek informs Marianna, teachers teach children to forget what they themselves forgot earlier. The graduation diploma only certifies that amnesia has taken place. Marianna's journey towards remembrance starts with this recognition. The spatial indication of going under the surface of things is the topography of the town. Turek and his gang meet in a former German shelter from the Second World War. Marianna ventures down into the shelter, and here she discovers the other side to Turek. In fact, her final exit from the text is connected with the desire to follow him after he disappeared into a world of his own invention.

The destructive role of school is also obvious to Marianna's teacher who studies the eighteenth-century manual of pedagogy and discovers that teaching strategies have not really changed. The children's spirit is broken to make them forget about their free will.[32] Like her pupil, the teacher realizes the collusion of adults who forgot how lonely and helpless they used to feel as children. The result of collusion in amnesia is the gradual destruction of the children's souls.

Defying the attempts to kill her spirit, Marianna ventures into a different world, bringing to mind a gnostic illumination. In this uncanonical experience the teenage girl enters her private apocryphal tale, mediated by another female character. At the end of the book Marianna encounters Aldona, her dead grandmother, who now announces the promise of the eighth earth to her granddaughter. Aldona admits that her previous exercise in Catholic devotion was a sham as a result of which she could have ended up in a different heaven than the one she really wanted. Aldona's metamorphosis is connected with a radical movement away from the centre. Part of her message for Marianna is that she must become her own gateway to a better reality. Marianna decides to swap with Aldona's daughter who died in childhood, beaten to death by the secretary's father. Aldona brings her daughter from the world of the dead and leaves her at the secretary's household as Marianna's proxy until her granddaughter decides to come back from her quest. The book ends with the message that forgetting is the clumsiest way to escape reality. Marianna goes away without looking back.[33]

Coda

Like *The Diviners*, *Absolutna amnezja* is concerned with the female protagonist's progress towards her own self. Bringing Filipiak's Polish fiction into interaction with Laurence's Canadian message does not lead to a reductive comparison of dissimilar authors from completely different contexts, but to the illustration of the condition that Laurence attempts to transcend. Morag Gunn divines herself out of the elements that have become discarded shards in the nuisance grounds of culture. Not unlike Christie, who structures his household out of redeemed garbage, Morag selects the components of her new self from the codes that have been rejected, marginalized or suppressed. She is a single mother, and her baby's father is a racial nuisance to the xenophobic, white community. The physiology which she can experience untramelled after her break-up with Brooke clearly feeds into her creativity. Bit by bit she retrieves her full self from conventions. She marks out her territory, divines and celebrates herself.

Marianna, her Polish teacher, Miss Lisiak, and Izolda are all diviners, trying to gain access to a reality beyond stereotype and ideology. Yet, whatever they select as a potential component of their selves proves to be contaminated or irretrievable. Izolda's failure to enjoy motherhood results in an escape-like exit from hospital and married life. The teacher's artistic role consigns her to the role of an inmate in the psychiatric hospital, much like the Countess from *Nie-Boska komedia*.[34] Marianna's quest for a different world results in a kind of gnostic migration into the remote 'there' rather than the transformation of the 'here'. At the time of the publication of her stories, the author resided in New York, where she actually wrote *Absolutna amnezja*. Thus Filipiak personifies her response to the condition in which the only way to avoid the imprisonment of Polish femininity is to leave.

Yet this self-imposed exile reinforces the self-fulfilling prophecy of female exclusion. Filipiak's women protagonists confront different aspects of female experience which they later reject because it is offered to them on somebody else's terms. Still, the scenario of complete exile leaves them in a vacuum, in no man's and no woman's land.

Filipiak's message is undercut by the romantic stereotype it seeks to disavow. According to Aldona, the absolute amnesia affects the angels that fell on to the earth where they forgot about their divine origin. Aldona's daughter who remains in the secretary's house as Marianna's proxy is supposed to exist as a physical creature, the maltreated body, while Marianna's spirit migrates elsewhere. The rift between the spirit and the body is not healed, but perpetuated. In Filipiak's fiction, the female body is irremediably caught in the web of negative signification.

In this context, Laurence's message offers an alternative. Even though the crucified woman and the crucified doll come disturbingly close to being the two sides of the same interpretative coin, Laurence's message places the female subject in the particularity of her physical context, which allows a female character to connect with the divine on her own terms. In the writing of both authors, women protagonists come to realize the distortions enshrined in culture, religion and everyday rituals. In both cases, their response necessitates divining the elements that were lost, buried or forgotten; and first of all, this means divining the female self. Laurence's heroines come to engage with their restricted condition and transmute it through the creation of a spiritual quest for autonomy. The result is not necessarily a different world, but 'a room of her own' in a situation where no room seemed available. Thus the interaction with Laurence's text becomes a form of therapy in the face of the aporias which haunt contemporary women in a Polish context.

Notes

1   M. Laurence, *The Diviners*, Toronto: McClelland & Stewart Inc., 1988.
2   L. Venuti, *Translator's Invisibility: A History of Translation*, London: Routledge, 1995, pp. 22–25.
3   G. Steiner, *After Babel. Aspects of Language and Translation*, Oxford: Oxford University Press, 1998, p. 28.
4   L. Venuti, *Translator's Invisibility*, pp. 19–27.
5   Ibid., p. 8.
6   A local phrase from Laurence's prairie home town, 'nuisance grounds' signifies the dump ground a little above the town and on the same hill as the cemetery. This is where Christie buries an aborted baby girl he found in the garbage (as an unwanted 'nuisance') outside a respectable house. This is

where Morag and her friend Tonnerre exchange the stories of their origin and thus mythologize their past and backgrounds.

7   Laurence, *The Diviners*, p. 276.

8   Ibid., p. 292.

9   C. Howells, *Reading Margaret Laurence in England*, Canadian Woman Studies, 1987, Fall (8, 3), 38–39.

10   A. Graff, *Świat bez kobiet. Płeć w polskim życiu publicznym*, Warszawa: WAB, 2001.

11   While indebted to Janion for this juxtaposition of texts and for her insights, my analysis emphasizes different dimensions of both texts. Janion reads *Absolutna amnezja* as a revisionary interpretation of Polish romantic myth. See M. Janion, *Kobiety i duch inności*, Warszawa: Wydawnictwo Sic, 1996, pp. 321–343.

12   Z. Krasiński, *Nie-Boska komedia* in, *Nie-Boska komedia, Irydion*, Warszawa: Wydawnictwo MEA, 2001, pp. 31–35.

13   Laurence, *The Diviners*, p. 277.

14   Krasiński, *Nie-Boska komedia*, pp. 132–134.

15   M. Laurence, *Dance on the Earth. A Memoir*, Toronto: McClelland & Stewart, 1998, pp. 14–15.

16   Howells, *Reading Margaret Laurence*, p. 38.

17   Laurence, *Dance on the Earth*, p. 15.

18   M. Laurence Fonds, Special Collections, McMaster University, Hamilton, Ontario, Box 10, Letter to Chinua Achebe dated 3 June, 1984.

19   Laurence, *Dance on the Earth*, p. 16.

20   Ibid., p. 17.

21   J. King, *The Life of Margaret Laurence*, Canada: Alfred Knopf, 1997, p. 396.

22   I. Filipiak, *Nic się nie stało* in: *Śwmierć i spirala*, Wrocław: Wydawnictwo A, 1992, p. 86.

23   Ibid., p. 86.

24   Ibid., p. 92.

25   K. Budrowska, *Kobieta i stereotypy. Obraz kobiety w prozie polskiej po roku 1989*, Białystok: trans. Humana Wydawnictwo Uniwersyteckie, 2000, pp. 127–128.

26   I. Filipiak, *Absolutna amnezja*, Poznań: Obserwator, 1995, pp. 182–184.

27   Ibid., pp. 227–228.

28   Ibid., pp. 26–29.

29   Ibid., pp. 22–23.

30   Ibid., pp. 150–155.

31   Ibid., p. 208.

32   Ibid., pp. 147–148.

33   Ibid., p. 246.

34   Filipiak was fully conscious of these implications as a former student of M. Janion's course on women and madness as creative transgression. She refers to Janion's seminar in *Absolutna amnezja*, while Janion herself comments on Filipiak's novel in *Kobiety i duch inności*.

Religious practice

Introduction

RELIGIOUS PRACTICE IS AN AREA much neglected by philosophers of religion.[1] The tendency in Anglo-American philosophy of religion has been to offer rather generalised views about the nature of religion, a stance that is, in practice, antipathetic to an engagement with concrete practices from specific religious traditions.[2] Instead, the focus has tended to be upon religious experience, rather than religious practice: the latter being considered the domain of anthropologists rather than philosophers of religion. And, indeed, the concern with religious experience has itself been addressed to the end of justification: to what extent do such experiences form the basis for religious belief? A rather different focus is developing in feminist philosophy of religion. As we have seen in the 'Approaches' section of this reader, feminists are increasingly concerned with particularity and the concrete, and the chapters that follow suggest something of this concern as each of the contributors attempts to take practice seriously.

Amy Hollywood offers what is in effect a prolegomenon for a feminist philosophy of religious practice. She argues that Anderson and Jantzen's ground-breaking works, like that of mainstream philosophers of religion, prioritise *belief* as the locus for philosophical discussions of religion. Despite their attempts to open up the field to the teachings of desire, neither, Hollywood claims, pay sufficient attention to 'the place of ritual and practice in religion' (p. 225). Hollywood's aim is to focus on precisely these aspects of religion, and by adopting this method she argues that we will come to 'understand religious belief and its objects in new ways' (p. 225). Applying the work of Marcel Mauss and Talal Asad to the practices of female mystics, Hollywood argues for the power of bodily practice to 'form subjectivity, inculcate virtue, and embody belief' (p. 230).

Vrinda Dalmiya's chapter continues this theme of the significance of studying religious practice by focusing on a specific example: that of the Goddess Kali. Her concern is less with Kali's significance for the intellectual engagement with the *idea* of the Goddess, and more on how the *devotee* approaches this Goddess: 'what is of feminist significance is not simply the paradoxes in the image of Kali but rather a devotee's worshipful *attitude* towards Kali, called *bhakti*' (p. 00). The devotee hopes for spiritual liberation through Kali-worship, and Dalmiya analyses what constitutes this liberation: liberation from the fear of death, or transcendent liberation? Both views are dependent upon a construction of personhood that Dalmiya wants to resist. Instead, she sees Kali-*bhakti* as promoting a 'liberative fearlessness' that overcomes the economic individuality of liberal personhood, and asserts in its place a relational concept of the self. But it is through engagement with the practice of Kali-*bhakti* that she is able to come to this conclusion, not through a merely intellectual engagement with the idea that Kali supposedly represents.

Notes

1   For example, E. Stump and M.J. Murray's *Philosophy of Religion: The Big Questions*, Oxford: Blackwell, 1999, includes only one article on the issue of practice: M.A. Oduyoye's 'The Value of Religious Beliefs and Practices for Christian Theology' (pp. 475–480). This, however, is significantly more than is offered in other readers in the subject, where it is belief, not practice, that forms the chief concern.

2   Even when prayer, for example, is addressed – as it often is – there is a sense in which what matters is less the practice of prayer itself, and more what this might tell us about God's relationship with the world (cf. E. Stump, 'Why Petition God?', in M. Peterson, W. Hasker, B. Reichenbach and D. Basinger (eds) *Philosophy of Religion: Selected Readings*, Oxford: Oxford University Press, 1996, pp. 568–577).

Chapter 15

Amy Hollywood

PRACTICE, BELIEF AND FEMINIST PHILOSOPHY OF RELIGION

T HE TWO MOST IMPORTANT and comprehensive feminist inter-
ventions in the philosophy of religion – Pamela Sue Anderson's *A Feminist Philosophy of Religion* and Grace Jantzen's *Becoming Divine: Toward a Feminist Philosophy of
Religion*[1] – follow the mainstream of analytic and Continental philosophy of religion in
focusing on belief.[2] Anderson arguably remains closer to that tradition than does
Jantzen. Rather than changing the aims of philosophy of religion, Anderson insists that
gender must become a crucial analytic category within accounts of the process of justification. More centrally (and more audaciously), she argues that philosophical arguments
grounded in feminist concerns must not only justify, but also evaluate belief and its
constitution. Jantzen, on the other hand, eschews justification, arguing that feminist
philosophy of religion has different aims than does its Anglo-American counterpart. For
Jantzen, philosophy of religion is theological and practical; properly pursued, it will
lead to the 'becoming divine' of women rather than the justification of religious belief.
Yet Jantzen too focuses her attention on 'religious discourse and the symbolic of which
it is a part'. The goal of feminist philosophy of religion is less to justify or to argue for
the truth or falsity of belief than to 'restructur[e] that myth in ways that foster human
dignity – perhaps in ways that oblige and enable us to become divine'.[3] Questions of
justification thereby give place to questions of moral or political adequacy. Jantzen suggests the primacy of moral or political over epistemological justification, whereas in
Anderson the two exist side by side.

Jantzen, however, is finally unable to avoid the epistemological issues she wishes to
displace. Ultimately she and Anderson both address the issue of the 'truth' or 'objectivity' of belief. Yet neither provides a satisfactory account of the ontological status of the
objects of religious belief. Both Anderson and Jantzen challenge the split between
reason and desire that would render belief solely a matter of rationality and conscious
cognition, yet they remain on the level of the discursive, the symbolic, or the mythic,
giving little attention to the place of ritual and practice in religion.

My contention here is that these two problems are closely related. The unsatisfac-
tory nature of current arguments about the ontological status of the objects of religious
belief is tied to the neglect of practice and ritual. Put in another way, attention to the
role of practice and ritual in religion will force feminist philosophers to understand

religious belief and its objects in new ways. Given the more immediately bodily nature of ritual and other forms of religious practice, moreover, any philosophy of religion attendant to them will be forced to acknowledge and to theorize those differences inscribed in and on bodies (often through rituals and bodily, mental, and spiritual practices themselves). We will then be better able to understand why religion is such an important site for the inculcation of bodily differences and to analyze the relationship between religious practice, belief, and sexual – as well as other – differences (themselves objects of belief inculcated on bodies through the bodily, mental, and discursive repetition of norms).[4]

The ontological status of the objects of religious belief

Anderson deals directly with the issue of the ontological status of the object of belief, asking in relationship to the work of Luce Irigaray, 'To what extent, if any, can one say that the female or feminine divine exists?' Anderson begins by distinguishing between a variety of different ways in which something might be said to exist. Existence might be:

1   real or empirical;
2   ideal;
3   fictional;
4   mythical;
5   illusory; or
6   historical (which for Anderson entails something like a collectively held illusion).[5]

Anderson will be most interested in the ideal and the mythical conceptions of existence, bringing them together in a modified Kantianism by means of which she attempts to safeguard the legitimacy of religious belief and the reality of its objects without committing herself to empiricist claims about the existence or nature of the divine.[6]

Anderson begins with Kant's assertion that transcendental ideas (like that of God's existence) do not constitute knowledge, but are regulative principles that direct human understanding toward the summation and limits of what can be known. Various post-Kantian accounts of the transcendental ideas as regulative principles, she argues, provide sufficient 'ground to treat myth as a regulative principle and not to equate it with constitutive knowledge of supersensible reality'.[7] When we talk about God or the divine we talk not about entities available to our senses and hence to empirical knowledge, but rather about the conditions of knowledge – both pure and practical (moral) – themselves. In stark contrast to Kant, Anderson wishes to allow an epistemological and moral role for desire. She insists, moreover, that this desire is neither psychologistic nor narcissistic, but grounded in the shared embodiment of human beings and hence susceptible to universalization. For feminist philosophy, she argues, 'authentically conceived and strongly objective theistic beliefs of women would not come from psychological need alone, nor from epistemological ignorance but, significantly, from a rational passion for justice.'[8] Moreover, 'reason, in its substantive form of yearning, represents the human potential for justice and freedom or liberty. These potentials are Enlightenment ideals; in Kantian terms, they are regulative ideals.'[9] When feminist philosophers talk about God, then, they are talking about the potential for human self-flourishing and human justice by means of which moral and political life should be regulated. In this sense, Anderson claims to maintain objectivity and ontological realism while at the same time avoiding any assertion of the empirical reality of supersensible beings at odds with the presumptions of her own Kantianism.

Anderson's inventive solution to the problem of theological realism and the ontological status of the divine depends on the close correlation of two central Kantian principles. Kant's argument about God's existence as a regulatory principle of pure reason occurs in the *Critique of Pure Reason*, yet Anderson's larger argument is grounded in his *Critique of Practical Reason* and its complex moral argument for the justification – even necessity – of accepting the postulate of God's existence.[10] The *Critique of Practical Reason* rests on two presumptions:

1   that reason in its practical dimension demands that human beings follow the moral law given to them by reason and
2   that rationality demands the moral law be capable of fulfillment (for Kant, it would be irrational for human beings to pursue an end they know is incapable of attainment).

Fulfillment of the moral law, however, depends on human freedom and the possibility of a perfect conjunction between virtue and happiness – the highest good, according to Kant. The latter in turns depends on the immortality of the soul and on the existence of God. Only if a being exists in which the phenomenal (the realm of happiness) and the noumenal (that of human freedom) come together can the highest end be possible. Although freedom, immortality, and God's existence cannot be known by pure reason, then, reason in its practical dimension requires that we postulate their existence. In this sense, moral ideals readily available to reason serve as the grounds for religious belief.

For Kant, we can never know God exists empirically. The very constitutive categories of understanding preclude knowledge of God, for God, as eternal and omnipresent, stands outside of these categories and thus can never become an object of knowledge. In the *Critique of Pure Reason*, Kant argues for God's existence as a regulative ideal of pure reason, that which marks the limits of reason and the sum total of its audacious – if unfulfillable – desire. The *Critique of Practical Reason* argues that we must accept as a postulate, a necessary hypothesis, that God exists, albeit in a manner never knowable by human beings. In both the *Critique of Pure Reason* and the *Critique of Practical Reason*, moreover, these ideals – be they epistemological or moral – are ideals the *existence of which* renders pure reason or practical reason and the moral life themselves rational. In other words, despite his insistence on the limitations of reason, Kant's God must be hypothesized as existing. Kant's realism is, then, arguably much more radical and far-reaching than Anderson's.

Despite crucial differences between Anderson's and Jantzen's projects, Jantzen falls back on a similar modified Kantianism when it comes to the question of the nature of divine existence. Rereading Ludwig Feuerbach's account of the divine as the projection of human ideal becoming, Jantzen argues that in speaking of the divine we 'speak . . . of ideals, indeed regulatory ideals in a Kantian sense. Projections need to be those which embody our best and deepest aspirations, so that we are drawn forward to realize them.'[11] Like Anderson, Jantzen brings together the concept of God's existence as an epistemological regulative ideal for pure reason with God's existence as a postulate necessary to the rationality of the moral law. Within the terms of practical reason, what is ideal is not the concept of God, but that of the moral law itself, its complete fulfillment, and its coincidence with absolute happiness (i.e. the highest good). God can only be said to be an ideal of practical reason in that God's existence renders the highest good possible.

Like Anderson, Jantzen also hopes to show that attention to the communities of faith for whom religious projections are meaningful enables feminist philosophy of religion to avoid the charge of relativism, arguing cogently that 'partiality of insight is not the same as absence of criteria' for adjudicating competing truth claims, or, as she prefers to put it, symbolic systems.[12] She is not interested in defending philosophical realism, however, and so saves herself from some of the worries faced by Anderson. Yet with Jantzen as with Anderson we are left with the problem that their accounts of belief – and most crucially their accounts of the ontological nature of the objects of religious belief – do not correspond to what people most often mean when they say that they believe in God. (This, incidentally, includes Kant. Although he gives different grounds for belief than would those not directly influenced by his work, his understanding of *what* is believed comes closer, I think, to the kind of theological realism espoused by many – if not most – religious people.)

Arguably, as constructive philosophical theologians, neither Anderson nor Jantzen need be concerned by my critique. They might easily respond that their projects entail an ameliorative reconception of what is meant by religious belief. Yet the question remains open as to what kind of power these putatively regulative ideals have if we do not believe in their realist instantiations. For Kant, once again, without belief in God's existence, reason becomes self-contradictory. Reason in its practical dimension, in particular, would demand a course of action that would be irrational to pursue, given that without God's existence the moral law's ends are unfulfillable. At the same time, however, Kant argues that to know God through pure reason would itself jeopardize morality, for we would then act out of a fear or love of God rather than from duty alone. (Hence Kant's insistence that we need to postulate the existence of God not in order to make moral action desirable, but rather to render it fully rational.)[13] Jantzen takes advantage of an ambiguity within the *Critical of Practical Reason* and argues that hope in the possibility of an ideal's realizability by human nature is all that is required for either religion or morality.

Jantzen's argument depends on the conflation of Feuerbach's theory of projection with a modified Kantianism. Yet she overlooks a crucial dimension of Feuerbach's theory of religion in her appeal to the divine as a realizable projection of human ideals. For Feuerbach, reason alone is inadequate to explain religious belief; *desire* motivates projection and with it the insistence on the ontological independence of that which is projected. As Van Harvey shows, for Feuerbach pain and ecstasy fuel humanity's projection of a divine other. When one human being encounters another,

> the individual I experiences a powerful inrush of two types of feeling: on the one hand, a painful feeling of limitation and inadequacy over against the unlimitedness of the species and, on the other, an ecstatic sense of the attractiveness of the

species, an attractiveness grounded in the individual's joy in the exercise of his/her own distinctive powers. But because the idea of the species is an abstraction and as such has very little emotional power, it is seized upon by the imagination and transformed into the idea of a single being. The individual, driven by his/her desire to live and his/her sense of finitude, finds in the perfection of the divine being a substitute for the true bearer of these predicates, the species, as well as an assurance of his/her worthiness and immortality as an individual.[14]

Unlike the forms of Christianity analyzed by Feuerbach, Jantzen is not interested in asserting the unlimitedness and immortality of the species. Yet ideals – however limited – remain abstract. Feuerbach suggests that to attain emotional force they require concretization in an object of belief held to be ontologically independent of the believer.[15]

Perhaps most importantly, what if we understand philosophy of religion less as an attempt to justify or redefine belief than as an attempt to account philosophically for those aspects of human existence broadly characterized as religious? Philosophy of religion understood in this way cannot move so quickly from the descriptive to the prescriptive, for it is responsible to religious phenomena as lived by practitioners and believers. From this perspective, the question of the ontological status of the objects of religious belief cannot be resolved by redefining the nature of divine existence in terms of regulative ideals (be they epistemological or moral). Nor can religion be equated solely with belief. For many religious people, practice takes precedence over belief; a philosophy of religion that does not account for the function and meaning of practice will never be adequate to its object.

As I suggested earlier, the issues of the ontological status of the objects of religious belief and of the centrality of practice to religion are intimately related. The early twentieth-century French sociologist, a son-in-law and intellectual heir of Emile Durkheim, Marcel Mauss makes the argument most starkly: 'I believe precisely that at the bottom of all our mystical states there are body techniques which we have not studied, but which were studied fully in China and India, even in very remote periods. This socio-biological study should be made. I think that there are necessarily biological means of entering into "communion with God".'[16] If mystical states are understood as God's existence made bodily and spiritually inescapable, then this leads to the possibility that skepticism about or disbelief in God's existence is itself, as Talal Asad puts it, 'a function of untaught bodies'.[17]

Bodily practice, the *habitus*, and practical reason

Asad uses Mauss's argument about the constitutive power of bodily practice in order to intervene in two related debates within contemporary anthropology, the first having to do with the supposed primacy of belief over practice and the second with the putative distinction between ritual and instrumental human actions. Both debates stem from modern Western European Protestantism's rejection of ritualism and insistence on the primacy of faith. Understanding religion primarily through the models provided by their own religious tradition (regardless of how distanced individual philosophers and proto-anthropologists may have been from that tradition), early students of religion assumed the centrality of belief to religion.[18] Ritual action, understood as a debased form of religiosity, needed to be distinguished from instrumental action; the former operates symbolically, the latter practically. In other words, rituals are understood to be actions that must be interpreted in terms of pre-existing systems of belief rather than described in terms of what they do (the presumption being that they do not do anything).[19] Mauss's rejection of the clear-cut distinction between instrumental and ritual action makes it possible for Asad to contest claims to the primacy of belief within religion (a contestation increasingly demanded by students of religion on empirical grounds – even, as I will show, in the study of Protestant Christianity).

For Mauss, 'the body is man's first and most natural instrument. Or more accurately, not to speak of instruments, man's first and most natural technical object, and at the same time technical means, is his body'.[20] Mauss is interested in those forms of bodily practice marked by culture (as well as by biology and psychology) yet not easily read in terms of symbolic meaning: gait, athletic styles, manners of sleeping and eating, clothing, and birth and nursing patterns. These forms of bodily practice form subjectivity, inculcate virtue, and embody belief. They constitute what Mauss calls the *habitus*:

> Please note that I use the Latin word . . . *habitus*. The word translates infinitely better than '*habitude*' [habit or custom], the '*exis*' the 'acquired ability' and 'faculty' of Aristotle (who was a psychologist). . . . These 'habits' do not vary just with individuals and their imitations; they vary especially between societies, educations, proprieties, and fashions, prestiges. In them we should see the techniques and work of collective and individual practical reason rather than, in the ordinary way, merely the soul and its repetitive faculties.[21]

As Asad explains, Mauss's understanding of the *habitus* enables social scientists 'to analyze the body as an assemblage of embodied attitudes, not as a medium of symbolic meanings'.[22] The distinction between bodily practices in the Maussian sense and ritual thus breaks down; for Asad both are disciplinary practices through which bodies, dispositions, and subjectivities are formed and transformed.[23] Rituals, like bodily practices, do not carry symbolic meanings but instead *do things*. They create certain kinds of subjects, dispositions, moods, emotions, and desires. Put in another way, they are like performative speech acts, for that to which they refer is constituted through the action itself.[24]

As Asad shows, Mauss provides the framework for a historicized Kantianism or 'an anthropology of practical reason'. Practical reason is not, as it is for Kant, a principle of universalizability by means of which ethical rules can be determined, but rather an

> historically constituted practical knowledge, which articulates an individual's learning capacities. According to Mauss, the human body was not to be viewed simply as the passive recipient of 'cultural imprints', still less as the active source of 'natural expressions' that are 'clothed in local history and culture', as though it were a matter of an inner character expressed in a readable sign, so that the latter could be used as a means of deciphering the former. It was to be viewed as the developable means for achieving a range of human objectives, from styles of

physical movement (e.g. walking), through modes of emotional being (e.g. composure), to kinds of spiritual experience (e.g. mystical states). This way of talking seems to avoid the Cartesian dualism of the mind and objects of the mind's perception.[25]

Mauss's arguments also de-stabilize any rigid distinction between 'body sense and body learning'.[26] Bodily experience is physiological and cultural; the body can – and arguably must – be taught and the various cultural lessons learned by the body shape one's experience. Physical pain, for example, is a universal physiological phenomenon, yet according to Asad anthropological and psychological research demonstrates 'that the perception of pain threshold varies considerably according to traditions of bodily training – and also according to the pain history of individual bodies.'[27] Pain, understood simultaneously as one of the most universal and one of the most subjective aspects of human experiences, is always also inflected by culture.[28]

Following Mauss, then, Asad embodies and historicizes practical reason and he does so by insisting on the centrality of bodily practices and rituals as forms of discipline. The body is humanity's first technical means and object because, through disciplined body practices, bodies acquire aptitudes, emotions, dispositions, and beliefs (although it should be noted that the relationship between dispositions and beliefs requires further discussion and refinement). On first sight, then, the *habitus* represents a much broader conception of practical reason than that found in Kant. One might argue that while Kant articulates reason in its practical dimension as providing a universally available means of determining the moral law (through the process of universalizability), Mauss and Asad show that practical reason also, and perhaps more fundamentally, involves learned modes of being in the body and in the world.[29] Seen from this perspective, Asad's work nicely complements that of Anderson and Jantzen, both of whom wish to expand the grounds for religious and moral reflection to include bodily affects, emotion, and desire. Asad, by insisting on the necessity of body practices and rituals to the formation of practical reason provides the concrete grounds for this extension in a way not provided by Anderson and Jantzen.

Yet to what extent and in what ways is Asad's conception of practical reason broader than Kant's? Asad's arguments are indebted to the work of philosopher and historian Michel Foucault as well as to that of Mauss. Foucault offers a rough typology of different modes of morality that might be helpful in elucidating the relationship between Mauss's and Asad's conception of practical reason and that of Kant. Foucault argues that the term 'morality' covers three different realities. First there are the values and rules of action that are set forth as normative for a particular group, a 'prescriptive ensemble' that Foucault calls a 'moral code'. Morality also refers to 'the real behavior of individuals in relation to the rules and values that are recommended to them', what Foucault terms 'the morality of behaviors'. Finally there 'is the manner in which one ought to "conduct oneself" – that is, the manner in which one ought to form oneself as an ethical subject acting in reference to the prescriptive elements that make up the code.'[30] In other words, social groups not only prescribe *what* one should do, but also attempt to form subjects who will perform certain kinds of actions in preference to others. The practices or exercises through which ethical subjects are formed also shape *how* and *toward what end* these subjects will act.

Descriptions of morality can be either descriptions of 'codes', of 'moral behaviors', or of 'ethics' and 'ascetics', understood as a history of the forms of moral subjectivation and of the practices of the self that are meant to ensure it'.[31] A history or anthropology of ethics and ascetics, of

> the way in which individuals are urged to constitute themselves as subjects of moral conduct would be concerned with the models proposed for setting up and developing relationships with the self, for self-reflection, self-knowledge, self-examination, for the decipherment of the self by oneself, for the transformation that one seeks to accomplish with oneself as object.[32]

One is called on not only to perform certain actions or to follow certain prohibitions, but *to be* a particular kind of moral subject, and within any given culture the models, techniques, and practices (remember that in ancient Greek, *askesis* means 'practice' or 'exercise') through which this form of subjectivity is inculcated can be uncovered by the historian or anthropologist. These practices not only form ethical subjects of a particular sort, but also promise them certain pleasures or goods. Thus Foucault argues, technologies of the self

> permit individuals to affect, by their own means, a certain number of operations on their own bodies, their own souls, their own thoughts, their own conduct, and this in a manner so as to transform themselves, modify themselves, and to attain a certain state of perfection, happiness, purity, supernatural power.[33]

Although certain cultures might give more weight to the 'code' and others more weight to 'askesis' and the formation of the self, generally both operate together within flourishing moral systems.

Seen in the light of Foucault's threefold account of morality, one might be tempted to argue that Kant's moral theory is all about codes, whereas Mauss and Asad create a space for thinking about askesis. Yet Kant does not simply provide a method for determining the maxims according to which one should act, but also argues that a particular mode of being in the world is decisive for determining the moral nature of one's actions. To behave on behalf of anything other than the moral law, Kant argues, is to act heteronomously. Morality depends on autonomy, on acting out of duty to the moral law itself. Human action must be determined solely by practical reason and the demands it makes on the subject. In providing the means for determining the moral law, then, Kant provides not only a code but also an askesis through which moral subjects are created. Kant not only tells us how to determine the proper moral code, but the very same operation also forms us as subjects who act in a particular way and toward particular ends. For Kant, then, code (or at least the means for determining the code) and askesis are inseparable. The form of askesis he recommends requires detachment from the body, emotion, and desire. It entails a bodily and mental discipline by means of which the subject becomes detached from his or her body. Thus Kant's form of askesis, like the notion outlined by Foucault, broadens Mauss's conception of practice to include mental and spiritual exercises that effect the body but are not generally acknowledged themselves to be bodily practices. (It is important to recognize, moreover, that the principle of universalizability is not reducible to the principle of detachment, although there are close relationships between the two. Moreover, there are aspects of body practice that go beyond the parameters of that with which Kant concerns himself in his writings on practical reason. The relationship between this more broadly construed conception of *habitus* and Kant's moral law requires further elucidation.) Kant generally does not acknowledge that the form of subjectivity he wishes to inculcate is a learned mode of being in the world. Instead he argues it is the mode of subjectivity demanded by human reason itself, rightly understood. Despite his insistence that morality requires a revolution in human disposition rather than its reform, Kant's deep interest in education as central to the work of enlightenment suggests that bodily and intellectual training is necessary to the successful attainment of moral subjectivity.

Mauss and Asad, in deuniversalizing the claims of practical reason, enable us to see that the moral law and moral dispositions – even those called for by Kant – are learned. An Asadian reading of Kant, then, would demand attention to his account of the practices – bodily and intellectual – through which the mind removes itself from the body, emotion, and desire in order to determine the moral law and to attain the proper disposition for its enactment. Seen from this perspective, Anderson's and Jantzen's critique of Kant is directed toward the debilitating effects of his particular account of the moral life. They both insist that the body, emotion, and desire must play a role in practical moral reasoning and in the religious life. What Mauss and Asad offer is an insistence on the role of bodily, mental, and spiritual practices and rituals in the transformation of the moral, religious, and intellectual life. Not only can we not fully understand Kant's moral philosophy and philosophy of religion without an understanding of the role of askesis within them, we also cannot hope to bring the body, emotion, and desire back into morality and religion solely through an analysis and critique of symbols and beliefs.

Embodying belief

Asad substantiates his claims about the constitutive role of practice in the formation of moods, emotions, dispositions, and beliefs through an analysis of medieval Christian monastic practice as codified within the *Rule of Benedict*.[34] As he argues, monastic practice formed and reformed Christian dispositions, among them humility, patience, and contrition. Following the *Rule*'s prescriptions involves undertaking a set of performative actions through which will, desire, intellect, and mind are transformed and (re)constituted. In other words, one becomes a certain kind of person, responds bodily, affectively, and intellectually in certain ways, and comes to hold certain beliefs by engaging in certain prescribed behaviors. (Of course, a certain set of beliefs determines one's decision to engage in these practices in the first place, rendering the relationship between body and practice even more complex than I can here articulate.) The monk who weeps over his sinfulness will become contrite; humiliating oneself before the abbot and the community (through manual labor, acts of homage to the abbot, and public confession) generates humility. Although Asad's detailed arguments are too complex for full elaboration here, his central, well-attested point is that 'emotions, which are often recognized by anthropologists as inner, contingent events, could be progressively organized by increasingly apt performances of conventional behavior'.[35]

Asad's examples focus on how subjects are constituted and/or transformed through practice, yet he follows Mauss in suggesting the more radical claim that religious experiences constitutive of and validating belief are constituted through practice.

Substantiating evidence for this claim can be found within the texts of the Christian Middle Ages, together with some evidence for the ways in which bodily differences – in this case sexual difference – may be both inculcated and presumed by prescriptive practices. Clear indications of the role of bodily practices and rituals in the inculcation of belief can be found in medieval meditative handbooks, saint's lives, and mystical texts. I'll focus here on just one example, chosen to highlight certain crucial features of meditative practice and the variable relationship between meditation and sexual difference within the later Middle Ages.

Margaret Ebner (1291–1351) was a German Dominican nun whose religious practice and experience followed closely the traditions of meditative practice and mystical experience found in the writings of thirteenth-century religious women. In her *Revelations*, however, Ebner provides more concrete descriptions of the relationship between meditative practice and mystical experience than we find in women's and men's mystical texts from the previous century. Ebner explicitly articulates the way in which her intense meditation on Christ's Passion leads to her inability *not* to see, hear, and feel Christ's Passion and ultimately to experience it in and on her own body.

The process begins with a conscious concentration of Ebner's energies on visual representations of Christ's suffering.

> Every cross I came upon I kissed ardently and as frequently as possible. I pressed it forcibly against my heart constantly, so that I often thought I could not separate myself from it and remain alive. Such great desire and such sweet power so penetrated my heart and all of my members that I could not withdraw myself from the cross. Wherever I went I had a cross with me. In addition, I possessed a little book in which there was a picture of the Lord on the cross. I shoved it secretly against my bosom, open to that place, and wherever I went I pressed it to my heart with great joy and with measureless grace. When I wanted to sleep, I took the picture of the Crucified Lord in the little book and laid it under my face. Also, around my neck I wore a cross that hung down to my heart. In addition, I took a large cross whenever possible and laid it over my heart. I clung to it while lying down until I fell asleep in great grace. We had a large crucifix in choir. I had the greatest desire to kiss it and to press it close to my heart like the others. But it was too high up for me and was too large in size.[36]

The one sister in whom Margaret confides this desire refuses to help her, fearing that the act would be too much for one as physically frail as Margaret. Yet, Margaret claims, what can't be possible while awake was granted to her in a dream:

> It seemed as if I were standing before the cross filled with the desire that I usually had within me. As I stood before the image, my Lord Jesus Christ bent down from the cross and let me kiss His open heart and gave me to drink of the blood flowing from His heart.[37]

The movement from actively pursued practice to unconsciously enacted experience first occurs, then, in Ebner's dream life. We see here a feature of religious practice suggested by Asad and highlighted by Saba Mahmood in her study of the modern Islamic women's piety movement in Egypt: the goal of consciously pursued bodily practices and rituals is ultimately to render conscious training unnecessary.[38] In Ebner, this movement nears completion when Christ's passion becomes inescapably present to her. In the Lent of 1340, while at matins, Margaret explains:

> the greatest pain came over my heart and also a sorrow, so bitter that it was as if I were really in the presence of my Beloved, my most heartily Beloved One, and as if I had seen his suffering with my own eyes and as if it were all happening before me at this very moment.[39]

Following in the meditative tradition on Christ's life and death promulgated by the Franciscan and Dominican orders during the later Middle Ages, Ebner seems here to have achieved a perfect *meditatio* in which external aides, be they visual or auditory, are no longer required in order for Christ's passion to be viscerally present to her.

Ebner goes even further, however, claiming not only to see Christ's passion, but to share in it. At first, she finds herself unable not to cry out when she hears of or sees (either through the physical eye or the mind's eye) Christ's Passion before her. These outcries lead to physical suffering that renders her body itself Christ-like.

> But when I was given to loud exclamations and outcries by the gentle goodness of God (these were given to me when I heard the holy suffering spoken about), then I was pierced to the heart and this extended to all my members, and then I was bound and ever more grasped by the silence. In these cases, I sit a long time – sometimes longer, sometimes shorter. After this my heart was as if shot by a mysterious force. Its effect rose up to my head and passed on to all my members and broke them violently. Compelled by the same force I cried out loudly and exclaimed. I had no power over myself and was not able to stop the outcry until God released me from it. Sometimes it grasped me so powerfully that red blood spurted from me.[40]

With blood gushing forth from her body, Margaret seems here to become a visible representation of Christ's suffering for those around her.[41] Her identification with the Passion shifts from identification with the onlookers to one with Christ himself.

Ebner claims, like Francis of Assisi a century before her, to achieve an identification with Christ's Passion in which her own body becomes a representation of Christ's suffering for those around her. This cross-gender identification occurs seemingly without question in Ebner's text, suggesting a gender fluidity that renders culturally plausible the valorization of women's suffering bodies.[42] In fact, the situation in the later Middle Ages is more complex than this sole example might suggest. Whereas women did finds ways to associate their suffering bodies and souls with that of Christ, other contemporary practices and discourses suggest that at least some men mistrusted these identifications and argued that women should identify, not with Christ on the cross, but with Mary at the foot of the cross.[43] Often couched in terms of concern for the danger done to women's bodies by their excessive suffering and asceticism, texts like Henry Suso's *Life of the Servant* reserve the role of Christ-like bodily and spiritual suffering for men (in this case, for Suso himself), with Suso's Christ-like body becoming itself the center of women's devotional life.

Early in his life, Suso had engaged in intense ascetic bodily practices, like Ebner rendering his body bloody in imitation of contemporary representations of Christ on the cross. In addition, he inscribed Christ's name on his chest with a stylus. In the second part of the *Life* he eschews such violent practices, particularly for his female followers, yet the sanctification of his body through these practices remains salient. So toward the end of his life we see his 'holy daughter' (Elsbet Stagel, who may have in part authored the *Life of the Servant*) sewing 'this same name of Jesus in red silk onto a small piece of cloth in this form, IHS, which she herself intended to wear secretly'. Moreover, she makes further images of the name of Jesus for distribution:

> She repeated this countless times and brought it about that the servant put them all over his bare breast. She would send them all over, with a religious blessing to his spiritual children. She was informed by God: whoever thus wore this name and recited an Our Father daily for God's honor would be treated kindly by God, and God would give him his grace on his final journey.[44]

Although Jeffrey Hamburger suggests that the displacement of wounds from the human body to cloth badges serves simply as a critique of Henry's early asceticism, the value of the badges depends on their contact with Suso's sanctified flesh.[45] Here we see a male saintly body replace the female body as the site of holiness. Women's role is now the dissemination of physical objects sanctified, not by their own actions or bodies, but by those of the male saint. Thus we can see the ways in which prescriptions for bodily and meditative practice can both depend on and shape gender ideologies.

My examples, like Asad's, come from the Christian Middle Ages, a period in which the centrality of liturgical and paraliturgical practices is largely unquestioned (although the role of these practices in inculcating religious experience and belief is only beginning to be studied). What of modern Protestantism, however, often understood as a religious tradition determined by its insistence on the centrality of faith – and hence of belief – alone? My contention that Kant's conception of practical reason depends on a particular form of askesis, one partially masked by its association with a putatively universal reason, suggests that similar forms of practice can be uncovered within Protestant Christianity. Again, I only have room here for a single example, one suggestive of the intense gendering of many Christian traditions of practice as well as of the limitations of studies of religion focused primarily on belief.

Marie Griffith's *God's Daughters: Evangelical Women and the Power of Submission* studies the Women's Aglow Fellowship, an interdenominational organization of charismatic Christian women founded in 1972 (although with roots in a smaller organization started in 1967). Women's Aglow meetings center on testimonials, singing, public prayer, tears, prophecy, exorcisms, and ecstatic transportation by the Holy Spirit. Griffith provides a fascinating account of the movement through analysis of the central themes articulated in oral testimonials and those printed in Women's Aglow Fellowship periodicals. She demonstrates the ways in which the Aglow women's stories of powerlessness, abuse, secrecy, and shame parallel those found in second-wave feminist literature, even as the two groups' strategies for coping with these issues fundamentally differ.[46] Her focus on narrative enables these comparisons and provides a useful locus for attempting to undermine the sharp divide between explicitly anti-feminist evangelical Christian women and U.S. feminists. From the perspective of my analysis of practice, ritual, and belief, however, Griffith too readily allows the Aglow women's self-understanding of the relationship between 'spontaneity' and 'ritual' to shape her telling of their story.

Griffith briefly describes a regular chapter meeting's fairly uniform schedule. Usually held in hotel conference rooms or other non-religious public spaces, meetings begin with music, followed by announcements, testimonies, an offering, a talk by a special speaker, and ending with more music and the reception of 'prayers from specially trained prayer counselors or coordinators'. Griffith argues that despite these formalized elements, 'the women continue to value and emphasize "spontaneity" over "ritual", believing the former to maintain openness to the spirit of God while the latter effectively hinders or even closes off such a possibility'.[47] Hidden by this account is the way in which the formalized movement from music and prayer to testimonials and then back to music and individualized prayer works to generate the tears, prophecies, and effusions of the spirit experienced by the Aglow women. In other words, their practice, more carefully observed and described, might be understood as itself strengthening belief in and engendering an experience of a judging, yet also munificent and forgiving God.

Attention to the constitutive power of practice might also help elucidate the seeming intractability of debates between non-feminist evangelical women and feminists. These differences are not simply the result of conflicting propositions about the world and women's place within it, but reflect deeply embodied dispositions, emotions, and beliefs. Appeals to reason will never be able fully to overcome the divide – a divide that tends toward an absolute refusal of debate – between the two groups. Recognition of the learned nature of one's *habitus* can begin to open spaces for understanding, yet it is the very nature of the *habitus* to cover over its own learned status. Belief successfully inculcated through bodily practice renders itself 'natural' and hence resistant to critique and change.[48] (Hence the insistence of the Aglow women that God engenders their experience rather than that their experience engenders God or an encounter with God.) Even if we begin to recognize the learned nature of many of our most deeply embedded dispositions and beliefs, new practices that enable a re-formation of the self will be required for their transformation. And as Feuerbach reminds us, religion appeals not only to reason, but to the body, emotion, and desire. This marks what is arguably the most crucial divide between the Aglow women and their secular feminist critics. Although the latter are also shaped by learned dispositions and beliefs grounded in emotion and desire, the epistemological and political assumptions of liberalism refuse to recognize the embodied nature of the *habitus*. From the standpoint of the religious believer, moreover, the consolations of liberalism are weak, insufficient to the desires satisfied, at least in part, by religion.[49]

Anderson and Jantzen both argue that we need not settle for a choice between forms of political liberalism cut off from the body, emotion, and desire and a wholesale relativism in which any claims to adjudication between competing practices and beliefs are eschewed. Desire and emotion themselves are shaped both by bodily practices and by reason (now no longer so easily differentiated), making it possible that new conceptions of practical reason and of the practices that inculcate it can be articulated and enacted. Yet without attention to bodily, mental, and spiritual practices and rituals, and their powerful shaping of the *habitus*, the transformation of practical reason and of religiosity demanded by feminist philosophers like Anderson and Jantzen will necessarily fall short.

Notes

1   P.S. Anderson, *A Feminist Philosophy of Religion: The Rationality and Myths of Religious Belief*, Oxford: Blackwell, 1998; and G. Jantzen, *Becoming Divine: Towards a Feminist Philosophy of Religion*, Blooming- ton, IN: Indiana University Press, 1999. See also P.S. Anderson, 'Gender and the Infinite: On the Aspiration to be All There Is', *Journal of Philosophy of Religion*, 50 (2001): 191–212; P.S. Anderson, 'Myth and Feminist Philosophy', in K. Schilbrack (ed.) *Thinking Through Myths: Philosophical Perspec- tives*, New York, NY: Routledge, 2002, pp. 101–122; and P.S. Anderson, 'Feminist Theology as Philosophy of Religion', in S.F. Parsons (ed.) *The Cambridge Companion to Feminist Theology*, Cam- bridge: Cambridge University Press, 2002, pp. 40–59. Philosopher Luce Irigaray's work is crucial to both Anderson and Jantzen. See, among other texts, L. Irigaray, *Speculum of the Other Woman*, trans. G. Gill, Ithaca, NY: Cornell University Press, 1985; L. Irigaray, *An Ethics of Sexual Difference*, trans. C. Burke and G. Gill, Ithaca, NY: Cornell University Press, 1993; L. Irigaray, *Sexes and Genealogies*, trans. G. Gill, New York, NY: Columbia University Press, 1993; and L. Irigaray, *I Love to You*, trans. A. Martin, New York, NY: Routledge, 1996. For other recent work on feminist philosophy of reli- gion, much of it also influenced by Irigaray, see the special issue of *Hypatia*, 9 (1994); D. Hampson, *After Christianity*, London: SCM Press, 1996; A. Hollywood, *Sensible Ecstasy: Mysticism, Sexual Dif- ference, and the Demands of History*, Chicago, IL: University of Chicago Press, 1991; and S. Coakley, *Powers and Submissions: Spirituality, Philosophy, and Gender*, Oxford: Blackwell, 2002.

   A question that remains unanswered in this literature is that of the relationship between philo- sophy of religion, philosophical theology, and theology. Like much contemporary analytic philosophy and, arguably, like the work of Irigaray, Anderson and Jantzen are engaged in philosophical theology, a point to which I will return in the chapter.

2   Most introductions to the philosophy of religion define the field in terms of the clarification and justi- fication of religious belief. This is also the case with anthologies for classroom use, which rarely, if ever, include sections on practice or ritual. Even the widespread interest in religious experience and mysticism ultimately reverts to questions of belief and justification, for the central philosophical dispute – the one to which all other questions lead – concerns whether religious experience can provide a means of justification for religious belief. See, for example, W. Proudfoot, *Religious Experience*, Berkeley, CA: University of California Press, 1985; W. Alston, *Perceiving God: The Epis- temology of Religious Experience*, Ithaca, NY: Cornell University Press, 1991; and M. Bagger, *Religious Experience, Justification, and History*, Cambridge: Cambridge University Press, 1999.

3   Jantzen, *Becoming Divine*, p. 22. Jantzen argues that her work does not focus on belief, yet given the centrality to her work of religious discourse and the symbolic, however broadly conceived, and the absence of any extended discussion of practice or ritual, it is difficult to see how she fully escapes the confines of more traditional forms of analytic philosophy of religion.

4   See A. Hollywood, 'Performativity, Citationality, Ritualization', *History of Religions*, 42 (2002): 93–115.

5   Anderson, *Feminist Philosophy of Religion*, p. 118.

6   Anderson distinguishes fiction, myth, and illusion in the following ways. Fiction she defines, rather flatly, as something that 'has been made up'. Illusions are defined in a quasi-Freudian way as ideas unconsciously generated 'from fear of the contingencies and losses in life'. Myths, finally, are complex configurations of narratives and concepts that 'constitute a people's meaningful, qualitative identity'. Anderson gives considerably attention to myth, articulating its relationship to embodi- ment, desire, and mimesis. Although I think these distinctions require more adequate conceptions of fiction and illusion to be fully convincing, the issue lies beyond the scope of my argument here. See Anderson, *Feminist Philosophy of Religion*, pp. 118, 127–164.

7   Ibid., p. 137.

8   Ibid., p. 213. Hence they are not illusions, as defined by Anderson.

9   Ibid.

10 See I. Kant, *Critique of Pure Reason*, trans. N.K. Smith, London: Macmillan, 1950, pp. 532–570; and I. Kant, *Critique of Practical Reason*, trans. Lewis White Beck, Indianapolis, IN: Bobbs-Merrill, 1956, pp. 130–138.

11 Jantzen, *Becoming Divine*, p. 92.

12 Ibid., p. 223. Essential for Jantzen are the 'criteria of trustworthiness and mutual accountability by which aspects of the symbolic can be tested against its fruitfulness in creating a space for the woman subject'. Such criteria arguably do not respond to all the problems raised by critics of moral and epis- temological relativism, but this issue will have to wait for exploration in another paper.

13 Kant, *Critique of Practical Reason*, p. 136. See G. Jantzen, 'Do We Need Immortality?', in A. Loades and L.D. Rue (eds) *Contemporary Classics in Philosophy of Religion*, La Salle, IL: Open Court Press, 1991, pp. 306–308.

14 V. Harvey, *Feuerbach and the Interpretation of Religion*, Cambridge: Cambridge University Press, 1995, p. 110.

15 For more on this issue as it applies to Irigaray's writings on religion and the ambivalent responses to them by feminists, see Hollywood, *Sensible Ecstasy*, pp. 234–235.

16 M. Mauss, 'Body Techniques', in B. Brewster, trans. *Sociology and Psychology: Essays*, London: Routledge, 1979, p. 122. Cited by T. Asad, *Genealogies of Religion: Disciplines and Reasons of Power in Christianity and Islam*, Baltimore, MD: The Johns Hopkins University Press, 1993, p. 76.

17 Asad, *Genealogies*, p. 77. Or perhaps better, of differently taught bodies.

18 See, for example, J.S. Preus, *Explaining Religion: Criticism and Theory from Bodin to Freud*, New Haven, CT: Yale University Press, 1987.

19 Asad, *Genealogies*, pp. 55–79.

20 Mauss, 'Body Techniques', p. 104. Cited by Asad, *Genealogies*, p. 75.

21 Mauss, 'Body Techniques', p. 101. Cited by Asad, *Genealogies*, p. 75. On the medieval reception of Aristotle and the doctrine of *habitus*, see C. Nederman, 'Nature, Ethics, and the Doctrine of "Habitus": Aristotelian Moral Psychology in the Twelfth Century', *Traditio*, 45 (1989–1990): 87–110.

22 Asad, *Genealogies*, p. 75.

23 Ibid., p. 131. Put another way, without claims to the primacy of belief over action and hence to the necessarily symbolic nature of ritual action, the distinction between ritual action and instrumental action breaks down and with it the need for a distinction between bodily practices and ritual. All that remains is the distinction between those actions that use the body as the instrument for transforming the body and those actions that use other instruments toward other ends.

24 For more on bodily practices and ritual as performative, see Hollywood, 'Performativity, Citationality, Ritualization'.

25 Asad, *Genealogies*, p. 76. Asad cites phrases from Mary Douglas's interpretation of Mauss's essay. M. Douglas, *Natural Symbols*, London: Barrie and Rockliff, 1970. Asad disagrees deeply with Douglas's account of Mauss and asks how, given his own reading of Mauss's essay, it has been understood as a founding document for symbolic anthropology. 'Was it,' Asad wonders, 'because "ritual" was already so powerfully in place as symbolic action – that is, as visible behavioral form requiring decoding?' (Asad, *Genealogies*, p. 77).

26 Ibid.

27 Ibid.

28 For an extremely influential proponent of this view, see E. Scarry, *The Body in Pain: The Making and Unmaking of the World*, Oxford: Oxford University Press, 1985.

29 From this standpoint, Mauss and Asad seem closer to an Aristotelian conception of practical reason. A longer version of my argument will require attention to both Aristotle's account of *habitus* and its deployment within medieval moral and sacramental theology. See Nederman, 'Nature, Ethics, and the Doctrine of "Habitus"'; and M. Colish, '*Habitus* Revisited', *Traditio*, 48 (1993): 77–92.

30 M. Foucault, *The History of Sexuality*, vol. 2, *The Use of Pleasure*, trans. R. Hurley, New York, NY: Vintage, 1986, pp. 25–26.

31 Foucault, *The History of Sexuality*, p. 29.

32 Ibid.

33 M. Foucault, 'Sexuality and Solitude', in M. Blonsky (ed.) *On Signs*, Baltimore, MD: The Johns Hopkins University Press, 1985, p. 367.

34 In the case of Benedictine monasticism, bodily practices and rituals are elaborated codified in a text; in other instances, prescribed modes of action are passed down through person-to-person interactions (and of course this kind of interaction also plays an essential role in monastic discipline, as the *Rule of Benedict* continually emphasizes).

35 Asad, *Genealogies*, p. 64. For full discussions of the role of humility in Christian monasticism, see pp. 125–167.

36 M. Ebner, *The Major Works*, trans. and ed. L. Hindsley, New York, NY: Paulist Press, 1993, p. 96; and P. Strauch (ed.) *Margaretha Ebner und Heinrich von Nördlingen: Ein Beitrag zur Geschichte der Deutschen Mystik*, Freiburg and Tubingen: Mohr, 1882, pp. 20–21.

37 Ebner, *Major Works*, p. 96; and *Margaretha Ebner*, p. 21. For the kiss of the heart and drinking blood from Christ's side wound/heart, see A. Hollywood, 'Sexual Desire, Divine Desire; Or, Queering

the Beguines', in G. Loughlin (ed.) *Queer Theology: New Perspectives on Sex and Gender*, Oxford: Blackwell, forthcoming.

38 On this point and the important corrective it provides to the work of Pierre Bourdieu, see S. Mahmood, 'Rehearsed Spontaneity and the Conventionality of Ritual: Disciplines of *Salat*', *American Ethnologist*, 28 (2001): 837–838.

39 Ebner, *Major Works*, p. 114; and *Margeretha Ebner*, p. 52.

40 Ebner, *Major Works*, p. 114; and *Margeretha Ebner*, p. 54.

41 On the salvific power of Christ's blood and the centrality of blood in representations of the Passion, see Hollywood, 'Queering'; and J. Hamburger, *The Visual and the Visionary: Art and Female Spirituality in Late Medieval Germany*, New York, NY: Zone Books, 1998.

42 For the fluidity of gender in the later Middle Ages, see C.W. Bynum, *Holy Feast and Holy Fast: The Religious Significance of Food to Medieval Women*, Berkeley, CA: University of California Press, 1987; C.W. Bynum, *Fragmentation and Redemption: Essays on Gender and the Body in the Later Middle Ages*, New York, NY: Zone Books, 1991; and A. Hollywood, *The Soul as Virgin Wife: Mechthild of Magdeburg, Marguerite Porete, and Meister Eckhart*, Notre Dame, IN: Notre Dame University Press, 1995.

43 The Franciscan-authored *Meditations on the Life of Christ*, for example, addressed to women, most often calls for readers to identify with Mary. As Robin O'Sullivan argues, Angela of Foligno, like Ebner, refuses this identification, instead insisting on her oneness with Christ on the cross. See R. O'Sullivan, *Model, Mirror and Memorial : Imitation of the Passion and the Annihilation of the Imagination in Angela da Foligno's Liber and Marguerite Porete's Mirouer des simples âmes*, University of Chicago Divinity School, Ph.D. Dissertation, 2002; and Hollywood, *Sensible Ecstasy*, pp. 69–74.

44 H. Suso, *The Exemplar, With Two German Sermons*, trans. Frank Tobin, New York, NY: Paulist Press, 1989, pp. 173–174; and for the German text, K. Bihlmeyer (ed.) *Heinrich Seuse: Deutsche Schriften*, Stuttgart: Kohlhammer, 1907, pp. 154–155.

45 Hamburger writes, 'the way in which the young – that is, spiritually immature – Suso so literally imitates Christ's passion bears an uncanny resemblance to the self-inflicted sufferings of numerous nuns' (Hamburger here cites only Elsbeth von Oye, although further examples are readily available from the hagiographical literature). Hamburger continues:

> By contrast in Part II of the Life, Suso deliberately distances himself from the extreme asceticism in which he indulged as a novice. The *imitatio Christi* is recast in ritualized, institutionalized forms, governed by texts and enacted through images. Instead of drawing blood, Stagel embroiders in red silk; rather than mortifying her flesh, she emulates her advisor's asceticism by adorning her body in his image.

Although I agree with Hamburger that this movement between Books I and II of the Life is decisive, it is crucial also to note that Suso's body remains the source of sanctification. Stagel adorns her flesh, but her flesh never gains the power evinced, still in Book II, by Suso's, a power gained precisely through the ascetic action against which he advises Stagel and his other followers. See Hamburger, *Visual and the Visionary*, pp. 263–266.

46 I follow Griffith here in generalizing about U.S. second-wave feminism, but with full recognition of the enormous variety of positions and practices that exist within it. Griffith seems most interested in the mainstream traditions of liberal feminism most visible to evangelical women and, arguably, most critical of fundamentalist Christian women.

47 R.M. Griffith, *God's Daughters: Evangelical Women and the Power of Submission*, Berkeley, CA: University of California Press, 1997, p. 27.

48 See P. Bourdieu, *Outline of a Theory of Practice*, trans. R. Nice, Cambridge: Cambridge University Press, 1977.

49 See also S. Mahmood, 'Feminist Theory, Embodiment, and the Docile Subject: Some Reflections on the Egyptian Islamic Revival', *Cultural Anthropology*, 16 (2001): 202–236.

Chapter 16

Vrinda Dalmiya

LOVING PARADOXES: A FEMINIST RECLAMATION OF THE GODDESS KALI

■ From **LOVING PARADOXES: A FEMINIST RECLAMATION OF THE GODDESS KALI**, *Hypatia*, 15: 1 (2000): 125–150.

T**HE FEMINIST SIGNIFICANCE** of the Goddess Kali lies in an indigenous worshipful attitude of 'Kali-bhakti' rather than in the mere image of the Goddess. The peculiar mother–child motif at the core of the poet Ramprasad Sen's *Kali-bhakti* represents, I argue, not only a dramatic reconstruction of femininity but of selfhood in general. The spiritual goal of a devotee here involves a deconstruction of 'master identity' necessary also for ethico-political struggles for justice.

I: Why Kali, again?

The iconography of the Goddess Kali from India comes as a dramatic relief in our search for alternative constructions of femininity and motherhood. Witness the following hymn describing Kali:

> Mother, incomparably arrayed,
> Hair flying, stripped down,
> You battle-dance on Shiva's heart,
> A garland of heads that bounce off
> Your heavy hips, chopped-off hands
> For a belt, the bodies of infants
> For earrings, and the lips,
> The teeth like jasmine, the face
> A lotus blossomed, the laugh,
> And the dark body billowing up and out
> Like a storm cloud, and those feet
> Whose beauty is only deepened by blood.
> So Prasād cries: My mind is dancing!

Can I take much more? Can I bear
An impossible beauty?
                    (Ramprasad 1982, 65)[1]

The feminine here is powerfully terrifying: A naked and intoxicated female – dark, bloodstained, and dishevelled – dancing on the prostrate body of Shiva, her husband, with her tongue lolling out, wearing nothing except a garland of human heads around her neck, a girdle of severed human hands around her waist, and infant corpses as earrings. Yet, strangely enough, the devotee sees in this macabre picture an 'impossible beauty' and a 'mother.' The mother here is anything but domestic (engaged as she is in a battle-dance) and anything but nurturing (adorned as she is with symbols of death – skulls, corpses, and blood). Yet, on beholding this grotesque form, the poet's 'mind is dancing.'

Such exuberant juxtaposition of polarities in the image of Kali has been interpreted by many[2] as holding feminist messages. Taken as signifying a rupture of water-tight exclusions, Kali has been brought on stage as the redeemer both of Nature and of women. The project in this paper is to rewrite her script for such redemption. Most reclamations of Kali concentrate on the *symbol* of the goddess as representing a collapse of typically 'Western' binary thinking. My claim here is that this understanding is not enough. I propose a shift from Kali as a spiritual icon taken out of context to an indigenous form of *Kali-bhakti*.[3] What is of feminist significance is not simply the paradoxes in the image of Kali but rather a devotee's worshipful attitude towards Kali, called *bhakti*. In order to make my argument, I take as an exemplar of *Kali-bhakti* the devotional poems (addressed to Kali) of Ramprasad Sen, an eighteenth-century Bengali poet. These poems, sung to a variety of set musical scores, figured very prominently in the spiritual life of Sri Ramakrishna, the modern nineteenth-century Indian Saint.[4] That they are not mere exotica is evidenced by their popularity even in contemporary Bengal. They are still sung in Bengali households and form an integral part of a living tradition constituted by modern devotees of Ramakrishna. Incidentally, the fact that Ramprasad (the composer of these songs) and Ramakrishna (the Saint who made extensive use of them as a means of devotional expression) are *men* is not unimportant for my analysis. We shall see that embedding the symbol of Kali in Ramprasad's *Kali-bhakti*[5] actually deepens the paradox and confluence of opposites that attracted the attention of feminists to the image of Kali in the first place.

Let us, however, first analyze just how or why Goddess Kali comes to be a site of apparent contradictions. First and foremost, Kali is both a wife and a mother. But she is also an *immodest*, *aggressive*, and *grotesque* wife and a *terrifying*, *violent*, and *self-absorbed* mother. Now Kali does not constitute a straightforward redefinition of the concepts of 'wife' and 'mother': that these concepts retain their usual connotations of conventional subservience (in the case of 'wife') and caring attentiveness (in the case of 'mother') becomes clear as Kali is constantly admonished for her deviations from societal norms definitive of wifehood and motherhood. Note Ramprasad's outbursts:

Kālī, why are You naked again?
Good grief, haven't You any shame?
Mother don't You have clothes?
Where is the pride of a king's daughter?

And Mother, is this some family duty –
This standing on the chest of Your man?
(1982, 46)

And then,

Rāmprasād asks: Who taught You to be so cold?
If You want to be like Your father –
Stone[6] – don't call Yourself
The Mother.

(1982, 32)

In effect, then, it is the adherence to very traditional expectations (associated with being a wife and mother), rather than their abandonment, that enables Kali to be a self-conscious representation of opposites. Thus, because Kali is a wife and mother in very conventional senses, she suggests passivity and tenderness. But her manifest form is violent and uncaring. Consequently, Kali comes to symbolize the paradoxical dyads: passivity/aggressiveness; traditionality/unconventionality; beautiful/grotesque; tender/terrifying.

Yet another paradox has to do not so much with Kali's image (or iconography) but with the bhakti lyrics in which she is invoked. While Kali is clearly Divine and deserving of the utmost obeisance, an expression of Ramprasad's Kali-devotion is often through poems that chide, berate, and scold her. Praying to Kali becomes a relentless litany of her faults and misdemeanors, and these are harped upon in the very act of seeking redemption through her! So not only is Kali paradoxical herself, but so also is the *love of* Kali. The question here is whether a devotional posture expressed in this odd form and addressed to an apparently odd Goddess can hold out any promises for social and environmental movements for justice. The more general issue is whether spirituality – this specific form of Goddess spirituality – can have any relevance for feminist agendas to end exploitation. To anticipate my conclusion: the devotee (like Ramprasad) expects, or hopes for, spiritual liberation (what I call here 'transcendent liberation') through Kali-worship. But the logical structure of such redemption (even when interpreted monistically as merging with an Absolute) is complex enough to entail an ethical stance that is consonant with feminism.

The advantages of the shift from Kali to *Kali-bhakti* will become clear as we go along. It is best to remind ourselves at this point that the use of spiritual symbols from the East (like the Kali icon) as an antidote for 'dualistic thinking' in the West is problematic in more ways than one. First, the move, in its attempt to overcome conceptual dualisms within 'Western' thought, underscores and reinforces a much deeper dualism and Orientalism – the *rationality* of the West versus the *spirituality* of the East. The rationality/spirituality divide mapped on to the West/East distinction comes in handy to deprive the 'East' of rationality and 'mind' which, in turn, reinforces a whole range of hierarchies. Second, it is too easy a transition from Kali as a symbol of contradictions to Kali as a symbol of an undifferentiated monism. But if transcendence of dualism is to be geared toward securing greater social justice, it is not clear how an appeal to an undifferentiated spiritual ooze can help. Spirituality could be now seen not just as the transcendence of dualism, but of the empirical, the political, and thereby of the very domain of justice itself. How can we meaningfully talk of just relationships if there is no plurality to order and relate? Third, do not the hopelessly oppressive institutions of the home cultures from which these symbols are transported bely their effectiveness as instruments of liberation? Since Kali co-exists quite happily with patriarchal structures and the oppression of women in India, can there be any real feminist potential in her symbolism or worship after all?

Each of these worries is important. But the pitfalls of trying to derive a politics from the realm of spirituality are far greater if we concentrate simply on the Kali-icon. It will become clear only at the end of the paper how relocating to *Kali-bhakti*, to an indigenous worshipful love for Kali, alleviates the first two objections. But let me begin by commenting briefly on the more general third charge made above – the objection that spiritual formations that co-exist with traditional patriarchal formations cannot be linked to liberatory politics.

I am not claiming that Kali in India *is* a feminist principle. As is well known, it has often been argued that the formulation of female divinity is a ploy to keep real power away from real women in the real world or that the terrifying image of Kali is a creation of phallocentric fear of female sexuality gone wild. By indicating how Goddesses have been otherwise appropriated, such arguments might also explain the hesitation that many Indian feminists feel about making use of Goddess symbols.[7] Now it is undeniable that the mere presence of spiritual phenomena – like Mother Goddesses or Bhakti saints[8] – do not, by themselves, ensure a just society. But simply because an image has been (and can be) manipulated to serve the ends of patriarchy does not imply that it has no positive value or that it cannot be further manipulated to serve other ends. It is the possibility of such an alternative encashing of a spiritual phenomenon that is being suggested here. Note also that what is controversial in the Indian context is not the relevance of Goddess symbols for political purposes per se. The Indian nationalist movement[9] and, more recently, the fundamentalist Hindu agenda[10] show quite clearly how Goddesses and spirituality *can* be used for political ends. What is in question is the attempted use of female spirituality for the *feminist* agenda.

Examples of how the 'Goddess phenomenon' has been manipulated to create particular instances of escape from oppression – of how the very predominance of Goddess worship in traditional Indian society creates interesting spaces for individual women in their struggle for survival – are not hard to find.

a   The Bengali short story by Mahasweta Devi, 'Sanjh Sakaler Ma' – literally, 'Mother of Dusk and Dawn' (Mahasweta Devi 1993) – tells the tale of a young destitute widow who decides in desperation to 'fake' possession by the Goddess and uses the offerings given to her-as-Devi by her devotees during the day to feed her (as-mortal-woman's) son at night. Thus it is the societal acceptance of her as a Divine Mother that enables her to function as a human mother in an overwhelmingly harsh environment.

b   Alternatively, in recounting her experience of domestic violence in the feminist journal *Manushi* (vol. 3, no. 2. Jan/Feb, 1983),[11] a young woman, Sumitra, relates how her mother-in-law claimed 'possession by the Goddess' when she tortured Sumitra. But, interestingly, we find Sumitra *herself* stepping into the Goddess's footprints in her attempt to summon up the courage to retaliate. This move is successful because, through it, she could create for herself at least a short respite while her abusive husband 'sat and listened with folded hands. He really believed that the goddess was speaking' (1983, 18).

c   On a more theoretical plane, Lina Gupta, in her very comprehensive paper, 'Kali, the Savior' (1991), ingeniously argues that Kali can embody the liberation of tradition itself from its patriarchal bias: 'Kali as a woman, as a wife, knows what her status should be. As she dances the dance of destruction she communicates her responses to the way things are and the way they should be. That is, in her destructive dance she creates her own reality' (37). Kali can thus symbolize the destruction of patriarchal interpretations of herself!

I do not pursue any of these arguments here. Rather, what I attempt is the derivation of an alternative model of self-construction and of self–other relationships from an analysis of a particular genre of devotional poetry addressed to Kali. This model of the self, we shall see, comes very close to the 'relational self' of some Western feminists. According to Rajeswari Sunder Rajan, the 'recuperation of the/an Hindu goddess as feminist is problematic at the present historical juncture both for its assumption of an undifferentiated "woman-power" as well as for its promotion of a certain radicalized Hinduism' (Sunder Rajan 1998, ws–34). The dialogue initiated here over the *metaphysics of the self* is neither of the above because it does not tap into an essentialized womanhood nor does it promote the formation of a '*Hindu*' self.[12] The spiritual motif here is quietistic and antithetical to instrumental rationality on one level; but, on another, it is suggestive of ontological transformations without which even very self-consciously adopted socio-political agendas for change might not be effective. So *Kali-bhakti* is being used here to deconstruct 'master identity' and to suggest an alternative.

The attempted deployment of *Kali-bhakti* could have another advantage specifically for certain strains of ecofeminism. Vandana Shiva, probably the most prominent of Indian ecofeminists, has focused on reclaiming the philosophical notion of *Prakṛti*. *Prakṛti* is the creative and dynamic ontological principle unique to a particular Indian worldview which, according to Shiva, entails an anti-Cartesian 'living, nurturing relationship between man and nature' (Shiva 1988, 39). But one of the problems with her analysis is that *Prakṛti* (the blueprint for liberatory practice, according to Shiva), is an abstract metaphysical principle of high philosophy, codified in Sanskrit texts accessible only to an elite. This naturally raises the question of how marginalized, rural women most affected by environmental degradation can ever access this key to their redemption. Of course, Shiva herself is careful to deny the separation between the popular and elite imaginations and to emphasize the knowledge of *Prakṛti* through gendered and non-intrusive practices of sylviculture and agriculture still prevalent in Indian villages. In spite of this very important epistemic concession, the *urban poor* remain cut off from *Prakṛti* because they are engaged neither in agricultural practices nor in classical scholarship. Replacing *Prakṛti* by *kali-bhakti* can broaden the epistemic base further and show how subjects engaged neither in textual scholarship nor in agriculture may still have cognitive access to a philosophical principle through worship and devotion.

To understand this epistemological importance of *Kali-bhakti*, it is necessary to underscore that Kali *is* a representation of *Prakṛti*. Even a simple devotee like Ramprasad is quite clear on the idol's representational significance: what is worshipped is not merely the image/idol/picture of Kali but what she stands for. For instance:

My mind dreams up this image
I could make with clay.
But is Mother clay?
. . .
Can an image of clay
Cool the mind's fever?
I've heard the hue of Her skin is black —
A black that lights the world.
Can an image of clay be made
That marvelous dark with a coat of paint?
Kālī cuts down evil
Is this the work of straw and clay?

(1982, 61)[13]

The intentional object of *bhakti* (the Goddess, Kali) – the idol fashioned out of clay – is grasped as being symbolic. Any ordinary devotee, in relating to the Goddess, understands that he or she is relating to the metaphysical truths that the Goddess stands for. In the spiritual moment, this truth is codified not in dead, lifeless propositions but in the form of the Goddess. So who/what is approached with 'love' in *bhakti* is not an 'image' made out of 'straw and clay' and covered with a 'coat of paint,' but something *more* that these externals are used to represent. What we have here, then, is a sort of 'emotional knowing' of fundamental truths. By emphasizing direct and personal contact with the Divine, the *bhakti*-movement itself arose in India, according to some, as a revolt against Brahmanical traditions that required scholarship and mediation of institutionalized priests for a contact with the deity. In *bhakti*, anyone – irrespective of caste, creed, learning, and gender – could qualify as a devotee and be capable of the appropriate emotion. Instead of with costly ritual offerings, the Goddess could now be worshipped just 'with tears.'[14] By focusing on this lived spiritual/devotional relationship to Kali, we have a solution to the epistemological problem thrown up by theories like that of Shiva's – the problem of how theoretical principles serving as the feminist fulcrum can be *known* from the fringes in a rigidly hierarchical society. Kali is representative of a philosophical truth. *Bhakti* is an egalitarian and personalized relationship with Kali. Consequently, through *Kali-bhakti*, the devotee – *anyone* who chooses to be a devotee – can access philosophical truth through a lived relationship. Kali-worship can thus bring together the metaphysical, the epistemological, and, as I shall argue (in the last two sections), an ethico-political vision. Before pursuing this line of thought, however, let us try to get a flavor of this lived relationship as found in Ramprasad's Kali-poetry.

II: Worshipping Kali/loving the mother

Personalization of the human–Divine relation which is the essence of *bhakti* can be captured by many motifs: an erotic bond between lovers; the playful comradeship between friends; the complete dependence of a slave/servant/valet on his master; or the attention-demanding petulance of a child before its mother. Though we do find devotional poetry in which the 'human' is a harried mother bringing up a mischievous and playful child-God (for example, SurDas identifying himself with Yashoda, Krishna's mother) or a lover yearning for union with a Divine Lover (MiraBai),[15] Ramprasad casts himself primarily as the *child* of a Divine Mother. Moreover, he is often a rebellious and quarrelsome child, throwing tantrums, feeling neglected, and flinging accusations. This graphic expression of all the ambivalences of childhood, in some beautiful poetry, *is* his devotion. Here are some samples:

> You think motherhood is child's play?
> One child doesn't make a mother if she is cruel.
> Mine carried me ten months and ten days
> But doesn't notice where I've gone when it's time to eat.
> When a child is bad, his parents correct him,
> But You can watch Death come at me
> With murder in His heart
> And turn away yawning.
>
> (1982, 32)

> You'd snatch the fruit out of the hand
> of a child, eat it Mother, and cheat him.
>
> (1982, 34)

> I'm not calling you Mother anymore,
> All You give me is trouble.
> I had a home and a family, now
> I'm a beggar – what will You think of
> Next, my wild-haired Devi?
> I'll beg before I come to You,
> Crying 'Mother.' I've tried that
> And got the silent treatment.
> If the mother lives should the son suffer,
> And if she's dead, hasn't he got to live somewhere?
> Rāmprasād says: What's a mother
> Anyway, the son's worst enemy?
> I keep wondering what worse You can do
> Than make me live over and over
> The pain, life after life.
>
> (1982, 35)

> What's so good in You
> That You deserve to be called Mother?
> . . .
> Because of You, Mother, Father is crazy,
> With Stepmother[16] sitting on His head.
> Twice-born Rāmprasād says: people mock me.
> They say: 'If your mother is Annapurna,[17]
> Why isn't there food in your father's house?'
>
> (1982, 45)

One could try to analyze the poetic function of such insults and accusations in an expression of devotional passion or to address the more general question of why such petulance, bordering on the blasphemous, could ever be prayer. My concern, however, is primarily whether this mother–child motif central to Ramprasad's *Kali-bhakti* can help to sustain self transformations that can, in turn, undercut exploitation. I look, therefore, at the idiosyncracies of the kind of *mother* Kali is and the kind of *child* Ramprasad is, in order to grasp the full significance of the kind of *mother–child* nexus being spoken of here.

III: The 'mother' of the child

Of course, the valorization of motherhood is not unproblematic for feminism. Motherhood is, more often than not, the site for the oppression of women, and hence becomes controversial as a feminine symbol of womanhood.[18] However, the root of Ramprasad's devotional outbursts is the fact that his mother is really a 'bad' mother. And herein lies his redemption! What we should remember, then, is that the addressee of Ramprasad's devotion, Kali, is not a simple mother but the 'terrible,' 'crazy,' or 'mad' mother. She exceeds what is allowed by the traditional construction of 'mother.' The extra connotation (as noted earlier) is not usually something consistent with motherhood ordinarily conceived – which makes the object of Ramprasad's devotion a self-consciously constructed paradox.

Gods and Goddesses in the Indian tradition are generally constituted in three layers.[19] On one level (*ādhidaivika*), they are iconographically represented celestial beings whose intricate biographies are narrated in mythological tales. On the second level (*ādhyātmika*), they are vital principles of the lived-body of the devotee. Finally, on the third level (*ādhibhautika*), they are principles in the environment or cosmos. Thus a Devi (Goddess) is not only a suprahuman deity but is simultaneously a principle in the inner and outer realms. An act of worship thus consists in dwelling on a deity, on a vital principle (internal to the body) and on a cosmic principle all at once.

On the *ādhidaivika* level, Kali is the naked Goddess iconographically represented in the manner spelled out at the beginning of the paper. There are numerous and fascinating stories as to why she came to be that way. I shall not go into the detailed accounts of her celestial biography that draw out the kinship relations between Kali and the other members of the Hindu pantheon.[20] Ramprasad, however, takes even this *ādhidaivic*, or 'deity-aspect', to be representational. Whatever else Kali might be, it is clear that, according to him, she stands in for *all* women:

> You'll find Mother
> In any house.
> Do I dare say it in public?
>
> . . .
>
> She's mother, daughter, wife, sister —
> Every woman close to you.
> What more can Rāmprasād say?
> You work the rest out from these hints.
>
> (1982, 60)

As the symbol of femininity, Kali may be read in two ways: as serving patriarchal purposes and emerging from male fear of female sexuality: or as a genuine feminine self-assertion and power, a mother who is not afraid of stepping out of the conventions of motherhood to express herself – her rage and her needs. But the point to be emphasized is that Kali always signifies *more* than the feminine.

The *ādhyātmika* aspect of Kali is spelled out by the meditational metaphysics of Tantra.[21] Kali is now a vital force (*kulakundalini* or 'serpent power') at the base of the spinal column. An elaborate 'geography of the body' indicates different 'centers' and 'pathways' through which this vital force can flow and be guided. Spiritual progress is equivalent to yogic control of the *kulakundalini*, making it rise to the 'highest center' in the crown of the head. This is the state of blissful repose.

> Now cry Kālī and take the plunge!
> O, my Mind, dive into this sea,
> . . .
> . . . Now, hold your breath
> And jump! Kick down to where She [Kulakundalini] sits
> Deep in the wise water, a great pearl.
>
> (1982, 54)[22]

The ascent of the *kundalini* to its peak is represented iconographically by the dancing Kali frozen into immobility (achievement) upon stepping on Shiva (the 'highest center').

In Her outer/ecological, or *ādhibhautika*, aspect, Kali is simply 'nature' – the word for which, in some of the vernaculars, is *prakṛti*. The mad Goddess is now wild, unpredictable, and capricious *nature*, the 'storm-cloud' that can cause floods (by her presence) or famine (by her absence). Her frenzied dance is the eternal change of the natural order. Her terrifying form is a pictorial expression of the brutal fact that everything in nature is constantly changing – and change is really decay and finally death.

Analyzed in this way, the Goddess Kali is simultaneously an *internal* principle and everything *outside*. Obviously, such identification can make sense only within a certain metaphysical framework. This metaphysical vision implicit in Kali-worship is articulated in the ontological principle of *Prakṛti*. Kali as *Prakṛti* (with a capital P) is to be distinguished from nature or *prakṛti* (with a small p). Kali/*Prakṛti* is the Ultimate monistic stuff from which everything emerges but which nevertheless is distinct from and transcends these emergents. Just as the Spinozistic *natura naturans* from which the world of plurality or *natura naturata* emerges remains distinct from its evolutes, the Ultimate metaphysical *Prakṛti* is not to be reduced to the plurality of nature that evolves out of it. *Prakṛti* gives birth to, but is not exhausted by, the plural nature around us. Kali as *Prakṛti* is the source of everything and is thus a metaphysical 'Mother.'

> . . . You are the Mother of all
> And our nurse. You carry the Three Worlds
> in Your belly.
>
> (1982, 28)

The nudity of Kali is now explained by the utter privacy of her being the 'First' and the 'Only' one. Can there be modesty where there is no multiplicity? Shame is generated by the gaze of others; in the primal moment, since there is no one other than Herself in the total self-absorption of the moment of giving birth, there is and can be no shame. It is interesting that in a poem quoted earlier, Ramprasad, exasperated by Kali's nakedness, goes on to plead

> O, Mother, *we* are dying of shame,
> Now put on Your woman's clothes.
>> (1982, 46, emphasis mine)

It is important to note that Kali's metaphysical motherhood is very different from biological motherhood. The latter not only requires impregnation by a male but is also constructed as being the more passive of the two roles in procreation. In the former, emanation from *Prakṛti* is not dependent on a male – being the source of everything, *Prakṛti* is prior to even the male. Secondly, *Prakṛti* is definitely the active principle in generation. Shiva, the male, is clearly subordinate to Kali – note the *dance* (activity) of Kali on a passive Shiva's chest. Look at Ramprasad's explanation of how Kali got to step on Her husband's body:

> All right, You crazy woman,
> Get down off the Great Lord's chest!
> . . .
> Now get down before His ribs cave in –
> O Shiva's Woman, You're pitiless, pitiless.
> . . .
> Rāmprasād thinks He's playing dead
> Just to have Your feet touching Him.
>> (1982, 47)

Shiva here is clearly in *need* of Kali's touch and is utterly powerless lying under her.

However, Shiva symbolizes *cit*, or consciousness. And one may worry whether this is not, once again, the age-old association of 'mind' with the masculine and the 'stuff/matter' with the feminine. A crucial question here is whether Shiva's dependence on Kali and his ineffectiveness without Her signify a metaphysical dualism after all – whether Shiva and Kali are not two distinct ontological categories that must cooperate for the creation of the world. In the dualistic Samkhya system, for example, a motionless but conscious Puruṣa[23] must conjoin with a dynamic but material *Prakṛti* to generate the world. But since Ramprasad's conception of *Prakṛti*/Kali is housed in the sharply different metaphysics of Tantra, Kali, as the primordial stuff, is not only dynamic energy but is also conscious and has will. By Her own desire to create, She differentiates Herself into a male and a female whose subsequent union creates the world. Thus the representation of such an ontology cannot be just Kali, nor Kali and Shiva together but of Kali-dancing-on-Shiva.[24] What we have is a monistic principle whose internal complexity is represented by two divine figures.

The dance of Kali is an important metaphor. A dance suggests playfulness and light-heartedness. Equally importantly, it is constant movement or change. Etymologically, *Kali* is a feminine form of *kāla*, which means time. But time and change are just euphemisms for decay and death. Kali is thus the paradox: She is the Primal

Mother who brings forth all life even while she signifies Death. Everything that there is, everything 'natural,' is the vale of Death even though it is nothing other than Kali/*Prakṛti*, the source of life.

IV: The 'child' of the mother

True to the convention of *bhakti*-poetry, Ramprasad writes himself into his lyrics in the signature lines (*bhanitā*) at the end of each poem. This helps to personalize the emotion and establish an intimacy with the addressee of the poem. The most striking aspect of Ramprasad's *bhakti* poetry, however, is that his voice is that of a child.

This is significant in more ways than one. Though it is true that Ramprasad thinks of himself as a 'son,' the self-conscious posture of a child suggests an attempt to step out of the gendered identity of a 'man.' Ramprasad *is* a man but he has to *become* a child in approaching Kali. Not only that; he is a 'bad,' weak, suffering, and needy child:

> What am I – a rickety thing
> Born a month early?
> > (1982, 49)

> A blind man clutches the cane he's lost
> Like a fanatic. So I clutch You, Mother.
> > (1982, 25)

All this is quite consistent with the general temper of *bhakti* in which the devotee approaches the deity with the utmost humility and in complete surrender. In male *bhakti* saints this leads to an interesting scenario. Since being male is usually associated with social power, a male saint not only has to cast off the usual forms of security and ego, but has also to abandon his maleness to attain the powerlessness required for *bhakti*. Interestingly,[25] in a few poems, Kali and Ramprasad switch roles: Kali becomes the girl-child (called Uma) and Ramprasad himself becomes the mother complaining to her husband.

> O Giri,[26] I can't comfort
> Your Umā anymore.
> She cries and pouts,
> Won't touch the breast,
> Won't touch Her *khir*
> And shoves away Her cream.
> > (1982, 41)

Here we have a double move: Not only does Ramprasad consciously adopt the posture of a female (that of social powerlessness), but, in the classic stance of a true *bhakta*, appears powerless before a Deity who is now a self-willed little girl! Thus the 'child' in Ramprasad's poetry signifies a deconstruction of the power. We are in a form of devotion in which being feminine is seen as an advantage.[27] Intriguingly, when Ramprasad becomes the mother, he does not assume Kali's great style. He is a typically 'good' mother complaining helplessly to 'her' husband, Giri. Ramprasad-as-mother does not claim for himself, even in poetic role-playing, the power of Kali, the Mother.

What emerges now is an interesting contradiction in Ramprasad's own posture: he is a demanding, adamant, and fearless one even while being aware of his helplessness.

> Prasād says; find a half-wit
> And fool him if You want,
> But if You don't save me
> I'm going to get Shiva to spank You.
> > (1982, 34)

> And if You aren't loving, why shouldn't I go
> To Stepmother and if she takes me up
> You won't see me around here anymore.
> > (1982, 29)

Ramprasad, the child, is as much a paradox as Kali herself. He is secure and strangely empowered even in the realization of his utter helplessness and complete dependence.

Thus Ramprasad's *Kali-bhakti* is an effusion of paradoxes. The object of worship, Kali, signifies the apparent contradictions of Life and Death; the worshiper, child-Ramprasad, is an exemplification of the opposites of helplessness and confidence; and the very act of worship, *bhakti*, is a mixture of love and hate. What purpose can such a phenomenon, an intensely ambivalent and intimate relationship between such a child and such a Mother, serve?

V: The 'mother'–'child' nexus: redemption, spiritual and earthly

Let us begin with the spiritual, where specifying a utilitarian motive for devotion is very much in order in the genre under consideration. Over and over again, the one thing that leaps out in Ramprasad's verses is the experience of mortality or the inevitability of death. Ramprasad's search for Kali is frankly because of this.

> Pitying Mother, do I worship You
> Out of my own free will?
> Nobody would
> If it weren't for the terror
> Of death.
> > (1982, 21)

Or in a less ironical and a more plaintive vein:

> The fisherman has cast his net
> And sits there waiting, waiting.
> What will become of me,
> Mother, in this world?
>
> . . .

Rāmprasād says: Call the Mother,
She can handle Death.

(1982, 33)

The Mother is an object of adoration because it is believed that she can 'handle Death' or (as in the earlier poem) help us handle the 'terror of Death.' But Kali, we saw, *is* Death. So Ramprasad ends up craving a proximity to that which he dreads the most. Two distinct responses that trade on the difference between overcoming the 'terror of death' and overcoming 'death itself' are forthcoming to dissolve the apparent paradox here. They give us alternative conceptions of what spiritual liberation attained through *Kali-bhakti* is. Both interpretations occur in the tradition but are very often not kept distinct.

According to the first, confrontation is a strategy for overcoming our fear. For example, I may not face the fact that I need surgery because of my fear of the anticipated pain. When I come to accept the necessity of surgery, what I feared, i.e., the anticipated pain, does not disappear: This acceptance just enables me to get on with life in spite of the pain. What I have overcome, then, is not the pain of surgery but only my crippling fear of that pain. In a similar vein, acceptance of Kali can be a confrontation of what I fear most – inevitable death. Such acceptance is not an overcoming of death but only of my fear of it. 'Through self-surrender (*Prapatti*) he (Ramprasad) loses his *fear of death* of self, which is all death really is' (Kinsley 1975, 119, emphasis mine).

Prasād says: I don't know what
It's all about, so do what You have to.
But shake me loose from this fear of death.

(1982, 48)

A snake afraid of a frog? – What rubbish!
Can you, your Mother's son, fear Death?
You're mad – [can] anyone whose mother
Is the Mother be afraid of Death?

(1982, 53)

Spiritual liberation through Kali-worship, according to this first interpretation, is a state of fearlessness (about mortality) that enables us to live life even as it comes mixed with death and decay. Call this 'liberative fearlessness.'

Alternatively, longing for Kali may be seen as a desire for immortality or a longing to overcome death itself. Liberation now consists in realizing that

. . . you end, brother,
Where you began, a reflection
Rising in water, mixing with water,
Finally one with water.

(1982, 20)[28]

The I, a mere 'reflection,' is the psycho-physical organism that dies. But what remains, 'the water,' is eternal and deathless. In realizing that I am not this necessarily-decaying, psycho-physical organism, I grasp my own hidden immortality. Embracing Kali as Death is a gesture of embracing the inevitable annihilation of the psycho-physical organism and clearing the way, as it were, for the 'mixing' of the ego in the Infinite. 'Kālī confronts one with a vision of the world as chaotic and out of control and thereby urges one to see beyond it to what is permanent and eternal. In this sense, Kālī is both the embodiment or mistress of this ephemeral, magically created world and the stimulus to resolve to transcend it' (Kinsley 1975, 136). The state of spiritual liberation, in this second interpretation, is a transcendence of empirical selfhood, of realizing that what dies is really not one's true self. It is understanding one's deathlessness and thereby overcoming death itself. Call this 'transcendent liberation.'[29]

The stage is now set for our final question: How can either 'liberative fearlessness' or 'transcendent liberation' (in other words, what a devotee aspires for through *Kali-bhakti*) be relevant in struggles against oppression? A criticism voiced in Section I rears its head here: Spirituality and politics seem to fall apart on either of these two construals of the spiritual goal. 'Transcendent liberation' is an overcoming of death achieved through transcendence of the empirical. This is virtually a *going beyond* the political rather than an engagement with it. Alternatively, 'liberative fearlessness,' which is overcoming the fear of death, avoids an other-worldly leap, no doubt, but does not seem to underscore any kind of responsible political action. The fear of death, along with the Hindu belief in *karma* and rebirth, serves as an impetus to be moral. If future incarnations are shaped by karmic influences acquired in the present life, then our impending death gives an urgency to being good. In this context, an overcoming of the fear of death, a forgetfulness about it, might well induce a carefreeness which, in turn, could very well push us into moral and political irresponsibility – the life of crude and uncommitted hedonists living only for the moment.[30] In this mode, Ramprasad would be quite consistent in taking as he says,

> . . . these few things –
> The sort Shiva carries[31] – and singing:
> 'Hurrah for Kālī,' (I'll) just dance off.
> (1982, 39)

The following depiction of salvation by David Kinsley echoes just this possibility: 'To accept one's mortality,' he says, 'is to be able to act superfluously, to let go, to be able to sing, dance, and shout. To win Kali's boon is to become childlike, to be flexible, open, and naive like a child. It is to act and be like Ramakrishna, who delighted in the world as Kali's play, who acted without calculation and behaved like a fool or a child' (1975, 145). Thus the critic constructs the following destructive dilemma: *Kali-bhakti* either leads to a straightforward transcendence of the social order (in 'transcendent liberation') and hence to a transcendence of socio-political consequences altogether; or its effect on us (in 'liberative fearlessness') is to make us naive (like a *fool/child*) and to suggest a life of irresponsibility rather than the stuff that politics is made of. On neither interpretation, then, is *Kali-bhakti* socially efficacious.

In order to respond to this let us step back for a moment to a diagnosis of exploitative relationships. According to Val Plumwood (1993), self–other relationships (oppressive or not) flow from the structure of self-identity. It has often been emphasized that a self defined in terms of Reason (which in turn is conceived in opposition to, and as higher than, the domain of the non-rational) is bound to have an exploitative 'master-identity.' The archetypical 'other' to reason is of course nature, whose comparative inferiority is variously conceptualized as lower than Reason (in the Platonic context), as inert, mechanical, and devoid of teleology (in the mechanistic philosophy fuelled by Descartes and the Enlightenment), or as private property that can be 'owned' and hence unabashedly appropriated by the self (in the liberal and contemporary context of capitalism). Whatever (or whoever) is associated with nature – women, indigenous cultures, emotionality, sexuality – is consequently perceived as being in need of control and ultimately is appropriated and owned. In this way, pervasive and widespread forms of domination are generated. Plumwood ultimately traces the construction of such a domineering self-identity to Western man's response to death. The problem, according to Plumwood, stems from a fear of mortality and the failure to acknowledge that life and death are intertwined. In an attempt to overcome death, man – as far back as Plato – has sought self-definitions in forms that deny his embeddedness and necessary dependence on nature (the realm of decay and death). The Platonic move to transcend the 'prison of the body,' the Cartesian search for 'pure rational objectivity' to make nature transparent, and, finally, contemporary man's insatiable desire for 'private property and consumption' are all attempts at attaining immortality and personal continuity while denying our necessary dependence on Death/Nature.

What is important is that, in this analysis, a solution to exploitation would obviously lie in an alternative self-construction. And 'any attempt to rework the Western tradition's account of human identity and its relations to nature must confront the anti-life themes implicit in its major traditions of death' (Plumwood 1993, 102). Ramprasad's *Kali-bhakti* becomes promising at this point because it encapsulates, as we have seen, the drama of his confronting Death. The wisdom in the symbolism of Kali is that *life and death are intertwined*. An acceptance of Kali is an acceptance of Death which is concomitant with Life. It is the realization that any attempt to defy Death amounts to denying Life itself. But does such Life/Death-acceptance (through acceptance of Kali) lead to a genuinely different self-construction not modelled on the master-identity? *Is there really a radically different picture of the self, and hence of interpersonal relationship, lurking in *Kali-bhakti*? Or are we reading too much into it?*

The mother–child nexus of Ramprasad's devotional lyrics can actually serve as a rich motif for both methodological and substantial changes. While ordinary conceptions of motherhood do not suggest an alternative self-construction, the dynamic between child-Ramprasad and Mother-Kali can do so in substantial ways. Methodologically, the child–mother motif underscores the importance of the personal, the private, and the particular over the abstract universalism of rationalism. Hence, if the argument here works, an archetypical instance from the 'private' domain – the mother–child bond – would represent self-identity relevant for the 'public' sphere. But let us see if this can be made more plausible through the following claims.

A. The ontological

Ramprasad's Kali is a mother who is not denied assertiveness. The danger of the mother losing herself in her cared-fors is expertly avoided by Kali. We have not only a Mother who is not self-sacrificing, but we are also faced with an assertive and demanding child. Yet, this is not a bond between 'equals' but a bond articulated by one who is irrevocably dependent and aware of his dependence on an immensely more powerful other. However, Ramprasad's indebtedness to and dependence on Kali does not lead to his enslavement. The weaker individual in the relationship makes claims and demands of the more powerful one, who, even while discharging her responsibility, does not turn into a self-effacing martyr. Let us remember that Ramprasad's chosen metaphor for the Divine–human bond is that of Mother–child and not that of Beloved–lover (as in some other *bhakti*-saints). While it is understandable for a lover to desire union with his or her beloved, it is more usual for a child to fight his Mother – to crave her proximity even while struggling for independence. So the child–mother motif of Ramprasad's *Kali-bhakti* clearly points to an interrelatedness between different centers of interest conscious of this difference and continually negotiating an optimally beneficial nexus in which none is effaced or sacrificed. In fact, each is committed to the welfare of the other and in turn is assured of the other's concern for her. Kali's whimsicality is a constant reminder of her autonomy so that her children do not appropriate her completely as care-giver. Child-Ramprasad's demands, on the other hand, serve as a reminder of the existence of 'another' that Kali must, and ultimately does, take into account. We clearly avoid here a dysfunctional dualism that impels us to negate and assimilate genuine others into our projects. In stark contrast to the 'master-identity,' Ramprasad's metaphor signifies a 'relational identity' that may well curb the excesses of the domineering self.

B. The ethical

The balance achieved between child-Ramprasad and Kali also suggests a revised moral terrain that breaks down the usual egoism–altruism divide. Kali, as we have seen, is not denied the competitiveness and self-assertiveness generally associated with a self-serving egoism. Yet, she is Ramprasad's Savior and looks to his interests as is required by a self-sacrificing altruism. Kali is thus both self-serving and other-serving at once. What is more, her altruism is not based on any exchange or contract. The strange Mother in question has not earned Ramprasad's devotion in any way – in fact, she seems to have done enough *not* to deserve it. Similarly, the child-Ramprasad's confidence that he will be acknowledged also comes not from the fact that he has done anything to deserve the Mother's attention (other than simply love and depend on her), but from the fact that it is her nature to attend to his needs, albeit in her inscrutable way. For example:

> Rāmprasād says: In this game
> The *end was a foregone conclusion*
> Now, at dusk, take up Your child
> In Your arms and go home.
>   (1982, 23, emphasis mine)

The 'child,' through all his chiding and chaffing, is bound unconditionally to the 'Mother,' who, in spite of all her eccentricity, does take care of him when all is said and done. What transpires is community not based on prudential curtailment of self-interest: Kali's taking care of Ramprasad is continuous with her self-assertion and Ramprasad's outbursts against Kali's waywardness might be prompted by his care and concern for *her*. What we have here, then, is a notion of serving interests of others as part of our own self-interests. The common good becomes a responsibility that each individual discharges in the formation of his or her 'relational self.' And the ground of such responsibility lies in what we are: essentially connected beings.

C. The environmental

The above ontological and ethical consequences have very important implications for environmental philosophy. Remember that one of the significances of Kali is *prakṛti*, or nature. A relational self modelled in and through a dialogue with Kali-as-nature thus becomes an ecological self. The 'water' we, as droplets, come out of and the water we go back to is the deep blue ocean of Kali – the primordial Nature (*Prakṛti*). Our relation to the natural realm is intrinsic to who and what we are. This is not a holistic absorption of ourselves in nature. Rather, we have a self-construction that recognizes its embeddedness in the natural and yet does not shy away from asserting interests that are sometimes antithetical to that of nature. Similarly, nature too can sometimes be hostile and uncaring of our wants. Growth consists in negotiating these differences, in sometimes even using nature, but with a full awareness of our intrinsic relation to her and nature's own (sometimes opaque to us) teleology. Environmental ethics becomes not a simple extensionist or utilitarian move where we curb exploitative tendencies for our own long-term interests. Rather, it is grounded in an indebtedness to and acknowledgment of embeddedness in nature that makes responsibility to care for it natural.

D. The social

The motif of Ramprasad's *Kali-bhakti* contains the seeds of a selfhood that is not dependent on possessions and is not consumed by greed. Look at Ramprasad's suggestions for an aspiring devotee:

> 'I'm this. This is mine.'
> Idiot thoughts.
> O Mind, you imagined all that stuff was real
> And carelessly tangled the heart!
> 'Who am I? Who is mine?
> Who else is real?'
> . . .
> O Mind, the light in a dark room
> Is snuffed by possessions.
> . . .
> Rāmprasād says:
> Lift the mosquito net and look at yourself.
> (1982, 44)

'Looking at myself' is looking at my mortality. And really to *look* at mortality is to understand the futility of acquisitiveness, to grasp the 'idiocy' of possessiveness, of claiming things and persons as 'mine.' Developing this further, Ramprasad says:

> The bee's blunder when it goes for
> The painted version of the lotus.
> You've given me bitter leaves,
> Swearing they were sweet, and my old
> Sweet tooth has cost me a whole day
> Spitting the bitterness out.
> Mother, You lured me into this world,
> You said: 'Let's play,' only to cheat
> My hope out of its hope with Your playing.
>   (1982, 23)

The key idea here is the end of hope in the salvific powers of 'commodities.' But this naturally signals the end of 'grasping,' of overconsumption, of selfishness – the girdle of severed hands around Kali's waist. Giving up the quest for 'possessions' and property is the deconstruction of the economic self which, as mentioned earlier, is the modern incarnation of the 'master identity.' The basic idea is that a self that does not want to possess for oneself is a self that does not need to appropriate, exploit, or oppress others, and, of course, is also one that does not fear loss. What emerges is really a counter to the classic picture of liberal man who is a 'person' only to the extent that he has property and the freedom to enjoy wealth as he chooses or contracts to do.

What we are moving towards is a rejection of the second horn of the critic's dilemma noted earlier. Recollect that 'transcendent liberation' was said to lead to a transcendence of ethics and politics (by collapsing all differences), while 'liberative fearlessness' led to the undermining of political life (by advocating a life of an irresponsible child or fool). But once we note how deep rooted the liberal notion of personhood is, we see why its rejection can be perceived as naive and akin to the behavior of a fool. Actually, the devotee, in 'acting like a child,' is really enacting an alternative model of self-hood. The motif of the child has suggested to some critics the rejection of manliness and a regression to the 'spiritual clutching of the babe.'[32] Read positively, however, it is a new construction of subjectivity and a new vision of freedom. 'Liberative fearlessness,' then, holds the key to an alternative social order by implying a new metaphysics of self. Ramprasad's mother–child motif is not a model of discrete centers of interests (at best) working out a contract for maximization of individual freedom. It is a system of interdependencies, of mutual indebtedness and responsibility dancing the cosmic dance of Life/Death. And this model is constitutive of the spiritual salvation that Ramprasad envisages in and through his poetry.

To sum up: What the devotee strives for is 'liberative fearlessness.' Spiritual practice is about overcoming greed and about restraining the drive to accumulate material possessions. It is giving up the constraints and pretensions of an 'adult' lifestyle and coming close to the 'foolish' playfulness of childhood. This undermining of economic individuality does not entail a negation of metaphysical individuality (or plurality) but is a crucial step in deconstructing exploitative social systems that are kept in place by defensive reactions to our imminent mortality.

VI: Some objections answered

The relevance of spiritual life for liberatory agendas through the notion of 'liberative fearlessness' is not without its problems. A concept of relational self culled from Ramprasad's *bhakti* seems to sit uncomfortably with the metaphysical context of his devotion. It appears to undermine the very possibility of 'transcendent liberation' which, after all, does find expression in his poetry. Note that 'transcendent liberation' is nothing but a dissipation of the individual/empirical ego and its final subsumption in the Infinite. Hence, it is a quest for the destruction of metaphysical individuality – not just of economic individuality, as argued in the previous section. Any attempt, therefore, to construe the devotionalism under question as a metaphor for the construction of *individual self-identities* (no matter how 'relationally' conceived) is utterly wrongheaded as long as 'transcendent liberation' is part of the complete context of *Kali-bhakti*. For better or for worse, Ramprasad's spirituality seems to entail the kind of transcendence that belies any ethics or politics. In different, but in no uncertain terms, it remains a denial of ordinary life as much as of Plato.

Ignoring scholarship about the possibility of *bhakti* within a dualistic ontology and even setting aside the debate over whether Ramprasad's own ontology is dualist or monist, I would like to concede here the metaphysical monism of Ramprasad's spirituality and the significance of 'transcendent liberation,' while adhering at the same time to the formation of a relational self as its ethico-political message. This move relies on considering the two interpretations of spiritual redemption ('transcendent liberation' and 'liberative fearlessness') not as discrete alternatives but as interrelated to constitute a more textured and complex notion of devotional life.

To the extent that spirituality is a practice and something to be engaged in, it assumes the reality of effort, action, and failure – all of which, in turn, require the reality of the self (and of other selves). Thus, in a sense, 'transcendent liberation' cannot be involved in the *practice* of spirituality because it entails a dissolution of the concepts of effort and action through the ultimate dissolution of the psycho-physical self. But, undeniably, it is the ultimate *end* of spiritual training and what the devotee hopes for. However, to hope for something is not necessarily to aim at it, and, in fact, we sometimes hope for that which we cannot aim at. In the Kantian system, for example, it is hoped that ultimate happiness will be granted to the virtuous; yet a moral person is not supposed to do her duties *for the sake of* happiness, and, in fact, is not moral if she does so. By aiming at doing duty simply for the sake of duty, we become worthy of happiness which might be granted by God.[33] Thus 'transcendent liberation' is only what the devotee *hopes* will be the result of his or her spiritual quest. It is the *telos* of spiritual life. However, it would be self-defeating to *aim* for it directly. What the devotee *can* attempt to do is to restructure her life and projects according to the less grandiose 'liberative fearlessness.' Constituting a relational self and deconstructing egotistical individuality is something which can be aimed at and consciously strived for. By achieving this, the devotee might become actually worthy of being led to a metaphysical monism through grace. Thus even if transcendence is the rationale of a spiritual life, it can be obtained only through the ethico-politically sensitive 'fearlessness.'

Such intertwining of 'liberative fearlessness' and 'transcendent liberation' makes excellence in ethics an integral part of being spiritual. This leads us to a non-dualistic understanding of the phenomena of spirituality itself. We are usually inclined to take the spiritual realm as sharply distinct from and beyond the 'ordinary' moral realm. But on our reading of Ramprasad's devotionalism, to be (ethically) 'good' – and sometimes even 'bad' – in very ordinary senses is to be spiritual. Given the centrality of the ethico-political in spiritual life, I wonder now whether the tables might not be turned. In other words, could we say that the other-worldly promise of a monistic bliss – a concept of 'transcendent liberation' – is really in the service of the more empirically grounded peace of 'liberative fearlessness'? Maybe the purpose of a spirituality non-dualistically conceived is excellence in interpersonal relationships, and the hope of a transcendent bliss is simply a Regulative Ideal to encourage our ethico-political struggles.

Whether or not we want to go this far, it is because of this dynamic between the empirical and the transcendent that the *bhakti* poetry which we have examined has feminist relevance in spite of the metaphysically esoteric and world-denying strands within it. And it is also because of this that it is a little off-track to quote 'eastern spirituality' as a transcendence of all duality. Certainly, Ramprasad's spirituality can provide us with an antidote for patriarchal thinking, but only because it has an internal complexity. Instead of the 'two,' it gives us 'many-in-relation.' At the core of such spirituality lies not just a logic but a deviant logic of interrelationship. And it is this logic within spiritual experience that holds out hope for more just social interactions. For Ramprasad, spiritual redemption seems continuous with political redemption. *Kali-bhakti*, thus, can be a symbol for both. As

> Prasād says: On Kālī's tree
> Goodness, wealth, love and release[34]
> Can be had for the picking.
> (1982, 59)

But note that 'goodness, wealth, love,' on the one hand, and 'release,' on the other, are radically different species of fruit.

Notes

I am grateful to Lynda Sexson, Arindam Chakrabarti, Christopher Chapple, and the referees and editors of *Hypatia* for comments on an earlier version of this paper.

1   All the verses cited here were written in Bengali by Ramprasad Sen and translated by Leonard Nathan and Clinton Seely (1982). The references are to this anthology. I also note the places where I have changed the translations a bit to capture the original better. Translation modified by one word here.

2   See, for example, Irene Javors (1990); Rachel Fell McDermott (1996); Lina Gupta (1991); Rita M. Gross (1983); C. Mackenzie Brown (1983); and Barbara G. Walker (1985).

3   *Bhakti* is an expression of devotion in a direct, personal, and experiential communication with the divine. This can take widely divergent forms. Such contextualization of Kali guards against what Greta Gaard calls 'cultural cannibalism' (1993).

4   See Sumit Sarkar (1993).

5   It should be noted that Kali is a Goddess in the Hindu pantheon and the popularity of Ramprasad's songs falls within a broadly Hindu devotional context. However, Kazi Nazrul Islam, a very popular *Islamic* poet of Bengali, has also written on Kali (1968). The very intriguing and complex issues of Kali's apparent travels to and within theological worlds other than her own will not be explored here.

6 Mythologically, the Goddess is the daughter of the mountains – the Himalayas.
7 See Rajeswari Sunder Rajan (1998).
8 For the complexities here, see, for example, Kumkum Sangari (1990).
9 See Jashodhara Bagchi (1990).
10 See, for example, Tanika Sarkar (1995) and Lisa Mckean (1996).
11 I am grateful to Ruth Vanita for this reference.
12 Once again note that, historically, Kali worship has not been restricted to the Hindus. Also, as Sarkar points out, even in Ramakrishna, who is a century after Ramprasad, 'there is no developed sense of a sharply distinct "Hindu" identity, let alone any political use of it. . . . Either out of innocence or deliberate choice, Ramakrishna represented a kind of protest against the creation of sectarian walls' (1993, 46). Of course, he adds that Ramakrishna's 'catholicity *would soon come to be displayed* as a timeless essence of Hinduism' (1993, 46, emphasis mine), though this appropriation requires the mediation of other historical figures and events.
13 Translation altered.
14 See, for example, Kumkum Sangari (1990) and *Manushi* (Tenth Anniversary Issue, 1989).
15 See *Manushi* (1989).
16 This is a reference to the river Ganges (Ganga), who, the story goes, descended from the heavens on Siva's head so as not to rupture the Earth with the force of her descent.
17 Literally 'full of food.' The form of the goddess through which she symbolizes plenitude of food.
18 See, for example, Sukumari Bhattacharji (1990).
19 See Brian K. Smith (1989, 46–47) and Taittirya Upanisad 1:7:1.
20 See Lina Gupta (1991) and Kinsley (1975).
21 For expositions of Tantra philosophy, see Arthur Avalon (Sir John Woodroffe) (1978), M.M. Gopinath Kaviraj (1990), and Kamalakar Mishra (1981).
22 Translation altered.
23 Also means 'man.'
24 The bisexuality implicit in this image has not been explored here.
25 See Sangari (1990).
26 'Giri' means 'mountain' and signifies the Himalayas here. The Goddess is said to be the daughter of the mountain.
27 This is further corroborated by the life of the modern Saint Sri Ramakrishna, who oftentimes dressed as a woman.
28 Contrast this with

> . . . and what's this salvation
> If it swallows the saved like water
> In water. Sugar I love
> But haven't the slightest desire
> To merge with sugar.
>   (1982, 62)

29 I owe this terminology to Christopher Chapple.
30 The Carvaka school of philosophy in Classical India exemplifies this possibility. In some interpretations, the Carvakas were egoistical hedonists whose ethics of 'eat, drink and be merry' was based on the acceptance of death as the inevitable end of life.
31 Shiva is an ascetic – someone who has renounced the world. Thus, the 'sort of things' Shiva carries amounts to a begging bowl and a tiger-skin mat for meditation.
32 This phrase is by Heinrich Zimmer. Quoted in Kinsley (1975, 130).
33 This point is argued for in Arindam Chakrabarti (1988).
34 The word 'release' signifies what we have termed here 'transcendent liberation.' It is the release from the cycle of birth–death which amounts to the transcendence of the psycho-physical self.

References

Avalon, Arthur. 1978. *Shakti and shakta*. New York: Dover Publications.

Bagchi, Jashodhara. 1990. Representing nationalism: Ideology of motherhood in colonial Bengal. *Economic and Political Weekly* 20 (27): Ws 65–Ws 71.

Bhattacharji, Sukumari. 1990. Motherhood in ancient India. *Economic and Political Weekly* 20 (27): Ws 50–Ws 57.

Chakrabarti, Arindam. 1988. The end of life: A Nyaya-Kantian approach to the *Bhagavadgita*. *Journal of Indian Philosophy* 16: 327–334.

Gaard, Greta. 1993. Ecofeminism and Native American cultures. In *Ecofeminism*, ed. Greta Gaard. Philadelphia: Temple University Press.

Gross, Rita M. 1983. Hindu female deities as a resource for the contemporary rediscovery of the Goddess. In *The Book of the Goddess Past, and the Present: An introduction to Her religion*, ed. Carl Olson. New York: Crossroad.

Gupta, Lina. 1991. Kali the Savior. In *After patriarchy: Feminist transformations of world religions*, ed. Paula M. Cooey, William R. Eakin, and Jay B. McDaniel. Maryknoll, N.Y.: Orbis Books.

Jarvos, Irene. 1990. Goddess in the metropolis: Reflections on the sacred in an urban setting. In *Reweaving the world: The emergence of ecofeminism*, ed. Irene Diamond and Gloria Feman Orenstein. San Francisco: Sierra Club Books.

Islam, Kazi Nazrul. 1968. *Debistuti* (in Bengali), ed. Netai Ghatak. Calcutta.

Kaviraj, M.M. Gopinath. 1990. Sakta philosophy. In *Selected writings of M.M. Gopinath Kaviraj*, ed. M.M. Gopinath Kaviraj. Centenary Celebration Committee. Varanasi.

Kinsley, David R. 1975. *The sword and the flute*. Berkeley: University of California Press.

Mackenzie Brown, C. 1983. Kali, the mad Mother. In *The Book of the Goddess past and present: An introduction to Her religion*, ed. Carl Olson. New York: Crossroad.

Mahasweta Devi. 1993. Sanjh sakaler ma. In *Mahasweta Devir Chhotogalpo* (in Bengali). New Delhi: National Book Trust.

Manushi. 1989. Tenth anniversary issue on women saints: 50–52.

McDermott, Rachel Fell. 1996. The western Kali. In *Devi: Goddesses of India*, ed. John S. Hawley and Donna M. Wulff. Berkeley: University of California Press.

Mckean, Lisa. 1996. Bharat Mata: Mother India and Her militant matriots. In *Devi: Goddesses of India*, ed. John S. Hawley and Donna M. Wulff. Berkeley: University of California Press.

Mishra, Kamalakar. 1981. *Significance of the Tantric tradition*. Varanasi: Ardhanarisvara Publications.

Nathan, Leonard and Clinton Seely. 1982. *Grace and mercy in Her wild hair: Selected poems to the Mother Goddess*. Boulder: Great Eastern.

Plumwood, Val. 1993. *Feminism and the mastery of nature*. London: Routledge.

Sangari, Kumkum. 1989. Mirabai and the spiritual economy of bhakti. *Economic and Political Weekly* July 7: 1464–1474; July 14: 1537–1551.

Sarkar, Sumit. 1993. *An exploration of the Ramakrishna Vivekananda tradition*. Occasional Paper I. Shimla: Indian Institute of Advanced Study.

Sarkar, Tanika and Urvashi Butalia, eds. 1995. *Women and the Hindu right*. New Delhi: Kali for Women.

Shiva, Vandana. 1988. *Staying alive*. New Delhi: Kali for Women.

Smith, Brian K. 1989. *Reflections on resemblance, ritual, and religion*. New York: Oxford University Press.

Sunder Rajan, Rajeswari. 1998. Is the hindu goddess a feminist? *Economic and Political Weekly* October 31: Ws 34–Ws 38.

Walker, Barbara G. 1985. *The crone: Women of age, wisdom and power*. San Francisco: Harper and Row.

Guide to further reading

Part one

Background readings for feminist approaches to philosophy of religion

Anderson, P.S., *A Feminist Philosophy of Religion: the Rationality and Myths of Religious Belief*, Oxford: Blackwell, 1998.

Anderson, P.S., 'Feminist Theology as Philosophy of Religion', in Susan Frank Parsons (ed.) *The Cambridge Companion to Feminist Theology*, Cambridge: Cambridge University Press, 2002, pp. 40–59.

Armour, E., *Deconstruction, Feminist Theology and the Problem of Difference: Subverting the Race/Gender Divide*, Chicago, IL: University of Chicago Press, 1999.

Cavarero, A., *Relating Narratives: Storytelling and Selfhood*, London: Routledge, 2000.

Fairweather, A. and Zagzebski, L. (eds), *Virtue Epistemology:Essays on Epistemic Virtue and Responsibility*, Oxford/New York, NY: Oxford University Press, 2001.

Harris, H. and Insole, C. (eds), *Faith and Philosophical Analysis: A Critical Look at the Impact of Analytical Philosophy on the Philosophy of Religion*, Aldershot, Hampshire: Ashgate Publishing Ltd, forthcoming.

hooks, b., *Remembered Rapture: The Writer at Work*, London: The Women's Press, 1999.

Jantzen, G., *Becoming Divine: Towards a Feminist Philosophy of Religion*, Manchester: Manchester University Press, 1998.

Part two

Suggested Readings

Topic one: divinity

Beattie, T., *God's Mother, Eve's Advocate: A Marian Narrative of Women's Salvation,* London and New York, NY: Continuum, 2002.

Daly, M., *Beyond God the Father: Toward a Philosophy of Women's Liberation*, London: The Women's Press, 1986.

Irigaray, L., 'Divine Women', *Sexes and Genealogies*, trans. G.C. Gill, New York, NY: Columbia University Press, 1993, pp. 55–72.

Julian of Norwich, *Revelations of Divine Love*, trans. Clifton Wolters, London: Penguin Books, 1996.

Raphael, M., *Thealogy and Embodiment: The Post-Patriarchal Reconstruction of Female Sacrality*, Sheffield: Sheffield Academic Press, 1996.

Soskice, J.M., 'Trinity and the "Feminine Other"', *New Blackfriars* (January 1993): 2–17.

Topic two: embodiment

Clack, B., *Sex and Death*, Cambridge: Polity Press, 2002.

Coakley, S. (ed.), *Religion and the Body*, Cambridge: Cambridge University Press, 1997.

Jasper, A., *The Shining Garment of the Text: Gendered Readings of John's Prologue*, Sheffield: Sheffield Academic Press, 1998.

Kristeva, J., *Powers of Horror: An Essay on Abjection*, trans. Leon S. Roudiez, New York, NY: Columbia University Press, 1982.

O'Grady, K., Gilroy, A. and Gray, J. (eds), *Bodies, Lives, Voices: Gender in Theology,* Sheffield: Sheffield Academic Press, 1998.

Walker Bynum, C., *Fragmentation and Redemption: Essays on Gender and the Human Body in Medieval Religion*, New York, NY: Zone Books, 1991.

Topic three: autonomy and spirituality

Anderson, P.S., 'Autonomy, Vulnerability and Gender', *Feminist Theory*, special issue. Ethical Relations: Agency, Autonomy, Care, edited by Sasha Roseneil and Linda Hogan, 4:2 (August 2003): 149–164.

Coakley, S., *Powers and Submissions: Spirituality, Philosophy and Gender,* Oxford: Blackwell, 2002.

Hampson, D., 'On Autonomy and Hereonomy', in D. Hampson (ed.) *Swallowing the Fishbone*, London: SPCK, 1996, pp. 1–16.

hooks, b., *Wounds of Passion: A Writing Life*, New York, NY: Henry Holt and Company, 1997.

Murdoch, I., *The Sovereignty of the Good*, London: Routledge & Kegan Paul, 1970.

Weil, S., *Waiting on God*, London: Collins, Fontana, 1959.

Topic four: religious practice

Asad, T., *Genealogies of Religion: Disciplines and Reasons of Power in Christianity and Islam*, Baltimore, MD: The Johns Hopkins University Press, 1993.

Butler, J., *Excitable Speech: A Politics of the Performative*, London: Routledge, 1997.

Dalmiya, V., 'Dogged Loyalties: A Classical Indian Intervention in Care Ethics', in Joseph Runzo and Nancy M. Martin (eds) *Ethics in the World Religions.* Volume III, in 'The Library of Global Ethics and Religion', General Editors, Runzo and Martin. Oxford: One World, 2001, pp. 293–308.

Hollywood, A. *Sensible Ecstasy: Mysticism, Sexual Difference and the Demands of History*, Chicago, IL: University of Chicago Press, 2002.

Hollywood, A. 'Performativity, Citationality, Ritualization', *History of Religions*, 42 (2002): 93–115.

Joy, M., O'Grady, K. and Poxon, J.L., *French Feminists on Religion: A Reader*, London: Routledge, 2000.

Mahmood, S., 'Rehearsed Spontaneity and the Conventionality of Ritual: Disciplines of Salat', *American Ethnologist*, 28 (2001): 827–853.

Index